[THE SOURCEBOOKS SHAKESPEARE]

King Lear

TEXT EDITOR
DOUGLAS A. BROOKS

ADVISORY EDITORS
DAVID BEVINGTON AND PETER HOLLAND

SERIES EDITORS
MARIE MACAISA AND DOMINIQUE RACCAH

William Shakspeare

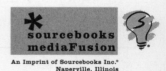

**sourcebooks
mediaFusion**

An Imprint of Sourcebooks Inc.®
Naperville, Illinois

Published by Sourcebooks MediaFusion, an imprint of Sourcebooks, Inc.
P.O. Box 4410, Naperville, Illinois 60567-4410
(630) 961-3900
Fax: (630) 961-2168
www.sourcebooks.com
www.sourcebooksshakespeare.com
For more information on The Sourcebooks Shakespeare, email us at shakespeare@sourcebooks.com.

Library of Congress Cataloging-in-Publication Data

Shakespeare, William, 1564-1616.
  King Lear / William Shakespeare ; text editor, Douglas A. Brooks ;
advisory editors, David Bevington and Peter Holland.
     p. cm. -- (The Sourcebooks Shakespeare)
  ISBN 978-1-4022-0830-0
 1. Lear, King (Legendary character)--Drama. 2. Inheritance and
succession--Drama. 3. Fathers and daughters--Drama. 4. Kings and
rulers--Drama. 5. Aging parents--Drama. 6. Britons--Drama. I. Brooks,
Douglas A. II. Bevington, David M. III. Holland, Peter, 1951- IV. Title.

PR2819.A2B75 2007
822.3'3--dc22

2007025522

Printed and bound in the United States of America.
LB 10 9 8 7 6 5 4 3 2 1

To students, teachers, and lovers of Shakespeare

Contents

ABOUT SOURCEBOOKS MEDIAFUSION

Launched with the 1998 *New York Times* bestseller
We Interrupt This Broadcast and formally founded in 2000,
Sourcebooks MediaFusion is the nation's leading publisher
of mixed-media books. This revolutionary imprint is dedicated
to creating original content—be it audio, video, CD-ROM,
or Web—that is fully integrated with the books we create.
The result, we hope, is a new, richer, eye-opening,
thrilling experience with books for our readers.
Our experiential books have become both bestsellers
and classics in their subjects, including poetry (*Poetry Speaks*),
children's books (*Poetry Speaks to Children*),
history (*We Shall Overcome*), sports (*And The Crowd Goes Wild*),
the plays of William Shakespeare, and more.
See what's new from us at www.sourcebooks.com.

About the Text

There are two key versions of *King Lear*, a quarto of 1608 (the First Quarto or Q1) and the Folio version of 1623 (F1). There are significant differences between the First Quarto and the First Folio, and each version of the play has a claim upon our attention. While the Oxford editors Wells and Taylor (1988) have argued that the two versions of *Lear* are separate and equally authentic, most editors, dating as far back as Alexander Pope (1725), have opted for a composite text, combining the beauties of both versions. This edition follows in that tradition.

However, my sense of "Shakespearean" differs, and given the changes in aesthetics over the centuries, it is no great surprise that my text looks very little like Pope's composite. I have used, for the most part, the early performance-based Q1 for reasons I articulated in an article about the "Good" quarto of *Lear*, and I have added passages from the longer F1. This text is an edition for the present and does not claim to have solved the "mystery of things" relating to *Lear*. My choices are explicit, and I encourage the reader who wants to explore the text to go online to the Sourcebooks Shakespeare web site, where it is reproduced with enhanced color-coded features that show my Q1 and F1 selections clearly.

I have modernized Shakespeare's spelling and punctuation along the principles espoused in Stanley Wells' *Modernizing Shakespeare's Spelling* (1979) and his *Re-Editing Shakespeare for the Modern Reader: Based on Lectures Given at the Folger Shakespeare Library, Washington, D.C.* (1984). However, where modernization strips a word of its original meaning, the archaic spelling has been retained: see, for example, "villein" (3.7.74).

Like any composite text, deciding what to keep and what to let go is a fraught and time-consuming process. Conflating Q1 and F1 has necessitated some relineations, but lineations are already suspect; editors regularly turn two half-lines into one full line, etc. I have, however, attempted to retain the Quarto's transitions from prose to verse, hoping, perhaps fruitlessly, that some of Shakespeare's original intention survived the various exigencies of the journey it was compelled to take from the playhouse to the printing house.

Douglas A. Brooks

On the CD

1. Introduction to the Sourcebooks Shakespeare *King Lear*: Sir Derek Jacobi

ACT 1, SCENE 1, LINES 44-106

2. Narration: Sir Derek Jacobi
3. Trevor Peacock as Lear, Penny Downie as Gonoril, Julia Ford as Cordelia and Samantha Bond as Regan
   The Complete Arkangel Shakespeare • *2003*
4. Paul Scofield as Lear, Harriet Walter as Gonoril, Emilia Fox as Cordelia, and Sara Kestelman as Regan
   Naxos AudioBooks • *2002*

ACT 1, SCENE 1, LINES 136-176

5. Narration: Sir Derek Jacobi
6. Anton Lesser as Kent and Trevor Peacock as Lear
   The Complete Arkangel Shakespeare • *2000*
7. David Burke as Kent and Paul Scofield as Lear
   Naxos AudioBooks • *2002*

ACT 1, SCENE 2, LINES 1-22

8. Narration: Sir Derek Jacobi
9. Simon Russell Beale as Edmund
   Naxos AudioBooks—Great Speeches and Soliloquies • *1994*
10. Toby Stephens as Edmund
    Naxos AudioBooks • *2002*

ACT 1, SCENE 4, LINES 249-264

11. Narration: Sir Derek Jacobi
12. Laurence Olivier as Lear
    Granada International • *1984*

Act 1, Scene 5, Lines 6-36

13. Narration: Sir Derek Jacobi
14. Paul Scofield as Lear, David Burke as Kent, and
    Kenneth Branagh as the Fool
    Naxos AudioBooks • 2002
15. Laurence Olivier as Lear, Colin Blakely as Kent,
    and John Hurt as the Fool
    Granada International • 1984

Act 2, Scene 1, Lines 13-36

16. Narration: Sir Derek Jacobi
17. Gerard Murphy as Edmund and David Tennant as Edgar
    The Complete Arkangel Shakespeare • 2003
18. Toby Stephens as Edmund and Richard McCabe as Edgar
    Naxos AudioBooks • 2002

Act 3, Scene 2, Lines 1-24

19. Narration: Sir Derek Jacobi
20. Donald Wolfit as Lear and Job Stewart as the Fool
    Living Shakespeare • 1962
21. Paul Scofield as Lear and Kenneth Branagh as the Fool
    Naxos AudioBooks • 2002

Act 3, Scene 4, Lines 37-69

22. Narration: Sir Derek Jacobi
23. David Tennant as Edgar, John Rogan as the Fool, Anton Lesser
    as Kent, and Trevor Peacock as Lear
    The Complete Arkangel Shakespeare • 2003
24. Richard McCabe as Edgar, Kenneth Branagh as the Fool,
    David Burke as Kent, and Paul Scofield as Lear
    Naxos AudioBooks • 2002

Featured Audio Productions

NAXOS AUDIOBOOKS (2002)

King Lear	Paul Scofield
Gonoril	Harriet Walter
Regan	Sara Kestelman
Cordelia	Emilia Fox
Duke of Albany	Peter Blythe
Duke of Cornwall	Jack Klaff
Earl of Gloucester	Alec McCowen
Edgar	Richard McCabe
Edmund	Toby Stephens
Earl of Kent	David Burke
Fool	Kenneth Branagh
Duke of Burgundy	John McAndrew
King of France	Simon Treves
Oswald	Matthew Morgan

THE COMPLETE ARKANGEL SHAKESPEARE (2003)

King Lear	Trevor Peacock
Earl of Gloucester	Clive Merrison
Earl of Kent	Anton Lesser
Gonoril	Penny Downie
Regan	Samantha Bond
Cordelia	Julia Ford
Edmund	Gerard Murphy
Edgar	David Tennant
Fool	John Rogan
Duke of Albany	David Horovitch
Duke of Cornwall	Rob Edwards
Oswald	Jonathan Tafler
Gentleman	Clifford Rose
King of France	John McAndrew
Duke of Burgundy	Christopher Gee

LIVING SHAKESPEARE (1962)

King Lear	Donald Wolfit
Gonoril	Coral Browne
Regan	Barbara Jefford
Cordelia	Rosalind Iden
Earl of Kent	Derek Francis
Earl of Gloucester	Joseph O'Conor
Duke of Burgundy	Mark Kingston
King of France	Brian Spink
Duke of Albany	David Dodimead
Duke of Cornwall	Peter Eyre
Fool	Job Stewart
Edgar	Thomas Johnston
Edmund	Mark Brackenbury

GRANADA INTERNATIONAL (1984): Laurence Olivier as King Lear
Naxos AudioBooks—Great Speeches and Soliloquies (1994): Simon Russell Beale as Edmund

Note from the Series Editors

For many of us, our first and only encounter with Shakespeare was in school. We may recall that experience as a struggle, working through dense texts filled with unfamiliar words. However, those of us who were fortunate enough to have seen a play performed have altogether different memories. It may be of an interesting scene or an unusual character, but it is most likely a speech. Often, just hearing part of one instantly transports us to that time and place. "Friends, Romans, countrymen, lend me your ears", "But, soft! What light through yonder window breaks?", "To sleep, perchance to dream", "Tomorrow, and tomorrow, and tomorrow".

The Sourcebooks Shakespeare series is our attempt to use the power of performance to help you experience the play. In it, you will see photographs from various productions, on film and on stage, historical and contemporary, known worldwide or in your community. You may even recognize some actors you don't think of as Shakespearean performers. You will see set drawings, costume designs, and scene edits, all reproduced from original notes. Finally, on the enclosed audio CD, you will hear scenes from the play as performed by some of the most accomplished Shakespeareans of our time. Often, we include multiple interpretations of the same scene, showing you the remarkable richness of the text. Hear Paul Scofield's authoritative and measured Lear banish Kent in the 1962 Living Shakespeare series. Compare the same speech to the wrenching rendition by Laurence Olivier in his 1984 performance. The actors create different meanings, different characters, different worlds.

As you read the text of the play, you can consult explanatory notes for definitions of unfamiliar words and phrases or words whose meanings have changed. These notes appear on the left pages, next to the text of the play. The audio, photographs, and other production artifacts augment the notes and they too are indexed to the appropriate lines. You can use the pictures to see how others have staged a particular scene and get ideas on costumes, scenery, blocking, etc. As for the audio, each track represents a particular interpretation of a scene. Sometimes, a passage that's difficult to comprehend opens up when you hear it out loud. Furthermore, when you hear more than one version, you gain a keener understanding of the characters. Is Lear a greedy patriarch or a misunderstood father? Are his daughters the victims of his misogynistic cruelty or the deserving targets of his ire? The actors made their choices and so can you. You may even come up with your own interpretation.

The text of the play, the definitions, the production notes, the audio—all of these work together, and they are included for your enjoyment. Because the audio consists of performance excerpts, it is meant to entertain. When you see a passage with an associated clip, you can read along as you hear the actors perform the scene for you. Or, you can sit back, close your eyes, and listen, then go back and reread the text with a new perspective. Finally, since the text is a script, you may find yourself reciting the lines out loud and doing your own performance!

You will undoubtedly notice that some of the audio does not exactly match the text. Also, there are photographs and facsimiles of scenes that may not be in your edition. There are many reasons for this, but foremost among them is the fact that Shakespearean scholarship continues to progress, and the prescribed ways of dealing with and interpreting texts are always changing. Thus a play that was edited and published in the 1900s will be different from one published in 2007. Finally, artists have their own interpretation of the play, and they too cut and change lines and scenes according to their vision.

The ways in which *King Lear* has been presented have varied considerably through the years. We've included essays in the book to give you glimpses into the range of productions, showing you how different artists have approached the play and providing examples of what changes were made and how. Bradley Ryner writes of Michael Kahn's compelling 1999 interpretation, performed by the Shakespeare Theatre Company, in which the deaf actress Monique Holt plays a deaf Cordelia. He discusses how her deafness textures the father-daughter relationship, creates closeness with the Fool (who interprets her sign language), and emphasizes one of the play's thematic concerns: the breakdown of communication. "In Production," an essay by our text editor, Douglas Brooks, provides an overview of how the play has been performed, from Nahum Tate's early adaptation that created a long-standing tradition of *Lear* ending happily to Paul Scofield's seminal performance in the 1962 RSC production that reversed that trend. Exploring the origins and legacy of the happy ending, Brooks examines its effect on the relationship between the text and the realization of the play in performance. In his essay on *King Lear* in popular culture, Douglas Lanier cites adaptations of Lear's story, introducing productions that alter the play's geographic or chronological location while retaining the central themes of fatherhood, inheritance and the melodrama of familial relations. In *Broken Lance* (1954), for example, Lear's daughters are supplanted with cattlemen's sons; *Harry and Tonto* (1974) replaces the Fool with a cat; *My Kingdom* (2001) sets the drama of *Lear* in the context of a Liverpudlian mob family. The list goes on. Finally, for the actor in you, (and for those who want to peek behind the curtain), we have an essay that you may find especially intriguing. Andrew Wade, voice coach of the Royal Shakespeare Company for sixteen years, shares his point of view on how to understand the text and speak it. You can also listen in on him working with Myra Lucretia Taylor on a speech from the play; perhaps you too can learn the art of speaking Shakespeare. The characters come to life in a way that's different from reading the book or watching a performance.

One last note: we are frequently asked why we didn't include the whole play, either in audio or video. While we enjoy the plays and are avid theatergoers, we are trying to do something more with the audio (and the production notes and the essays) than just presenting them to you. Our goal is to provide you tools that will enable you to explore the play on your own, from many different directions. Our hope is that the different pieces of audio, the voices of the actors, and the production photos and notes will engage you and illuminate the play on many levels, so that you can construct your own understanding and create your own "production," a fresh interpretation unique to you.

Though the productions we referenced and the audio clips we have included are but a miniscule sample of the play's history, we hope they encourage you to further delve into the works of Shakespeare. New editions of the play come out yearly; movie adaptations are regularly being produced; there are hundreds of theater groups in the U.S. alone; and performances could be going on right in your backyard. We echo the words of noted writer and poet Robert Graves, who said, "The remarkable thing about Shakespeare is that he is really very good—in spite of all the people who say he is very good."

Dominique Raccah

Marie Macaisa

Dominique Raccah and Marie Macaisa
Series Editors

track 1

Introduction to the Sourcebooks Shakespeare **King Lear**
Sir Derek Jacobi

In Production

King Lear THROUGH THE YEARS

Douglas A. Brooks

Few records of the earliest performances of Shakespeare's plays have survived, but we are fortunate in the case of *King Lear*. The title page of the play, as it was initially published in 1608, provides us with some important details about the first performance of the play, who was in the audience, and even the basic plot of the play. While we have come to see *Lear* as one of Shakespeare's greatest tragedies, the title page of the 1608 edition (Q1) refers to the play not as a tragedy, but as the *"True Chronicle History of the life and death of King Lear, and his three Daughters"*, adding that it also tells the story of *"the unfortunate life of Edgar, sonne and heire to the Earle of Glocester, and his sullen and assumed humour of TOM of Bedlam"*. Whoever might have had an interest in purchasing a printed version of the play in 1608 certainly knew what to expect. Such a potential reader would have also learned that not only was the first performance of *Lear* "plaid before the Kings Majesty at White-Hall, upon S. Stephens night, in Christmas Hollidaies," but also that it was performed by "his majesties Servants, playing usually at the Globe on the Banck-side." In other words, the first performance of *King Lear* was a special production by Shakespeare's company, The King's Men, for James I at Whitehall Palace on December 26, 1606. The only other thing we know for certain about this performance was that Shakespeare's friend and fellow actor, Richard Burbage, one of the great tragedians of the English Renaissance stage, played the role of Lear that night.

Our good fortune begins and ends there. Apart from a production of the play that may have been put on in Yorkshire in 1610 (1), there is no reliable evidence that the play was performed again during Shakespeare's lifetime.

"BUT NOW IN THE DIVISION OF THE KINGDOMS"
When the theaters reopened shortly after the ascension of Charles II to the throne in 1660, *Lear* returned to the stage and was performed only twice in

the next decade or so in ways that Shakespeare might have recognized, once in 1664 and then again in 1675. The playwright, William Davenant, was

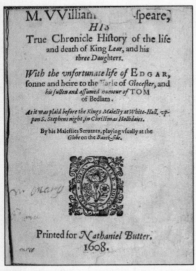

Title page of *King Lear* (1608)
Courtesy of the Horace Howard Furness Memorial Library, University of Pennsylvania

behind the first of these two largely unsuccessful attempts to put on stage what Shakespeare had written. Such an adherence to the playwright's text was to be short-lived. Along with the restoration of England to monarchic rule came an intensive effort to adapt and change Shakespeare's plays both for theater audiences and readers, and *Lear* did not escape unscathed. In 1681, Nahum Tate's now infamous adaptation appeared in print as *The History of King Lear* and proclaimed itself as containing the play as "acted at the Duke's Theater", a production mounted by the Duke's Company at their playhouse, with Thomas Betterton in the title role. I used the word "infamous" because although Tate's version greatly appealed to Restoration theater-goers and was more or less the only *Lear* audiences saw during the eighteenth and early nineteenth century, it has not fared well with Shakespearean critics. Rather, such critics have often disparaged the profound distortions Tate's adaptation imposed on the original—distortions, as Tate himself indicated, aimed at "making the Tale conclude in a Success to the innocent distrest Persons: Otherwise I must have incumbred the Stage with dead Bodies" (2). It is hard to imagine how some of the great, dark, often proto-existentialist early twentieth-century criticism of *Lear* by G. Wilson Knight or A.C. Bradley, for example, could have been written had they been responding to a play that concludes, as Tate's does, not only with Lear restored to the throne of the realm he had torn asunder, but also with Edgar and Cordelia destined for conjugal bliss. How odd all of this might seem to modern audiences who are sometimes taken aback by the crude and bawdy language that characterizes the banter between Edmund, Gonoril, and Regan. On the other hand, it would have surprised Shakespeare to see three female actors on stage playing Gonoril, Regan, and Cordelia in performances of Tate's *Lear* at the Duke's Theater. Prior to the closing of the theaters in 1642, numerous, widely circulated anti-theatrical pamphlets repeatedly upbraided players and playing companies for promoting wickedness, lewd behavior, and Papist (Catholic) beliefs. "Proper" women attended plays at their own moral peril, and no woman of any class would have been allowed to appear on stage, all female parts being played by boy actors. Indeed, it has been speculated that the Fool mysteriously vanishes from the play after the mock-trial scene (in Q1) because Shakespeare knew that the same boy actor playing him would also play Cordelia. When the Fool disappears after 3.6, Cordelia reappears. In Tate's *Lear*, which gives Cordelia more prominence than Shakespeare's, such juggling of roles would not have been necessary for two reasons: 1) an actress played Cordelia, and 2) Tate cut the role of the Fool altogether because he felt that such a character had no place in tragedy, regardless of the fact that his adaptation turned the play into a comedy.

Writing nearly a century after the earliest performances of Tate's play, Samuel Johnson noted what eighteenth-century audiences wanted from their *Lear*: "the publick has decided. Cordelia, from the time of Tate, has always retired with victory and felicity. And, if my sensations could add any thing to the general suffrage, I might relate, that I was many years ago so shocked by Cordelia's death, that I know not whether I ever endured to read again the last scenes of the play till I undertook to revise them as an editor" (3). Given the chaos that threatened to engulf England during the interregnum (1649-60), perhaps Tate's Lear best expresses the yearnings of Restoration audiences when he exclaims to Kent near the conclusion of the play, "Why I have News that will recall thy Youth; / Ha! Didst Thou hear't, or did th'inspiring Gods / Whisper to me Alone? Old *Lear* shall be / A King again" (5.6.104-7 in Tate's edition).

Perhaps the most celebrated productions of *Lear* in the eighteenth century starred David Garrick (1717-79), the actor, playwright, and theater mogul who dominated theatrical practices and tastes during his lifetime and after. Prior to Garrick, performers commonly declaimed their lines, rarely feeling compelled to modulate their approach for the sake of representing the nuances of a role. Garrick introduced theater-goers to a more natural approach to acting, one that sought to realistically communicate the shifting emotional registers of a part. Audiences loved what they saw. Describing the final scene of a performance of *Lear* (Tate's version) he attended in 1747, the actor and theater critic Thomas Davies (1712-85) wrote, "The half breathing and panting of Garrick, with a look and action which confessed the infirmity of old age, greatly heightened the picture...Who could possibly think of depriving an audience, almost exhausted with the feelings of so many terrible scenes, of the inexpressible delight which they enjoyed, when the old King, in rapture, cried out – 'Old Lear shall be a king again!'" (4). Another audience member (Thomas Wilkes) who saw Garrick perform Lear some years later, wrote, "his old grey hair standing, as it were, erect on his head, his face filled with horror and attention, his hands expanded, his whole frame actuated by a dreadful solemnity...methinks I share his calamities, I feel the dark drifting rain and the sharp tempest" (5). The natural style had literally taken the theater by storm, and Garrick's approach to preparing for the role suggests that method acting, so popular with contemporary film actors, has important antecedents in the performance history of *Lear*. On Garrick's assertion that his portrayal of Lear's madness was based on the real-life tragedy of a father who accidentally dropped his baby daughter out of a window and killed her, Thomas Davies reports that Garrick, "frequently went to see his distracted friend, who passed the remainder of his life in going to the window, and there playing in fancy with his child. After some dalliance, he dropped it, and, bursting into a flood of tears, filled the house with shrieks of grief and bitter anguish. He then sat down, in a pensive mood, his eyes fixed on one object, at times looking slowly round him, as if to implore compassion" (6). And so, art, it would seem, was imitating life.

Nevertheless, Garrick's portrayal of Lear was not without its detractors. In a review of Garrick's performance in the same production Davies found so moving, Samuel Foote (1720-77), a playwright, actor, and theater manager well-known in his day for penning popular farces, criticized Garrick's naturalistic style of acting as inadequate for representing the grandeur of kingship. Especially troubled by Garrick's handling of Lear's madness, Foote asserted that everything an actor does onstage to play the king "should express an Extravagance of State & Majesty...but no Sign of Equality, no Familiarity, no sitting down Cheek by Jowl" (7). Foote, whose 1741 performance of Shylock in *The Merchant of Venice* mesmerized London audiences, was in direct competition with Garrick, though he was far less financially successful. As such, professional bitterness may have fueled his critique. Whichever critic is more credible, there is no disputing Lear earned Garrick more acclaim than perhaps any other role he attempted, and he performed it regularly for more than three decades.

It is important to remember here that all such eyewitness accounts of *Lear* in the theater describe performances of what was essentially Tate's version of the play. During the many years he portrayed the king, Garrick increasingly incorporated more and more of Shakespeare's play into the performance texts he and his fellow actors relied on for a given production, but he could not bring himself to do without Tate's happy ending. Nor was he willing to allow the Fool to return from the exile imposed on him since 1681 because, as he put it, "the feelings of Lear would derive no advantage from the buffooneries of the parti-coloured jester" (8).

Garrrick's successor, John Philip Kemble (1757-1823), who first performed the role on January 21, 1788, agreed with him. Indeed, Kemble not only kept Tate's ending, but also restored some of the plot twists that Garrick had deleted, including Cordelia's marriage to Edgar. The theater critic George Daniel did not approve. Although Daniel praised Kemble for the realism of his performance, noting how the actor's "figure, countenance, and manner all conspired to give truth to the resemblance..." he was less moved, however, by Kemble's choice of Tate's version. Critizing the marriage that Tate created, which erased Cordelia's death, Daniel observed, "The daring presumption that marred this glorious drama, deprived us of Mr. Kemble's exertions in the scene where Lear enters bearing in the dead body of Cordelia. What this would have been in the hands of *such* an actor, we can only anticipate. But we deeply regret that Mr. Kemble's correct taste did not brush away this vile interpolation, and restore the original text of Shakespeare" (9). If only, as we shall see, Daniel could have avoided seeing *Lear* for another eight years.

Beginning in 1810 performances of *Lear,* regardless of the text on which they were based, were banned for the next decade out of concern that the representation of a monarch descending into madness would be insensitive at a time when King George III (r. 1760-1820), who suffered from recurrent bouts of mental illness in the later years of his reign, lapsed into a permanent state of incompetence during the final ten years of his rule. Upon his death in 1820, *Lear* would return, though not quite Shakespeare's *Lear.* In the year the ban was lifted, the widely acclaimed nineteenth-century English actor Edmund Kean (1787-1833) mounted a production of the play that relied heavily on the original texts, but still followed Tate in terms of its comic ending. Kean's performance was celebrated by a number of critics, but it was his portrayal of Lear's madness that was singled out for critical praise. One reviewer writing in the *New York Post* about Kean's 1820 production observed: "Nature, writhing under the poignancy of feeling, and finding no utterance in words or tears found a vent at length…in a spontaneous, hysterical, idiot laugh. The impressions made upon all who were present, will never be forgotten. His dreadful imprecations upon his daughters, his solemn appeals to heaven, struck the soul with awe" (10). Like Garrick before him, Kean had done a little preparation of his own, for it was widely reported at the time that "he was studying the character [of Lear] with great care, even visiting lunatic asylums to observe the effects of madness…He disturbed [his wife] Mary by wandering about the house with his eyes alternately vacant and filled with fierce light" (11). Emboldened by the favorable reception of this production and hoping to display fully his virtuosity as an actor by plunging himself into the depths of Shakespeare's *Lear*, Kean staged the play with its tragic ending in 1823. Virtuosity or not, the production proved so unpopular with audiences that after only three performances Kean was forced to return to Tate's version for the remainder of the run.

Despite this brief debacle, Kean's acting style continued to have a profound impact on stage actors in general, and on those who played Lear in particular. The impact extended to America, where the actor Edwin Forrest (1806-1872) fashioned himself Kean's disciple, even emulating his approach to preparing for a role as he readied himself to portray Lear's madness for a production during the 1827-28 theater season in New York. As a friend of the American actor recalled, "Mr. Forrest had studied the theory of insanity with a student's care…visited insane asylums and other places both here [in America] and in Europe, and with artistic exactness, carried out in his renditions all those mental peculiarities and eccentricities that critics recognize as truthful, and not as the mere ebullitions of a disposition and temper naturally fiery and irritable" (12). It was only a matter of time before Freud would come to rely on Shakespeare for some of his own theories of insanity.

"MEANTIME WE WILL EXPRESS OUR DARKER PURPOSES"

King Lear, as Shakespeare wrote it, would not return to the theater successfully until William Charles Macready (1793-1873) mounted a production, replete with the Fool and all of those "dead bodies" with which Tate had been loath to encumber the stage, in Drury Lane on January 25,1838 (13). An English actor who made his debut at the age of 16 playing Romeo at a theater in Birmingham, Macready went on to have a long and successful acting career, including three separate tours in America. While there, Macready attended performances of *Lear* starring Forrest. The English snob or the Shakespeare purist in him must not have liked what he saw, especially in front of the stage, because he later wrote, "The audience were very liberal, very vehement in their applause; but it was such an audience! – applauding all the disgusting trash of Tate as if it had been Shakespeare, with might and main" (14). It is unclear why Macready so disliked Tate's *Lear*, and why he subsequently expunged all of Tate's distortions from what amounted by now to a 150-year long performance tradition, but critical tastes were certainly shifting in the direction of his decision. And surely Daniel's rather damning review of Kemble's Tate-ish *Lear* could have made a persuasive case to anyone who might be planning to mount a production, like Macready, that it was time to bring Shakespeare back alive.

Perhaps the century that would produce the likes of Nietzsche, Marx, and Freud was finally ready for the "darker purposes" of the play Shakespeare gave us. Indeed, a work whose rallying cry seems to be, "Now gods, stand up for bastards" had suddenly become prescient of the decentering and illegitimacy that characterized the human condition in the West after Nietzsche's announcement of God's death had begun to ring in our ears.

Whether it was the critical winds that caught theatrical sails, or the proto-psychologism of the Romantic movement compelling us to look evermore inward to the point where God, if not dead, had at least been marginalized by our own self-deification—either way, the stage was being set for the moment when once again it would be littered with corpses, when once again Cordelia and Edgar would never speak to each other, when once again the king's initial longing to be "unburdened" so he can "crawl toward death," would, in his final dying words, be reduced to begging for help to "undo this button." Even the Fool would reappear, though in Macready's production it was a female character played by actress Priscilla Horton. It may not have been exactly what Shakespeare had in mind, but according to one reviewer, Horton brought the long-absent Fool back with a certain élan: "hers is a most pleasing performance, giving evidence of deep feeling; and she trills forth the snatches of song with the mingled archness and pathos of their own exquisite simplicity" (15). Significantly, all of the figurative hand wringing that brought Tate's *Lear* into the world and helped it to thrive so robustly on so many stages for so many years seems to have been for naught. As one reviewer who saw Macready's production on opening night made clear, a fully tragic *Lear* could make the journey from the page to the stage quite successfully.

Not only had Macready restored *Lear* to the theater in a form its playwright might have called his own, he was also inadvertently laying the foundation for a new set of performance traditions that would last well into the present. But beyond the textual choices that engendered this production, its back-to-the-futurism was also embodied in an important sense by the decisions that Macready made with regard to the play's setting. Now that "old Shakespeare" had finally returned, it was perhaps only fitting that his elderly king return to a stage that approximated the historical moment of his reign. Thus, as one reviewer who attended opening night appreciatively noted, the scenery "corresponds with the period, and with the circumstances of the text. The castles are heavy, sombre, solid; their halls adorned with trophies of the chase and instruments of war; druid circles rise in spectral loneliness out of the heath; and the 'dreadful pother' of the elements is kept up with a verisimilitude which beggars all that we have hitherto seen attempted" (16).

Lear was back in his element, and Macready's scenic efforts to re-locate the play in its mythic past proved infectious. Indeed, his attention to period details, "hitherto" unseen during the age of Tate, soon became *de rigueur* in a number of productions that were mounted during the second half of the nineteenth century, sometimes to the point of obsession. In one such production, Edmund Kean's son, Charles Kean (1811-1868) set out at mid-century to stage a *Lear* so heavily invested in recreating the King's Dark Ages that during rehearsals, he reportedly scolded the actor playing Edmund for inadequately denoting the play's historical moment. When that actor handed his key to Edgar, according to one account Kean exclaimed, "Good heavens! You give it to him as if it was a common room-door key. Let the audience see it, sir; make 'em feel it; impress upon 'em that it is a *key of the period*, sir" (17). Nature, it has been said, abhors a vacuum, and so with Tate's efforts to "rectifie what was wanting in the Regularity and Probability of the Tale" now expunged completely, this new fixation with making "'em feel" the temporal divide between their present and the play's present stepped in. It is probable that the great twentieth-century Shakespeare critic A.C. Bradley was hoping to un-fix this preoccupation when, in 1904, he essentially made *Lear* a refugee: "This world, we are told, is called Britain; but we should no more look for it in an atlas than for the place, called Caucasus, where Prometheus was chained by Strength and Force and comforted by the daughters of Ocean..." (18). If, like Prometheus, Shakespeare's *Lear* was homeless, then it was also timeless, and any theatrical attempt to shelter it within England's times of yore was likely to be as unaccommodating as the hovel into which the King and company escape from the storm. By deracinating the play from the moorings that had become ever more sturdy since Macready, Bradley was loosing the play onto the twentieth century. *King Lear*, to borrow from the title of Jan Kott's important critical study of Shakespeare, was about to become "our contemporary." The timing could not have been better.

In a production of the play that was first mounted at the Lyceum Theatre (London) on November 10, 1892 by the famous Victorian actor, Sir Henry Irving (1838-1905), what might be called the Macready curse—those who think they know *Lear*'s past are condemned to repeat it on stage as realistically as possible—was taken to something like its logical conclusion. Born, coincidentally, in the same year that Macready issued this curse, and dying a year after Bradley attempted to undo it, Irving was very clear about when he thought his *Lear* should be. Writing in the preface to an edition of the play he published in conjunction with the London premiere, Irving observed: "As the period of *King Lear* is fabulous, I have chosen, at the suggestion of Mr. Ford Madox Brown (who has kindly designed three scenes in the First and Second Acts) a time shortly after the departure of the Romans, when the Britons would naturally inhabit the houses left vacant" (19). Accordingly, Irving's Lear divested himself of his rule over a desolate fifth-century wasteland, peopled by hordes of barbarians and squatters making do among Roman ruins. No matter that one of the key historical references from which Shakespeare drew the basic elements of the story, *The History of the Kings of Britain* (1138) by Geoffrey of Monmouth ((c.1100-c.1155), tells of a King Leir who reigned from 861 BCE to 801 BCE, but then lost his kingdom when he attempted to divide it amongst his three daughters. In other words, nearly thirteen hundred years separate Geoffrey's historical Leir from the Lear imagined by Irving and Brown. Charles Kean, who was comparably concerned with accurately staging the play's historical moment, set his production in 800 AD, some 1600 years after the reign of the historical king. As if all of this emphasis on making the play "of the period, sir," as Kean put it, was not confusing enough, one of the painted backdrops Brown designed for Irving's Lyceum production consisted of "huge stones roughly laid upon each other in the Stonehenge fashion" (20). But if the anachronisms that inevitably emerged out of Macready and his successors' efforts to get it right bothered the audiences that attended Irving's *Lear*, they did not let on: the play ran for 76 performances, closing on February 1, 1893. And although the craving for historical authenticity that accompanied the return of Shakespeare's tragic *Lear* to the theater in the mid-nineteenth century did not completely disappear after Irving's production—indeed there was no shortage of period productions that were to follow—there was a significant shift in the locus of that craving from the stage to the page.

Within the same decade that Irving's *Lear* appeared, a newly intensified effort at getting Shakespeare right was underway. Textual scholarship, which began to emerge as a coherent discipline not long after Macready resurrected Shakespeare's *Lear*, had spent much of the second half of the century focusing its attention on Biblical texts. By the end of the century, that scholarly project well established, its various methodologies tried and tested, a new set of "sacred" texts was needed. Enter Shakespeare. Thus began an intensive scholarly effort, led initially by A. W. Pollard, R. B. McKerrow and W. W. Greg, aimed at determining the most authentic texts of Shakespeare's works, then producing authoritative editions of those works. Because the burden of authenticity had been relocated to Shakespeare's texts, the theater was now free to pursue other concerns. Once again, the timing could not have been better.

"IN THY BEST CONSIDERATION"
In important ways, the twentieth century belonged to *King Lear*. Freed from the obligation to recall a specific moment in the distant English past, the play—its splintered nationalism, its decentered authority and the resulting scramble for power, its representation of the generational impiety that tears apart bonds of family and state, its juxtaposition of nature's fury and human insignificance, its relentless portrait of human cruelty, and its stubborn insistence that our yearning for justice is the only salve against gods who amuse themselves with our suffering—had everything we needed to make it a cipher for what was on the minds of many people in many societies. Bound by the caprices of authority, blinded by propaganda, and often seeing death as the only escape from misery, those who struggled to survive in the gulags of the era could find the truth of their lives in Gloucester. Or naked, starving, and at the mercy of forces that seemed incognizant of their humanity, those "unaccommodated" beings who somehow lived to recall the charnel houses that sprang up in so many countries, yet offered no shelter, could find a kindred soul in Lear. And, tragically, for so many, the justice the king so vehemently pursues in the mock-trial scene, a trial that only really takes place in his anguished mind, typified the imaginary legal systems through which they were compelled to seek compensation in the darkness of sleepless nights. Perhaps more than any other of Shakespeare's

plays, *Lear* became for the age "a mirror up to nature," to borrow a phrase from *Hamlet*. Accordingly, it quickly became among the most popular of Shakespeare's plays to be staged.

"SUCH UNCONSTANT STARTS ARE WE LIKE TO HAVE"

The twentieth century witnessed an extraordinary proliferation of important productions of *Lear*, both on stage and on film, the new medium that was profoundly well suited to Shakespeare. What follows are brief descriptions of those that have powerfully articulated the geist of its era.

The great Shakespeare critic A.C. Bradley set the stage for many *Lears* to come by freeing the play from the bondage of representing England's ancient past. But in cutting those chains, Bradley acknowledged that "*King Lear* is too huge for the stage," further observing: "there is something in its very essence which is at war with the senses, and demands a purely imaginative realization" (21). There would be no shortage of attempts at such realizations, and if in fact the play was too big for any stage, perhaps a movie camera could give it the space it needed.

Art rarely cooperates with arbitrary periodization, so perhaps it is only appropriate that the most important British theater director and producer of the first half of the twentieth century, Harley Granville-Barker (1877-1946), actually began his acting career at the age of fourteen in the previous century. In 1900, Granville-Barker joined the experimental Stage Society, and a decade or so later began a series of productions of Shakespeare's plays at the Savoy Theatre that would prove to be enormously influential. *Lear* was not among those productions, but Granville-Barker's significance in the performance history of the play would come a little later. Arguably, that significance would move indirectly from his stage to other stages by making an appearance on the page in the form of his *Prefaces to Shakespeare*, a series of studies focusing on issues of staging Shakespeare's plays that began to appear in 1927. In the specific case of *Lear*, Granville-Barker discussed the play at length in the first of these volumes, and much of what he said continues to impact productions of the play today. As Stanley Wells observes, "Barker's *Preface* of 1927, one of the most practically efficacious pieces of drama criticism ever written, is a landmark in the history of the reception of King Lear" (22).

I have suggested above that *Lear* would speak powerfully to twentieth century audiences. However, its ability to do so was complicated by a question textual scholars had begun to raise in earnest: Which *Lear*? Having taken over the craving for authenticity that had preoccupied Macready and his successors in the previous century, these scholars began to demonstrate in considerable detail that the play had come down to us in two substantially different versions: the First Quarto version of 1608 (Q1) and the First Folio version of 1623 (F1). This was not, of course, new information. As early as 1725, Alexander Pope had noted a number of differences between the two versions, including the fact that F1 was missing a number of substantial passages that appeared in Q1. One such section of missing text was Lear's mock trial of Gonoril and Regan (3.6.30-74). It is hard to conceive of a *Lear,* focused as the play is on the human longing for justice, that does not allow the King the consolation of demanding to "see their trial first", but F1 does not, in fact, offer him such comfort. Nevertheless, the seriousness of purpose displayed by early twentieth-century textual scholars, a seriousness inherited from the discipline's origins in Biblical studies, guaranteed that the differences between Q1 and F1 *Lear* would be taken seriously.

Thus, in precisely the same historical moment, both the atom and *King Lear* were being split, and the resulting fragmentation would have profound implications in each context. The kingdom had been divided yet again, and no one attempting to bring the play to the stage could ignore the new lines being drawn on the textual map. After 1681, there were two different versions of the *Lear*, one by Shakespeare, the other by Tate; anyone planning to mount a production of the play either had to choose between them or, subsequently, to choose how to conflate them. History was repeating itself, only now it was a matter of choosing between two Shakespeare plays – the 1608 Quarto and the 1623 Folio – or choosing how to conflate them. The decision that haunted Lear throughout the play seemed to haunt the performance history of the play itself. Or, as Granville-Barker would put things in the newly sophisticated language of textual scholarship, "a producer must ask himself whether these two versions do not come from different prompt-books, and whether the Folio does not, both in cuts and additions, sometimes represent Shakespeare's second thoughts" (25). Such second thoughts, as theorized by textual scholars who influenced Granville-Barker's thinking here, presumed that because the

F1 was printed after Q1, it reflected the play as Shakespeare himself chose to revise it upon seeing the earlier version staged. Regardless of whether this presumption can be substantiated (a topic of intense scholarly debate still) what matters is that Granville-Barker was persuaded that F1 was the superior of the two texts. Accordingly, he recommended that it be the basis of theatrical productions, though he also cautioned that directors should pick and choose readings from Q1 as well.

One of the first people to follow Granville-Barker's advice was Russian theatrical director and designer Theodore Komisarjevsky (1882-1954), who in 1936 staged a widely acclaimed production at the Memorial Theatre in Stratford-upon-Avon. Starring Randall Ayrton in the title role, the text upon which the performance was based suggests that Komisarjevsky rearranged several of the lines of the play and cut many others. As Ralph Berry notes, Komisarjevsky turned Lear's knights into "a Chorus commenting on the futility of the old king's aims. They repeated, in unison, the Fool's songs and sayings" (26). Though Komisarjevsky himself told the press before his first production at the Memorial Theater, "I am not in the least traditional" (27), he was not above relying on recently established traditions. Granville-Barker was clearly the source of one such tradition with regard to what a director could do with the two texts of *Lear*; A.C. Bradley may have been the source of another. Komizarjevski's Stratford production received a great deal of attention for its abstract, geometric set and imaginative use of lighting, and for placing the play altogether outside of time and beyond geography. It was, in other words, the realization of what Bradley had argued some three decades earlier.

In 1940, Granville-Barker would finally have the opportunity, as Wells observes, "to translate his *Preface* into theatrical practice and to show that it was possible to perform an almost complete text [of *Lear*], in Elizabethan costume, with great theatrical success when, in collaboration with Lewis Casson, he directed John Gielgud (1904-2000) as Lear at the Old Vic" (26). Born in the same year that Bradley unchained the play from Stonehenge, Gielgud was only thirty-five when he played the elderly king, and had first performed the role ten years earlier. In 1950, collaborating with the English actor and director, Anthony Quayle (1913-1989), Gielgud directed and starred in a critically acclaimed production of *Lear* at the Memorial Theatre in Stratford. That production, which did much to confirm Gielgud's reputation as one of the great English actors of his generation, also effectively demonstrated that Lamb's oft-cited indictment (that *Lear* "cannot be acted") had reached its statute of limitation. *Lear*'s day on stage had finally arrived, though in fact it had been there all along. Three years later, the English actor/theater manager Michael Redgrave (1908-85) brought another production to the Old Vic with himself in the lead. The influential theater critic Kenneth Tynan (1927-1980) praised Redgrave's performance even as he reminded readers of the play's checkered theatrical past: "Michael Redgrave has played King Lear and won...*Lear* is a labyrinthine citadel, all but impregnable, and it needed a Redgrave to assault it" (27).

"UNFRIENDED, NEW-ADOPTED TO OUR HATE"

Emboldened by the recent successes of Gielgud, Redgrave, Olivier, and others at staging a play that was for so long considered hostile to the theater, an increasing number of directors would try their luck, and some of the great productions of the century would follow soon after. There is tremendous critical consensus that one of the greatest of these productions is the one mounted by Peter Brook in 1962 for the Royal Shakespeare Company, and subsequently directed by him for the 1971 film version. Influenced by Jan Kott's bleak critical interpretation of *Lear*, the plays of Samuel Beckett, and, more generally, the Theatre of the Absurd, Brook declared "he wished to give his audiences 'no aesthetic shelter'. The house-lights were brought up mercilessly as the bleeding, blinded Gloucester crawled slowly off stage, with no help or words of comfort from the indifferent servants" (28). Gone was the Elizabethan costume of Granville-Barker's Old Vic staging, replaced by a cast dressed in furs and leathers, compelled to eke out survival in a primitive world and "gathered in ritualistic ceremony around the King's huge, boulder-like throne." Lear, played by Paul Scofield, "was a dangerous, tough king, with an inscrutable face, close-cropped grey hair and a terrifying voice" (29).

Like Macready more than a century earlier, Brook thrust the play back into the barbaric past, but not for the sake of making the production correspond "with the period, and with the circumstances of the text," as the 1838 staging had sought to do. Rather, Brook had something more contemporary in mind. In keeping with this vision, Brook chose sets that transformed the stage into a kind of stone-age junkyard, full of rusting metal, tattered, worn-out looking costumes, and beat-up furniture. Like the sets, Scofield's Lear wondered the stage, "a character stripped to its muscles and sinews, lacking ornament of any kind," according to Kevin Hagopian. "His world is clearly in austere yet meaningful order. Instantly, with his attempt to divide his kingdom equitably, that order starts to disintegrate. By the end of the play, with Lear descending deeper into emotional and physical disability, Brook's scene design choices, and his understanding of his protagonist, come together in a collision of dread and insight…Surreal, horrifying, deadly, Lear's world dissolves into a fractured series of glimpses of the inferno, splinters of a world gone mad" (30). By the end of that decade Brook would take the cast of the stage production to North Jutland in Denmark to film the play in a cold, winter landscape that was as unaccommodating and abstract as his stage had been. The result, according to Hagopian, was a film "that touched the minor chords of its age. Brook's *Lear* is the late 1960s everyman, toppled from sanity and sureness by the whirlwind of change" (31).

As was the case with Macready's *Lear*, which rendered so many of the previous efforts to commingle Shakespeare and Tate's versions obsolete, it can be argued that Brook's RSC production and subsequent film essentially erased the performance history of the play, forcing at least a generation of directors and actors who followed to negotiate with his/Scofield's Lear. One had to emulate it, build on it, or reject it; but there was no ignoring it. Thus Trevor Nunn's 1968 RSC production set the play in an ancient Bronze age kingdom, recalling the primitivism of Brook's set; but Nunn countered his effort to suggest decay perhaps by emphasizing just how far Lear would fall. Eric Porter's white-haired/-bearded king and the other characters appear onstage initially dressed in sumptuous gold robes. This was not Beckett's Lear. When Nunn returned to the play in 1976 to direct an RSC production starring Donald Sinden, the ancient past was gone, replaced by a late nine-teenth-century kingdom.

Coming nearly three decades after Brook, perhaps Nicholas Hyntner's 1990 RSC production, with John Wood in the title role, sought in part to wipe the slate clean and restart the play from a vacuum. The minimalist set, consisting of a white open-sided box, "provided a painfully bright, white space for the action, isolating and alienating the characters within" (32). An empty white box brilliantly anticipates the absence that dominates so much of the linguistic, emotional, and spiritual content of the play once Cordelia informs her father that she has "nothing" to say. But might it also suggest the emptiness of a world rapidly becoming virtual—a world in which we, like the king who inadvertently turns his daughter into a prophet by being reduced to nothing, are moving inexorably toward—a divided kingdom consisting of and ruled by nothing more than 0s and 1s? Or should we "look up," as Edgar instructs Lear to do right before he dies? Maybe we should see the open-sided box of Hyntner's production as a space of possibility, an open invitation to re-start the history of *Lear* on stage, thereby doing all we really can do: domesticate the nothingness and the division in all our kingdoms by staging them again and again.

Notes:
1. See C.J. Sisson, "Shakespeare's quartos as prompt-copies, with some account of Cholomey's players, and a new Shakespeare allusion," Review of English Studies 18 (1942): 129-43.
2. From the "Dedicatory Epistle" to *The History of King Lear, Acted at the Duke's Theatre. Reviv'd with Alterations* (London: printed for E. Flesher, 1681)
3. *The Preface to Shakespeare: Together with selected notes on some of the plays* (1765).
4. *Dramatic Miscellanies* (Dublin, 1784), p. 212. Quoted in Barbara Freeman, "Performing the Bodies of King Lear." Studies in Philology (45).
5. Quoted in http://www.rsc.org.uk/lear/about/stage.html
6. *Memoirs of the life of David Garrick, Esq Interspersed with characters and anecdotes of his theatrical contemporaries. The whole forming a history of the stage, which includes a period of thirty-six years* (London, 1784), I: 49-50
7. Quoted in Freeman, "Performing."
8. Quoted in http://www.rsc.org.uk/lear/about/stage.html
10. *King Lear: A Tragedy in Five Acts*, By William Shakespeare, in *Cumberland's British Theatre*, Volume 6 (London: John Cumberland, 1830), p. 8. Quoted in *William Shakespeare's King Lear: A Sourcebook*, ed. Grage Ioppolo (London: Routledge, 2003), p. 78.
12. George C. D. Odell, *Annals of the New York Stage* 10 vols (New York: Columbia University Press, 1927-49), II: 588

13. Raymund FitzSimons, *Edmund Kean: Fire From Heaven* (London: Hamish Hamilton Ltd., 1976), p. 138.

14. James Rees, *The Life of Edwin Forrest. With Reminiscences and Personal Recollections* (Philadelphia: T.B. Peterson & Brothers, 1874), p. 168.

15. F. E. Halliday, *A Shakespeare Companion 1564-1964* (Baltimore, Penguin, 1964), pp. 265-66.

16. William Macready. *The Diaries of William Charles Macready 1833-1851*, ed. William Toynbee, 2 vols. (New York: G.P. Putnum's Sons, 1912), II: 229.

17. Odell, *Annals*, II: 195

18. Odell, *Annals*, II: 210-11

19. Wingate, Charles E.L. Wingate, *Shakespeare's Heroes on the Stage* 2 vols. (New York: Thomas Y. Crowell & Company, 1896), I: 93.

20. *Shakespearean Tragedy* (New York: Meridian Books/St. Martin's Press, 1960), 210.

21. *King Lear, A Tragedy in Five Acts, By William Shakespeare, as arranged for the stage by Henry Irving, and presented at The Lyceum Theatre, On November 10, 1892* (London: Nassau Steam Press, Ltd., 1892), p. 5.

22. Odell, *Annals*, II: 446

23. *Shakespearean Tragedy*, pp. 200, 201.

24. *The Oxford King Lear* (USA: Oxford University Press, 2002), p. 72.

25. *Prefaces to Shakespeare* (London: Sidwick & Jackson, Ltd, 1927), p. 229.

26. "Komisarjevsky at Stratford-upon-Avon," *Shakespeare Survey* 36 (1983): 73-84; p. 79.

27. Quoted in Berry, "Komisarjevsky," p. 73.

28. Wells, *Lear*, p. 73.

30. Quoted in http://www.rsc.org.uk/lear/about/stage.html

31. *Exploring Shakespeare/RSC*: http://www.rsc.org.uk/explore/kinglear/2817_2814.htm

32. *Exploring Shakespeare/RSC*: http://www.rsc.org.uk/explore/kinglear/2817_2814.htm

34. *New York Institute: Film Notes – King Lear*: http://www.albany.edu/writers-inst/fns98n11.html

35. *New York Institute: Film Notes – King Lear*: http://www.albany.edu/writers-inst/fns98n11.html

36. *Exploring Shakespeare/RSC*: www.rsc.org.uk/explore/kinglear/2817_2814.htm

As Performed

By the Shakespeare Theatre Company in Washington, DC in 2000

Bradley D. Ryner

In 2000, Michael Kahn, the Artistic Director of the Shakespeare Theatre Company, directed a production of *King Lear* that was highly original: without reducing the sweeping scope of Shakespeare's play to a domestic tragedy, Kahn placed a believably textured father-daughter relationship at the heart of the production.

Normally, the character of Cordelia is not the most memorable element of *King Lear*. The entire play hinges on her reluctance to speak, meaning she gets relatively few lines before disappearing for the majority of the play. The role was probably written for a third-string boy actor (the company's best two boys would have played Gonoril and Regan). How does one transform a role written for a young actor of modest talents into a more rounded and interesting character? For Kahn, the answer was to cast the deaf actress Monique Holt as a deaf Cordelia, who reads lips and communicates through sign language. In this production, the relationship between Cordelia and Lear was unusually nuanced because Lear's apparently genuine love for his favorite daughter had not extended to learning sign language in order to communicate with her directly.

THE ONSTAGE WORLD OF KAHN'S *Lear*

Because Kahn's production of *King Lear* stressed the significance of Cordelia's non-verbal communication, it seems appropriate to begin by looking at the production's own non-verbal signifying elements, such as setting, props, costumes, and the actors' physical appearances.

The bleak mood of the production was largely informed by Georgi Alexi-Meskhishvili's stage design, which suggested a post-industrial wasteland. The stage was littered with empty oil drums that served as chairs, tables, and hiding places for the characters. A large sheet of metal served as a backdrop, and one could easily imagine that the action was taking place inside a giant, rusty oil drum. The inorganic stage dressing fit with Kahn's idea that the protagonists "were all in purgatory" and must "go through a lot in order to emerge as real people, as humans with real human qualities" (1).

Most of the play's props seemed perfectly at home in this desolate world: a discarded tire in which to bind Gloucester and a leather blindfold to cover his empty eye sockets; wilted flowers for Lear to gather on the heath and a garland of dead weeds for him to wear in his madness. One memorable prop, however, stood out in sharp contrast to its surroundings. In the first act, Lear was presented with a giant, round birthday cake, decorated with a representation of England in lush green and electric blue frosting. It has become conventional to have a map of England onstage for the division of the kingdom scene. Some Lears have judiciously marked boundary lines on the map as they parceled out the land, and then angrily redrawn these boundaries to exclude Cordelia. Other Lears have furiously torn the map in two, flinging half to Gonoril and half to Regan. I found the cake's frosted map particularly effective, in part because it was such an obviously idealized vision of Lear's kingdom. It was very easy to feel sympathy for this childish, shortsighted Lear, who was unaware that by offering his daughters a slice of his fantasy world, he was simultaneously destroying it. Of course, a dream world made of confectioner's sugar and food coloring is ultimately no healthier a delusion than the nightmare world of metal and dead plants in which the protagonists of this production suffered.

The contrast between the starkly horrifying stuff of nightmares and the appealing but tawdry stuff of dreams was similarly evident in the production's costumes (also designed by Alexi-Meskhishvili). The male characters mostly wore vaguely pre-1945 military dress in blacks and grays. Lear and Gloucester both began the play in sleek, black formalwear and ended in tattered earth-toned rags. Gonoril and Regan, on the other hand, wore the garish trappings of 1950's and 1960's high fashion. They appeared mostly in cocktail dresses and high heels, accented with feathers and furs. Even when roused in the middle of the night to deal with Gloucester, Regan had taken the time to throw on an immense fur coat and stylish orange heels—though not the time to remove her beauty mask. Thus, the production established a simple gender division. The male characters were austere, at one with the inorganic, bleak world of the set. The female characters were glamorous, though their theatrical artifice was all too evident.

The Fool and Cordelia, however, failed to conform to this pattern. The Fool's costume was composed of rags and tatters, not unlike those that Lear and Gloucester wore by the end of the play, except that the Fool wore his with panache. Unlike Lear and Gloucester, who were forced to give up the sartorial markings of the conventional social order when they found themselves on the heath, the Fool had constructed himself outside this order from the beginning. He wore a bizarre skullcap with shining protuberances of hair or wire (it was impossible to tell which from a distance) jutting out from its top. The Fool's prosthetic hair seemed to parody Cordelia's actual hair, which was bleached white and spiked up in a punk hairstyle that was at least two decades more modern than the other characters. Her long jacket was

Tara Hicken as Gonoril
Courtesy of the Shakespeare Theatre Company

tailored to intimate the lines of a Jacobean doublet, but belonged to no actual historical period. Visually differentiated from the established order, the Fool and Cordelia were also exceptionally close in this production. Their closeness was underscored by the fact that the Fool, who appeared to be the only member of Lear's court who understood sign language, served as Cordelia's translator, so we heard the majority of her lines in his voice.

Clothes and hair were not the only markers that differentiated Cordelia from her sisters. Whereas Lear, Gonoril, and Regan were played by white actors, Holt was born in South Korea (2). Kahn reportedly wanted Cordelia to look "as if she was from a different family than [her] older avaricious sisters" (2). But how was the audience to know whether to read this difference metaphorically or literally? Should they have interpreted race as a metaphor for the differences in personality and temperament between Cordelia and the rest of her family? Or, should they have imagined that Cordelia was actually the product of a different marriage, or that she was a bastard, like Edmund? Contemplating these questions pulls us from the onstage world to the offstage world—the world of hypothetical narratives and real life biography.

THE OFFSTAGE WORLD OF KAHN'S *Lear*

Perhaps it is futile to speculate about what takes place offstage. After all, Cordelia, Lear, and the rest are fictional characters who have no independent lives offstage. When I saw this production, I assumed that Holt's race was being used metaphorically. Doing so seemed simpler than constructing an imaginary narrative that would account for Cordelia's biological difference from her sisters. However, it should be clear from what follows that such imaginary narratives are invaluable to actors, directors, and audience members trying to make sense of plays. Moreover, these imaginary narratives connect in profound ways to people's real life experiences.

In fact, Kahn only arrived at the idea of an imaginary deaf character because of his desire to cast a real-life deaf actor. Mary Vreeland, a deaf actor who had appeared in his production of *Mother Courage*, gave him a list of roles suited to deaf actors that included Cordelia (2). Using Lear's inability to understand sign language as a symbol for his failure to communicate with his daughter seemed perfect. As Kahn explains, "In the play's crucial first scene, people communicate by telling lies or use speech for

Ted van Griethuysen as Lear and Monique Holt as Cordelia
Courtesy of the Shakespeare Theatre Company

power or manipulation…The only daughter who tells the truth is banished. So I thought it might be interesting if indeed it was a person who didn't speak…" (2). Several very effective moments followed from this choice. Lear was able to chillingly silence Cordelia in the first act by grabbing her hands. In Act 4, the King of France's love for Cordelia was demonstrated by the fact that he had learned sign language. Lear himself, upon being reunited with Cordelia, attempted to invent signs by which to communicate with her. Clumsily signing to her, he exclaimed, "Do not laugh at me, / For as I am a man, I think this lady / To be my child, Cordelia" (4.7.66-68). At this point, Cordelia responded in a soft, unsteady voice with the irregular sound that results from not being able to hear one's own pronunciation, "And so, I am, I am" (4.7.68). This moment, in which each character tried to reach out to the other by using the other's mode of expression, was extremely moving.

Significantly, Holt approached Cordelia's deafness literally. As a result, she saw a problem that no one else seemed to notice: "Why would Cordelia sign if there were no one else to sign to?" wondered Holt, who pointed out that, "in real life, [she] would not sign to a non-signer" (3). To deal with this problem, Holt, Kahn, and the other actors created in imaginary backstory in which, "Lear had abandoned his responsibility for Cordelia by hiring teachers to instruct her in sign language, while remaining too distressed by her deafness to learn to sign himself." In this narrative, the Fool had secretly observed her lessons and learned how to communicate with her (Berson 48). Jessica Berson observes that this imaginary story is "a familiar one to those in the Deaf community" because "most hearing parents of deaf children never learn A[merican] S[ign] L[anguage]" (Berson 48). Thus, the imagined backstory, which is connected obliquely to Holt's lived experience, helps to frame the narrative within a set of real-world concerns.

The relationship between fictional and real-life narratives was also important to Ted van Griethuysen, who played Lear. Van Griethuysen is a student of Eli Siegel, whose theory of aesthetic realism involves seeing both the real world and works of art as structured by balanced oppositions (4). In van Griethuysen's words, "Lear is a certain relation of coolness and intensity…so am I. The way I'm cold and warm is different from the way Lear is cold and warm. But the opposites, the coldness and warmth, are universal" (4). To understand Lear's anger toward Cordelia, van Griethuysen remembered a time in his mid-twenties when he felt contempt for his mother. He said that aesthetic realism helped him to realize that this contempt stemmed from a more subtly pervasive contempt for "the whole world that was different from [himself]" (4). Recalling how difficult it was for him to learn to empathize with the outside world in his twenties, van Griethuysen extrapolated how devastating the lesson would have been for Lear in his eighties.

This fluid movement between the play and deeply personal real-world narratives must have been satisfying for Kahn, who staged the production in part because he wanted "to explore the issue of getting older and the issue of families" (1). He said that he was gratified to hear from audience members that the production "helped them understand their aged father, whom they'd just put in a nursing home" (1).

THE WORLD OF THE TEXT

As we have seen above, the director's, designer's, and actors' decisions about casting, characterization, sets, props, and costumes succeeded in creating an onstage world that connected meaningfully to the real lives of its cast and audience members. However, Shakespearean productions cannot generate meaning *ex nihilo*—as Lear knows, "Nothing can come of nothing" (1.1.87). Good productions, like this one, use the text as a framework: it serves a basis on which to build a new structure, but it also places limits on what shape that structure can take.

Obviously, Cordelia's deafness works within the framework of *King Lear* because one of its major thematic concerns is impediments to communication. Making the Fool her translator creates a new relationship between two characters that are never onstage at the same time in the text. Nonetheless, the affinity between the two is established in the text itself. They represent two opposed ways of speaking truth to Lear. Whereas Cordelia is laconic and reluctant to use rhetoric, the Fool employs highly wrought speeches filled with jests and wordplay. Both tell Lear what he does not want to hear, and Lear ignores them both. In the text, Lear's language conflates the two characters when he says of the dead Cordelia, "my poor fool is hanged" (5.3.306). During Shakespeare's time, "fool" was a term of endearment. Kahn's production literalized the association implicit in this line by bringing onstage the body of the Fool, who had apparently been hanged alongside Cordelia.

At one point, the production pushed the framework of the text almost to its breaking point. In the final scene, Lear, imagining that he hears the voice of his dead child, claims, "Her voice was ever soft, / Gentle, and low, an excellent thing in woman" (5.3.273-274). This line raised an unexpected set of questions in the context of Kahn's production. Why would Lear imagine hearing the voice of a daughter who almost never spoke? Moreover, was he imagining the soft, unsure voice that the audience had heard proclaiming "I am" in Act 4, or was he fantasizing about the voice he wished his daughter had? Although the text seemed to be pushing against the production choice at this moment, the resulting tension was highly effective, since it highlighted a tension already present in the text. On one hand, it is satisfying to see Lear, who failed to listen to his daughter early in the play, finally longing to hear her speak. On the other hand, he praises the qualities that diminish the forcefulness of her speech – its softness, gentleness, and lowness. Ultimately, I am forced to wonder if Lear ends by retreating into the same solipsistic fantasy world in which he began. In Kahn's production, these lines were even more troubling. Even if

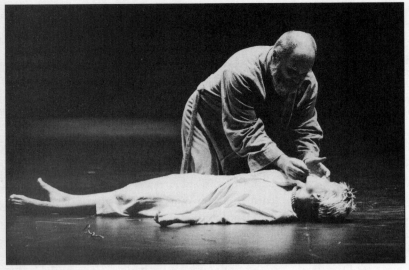

Ted van Griethuysen as Lear and Monique Holt as Cordelia
Courtesy of the Shakespeare Theatre Company

Lear was not imagining away Cordelia's deafness, he was choosing to praise her vocal expression at the expense of her more fluent use of sign language. Thus, the final tableau felt like a sad falling off from their fourth act reunion. This scene, like the production in general, managed to work within the framework of the text to create a uniquely compelling new narrative.

Notes:

1. Horwitz, Jane. "'Lear' & Dear to the Heart." *The Washington Post* 5 Oct. 99: C05.
2. Kuchwara, Michael. "Playing Cordelia in 'Lear.' *Associated Press* 21 Sep. 1999. *Lexis-Nexis Academic.* 13 Apr. 2007.
3. Berson, Jessica. "Performing Deaf Identity: Toward a Continuum of Deaf Performance." *Bodies in Commotion.* Ed. Carrie Sandahl and Philip Auslander. Ann Arbor: University of Michigan Press, 2005.
4. Triplett, William. "Lear and Present Danger." *The Washington Post* 5 Sep. 99: G01

"Unaccommodated Man"

King Lear IN POPULAR CULTURE

Douglas Lanier, University of New Hampshire

OLD KING LEAR AND YOUTH CULTURE

The Mount Everest of the Shakespearean canon, *King Lear* would seem to offer adaptors a wealth of material with which to work: a plotline which in schematic form resembles a fairy tale of a foolish king; character relationships grounded in archetypal tensions between fathers and children; durable themes such as neglected love, political authoritarianism, downfall and redemption, and the vagaries of cosmic justice; memorable stage images like Lear raging at the storm or carrying his dead daughter; thrilling scenes of battle, madness, intrigue and pathos; and some of Shakespeare's most indelible speeches and lines. Yet, of Shakespeare's five most popular tragedies (*Romeo and Juliet, Hamlet, Othello, King Lear*, and *Macbeth*) *King Lear* has proved the least accommodating to adaptation in modern popular culture, and there are several reasons for this resistance. Contemporary popular culture is predominantly youth-oriented, so Shakespeare's focus on the travails of two old men runs against the prevailing grain. Indeed, the absolute power of Lear and Gloucester as aristocratic fathers and their capacity to tyrannize their children and underlings so completely (at first) is foreign to the fathers typical of current popular culture, whose attempts to exert authority are often portrayed as ineffectual or comic. Lear's ferocious misogyny toward his daughters, however indicative it may be of his complex psychology of infantile projection and child-like rage, makes him strikingly unsympathetic to modern audiences familiar with feminism. And perhaps most importantly, the overwhelming sense of loss and hopelessness that pervades the final scene of this play, Shakespeare's bleakest tragedy, is difficult to square with the predominantly affirmational nature of popular culture, its preference for happy endings or for edifying, reassuring lessons to be drawn from misfortune.

The play's resistance to pop culture conventions, however, has made *King Lear* suitable for avant-garde or confrontational adaptations. Samuel

Beckett's *Endgame* (1957) features myriad echoes of Shakespeare's play, and several commentators have remarked that Peter Brook's bleak film *King Lear* (1971) owes much to Beckett. Howard Barker's *Seven Lears* (1989) offers an unconventional prequel to *King Lear*, tracing Lear's life through the "seven ages of man" and situating Lear's mother at the center of his tormented psychology. Jean-Luc Godard's 1987 adaptation uses the play to meditate on the fate of art in a post-modern world dominated by American culture. In Godard's film, William Shakespeare Jr. the Fifth, a modern reporter, attempts to recover the words of his famous ancestor, lost after a Chernobyl-like disaster, by listening to the Shakespearean exchanges between an American gangster, Don Learo, and his daughter Cordelia. The relationship between politics and brutality is particularly strong in two British theatrical adaptations: Edward Bond's *Lear* (1971), in which Lear's cruel authoritarianism prompts rebellion from two of his daughters only in the end to lead to Cordelia's reestablishment of a tyrannical regime; and Adrian Mitchell's *The Tragedy of King Real* (1982, filmed as *King Real and the Hoodlums* in 1983), a rock musical which converts Shakespeare's tragedy into a nuclear holocaust morality play. Kristian Levring's superb Dogme film *The King is Alive* (2000) also partakes of this adaptational tradition. It offers a savage critique of Western middle-class privilege by portraying the gradual psychological breakdown of a group of tourists stranded in the Namibian desert. To stave off boredom and despair, the group decides to perform scenes from *King Lear* that, ironically, only magnify their escalating antagonisms and madness. Arguably, Ian Pollock's comic book version of *King Lear* (1984) is also affiliated with this avant-garde tradition, for though it uses an uncut version of Shakespeare's text, its expressionist illustrations and barren landscapes are more reminiscent of Beckett and Brook than conventional comic books.

Paul Mazursky's film *Harry and Tonto* (1974) illustrates nicely how adaptors often struggle to resolve the mismatch between Shakespeare's tragedy and the conventions of popular culture. Mazursky's film tells the tale of aging widower Harry Coombes and his cat Tonto who become homeless when Harry's New York apartment is demolished. Stripped of his belongings and acquaintances, Harry journeys to his children's homes and in the process, encounters an American underclass he has never before known. Mazursky pointedly mutes the unsympathetic, irascible qualities of

Shakespeare's father-king. Unlike Lear, Harry is quietly philosophical about his lot, though at the moment of his eviction he angrily launches into Lear's "reason not the need" (2.2.426) and "blow, winds, and crack your cheeks" (3.2.1) speeches. Grafting elements of *King Lear* onto the sixties' road movie, Mazursky's target for critique is the American bourgeois mainstream, exemplified by Harry's dysfunctional children. Like *King Lear, Harry and Tonto* ends with a poignant death, that of Harry's beloved pet and traveling companion Tonto, a surrogate for Cordelia and the Fool. However, in keeping with the affirmational tone of popular culture Mazursky softens Shakespeare's tragic ending: Harry will move in with an eccentric cat lady he has just met, perhaps to begin a romance. The film's final tableau shows Harry watching a boy build sand castles on a beach as the sun sets, an image of age and youth in tandem and of fragile renewal for an unfinished life.

GANGSTER EPICS, WESTERNS, AND FAMILY MELODRAMAS

Finding an apt analogy for Shakespeare's tyrannous patriarch-king in the post-dynastic modern world has posed a challenge for popular adaptations of *King Lear*, but the gangster and the Western genres offer solutions. Two recent British gangster films have reimagined Lear as an aging kingpin struggling to maintain his criminal empire. *Shiner* (dir. John Irvin, 2000) uses motifs from *Lear* in its exploration of petty boxing promoter Billy "Shiner" Simpson who, after losing a desperate gamble on a fight, gradually discovers the depths of distrust and fear he has bred among his children and followers. *My Kingdom* (dir. Don Boyd, 2001) is a more thoroughgoing adaptation of Shakespeare's play. In it, Sandeman, an authoritarian Merseyside, England mob boss, becomes consumed with rage, paranoia and revenge when his beloved wife Mandy is killed in a mugging. Disowning his loyal daughter Jo, he falls to the mercy of his daughters Tracy and Kath, both of whom resent their father's tyrannical control and lack of love. Tracy's brutally sadistic husband Jug corresponds to Cornwall, and Kath's son plays the Fool, acting as Sandeman's confidante as he confronts the consequences of his treatment of his daughters. Like *Harry and Tonto, My Kingdom* evidences some of pop culture's discomfort with Shakespeare's bleak ending. Though Sandeman sets up an elaborate revenge upon his daughters and survives the final carnage, at film's end, his remaining daughter Jo abandons him on the quayside, suggesting the Pyrrhic nature of his victory.

Because land empires are often at issue, the Western provides adaptations of *King Lear* with an epic scope. Two revisionist Westerns by noted directors, Edward Dmytryk's *Broken Lance* (1954) and Anthony Mann's *The Man from Laramie* (1955), have used elements from Shakespeare's tragedy, the former from the Lear plot (as imagined from the perspective of a faithful son, Cordelia's equivalent), the latter from the Gloucester plot (including his blindness and misplaced trust of his duplicitous child). As might be expected from this masculine genre, Lear's daughters become cattlemen's sons in both films. The TV film *King of Texas* (dir. Uli Edel, 2002) is a close adaptation of *Lear* as a Western. In this version Lear's children remain daughters and Lear dies in the end, cradling his devoted daughter Claudia after she has been shot. Interestingly, the film provides an explanation for Lear's irascible temperament, making him somewhat sympathetic: his emotional hardness

Spencer Tracy as Matt Devereaux in the 1954 film *Broken Lance* directed by Edward Dmytryk
Courtesy of Douglas Lanier

comes from his sacrifices to preserve his ranching empire, struggles which earlier led to the deaths of his wife and only son.

Popular adaptors often jettison the political dimensions of Shakespeare's tragedy, recrafting the narrative as a family melodrama in a range of settings:

- **Randolph Stow's novel** *To the Islands* **(1958)** - chronicles the decline of Stephen Heriot, master of a mission station for Aborginals in Northwest Australia
- **Angus Wilson's novel** *Late Call* **(1964)** - retired hotel housekeeper Sylvia Calvert is forced to live with her son and retreat into memory
- **David Lowell Rich's** *Rosie!* **(1967)** - (from Ruth Gordon's play, *A Very Rich Woman*) a matriarch is nearly driven insane by her money-hungry daughters but is saved by her granddaughter and her lawyer
- **John Boorman's film** *Where the Heart Is* **(1990)** - tensions arise between a property developer and children over a building scheduled for demolition; the children and the father become dispossessed and eventually reunite
- **Jon Robin Baitz's play** *The Substance of Fire* **(1991)** - a family struggles over the fate of a small publishing house
- **Nagle Jackson's play** *Taking Leave* **(2000)** - a Shakespeare professor and his family are forced to confront his descent into Alzheimer's disease

"O, HOW THIS MOTHER SWELLS UP TOWARD MY HEART!": FEMINIST REINTERPRETATIONS

Of these family melodramas, Jane Smiley's distinguished novel *A Thousand Acres* (1991, filmed 1997) is perhaps the best known (it won the Pulitzer Prize for fiction and the National Book Critics Circle Award). As in adaptations to the Western genre, a land empire, here a thousand-acre farm in rural Iowa, is at the heart of this family conflict. Ruled by a bullying patriarch, Larry Cook, the farm remains fertile, but the aquifer underneath the land is contaminated with pesticides and fertilizers, a metaphor for the poisoned feelings that run beneath the Cook family's superficially civil relationships with each other. Though the novel remains faithful to Shakespeare's narrative in its first half, Smiley's adaptation has been controversial for several reasons. First, the story is retold from the perspective of Ginny, the novel's Gonoril figure. Unlike Gonoril's presentation in *King Lear*, Smiley presents Ginny sympathetically; by contrast, the devotion of Caroline (Cordelia) to her father is misguided and condescending to her sisters. Second, Smiley reshapes Ginny's tale into a narrative of feminist awakening and redemption. As events unfold, Ginny comes to resent her father's power over the family and the effects it has wrought on her life. Most controversially, Smiley radically remotivates the antagonism between Gonoril and Lear. In her version, Ginny turns on Larry when repressed memories of Larry's sexual abuse of Ginny and her sister Rose resurface. Though Smiley delineates the tragic ruin of the Cook family and their farming empire, she offers hope amidst the ruin. Like her Shakespearean counterpart, Ginny is tempted to poison her sister but changes her mind in time to save Rose; she also leaves a cold, unfruitful marriage with her good-hearted but ineffectual husband Ty for a menial job, which offers her a measure of independence. Despite these parallels, Smiley publicly distances her work from *King Lear* comparisons.

Nevertheless, Smiley's novel is one of several popular adaptations that have addressed the problematic gender and sexual politics of *King Lear*. Gordon Bottomley's prequel *Lear's Wife* (1915), a Georgian verse drama, provides a proto-feminist critique of Shakespeare's play. Diana Paxson's *The Serpent's Tooth* (1991), a fantasy retelling of the Lear story from the perspective of Cordelia (here Cridilla), reimagines Lear's meek daughter as a warrior princess who returns after being exiled by her father to save and eventually to rule the kingdom. Elaine Feinstein's play *Lear's Daughters* (1987, for the Women's Theatre Group) is more explicitly feminist in its politics, anatomizing the psychologies of Cordelia, Regan, and Gonoril by imagining their family life before Shakespeare's play begins. In Feinstein's version, King Lear is largely an absent father, preoccupied with travel and philandering. After the aloof Queen's death, a nurse who tells the girls fairy stories about mythic fathers fulfills the parental role. An androgynous Fool serves as narrator and sardonic commentator, and the action occurs within a claustrophobic tower that symbolizes the economic privilege and patriarchal mythology shaping the girls' development. In 2000, Toronto's Necessary Angel Theatre (NAT) created *Hysterica*, a free adaptation of *Lear* with matriarch Mama Leda, a Greek businesswoman, as tyrant over her two sons; this adaptation was an offshoot of NAT's several cross-gendered productions of *King Lear*.

Indeed, several companies have experimented with cross-gendered recasting, including *The Lear Project* (1998) for Shakespeare & Co. in Massachusetts and Mabou Mines' *Lear* (1990) in New York City. Taking the prison episode that opens *King Lear* 5.3 as its starting point, Scottish playwright Joan Ure's *Something in it for Cordelia* (1979) recasts Lear and Cordelia as modern shabby aristocrats. The feminist Cordelia convinces her father to give his wealth to charity and take up residence in a Highland retreat, where the two sign autographs and sell produce to tourists. The sexual politics of the play have also been explored in two theatrical adaptations concerned with homosexual themes: Alison Lyssa's *Pinball* (1980, in which a lesbian mother fights for custody of her child) and Reginald Jackson's *House of Lear* (1994, in which Lear is a drag queen dying of AIDS).

Several other popular adaptations warrant mention, if only to suggest the extraordinary ingenuity of the adaptors. One is "Lear the Giant-King" (2000), a game scenario for the Dungeons & Dragons game published by Mike Selinker in *Dungeon Adventures*. (Selinker has also created Shakespeare-themed game scenarios for *Macbeth* and *The Tempest*.) Another is Scot LaHaie's recent *Lear Reloaded* (2007), which crosses *King Lear* with motifs drawn from the film series *The Matrix* (1999-2003). Both of these versions eschew the family melodrama genre, instead treating Shakespeare's narrative in terms of fantasy and science fiction. Though it would seem particularly uncongenial to revise *Lear* as a comedy, parodies have appeared in episodes of *Do Not Adjust Your Set* (1968) and *Saturday Night Live* (1990).

Music has not been an amenable form for adapting *King Lear* either. Despite the nineteenth century vogue for operatic adaptations of Shakespearean tragedies, major composers *bypassed King Lear*, though Hector Berlioz, Mily Balakirev, and Paul Dukas produced overtures based on the play. It was only in the twentieth century that major operas of *Lear* were produced, by Aribert Reimann in 1978, Darijan Bozic in 1986, and Aulis Sallinen in 2000.

"MY TEARS BEGIN TO TAKE HIS PART SO MUCH, / THEY'LL MAR MY COUNTERFEITING": RE-ENACTING *Lear*

Another strategy for adapting *King Lear* has been to explore parallels between actors performing *Lear* and the roles they play. Though this approach has been used for many other Shakespeare plays, particularly the major tragedies, it has been especially prominent for *King Lear* wherein the aging Lear becomes symbolic of the theater, faced as it has been throughout the twentieth century with dispossession by its own upstart children, film and television. Ronald Harwood's acclaimed play *The Dresser* (1980, filmed 1983) illustrates this sub-genre well. It chronicles the last days of Sir, an aging actor-manager struggling through a performance of *King Lear* in wartime Britain, and his faithful dresser Norman, a closeted gay man devoted to Sir's care. Like Lear, Sir has led a self-centered life, ignorant and abusive of those who truly love him. At once powerful and pathetic, self-dramatizing and self-pitying, he has become with age half-mad, half-senile as he faces death and cultural obsolescence, sustained by Norman who, unlike Lear's Fool, faithfully maintains Sir's illusions about himself. Tragedy comes when, after Sir's performance, he falls dead and Norman learns that Sir has said nothing about him in his unfinished memoir. Norman's final howl "What about me?" pathetically echoes that of Lear with the dead Cordelia, but it also voices the demands of modernity in the face of a tyrannical, outmoded cultural institution. Reportedly, Harwood modeled "Sir" on Donald Wolfit, a noted Shakespearean for whom he served as dresser. Other adaptations concerning theatrical institutions include:

• **Hy Kraft's *Café Crown* (1942)** - set in the Lower East Side's once-thriving Yiddish theater district, a flamboyant director hopes to improve *Lear* by giving Shakespeare's protagonist a wife and palatial apartment
• **Desmond Rayner's novel *The Dawlish Season* (1984)** - examines parallels between family production of *King Lear* and tensions in the Dawlish family
• **Marc van der Velden's children's play *Cordelia* (1996)** - imagines that Cordelia takes on the Fool's role in disguise after he had died
• **James Patrick Kelly's story "Itsy Bitsy Spider" (1997)** - portrays the performance of a scene from *Lear* between an aging Shakespearean and an android replacement for his deceased daughter
• **Fred Curchack and Shannon Kearns's multimedia play *Lear's Shadow* (2000)** - an aging actor becomes unhinged by memories of his dead lover as he watches a videotape of himself auditioning for *Lear*

• **Season 3 of the Canadian TV series** *Slings and Arrows* **(2006)** - chronicles the struggles of the resident company of the New Burbage Festival to perform *Lear*, with parallels between characters and actors

"THOU BEACON TO THIS UNDER GLOBE": CROSS-CULTURAL ADAPTATIONS OF *King Lear*

In contrast to *Lear*'s somewhat anemic afterlife in modern Anglo-American popular culture, *Lear* has been one of the favorite Shakespearean plays to adapt in several non-English speaking cultures, particularly in those where traditions of reverence and respect toward the elderly remain strong. For example, Yiddish adaptations of *King Lear*, particularly Jacob Gordin's *Der Yiddisher Koenig Lear* [*The Yiddish King Lear*, 1892] and *Mirele Efros* [*The Yiddish Queen Lear*, 1898], enjoyed considerable popularity, enough so that Harry Thomashefsky produced a film version of *The Yiddish King Lear* in 1935. Vestigial memory of that tradition lives on in popular culture, not only in Julia Pascal's play *The Yiddish Queen Lear* (1999, which portrays the efforts of a Jewish actress to establish a Yiddish theater in New York and the machinations of her daughters to depose her) but also in "Guess Who's Coming to Criticize Dinner" (1999), an episode of *The Simpsons* in which Krusty the Clown, the show's resident Jewish comic, performs his version of *King Lear* at a dinner theater. *The Kathakali King Lear* (1990), a multinational production by Annette Leday, David McRuvie, Kalamandalam Padmanabhan Nair, and K. Kumaran Nairthe, hybridized Shakespeare's tragedy with Kathakali, the traditional Southern Indian dance-drama form. This production was performed in the new Globe Theatre in London in its opening season in 1999. It might be fruitfully compared to the adaptation of Hindi director Amal Allana, *Maharaja Yashwant Rao* (1989), which reconceives Lear as an arrogant Rajput prince.

East Asian adaptations of *King Lear* have been equally robust. The affinities between Asian theatrical traditions and *King Lear* have long been recognized. John Gielgud's 1955 production of the play at Stratford-upon-Avon, for example, visually referenced the iconography of traditional Japanese Kabuki theater. When Singaporean director Ong Keng Sen wanted to create a pan-Asian play for the Perth Festival in 1997, he turned to *King Lear* because he regarded it as a fable of "universal significance" equally relevant to the six cultures he referenced. The result was *Lear*, a work in which Shakespeare's characters were inflected not only through traditional archetypes of Asian theater (e.g., the Old Man of Japanese Noh Theater, the Young Daughter of Thai dance-theater, and the older daughter of Chinese opera) but also through cultural stereotypes of modern Asia, such as the Fool, a girl in a jogging suit carrying a camera. Sen uses *King Lear* to provide not only an example of Asian interculturalism but also a portrait of

Kalamandalam Padmanabhan Nair as Lear, Kalamandalam MPS Namboodiri as Gonoril, and Kalamandalam Manoj Kumar as the Fool in "The Kathakali King Lear"
Photo: Donald Cooper

Asian conflicts between traditionalism and modernity. Several recent productions have offered imaginative transpositions of *King Lear* into Chinese operatic styles: Wang Lian and Wang Yongshi's *King Qi's Dream* (1995); Wu Hsing-kuo's tour-de-force one-man show *King Lear* (2000, a.k.a. *Lear Alone*), produced for the Contemporary Legend Theater; and Lu Jiang's *King Liguang* (dir. Yu Shengpu, 2002).

KOZINTSEV'S *Koral Lir* AND KUROSAWA'S *Ran*

Two non-English film adaptations of *King Lear*, Grigori Kozintsev's Russian adaptation *Korol Lir* (1969) and Akira Kurosawa's Japanese adaptation *Ran* ([*Chaos*], 1985), have been widely regarded as masterpieces of the cinematic adaptation of Shakespeare. Using Boris Pasternak's translation, Kozintsev favors a faithful period production of Shakespeare's tragedy, which stresses the play's political themes. Even so, the film reflects Russian cultural traditions in several respects: the yawning gap between the extravagance and heartlessness of the aristocrats and the abject poverty of the homeless peasants accords with Soviet critiques of bourgeois decadence, (and covertly critiques the corruption of the Soviet regime itself); the eccentricity and eerie appearance of Lear's Fool is reminiscent of the Russian artistic tradition of the *yurodivy*, the holy fool, a link also indicated by the predominance of Christian imagery throughout the film; and the pervasive fatalism of the film seems distinctively Slavic in its outlook.

In *Ran*, Kurosawa transposes *Lear*'s action to feudal Japan, where warlord Hidetora Ichimonji resolves to cede his royal authority to his eldest son Taro and divide his kingdom among his two younger sons, Jiro and Saburo, punctuating his decision with a parable of three arrows taken from Japanese medieval legend. When Saburo warns his father of his folly, Hidetora exiles him along with his own loyal servant Tango, setting in motion the patriarch's precipitous downfall. Rather than muting Shakespeare's misogyny, Kurosawa amplifies it, making Taro's scheming wife, the terrifyingly ruthless Lady Kaede, a catalyst for the betrayals by Hidetora's sons; Kyoami, Hidetora's Fool, is pointedly androgynous, neither fully male nor female. The film is renowned for its exceptional scenic beauty, particularly in the opening boar hunt and in the extraordinarily lavish battle scenes. Yet for its debt to samurai epics and Kabuki theater, *Ran* also weds *King Lear* to Buddhist philosophy, emphasizing the essential transience and precariousness of human existence, a point made visually by repeated shots of clouds passing in the sky. It is one of the few popular adaptations to engage the metaphysical questions so powerfully raised by Shakespeare's tragedy, questions articulated directly by Kyoami and Hideotara as they wander the landscape. The film ends with an unforgettable image: Tsurumaru, a man who Hidetora blinded and exiled as a child, awaits the arrival of his sister

Tatsuya Nakadai as Lord Hidetora Ichimonji and Shinnosuke "Peter" Ikehata as Kyoami in the 1985 film
Ran directed by Akira Kurosawa
Courtesy of Douglas Lanier

Lady Sué, unaware that she has been killed. Edging toward a precipice without a guide, he stumbles on the brink, dropping a Buddhist scroll meant to protect and comfort him. As the sun sets behind him, Tsurumaru stands alone, his arms outstretched into the void, motionless lest he fall, a bleak yet beautiful metaphor for humankind's mortal circumstance. Kozintsev's and Kurosawa's films of *King Lear* point to the continuing vitality of Shakespeare's tragedy, the play's stature outside of Anglo-American popular culture as one of the great cross-cultural fables of the world.

Dramatis Personae

KING LEAR, King of Britain

GONORIL, Lear's eldest daughter
DUKE OF ALBANY, husband to Gonoril

REGAN, Lear's second daughter
DUKE OF CORNWALL, husband to Regan

CORDELIA, Lear's youngest daughter
KING OF FRANCE, suitor to Cordelia, later her husband
DUKE OF BURGUNDY, suitor to Cordelia

FOOL, servant to Lear

EARL OF KENT

EARL OF GLOUCESTER

EDGAR, son to Gloucester
EDMUND, bastard son to Gloucester

CURAN, a courtier

OSWALD, steward to Gonoril

OLD MAN, tenant to Gloucester

DOCTOR

CAPTAIN, employed by Edmund

GENTLEMAN, attendant on Cordelia

HERALD

SERVANTS TO CORNWALL

KNIGHTS OF LEAR'S TRAIN, Gentlemen, Officers, Messengers,
Soldiers, and Attendants

[King Lear

Act 1

0: Location: King Lear's Palace

0: Scene: In the production starring Laurence Olivier (1984), the set resembled Stonehenge. The set of Director Robin Philips's *King Lear* (Stratford, Ontario, 1979) was Victorian and the acting, prosaic. King Lear did not descend from a high throne to unfurl a ceremonial map; instead, Peter Ustinov begins by signing and stamping an order, as if he were a midlevel clerk in an import/export firm.

1: **more affected**: preferred

4: **equalities**: the division of the kingdom based on worth (perhaps connected to "equity")

6: **moiety**: portion

8: **breeding**: fathered; **charge**: expense, and perhaps a bawdy joke—the *dis*charge of semen

9: **brazed**: brazen, without shame

10: **conceive**: understand

12: **ere**: before

14: **issue**: 1) offspring, and 2) result; **proper**: upstanding, well-made

15: **a son by order of law**: a legitimate son, born within wedlock

16: **in my account**: in my eyes

17: **knave**: endearing term, akin to "rascal"; **something saucily**: under impolite circumstances, a reference to Edmund's bastardy

Act 1, Scene 1]

Enter [the Earl of] KENT, [the Earl of] GLOUCESTER,
and Bastard [EDMUND]

KENT
I thought the King had more affected the Duke of Albany than
Cornwall.

GLOUCESTER
It did always seem so to us but now in the division of the kingdoms
it appears not which of the Dukes he values most; for equalities are
so weighed, that curiosity in neither can make choice of either's   5
moiety.

KENT
Is not this your son, my lord?

GLOUCESTER
His breeding, sir, hath been at my charge. I have so often blushed
to acknowledge him that now I am brazed to it.

KENT
I cannot conceive you.   10

GLOUCESTER
Sir, this young fellow's mother could, whereupon she grew round-
wombed and had indeed, sir, a son for her cradle ere she had a
husband for her bed. Do you smell a fault?

KENT
I cannot wish the fault undone, the issue of it being so proper.

GLOUCESTER
But I have, sir, a son by order of law, some year elder than this,   15
who yet is no dearer in my account. Though this knave came
something saucily into the world before he was sent for, yet was

18: **fair**: attractive

19: **whoreson**: i.e., whore's son (bastard); used here affectionately, as in "knave"

24: **services**: duty

25: **sue**: beg your permission

26: **study deserving**: strive to merit

Set design for the 1959 production at the Shakespeare Memorial Theatre in Stratford-upon-Avon directed by Glen Byam Shaw

Rare Book and Special Collection Library, University of Illinois at Urbana-Champaign

29: **Attend**: accompany

31: **we**: i.e., the Royal "we", the King speaking on behalf of himself and his people; **darker**: secret, gloomy

33: **first**: primarily; the Folio prints "fast", meaning firm or resolute

his mother fair, there was good sport at his making, and the
whoreson must be acknowledged. [*To EDMUND*] Do you know
this noble gentleman, Edmund?   20

EDMUND
No, my lord.

GLOUCESTER
[*To EDMUND*] My Lord of Kent. Remember him hereafter as my
honorable friend.

EDMUND
[*To KENT*] My services to your lordship.

KENT
I must love you, and sue to know you better.   25

EDMUND
Sir, I shall study deserving.

GLOUCESTER
[*To KENT*] He hath been out nine years, and away he shall again.
                                                 Sound a sennet
The King is coming.
                    Enter one bearing a coronet, then [King] LEAR,
                    then the Dukes of ALBANY and CORNWALL; next
                    GONORIL, REGAN, CORDELIA, with followers

LEAR
Attend my lords of France and Burgundy, Gloucester.

GLOUCESTER
I shall, my liege.   30
                                                              [Exit]

LEAR
Meantime we will express our darker purposes.
Give me the map there. Know that we have divided
In three our kingdom, and 'tis our first intent

tracks 2–4

44–106
*Trevor Peacock as Lear, Penny Downie as Gonoril, Julia Ford as Cordelia
and Samantha Bond as Regan*
*Paul Scofield as Lear, Harriet Walter as Gonoril, Emilia Fox as Cordelia,
and Sara Kestelman as Regan*

34: Scene: **age**: John Philip Kemble (1757-1823), while initially favoring athleticism, eventually played Lear as aged and infirm; Henry Irving's Lear (1838-1905) played the King as "a scared, eccentric, lunatic shamble." In his book *On Acting* (1983), Laurence Olivier wrote: "Lear is easy. He's like all of us, really: he's just a stupid old fart."

35-40: **while we...now**: from the First Folio

36: **son**: i.e., son-in-law

38: **constant**: unwavering or long-planned

39: **several**: respective

3: **amorous sojourn**: courtship

45-46: **Since now...state**: from the First Folio

46: **Interest of**: management of

48-49: **doth with merit challenge**: rewards according to merit

56: **makes breath poor**: is dearer than life, outpaces expression

60-61: **champaigns riched...meads**: large tracts of rich, fertile land

62: **issue**: i.e., children (see line 14)

To shake all cares and business off our state,
Confirming them on younger years, while we   35
Unburdened crawl toward death. Our son of Cornwall,
And you, our no less loving son of Albany,
We have this hour a constant will to publish
Our daughters' several dowers, that future strife
May be prevented now. The two great princes,   40
France and Burgundy—
Great rivals in our youngest daughter's love—
Long in our court have made their amorous sojourn,
And here are to be answered. Tell me, my daughters,
Since now we will divest us both of rule,   45
Interest of territory, cares of state—
Which of you shall we say doth love us most,
That we our largest bounty may extend
Where merit doth most challenge it?
Gonoril, our eldest born, speak first.   50

GONORIL
  Sir, I do love you more than words can wield the matter;
  Dearer than eyesight, space, or liberty;
  Beyond what can be valued, rich or rare;
  No less than life; with grace, health, beauty, honor;
  As much as child e'er loved, or father, friend;   55
  A love that makes breath poor and speech unable.
  Beyond all manner of so much I love you.

CORDELIA
  [*Aside*] What shall Cordelia do? Love and be silent.

LEAR
  [*To GONORIL*] Of all these bounds even from this line to this,
  With shady forests and with champaigns riched,   60
  With plenteous rivers and wide-skirted meads,
  We make thee lady. To thine and Albany's issue
  Be this perpetual.—What says our second daughter?
  Our dearest Regan, wife to Cornwall, speak.

tracks 2–4

44–106
*Trevor Peacock as Lear, Penny Downie as Gonoril, Julia Ford as Cordelia and
Samantha Bond as Regan*
*Paul Scofield as Lear, Harriet Walter as Gonoril, Emilia Fox as Cordelia and
Sara Kestelman as Regan*

66: **mettle**: disposition
71: **square**: measure
72: **felicitate**: made happy (from "felicity")

73: Scene: **poor Cordelia**: In Kozintsev's 1969 film, Valentina Shendrikova's Cordelia is
first seen quietly playing guitar. Granville-Barker (1877-1946) suggested one of two
possibilities: that Cordelia is taken utterly by surprise when hearing Lear's plan to
divide the kingdom and is thus choked into silence; or, that her failure to respond is
the result of hours of deliberation.

76-77: "To thee and thine...our fair kingdom": the Ensemble in the 2000
Shakespeare Theatre Company production directed by Michael Kahn
Photo: Carol Rosegg

80-82: **to whose...interested**: from the First Folio
81: **vines**: vineyards; **milk**: fertility, hence, fertile lands
85-86: **Nothing? / Nothing.**: from the First Folio

REGAN
Sir, I am made   65
Of the self-same mettle that my sister is,
And prize me at her worth. In my true heart
I find she names my very deed of love—
Only she came short, that I profess
Myself an enemy to all other joys   70
Which the most precious square of sense possesses,
And find I am alone felicitate
In your dear Highness' love.

CORDELIA
                    [*Aside*] Then poor Cordelia—
And yet not so, since I am sure my love's
More richer than my tongue.   75

LEAR
[*To REGAN*] To thee and thine hereditary ever
Remain this ample third of our fair kingdom,
No less in space, validity, and pleasure
Than that confirmed on Gonoril. [*To CORDELIA*] But now our joy,
Although the last, not least in our dear love, to whose young love   80
The vines of France and milk of Burgundy
Strive to be interessed; what can you say to win
A third more opulent than your sisters? Speak.

CORDELIA
Nothing, my lord.

KING LEAR
Nothing?   85

CORDELIA
Nothing.

KING LEAR
How? Nothing can come of nothing. Speak again.

tracks 2–4

44–106
Trevor Peacock as Lear, Penny Downie as Gonoril, Julia Ford as Cordelia and
Samantha Bond as Regan
Paul Scofield as Lear, Harriet Walter as Gonoril, Emilia Fox as Cordelia and
Sara Kestelman as Regan

90: **bond**: natural obligation, duty

Ian McKellen as Lear, Romola Garai as Cordelia, and the Ensemble in the 2007 Royal
Shakespeare Company production directed by Trevor Nunn
Photo: Donald Cooper

93: **bred me**: raised me
94: **fit**: appropriate
97: **Haply**: perhaps
98: **plight**: pledge of marriage

102-118: Scene: **But...sometime daughter**: In Peter Brook's 1971 film, Paul Scofield
"chewed on his bitterness, ground out his plans with methodical anger"; William C.
Macready (1773-1873) hurried on to other matters; Sir Lawrence Olivier (1907-1989) flung
his crown to the ground in rage. The Italian actor Tommaso Salvini (1829-1915) drew
Cordelia aside with great warmth and intimacy; the American actor, Edwin Forrest
(1806-1872), feebly walked to Cordelia and caressed her, begging her to reconsider.

106: **dower**: a traditional gift given by the father of the bride (from "dowry")
108: **mysteries**: sacred rituals; **Hecate**: goddess of witches and the underworld; also
mentioned in *Macbeth*: "Pale Hecate's offerings" (2.1.53)
109: **operation of the orbs**: influence of the planets and stars

CORDELIA
    Unhappy that I am, I cannot heave
    My heart into my mouth. I love your Majesty
    According to my bond, nor more nor less.   90

KING LEAR
    Go to, go to, mend your speech a little
    Lest it may mar your fortunes.

CORDELIA
                            Good my lord,
    You have begot me, bred me, loved me.
    I return those duties back as are right fit—
    Obey you, love you, and most honor you.   95
    Why have my sisters husbands if they say
    They love you all? Haply when I shall wed
    That lord whose hand must take my plight shall carry
    Half my love with him, half my care and duty.
    Sure, I shall never marry like my sisters,   100
    To love my father all.

LEAR
    But goes this with thy heart?

CORDELIA
    Ay, good my lord.

LEAR
    So young and so untender?

CORDELIA
    So young, my lord, and true.   105

LEAR
    Well, let it be so. Thy truth then be thy dower;
    For by the sacred radiance of the sun,
    The mysteries of Hecate and the night,
    By all the operation of the orbs
    From whom we do exist and cease to be,   110

111: "Here I disclaim all my paternal care": Kevin Kline as Lear, Kristen Bush as Cordelia, and the Ensemble in the 2007 Public Theater production directed by James Lapine
Photo: Michal Daniel

112: **Propinquity**: blood ties
114: **Scythian**: The Scythians were horse-riding nomads who inhabited Eurasia between the eighth century BCE and the second century CE. The reference here implies an uncivilized person.
115: **makes his generation messes**: i.e., makes his own children into food (messes) to be eaten; used similarly in *Othello*: "I will chop her into messes. Cuckold me!"(4.1.201)
118: **sometime daughter**: former daughter
119: **dragon**: a traditional sign, along with the lion, of kingship; a symbol of power
120: **set my rest**: rely on completely; the phrase comes from playing cards and refers to betting everything
121: **nursery**: care
123: **France**: i.e., the King of France; **Burgundy**: i.e., the Duke of Burgundy
126: **plainness**: the quality of being plain spoken or frank
128: **large effects**: outward signs
130: **With reservation**: reserving the right to be accompanied by
136: **crownet**: coronet (the Crown), which represents Cordelia's dowry

136–176
Anton Lesser as Kent and Trevor Peacock as Lear
David Burke as Kent and Paul Scofield as Lear

tracks 5-7

Here I disclaim all my paternal care,
Propinquity, and property of blood,
And as a stranger to my heart and me
Hold thee from this for ever. The barbarous Scythian,
Or he that makes his generation messes   115
To gorge his appetite, shall to my bosom
Be as well neighbored, pitied, and relieved
As thou, my sometime daughter.

KENT

                            Good my liege—

LEAR

Peace, Kent. Come not between the dragon and his wrath.
I loved her most, and thought to set my rest   120
On her kind nursery. [*To CORDELIA*] Hence, and avoid my sight!—
So be my grave my peace as here I give
Her father's heart from her. Call France. Who stirs?
Call Burgundy.

                                             [Exit one or more]
                    Cornwall and Albany,
With my two daughters' dowers digest this third.   125
Let pride, which she calls plainness, marry her.
I do invest you jointly in my power,
Pre-eminence, and all the large effects
That troop with majesty. Ourself by monthly course,
With reservation of an hundred knights   130
By you to be sustained, shall our abode
Make with you by due turns. Only we still retain
The name and all the additions to a king.
The sway, revenue, execution of the rest,
Beloved sons, be yours, which to confirm,   135
This crownet part betwixt you.

KENT

                        Royal Lear,
Whom I have ever honored as my king,
Loved as my father, as my master followed,
As my great patron thought on in my prayers—

136–176
Anton Lesser as Kent and Trevor Peacock as Lear
David Burke as Kent and Paul Scofield as Lear

Costume rendering for Lear by Susan Tsu from the 2004 Oregon Shakespeare
Festival production directed by James Edmondson
Courtesy of the Oregon Shakespeare Festival

140: **bow is bent and drawn**: plan is already underway; **make from**: move out of the way of

141: **fall**: hit; **fork**: two-pronged head of an arrow

142: **unmannerly**: impolite, forthright

143: **mad**: unreasonable, angry

147: **in...consideration**: with much thought; **check**: hold back

150: **empty-hearted**: with empty or hollow words

151: **Reverbs no hollowness**: reverberates or echoes like something hollow; thus insincerely

152: **pawn**: worthless piece, to be used as the player (i.e., King Lear) decides

153: **wage**: wager, risk in battle

156: **blank**: white circle at the center of a target; **Apollo**: the ancient Greek and Roman god of light, healing, music, poetry, prophecy

158: **Vassal**: wretch; **recreant**: traitor

158: **Vassal, recreant!**: appears only in the First Quarto

LEAR

    The bow is bent and drawn; make from the shaft.   140

KENT

    Let it fall rather, though the fork invade
    The region of my heart. Be Kent unmannerly
    When Lear is mad. What wilt thou do, old man?
    Think'st thou that duty shall have dread to speak
    When power to flattery bows? To plainness honor's bound   145
    When majesty stoops to folly. Reverse thy doom,
    And in thy best consideration check
    This hideous rashness. Answer my life my judgment,
    Thy youngest daughter does not love thee least,
    Nor are those empty-hearted whose low sound   150
    Reverbs no hollowness.

LEAR

                    Kent, on thy life, no more!

KENT

    My life I never held but as a pawn
    To wage against thy enemies, nor fear to lose it,
    Thy safety being the motive.

LEAR

                    Out of my sight!

KENT

    See better, Lear, and let me still remain   155
    The true blank of thine eye.

LEAR

                    Now, by Apollo—

KENT

    Now, by Apollo, King, thou swear'st thy gods in vain.

LEAR [*Making to strike him*]

    Vassal, recreant!

136–176
Anton Lesser as Kent and Trevor Peacock as Lear
David Burke as Kent and Paul Scofield as Lear

158: **Dear sir, forbear**: from the First Folio

158-159: **kill thy physician...foul disease**: akin to "don't blame the doctor for diagnosing the illness from which you suffer"

160: **vent clamor**: cry out

165: **Our sentence**: i.e., the sentence passed down by a judge

172: **trunk**: body

173: **By Jupiter**: an oath, as in "By heaven and earth I swear"; Jupiter is the King of the gods

174: **This shall not be revoked**: Lear's threat is ironic because Jupiter is known, in Roman mythology, for changing his mind often.

175: **since**: if

176: Scene: **banishment is here**: When Sir John Gielgud (1904-2000) played Lear, Kent kissed the King's sword before taking his leave. Carnovsky's Lear (American Shakespeare Festival, 1965) was so upset by Kent's departure that he threw down his sword, but in Peter Brook's 1971 film, Paul Scofield's Lear "ground crisply on, seemingly as tough as ever."

177: **protection**: shelter

179: **large**: unrestrained; **approve**: confirm

ALBANY *and* CORDELIA
>   Dear sir, forbear.

KENT
>   [*To LEAR*] Do, kill thy physician,
> And the fee bestow upon the foul disease.
> Revoke thy doom, or whilst I can vent clamor   160
> From my throat I'll tell thee thou dost evil.

LEAR
> Hear me, recreant; on thine allegiance hear me!
> Since thou hast sought to make us break our vow,
> Which we durst never yet, and with strayed pride
> To come between our sentence and our power,   165
> Which nor our nature nor our place can bear,
> Our potency made good take thy reward.
> Four days we do allot thee for provision
> To shield thee from diseases of the world,
> And on the fifth to turn thy hated back   170
> Upon our kingdom. If on the next day following
> Thy banished trunk be found in our dominions,
> The moment is thy death. Away! By Jupiter,
> This shall not be revoked.

KENT
> Why, fare thee well, King; since thus thou wilt appear, 175
> Friendship lives hence, and banishment is here.
> [*To CORDELIA*] The gods to their dear protection take thee, maid,
> That rightly thinks, and hast most justly said.
> [*To GONORIL and REGAN*] And your large speeches may your deeds
>   approve,
> That good effects may spring from words of love.   180
> Thus Kent, O princes, bids you all adieu;
> He'll shape his old course in a country new.
>   *[Exit]*
>   *Enter the [the King of] FRANCE and [the Duke of]*
>   *BURGUNDY, with GLOUCESTER*

GLOUCESTER
> Here's France and Burgundy, my noble lord.

185: **address**: address ourselves, here used in the plural form to denote Lear's status as king
186: **rivaled**: competed
187: **in present**: immediate

Costume rendering for Lear from the 1959 production at the Shakespeare Memorial Theatre in Stratford-upon-Avon directed by Glen Byam Shaw

Rare Book and Special Collection Library, University of Illinois at Urbana-Champaign

193: **little-seeming substance**: implying that Cordelia is not what she seems; **aught**: anything
194: **pieced**: added on
195: **fitly like**: properly please
197: **infirmities**: corrupt qualities
199: **strangered with**: isolated from us by
201: **Election...conditions**: i.e., No other choice is possible given the circumstances.
203: **great King**: in reference to the King of France
204: **make such a stray**: go so far away
205: **beseech**: I beseech

LEAR

My Lord of Burgundy,
We first address towards you, who with a king   185
Hath rivaled for our daughter. What in the least
Will you require in present dower with her
Or cease your quest of love?

BURGUNDY

Most Royal Majesty,
I crave no more than what your Highness offered;
Nor will you tender less.

LEAR

Right noble Burgundy,   190
When she was dear to us we did hold her so;
But now her price is fallen. Sir, there she stands.
If aught within that little-seeming substance,
Or all of it, with our displeasure pieced,
And nothing else, may fitly like your grace,   195
She's there, and she is yours.

BURGUNDY

I know no answer.

LEAR

Sir, will you with those infirmities she owes,
Unfriended, new-adopted to our hate,
Covered with our curse and strangered with our oath,
Take her or leave her?

BURGUNDY

Pardon me, royal sir.   200
Election makes not up on such conditions.

LEAR

Then leave her, sir; for by the power that made me,
I tell you all her wealth. [To FRANCE] For you, great King,
I would not from your love make such a stray
To match you where I hate, therefore beseech you   205

206: **avert your liking**: turn your love
209: **strange**: odd
210: **best object**: favorite; **argument**: central focus
211: **balm**: comfort
212: **trice**: instant
214: **folds**: levels, depth
216: **monsters it**: makes it monstrous; **fore-vouched:** previously affirmed
221: **want**: lack; **glib and oily**: smooth, insincere
222: **purpose not**: have no intention of doing
223: **acknow**: acknowledge
224: **blot**: stain
228: **still-soliciting**: always begging

231: "Better thou hadst not been born than not to have pleased me better":
Ian McKellen as Lear, Romola Garai as Cordelia, and Peter Hinton as Burgundy in
the 2007 Royal Shakespeare Company production directed by Trevor Nunn
Photo: Donald Cooper

230: **Go to, go to.**: from the First Folio
232: **tardiness**: reluctance to speak
233: **That**: what

To avert your liking a more worthier way
Than on a wretch whom nature is ashamed
Almost to acknowledge hers.

FRANCE
This is most strange, that she that even but now
Was your best object, the argument of your praise,   210
Balm of your age, most best, most dearest,
Should in this trice of time commit a thing
So monstrous to dismantle
So many folds of favor. Sure, her offense
Must be of such unnatural degree   215
That monsters it, or your fore-vouched affections
Fall'n into taint; which to believe of her,
Must be a faith that reason without miracle
Could never plant in me.

CORDELIA
[*To LEAR*] I yet beseech your Majesty,   220
If for I want that glib and oily art
To speak and purpose not—since what I well intend,
I'll do't before I speak—that you acknow
It is no vicious blot, murder, or foulness,
No unclean action or dishonored step   225
That hath deprived me of your grace and favor,
But even the want of that for which I am rich—
A still-soliciting eye, and such a tongue
As I am glad I have not, though not to have it
Hath lost me in your liking.

LEAR
                              Go to, go to.   230
Better thou hadst not been born than not to have pleased me better.

FRANCE
Is it no more but this—a tardiness in nature,
That often leaves the history unspoke
That it intends to do?—My Lord of Burgundy,
What say you to the lady? Love is not love   235

237: have her: marry her

Costume rendering for Burgundy by Susan Tsu from the 2004 Oregon Shakespeare Festival production directed by James Edmondson

Courtesy of the Oregon Shakespeare Festival

241: Nothing: recalling Cordelia's remarks at 1.1.84 and 1.1.86
241: I am firm.: from the First Folio
251: inflamed respect: feverish love
254: wat'rish: irrigated by rivers, but also lacking strength, as in "watered down"
256: though unkind: though they have not acted like a family

When it is mingled with respects that stands
Aloof from the entire point. Will you have her?
She is herself a dower.

BURGUNDY

Royal Lear,
Give but that portion which yourself proposed,
And here I take Cordelia by the hand,   240
Duchess of Burgundy—

LEAR

Nothing. I have sworn. I am firm.

BURGUNDY

[*To CORDELIA*] I am sorry, then, you have so lost a father
That you must lose a husband.

CORDELIA

Peace be with Burgundy; since that respects
Of fortune are his love, I shall not be his wife.   245

FRANCE

Fairest Cordelia, that art most rich, being poor;
Most choice, forsaken; and most loved, despised.
Thee and thy virtues here I seize upon.
Be it lawful, I take up what's cast away.
Gods, gods! 'Tis strange that from their cold'st neglect   250
My love should kindle to inflamed respect.—
Thy dowerless daughter, King, thrown to my chance,
Is queen of us, of ours, and our fair France.
Not all the dukes in wat'rish Burgundy
Shall buy this unprized precious maid of me.—   255
Bid them farewell, Cordelia, though unkind.
Thou losest here, a better where to find.

LEAR

Thou hast her, France. Let her be thine, for we
Have no such daughter, nor shall ever see
That face of hers again. Therefore be gone,   260

261: **benison**: blessing

"King Lear: Cordelia's Farewell"
Painting by Edwin Austin Abbey, 1898

263: **jewels**: tears; **washed**: tearful
266: **as they are named**: for what they really are
267: **professèd bosoms**: public assertions of love
274: **Fortune**: the goddess of luck, mentioned in *Hamlet*: "In the secret parts of Fortune? O, most true—she is a strumpet" (2.2.224). See also 2.1.39, 2.2.155-56, 4.6.211, 5.3.6 and 5.3.173; **scanted**: neglected
275: **well...wanted**: rightly deserve to be treated the way you have treated others
276: **unfold**: bring to light; **pleated**: folded, hidden

279-299: Scene: **Sister...i' th' heat**: The least compassionate rendering of these sisters is found in the Orson Welles film (dir. Peter Brook, CBS-TV, 1953), which cut Gonoril and Regan's discussion about Lear's growing unruliness and their own need to defend themselves. As a result, their actions seemed far more malicious, if only because they no longer have clear motives for what they do.

279: **appertains**: concerns

Without our grace, our love, our benison.—
Come, noble Burgundy.

[Flourish.] Exeunt LEAR and BURGUNDY [then ALBANY,
CORNWALL, GLOUCESTER, EDMUND, and followers].

FRANCE
                         [To CORDELIA] Bid farewell to your sisters.

CORDELIA
Ye jewels of our father, with washed eyes
Cordelia leaves you. I know you what you are,
And like a sister am most loath to call   265
Your faults as they are named. Use well our father.
To your professèd bosoms I commit him.
But yet, alas, stood I within his grace
I would prefer him to a better place.
So farewell to you both.   270

GONORIL
Prescribe not us our duties.

REGAN
Let your study
Be to content your lord, who hath received you
At Fortune's alms. You have obedience scanted,
And well are worth the worst that you have wanted.   275

CORDELIA
Time shall unfold what pleated cunning hides.
Who cover faults, at last shame them derides.
Well may you prosper.

FRANCE
                         Come, my fair Cordelia.
                         Exeunt FRANCE and CORDELIA

GONORIL
Sister, it is not a little I have to say of what most nearly appertains
to us both. I think our father will hence tonight.   280

285: **gross**: obvious

Costume rendering for Regan from the 1959 production at the Shakespeare
Memorial Theatre in Stratford-upon-Avon directed by Glen Byam Shaw

Rare Book and Special Collection Library, University of Illinois at Urbana-Champaign

289-290: **long-engrafted**: closely merged and longstanding

291: **choleric**: impatient, easily angered

292: **unconstant starts**: temper tantrums; **like**: likely

294: **compliment**: evidence or show

295: **hit**: concur; **authority**: power

297: **offend**: endangers

299: **i' th' heat**: immediately, as in "strike while the iron is hot"

REGAN
  That's most certain, and with you. Next month with us.

GONORIL
  You see how full of changes his age is. The observation we have
  made of it hath not been little. He always loved our sister most,
  and with what poor judgment he hath now cast her off appears
  too gross.   285

REGAN
  'Tis the infirmity of his age, yet he hath ever but slenderly known
  himself.

GONORIL
  The best and soundest of his time hath been but rash, then must
  we look to receive from his age not alone the imperfection of long-
  engrafted condition, but therewithal the unruly waywardness   290
  that infirm and choleric years bring with them.

REGAN
  Such unconstant starts are we like to have from him as this of
  Kent's banishment.

GONORIL
  There is further compliment of leave-taking between France and
  him. Pray you, let's hit together. If our father carry authority with   295
  such dispositions as he bears, this last surrender of his will but
  offend us.

REGAN
  We shall further think on't.

GONORIL
  We must do something, and i' th' heat.

                                                              Exeunt

0: Location: The Earl of Gloucester's house

0: Scene: Missing Edmunds: Orson Welles' film (dir. Peter Brook, CBS-TV, 1953) cut Edmund altogether. Oswald plays the cheat, betrays Gloucester, plans Cordelia's murder, and offers himself to both Regan and Gonoril.

tracks 8-10

1–22
Simon Russell Beale as Edmund
Toby Stephens as Edmund

1: **Nature**: here deified. Edmund may have in mind any number of goddesses. In classical Greek literature, Nature was associated with the sexually active and lawless women of *The Bacchae*.

3: **Stand...custom**: submit to or accept a hurtful practice or habit

4. **curiosity of nations**: arbitrary social rankings

5: **moonshines**: months (from the lunar calendar)

6: **Lag of**: lagging behind

7: **dimensions**: physical attributes or proportions

9: **honest**: virtuous, chaste

10: **base, base bastardy**: The siring of bastards indicates base or low morality; Edmund argues that these characterizations are unfounded.

11: **lusty stealth**: secret lust

11-12: **Who...quality**: Whose conception is more fully realized and strong

14: **fops**: fools

16: **your land**: i.e., the land Edgar is meant to inherit as Gloucester's legitimate heir

19: **speed**: succeed

20: **invention thrive**: plot succeeds

23: **choler**: anger

24: **to-night**: last night; **subscribed his power**: limited his own power (by giving it away)

25: **exhibition**: his pension or allowance

26: **Upon the gad**: suddenly

Act 1, Scene 2]

EDMUND
    Thou, Nature, art my goddess. To thy law
    My services are bound. Wherefore should I
    Stand in the plague of custom and permit
    The curiosity of nations to deprive me
    For that I am some twelve or fourteen moonshines   5
    Lag of a brother? Why "bastard"? Wherefore "base,"
    When my dimensions are as well compact,
    My mind as generous, and my shape as true
    As honest madam's issue?
    Why brand they us with "base, base bastardy,"   10
    Who in the lusty stealth of nature take
    More composition and fierce quality
    Than doth within a stale, dull-eyed bed go
    To the creating a whole tribe of fops
    Got 'tween a sleep and wake? Well then,   15
    Legitimate Edgar, I must have your land.
    Our father's love is to the bastard Edmund
    As to the legitimate. Fine word,—legitimate!
    Well, my legitimate, if this letter speed
    And my invention thrive, Edmund the base   20
    Shall to the legitimate. I grow, I prosper.
    Now gods, stand up for bastards!

Enter GLOUCESTER
[EDMUND reads a letter]

GLOUCESTER
    Kent banished thus, and France in choler parted,
    And the King gone to-night, subscribed his power,
    Confined to exhibition—all this done   25
    Upon the gad?—Edmund, how now? What news?

31: **Nothing**: again, echoing Cordelia at 1.1.84 and 1.1.86

32: **terrible dispatch**: attempt to hide quickly

36: **o'er-read**: finished reading

37: **liking**: approval

42-43: **assay or taste**: an effort to test

Set design for the 1959 production at the Shakespeare Memorial Theatre in Stratford-upon-Avon directed by Glen Byam Shaw

Rare Book and Special Collection Library, University of Illinois at Urbana-Champaign

EDMUND
So please your lordship, none.

GLOUCESTER
Why so earnestly seek you to put up that letter?

EDMUND
I know no news, my lord.

GLOUCESTER
What paper were you reading?   30

EDMUND
Nothing, my lord.

GLOUCESTER
No? What needs then that terrible dispatch of it into your pocket?
The quality of nothing hath not such need to hide itself. Let's see.
Come, if it be nothing, I shall not need spectacles.

EDMUND
I beseech you, sir, pardon me. It is a letter from my brother that I   35
have not all o'er-read; and for so much as I have perused, I find it
not fit for your liking.

GLOUCESTER
Give me the letter, sir.

EDMUND
I shall offend either to detain or give it. The contents, as in part I
understand them, are to blame.   40

GLOUCESTER
Let's see, let's see.

EDMUND
I hope for my brother's justification he wrote this but as an assay
or taste of my virtue.

[He gives GLOUCESTER] the letter

44: Stage Direction: *Reads*: David Sabin as Gloucester and Andrew Long as Edmund in the 2000 Shakespeare Theatre Company production directed by Michael Kahn
Photo: Carol Rosegg

44: **policy and reverence of**: mandatory policy of revering
45: **the best of our times**: i.e., our youth
46: **relish**: enjoy; **idle and fond**: worthless and foolish
47: **who sways**: which rules
48: **suffered**: allowed
53: **breed it**: hatch this plot
55: **casement**: window; **closet**: small room, often used for reading and writing
56: **character**: handwriting
57: **matter**: contents
58: **fain**: happily
61: **sounded you**: discussed with you
62: **fit**: suitable
63: **perfect age**: i.e., prime of life; **declining**: getting old
65: **Abhorred**: abhorrent or hateful, but also a pun on whore
66: **brutish**: ill-mannered

GLOUCESTER

[Reads] This policy and reverence of age makes the world bitter to
the best of our times, keeps our fortunes from us till our oldness 45
cannot relish them. I begin to find an idle and fond bondage in the
oppression of aged tyranny, who sways not as it hath power but as
it is suffered. Come to me, that of this I may speak more. If our
father would sleep till I waked him, you should enjoy half his
revenue forever and live the beloved of your brother, Edgar. 50
Hum, conspiracy! "Slept till I waked him, you should enjoy half
his revenue,"—my son Edgar! Had he a hand to write this, a heart
and brain to breed it in? When came this to you? Who brought it?

EDMUND

It was not brought me, my lord, there's the cunning of it. I found
it thrown in at the casement of my closet. 55

GLOUCESTER

You know the character to be your brother's?

EDMUND

If the matter were good, my lord, I durst swear it were his; but in
respect of that, I would fain think it were not.

GLOUCESTER

It is his.

EDMUND

It is his hand, my lord, but I hope his heart is not in the contents. 60

GLOUCESTER

Hath he never heretofore sounded you in this business?

EDMUND

Never, my lord; but I have often heard him maintain it to be fit
that, sons at perfect age and fathers declining, his father should be
as ward to the son, and the son manage the revenue.

GLOUCESTER

O villain, villain—his very opinion in the letter! Abhorred villain, 65
unnatural, detested, brutish villain—worse than brutish! Go, sir,
seek him, ay, apprehend him. Abominable villain! Where is he?

70: **testimony**: evidence; **run a certain course**: proceed more judiciously; **where**: whereas

73: **pawn down**: stake

74: **feel**: get a sense of

77: **judge it meet**: think it appropriate

77-78: **hear us confer**: eavesdrop on us

78-79: **have your satisfaction**: be assured

82-83: **To his father...earth!**: appears only in the First Quarto

83: **wind me into him**: gain his confidence

84: **frame**: plan; **after...wisdom**: according to what you think is best

84-85: **I would...resolution**: i.e., I would give up everything I have to know the truth.

86: **presently**: immediately; **convey**: undertake

87: **acquaint you withal**: inform you of everything as soon as I can

88: **late**: recent

90: **sequent effects**: horrible consequences

91: **mutinies**: rebellions

EDMUND

I do not well know, my lord. If it shall please you to suspend
your indignation against my brother till you can derive from him
better testimony of this intent, you shall run a certain course;   70
where if you violently proceed against him, mistaking his
purpose, it would make a great gap in your own honor and shake
in pieces the heart of his obedience. I dare pawn down my life for
him that he hath wrote this to feel my affection to your honor, and
to no further pretense of danger.   75

GLOUCESTER

Think you so?

EDMUND

If your honor judge it meet, I will place you where you shall hear
us confer of this, and by an auricular assurance have your satisfaction, and that without any further delay than this very evening.

GLOUCESTER

He cannot be such a monster.   80

EDMUND

Nor is not, sure.

GLOUCESTER

To his father, that so tenderly and entirely loves him—heaven and
earth! Edmund, seek him out, wind me into him. I pray you,
frame your business after your own wisdom. I would unstate
myself to be in a due resolution.   85

EDMUND

I shall seek him, sir, presently, convey the business as I shall see
means, and acquaint you withal.

GLOUCESTER

These late eclipses in the sun and moon portend no good to us.
Though the wisdom of nature can reason it thus and thus, yet
nature finds itself scourged by the sequent effects. Love cools,   90
friendship falls off, brothers divide; in cities, mutinies, in countries,

92: **discords**: conflicts
93-97: **This villain...graves**: from the First Folio
94: **bias of nature**: the natural order of things
97: **it shall lose thee nothing**: i.e., You will be generously rewarded.

Costume rendering for Edmund from the 1959 production at the Shakespeare Memorial Theatre in Stratford-upon-Avon directed by Glen Byam Shaw
Rare Book and Special Collection Library, University of Illinois at Urbana-Champaign

100: **foppery**: foolishness
100-101: **sick in fortune**: plagued by bad luck
101: **surfeit...behavior**: result of our lavish lifestyles
101-102: **make guilty of**: blame
104: **treacherers**: traitors; **spherical predominance**: influence of the planets on the future based on the hour of one's birth (from astrology)
106: **divine thrusting on**: blaming the supernatural
107: **evasion**: unwillingness to confront the truth; **goatish**: lecherous
108-109: **My father...Dragon's tail**: i.e., My parents had sex and conceived me under the constellation Draco (not one of the signs of the Zodiac).
109-110: **Ursa Major**: the constellation of the Great Bear or Big Dipper—also not a standard sign of the zodiac
110: **Fut!**: an oath, short for 'sfoot or Christ's Foot
111: **maidenliest**: most virginal
113: **catastrophe of the comedy**: climax of a play
114: **Bedlam**: a reference to Bethlehem Hospital in London, a lunatic asylum
115: **divisions**: conflicts in the family and culture; **fa, sol, la, mi**: notes in the musical scale (from the First Folio)

discords, in palaces, treason, and the bond cracked between son
and father. This villain of mine comes under the prediction: there's
son against father. The King falls from bias of nature: there's father
against child. We have seen the best of our time. Machinations, hol-   95
lowness, treachery, and all ruinous disorders, follow us disquietly to
our graves. Find out this villain, Edmund; it shall lose thee nothing.
Do it carefully. And the noble and true-hearted Kent banished, his
offense honesty! Strange, strange.

[Exit]

EDMUND
This is the excellent foppery of the world, that when we are sick   100
in fortune—often the surfeit of our own behavior—we make
guilty of our disasters the sun, the moon, and the stars, as if we
were villains by necessity, fools by heavenly compulsion, knaves,
thieves, and treacherers by spherical predominance, drunkards,
liars, and adulterers by an enforced obedience of planetary influ-   105
ence, and all that we are evil in by a divine thrusting on. An
admirable evasion of whoremaster man, to lay his goatish disposition to the charge of stars! My father compounded with my
mother under the Dragon's tail and my nativity was under Ursa
Major, so that it follows I am rough and lecherous. Fut! I should   110
have been that I am, had the maidenliest star of the firmament
twinkled on my bastardy. Edgar—

Enter EDGAR

And on's cue out he comes, like the catastrophe of the old comedy;
mine is villainous melancholy, with a sigh like Tom of Bedlam.—
O, these eclipses do portend these divisions! Fa, sol, la, mi.   115

EDGAR
How now, brother Edmund, what serious contemplation are you in?

EDMUND
I am thinking, brother, of a prediction I read this other day, what
should follow these eclipses.

EDGAR
Do you busy yourself about that?

120: **promise**: guarantee; **succeed unhappily**: are the unlucky result of

120-126: **as of...astronomical?**: appears only in the First Quarto

121: **dearth**: famine

123: **needless diffidences**: unfounded distrust of others

124: **dissipation of cohorts**: military desertions

126: **sectary**: sectarian or religious dissenter; **sectary astronomical**: believer in astrology

129: **Spake**: speak

132: **countenance**: demeanor

135: **forbear his presence**: stay away from him; **qualified**: reduced

137: **with the mischief of your person**: in combination with your presence; **allay**: reduce or calm

EDMUND

I promise you, the effects he writ of succeed unhappily, as of   120
unnaturalness between the child and the parent, death, dearth,
dissolutions of ancient amities, divisions in state, menaces and
maledictions against king and nobles, needless diffidences, banishment of friends, dissipation of cohorts, nuptial breaches, and I
know not what.   125

EDGAR

How long have you been a sectary astronomical?

EDMUND

Come, come, when saw you my father last?

EDGAR

Why, the night gone by.

EDMUND

Spake you with him?

EDGAR

Two hours together.   130

EDMUND

Parted you in good terms? Found you no displeasure in him by
word or countenance?

EDGAR

None at all.

EDMUND

Bethink yourself wherein you may have offended him, and at my
entreaty forbear his presence till some little time hath qualified   135
the heat of his displeasure, which at this instant so rageth in him
that with the mischief of your person it would scarcely allay.

EDGAR

Some villain hath done me wrong.

139-143: I pray you...brother?: from the First Folio

139: have a continent forbearance: stay far away from

140: till the speed of his rage goes slower: i.e., until he calms down

141: fitly: at the right time

142: stir abroad: i.e., leave your house

142: "If you do stir abroad, go armed": Brian Avers as Edgar and Logan Marshall-Green as Edmund in the 2007 Public Theater production directed by James Lapine
Photo: Michal Daniel

144: Brother and **Go armed:** appear only in the First Quarto

145: meaning: intention

150: credulous: easily fooled

153: practices ride easy: plots go smoothly; **the business:** the way to proceed

155: meet: appropriate; **fashion fit:** rely on to further my plans

EDMUND

That's my fear, I pray you, have a continent forbearance till the
speed of his rage goes slower; and, as I say, retire with me to my   140
lodging, from whence I will fitly bring you to hear my lord speak.
Pray ye, go. There's my key. If you do stir abroad, go armed.

EDGAR

Armed, brother?

EDMUND

Brother. I advise you to the best. Go armed. I am no honest man
if there be any good meaning towards you. I have told you what I   145
have seen and heard but faintly, nothing like the image and horror of it. Pray you, away.

EDGAR

Shall I hear from you anon?

EDMUND

I do serve you in this business.

Exit EDGAR

A credulous father, and a brother noble,   150
Whose nature is so far from doing harms
That he suspects none; on whose foolish honesty
My practices ride easy. I see the business.
Let me, if not by birth, have lands by wit.
All with me's meet that I can fashion fit.   155

Exit

0: Location: The Duke of Albany's Palace

Set design for the 1959 production at the Shakespeare Memorial Theatre in Stratford-upon-Avon directed by Glen Byam Shaw

Rare Book and Special Collection Library, University of Illinois at Urbana-Champaign

0: Scene: In the film adaptation of Peter Brook's 1962 RSC production, the knights are very disrespectful; Gonoril's house looks like a tavern.

5: **gross crime**: unwarranted offense

6: **riotous**: ill-behaved; **upbraids**: reproaches

9: **come slack**: fall short

10: **answer**: explain or take responsibility for

13: **come to question**: be turned into a point of discussion

16-20: **Not to be...abused.**: appears only in the First Quarto

16: **Idle**: ridiculous

17: **manage those authorities**: exercise those royal powers

19-20: **used / With...abused**: reprimanded rather than flattered when they take advantage of one's kindness

Act 1, Scene 3]

Enter GONORIL and Gentlemen [OSWALD]

GONORIL
Did my father strike my gentleman for chiding of his fool?

OSWALD
Yes, madam.

GONORIL
By day and night he wrongs me. Every hour
He flashes into one gross crime or other
That sets us all at odds. I'll not endure it.   5
His knights grow riotous, and himself upbraids us
On every trifle. When he returns from hunting
I will not speak with him. Say I am sick.
If you come slack of former services
You shall do well; the fault of it I'll answer.   10
[Hunting horns within]

OSWALD
He's coming, madam; I hear him.

GONORIL
Put on what weary negligence you please,
You and your fellow servants. I'll have it come to question.
If he dislike it, let him to our sister,
Whose mind and mine I know in that are one,   15
Not to be overruled. Idle old man,
That still would manage those authorities
That he hath given away! Now, by my life,
Old fools are babes again, and must be used
With checks as flatteries, when they are seen abused.   20
Remember what I tell you.

23: have colder looks: be treated as strangers

25-26: I would...speak: appears only in the First Quarto

25: occasions: opportunities

26: straight: right away

OSWALD
   Well, madam.

GONORIL
   And let his knights have colder looks among you.
   What grows of it, no matter. Advise your fellows so.
   I would breed from hence occasions, and I shall,   25
   That I may speak. I'll write straight to my sister
   To hold my very course. Go prepare for dinner.

                                                       Exeunt

0: Location: The Duke of Albany's Palace
2: **diffuse**: make unrecognizable
3: **May...issue**: will achieve the final result
4: **razed my likeness**: disguised myself
6: **come**: turn out that

Set design for the 1959 production at the Shakespeare Memorial Theatre in Stratford-upon-Avon directed by Glen Byam Shaw
Rare Book and Special Collection Library, University of Illinois at Urbana-Champaign

7: Scene: *Enter LEAR [and servants from hunting]*: Orson Welles's (1915-1985) Lear occupied himself with a falcon which was perched on his arm; Edmund Kean's (1787-1833) Lear, fresh from the hunt, held a boar spear.

8: **not stay a jot**: not wait a moment
11: **What dost thou profess?**: i.e., What is your profession or calling?
13: **honest**: honorable; **converse**: associate
14: **fear judgment**: be devout, as in fearing God's final judgment
14-15: **cannot choose**: i.e., have no choice but to fight; **eat no fish**: Because Catholics eat fish on Fridays, this may suggest that Kent identifies as a Protestant; it could also refer to a manly meat-and-potatoes diet.

Act 1, Scene 4]

Enter KENT, [disguised]

KENT
    If but as well I other accents borrow
    That can my speech diffuse, my good intent
    May carry through itself to that full issue
    For which I razed my likeness. Now, banished Kent,
    If thou canst serve where thou dost stand condemned,   5
    So may it come thy master, whom thou lov'st,
    Shall find thee full of labor.
               [Horns within.] Enter LEAR [and servants from hunting].

LEAR
    Let me not stay a jot for dinner. Go get it ready.
                                           [Exit one]

    [To KENT] How now, what art thou?

KENT
    A man, sir.   10

LEAR
    What dost thou profess? What wouldst thou with us?

KENT
    I do profess to be no less than I seem, to serve him truly that will
    put me in trust, to love him that is honest, to converse with him that
    is wise and says little, to fear judgment, to fight when I cannot
    choose, and to eat no fish.   15

LEAR
    What art thou?

KENT
    A very honest-hearted fellow, and as poor as the King.

24: **countenance**: noble facial expression and bearing

29: **honest counsel**: a secret; **mar a curious tale**: ruin an elaborate story

30-31: "That which ordinary men are fit for I am qualified in; and the best of me is diligence": Michael Cerveris as Kent in the 2007 Public Theater production directed by James Lapine

Photo: Michal Daniel

LEAR
   If thou be as poor for a subject as he is for a king, thou'rt poor
   enough. What wouldst thou?

KENT
   Service.   20

LEAR
   Who wouldst thou serve?

KENT
   You.

LEAR
   Dost thou know me, fellow?

KENT
   No, sir, but you have that in your countenance which I would fain call
   master.   25

LEAR
   What's that?

KENT
   Authority.

LEAR
   What services canst thou do?

KENT
   I can keep honest counsel, ride, run, mar a curious tale in telling
   it, and deliver a plain message bluntly. That which ordinary men   30
   are fit for I am qualified in, and the best of me is diligence.

LEAR
   How old art thou?

KENT
   Not so young, sir, to love a woman for singing, nor so old to dote
   on her for anything. I have years on my back forty-eight.

37: **knave**: jester

40: **clotpoll**: clodpole, an oafish person

45: **roundest**: most direct or blunt

48: **entertained**: treated

49: **abatement**: lessening

50: **dependants**: i.e., Gonoril's servants, including Oswald

LEAR

Follow me. Thou shalt serve me, if I like thee no worse after   35
dinner. I will not part from thee yet.—Dinner, ho, dinner! Where's
my knave, my fool? Go you and call my fool hither.

[Exit one]
Enter Steward [OSWALD]

You, you, sirrah, where's my daughter?

OSWALD

So please you—

[Exit]

LEAR

What says the fellow there? Call the clotpoll back.   40
[Exeunt SERVANT and KENT]
Where's my fool? Ho, I think the world's asleep.
[Enter KENT and a SERVANT]
How now, where's that mongrel?

SERVANT

He says, my lord, your daughter is not well.

LEAR

Why came not the slave back to me when I called him?

SERVANT

Sir, he answered me in the roundest manner he would not.   45

LEAR

A would not?

SERVANT

My lord, I know not what the matter is, but to my judgment your
Highness is not entertained with that ceremonious affection as
you were wont. There's a great abatement of kindness appears as
well in the general dependants as in the Duke himself also, and   50
your daughter.

LEAR

Ha, sayst thou so?

55: **rememberest**: reminds; **conception**: thought

56: **faint**: unenthusiastic

57: **jealous curiosity**: oversensitivity with regard to etiquette; **very pretense**: true intention

Costume rendering for Oswald from the 1959 production at the Shakespeare Memorial Theatre in Stratford-upon-Avon directed by Glen Byam Shaw
Rare Book and Special Collection Library, University of Illinois at Urbana-Champaign

67: **whoreson dog**: (a scathing insult)

70: **bandy looks**: exchange glances (as if Oswald sees himself as Lear's equal)

SERVANT

   I beseech you pardon me, my lord, if I be mistaken, for my duty
cannot be silent when I think your Highness wronged.

LEAR

   Thou but rememberest me of mine own conception. I have per-   55
ceived a most faint neglect of late, which I have rather blamed as
mine own jealous curiosity than as a very pretense and purport of
unkindness. I will look further into't. But where's this fool? I
have not seen him these two days.

SERVANT

   Since my young lady's going into France, sir, the fool hath much   60
pined away.

LEAR

   No more of that, I have noted it well. Go you and tell my daughter I would speak with her.

                                         [Exit one]

   Go you, call hither my fool.

                                         [Exit one]
               [Enter OSWALD, crossing the stage]

   O you, sir, you, sir, come you hither. Who am I, sir?   65

OSWALD

   My lady's father.

LEAR

   My lady's father? My lord's knave, you whoreson dog, you slave,
you cur!

OSWALD

   I am none of this, my lord; I beseech you pardon me.

LEAR

   Do you bandy looks with me, you rascal?   70

                          [LEAR strikes him]

OSWALD

   I'll not be struck, my lord—

72: **football**: low-class street game

74: **differences**: distinction in social rank

75: **If...again**: i.e., if you want to be knocked down again, you clumsy fool

76: **away...wisdom**: i.e., leave if you know what is good for you

77: Scene: ***Enter [Lear's] FOOL***: William C. Macready (1773-1873), seeking to soften the Fool's acerbic humor, cast a woman, Priscilla Horton (1818-1895), in the role. Granville-Barker (1877-1946) imagined the Fool to be agile and athletic, a gymnast; Alan Badel (1923-1982) as the Fool followed Orson Welles' Lear with dog-like loyalty.

78: **earnest of**: initial payment for

79: **coxcomb**: hat traditionally worn by fools

83-84: **Nay...shortly**: If you don't flatter those in power, you will be in trouble.

85: **banished...daughters**: lost two of his daughters

86: **done the third a blessing**: The fool implies that Cordelia is fortunate not to be associated with her sisters.

87: **nuncle**: mine uncle, an expression coined by the Fool for Lear

KENT

[*Tripping him*] Nor tripped neither, you base football player.

LEAR

[*To KENT*] I thank thee, fellow. Thou serv'st me, and I'll love thee.

KENT

[*To OSWALD*] Come, sir, arise, away. I'll teach you differences.
Away, away. If you will measure your lubber's length again, tarry;   75
but away if you have wisdom.

[Exit OSWALD]

LEAR

Now, my friendly knave, I thank thee.

Enter [Lear's] FOOL

There's earnest of thy service.

[He gives KENT money]

FOOL

Let me hire him, too. [*To KENT*] Here's my coxcomb.

LEAR

How now, my pretty knave, how dost thou?   80

FOOL

Sirrah, you were best take my coxcomb.

KENT

Why, fool?

FOOL

Why, for taking one's part that's out of favor. Nay, an thou canst
not smile as the wind sits, thou'lt catch cold shortly. There, take
my coxcomb. Why, this fellow hath banished two on's daughters   85
and done the third a blessing against his will. If thou follow him,
thou must needs wear my coxcomb. [*To LEAR*] How now, nuncle?
Would I had two coxcombs and two daughters.

LEAR

Why, my boy?

90: **If...myself**: i.e., If I gave away all of my property, I too would be a fool like you.

90-91: "There's mine; beg another off thy daughters": Kevin Kline as Lear and Philip Goodwin as the Fool in the 2007 Public Theater production directed by James Lapine
Photo: Michal Daniel

93: **Truth's...kennel**: i.e., Truth must be kept locked up.

94: **brach**: female hunting dog; **Lady...fire and stink**: idiomatic expression: A wet dog drying by the fire smells bad.

95: **pestilent gall**: painful truth

101: **thou owest**: you own

103: **trowest**: believe

104: **Set...throwest**: i.e., Do not bet everything on a single throw of the dice.

106: **in-a-door**: indoors

107-108: **more...a score**: A score is twenty, so more than two tens is a profit.

110-111: **like...for't**: i.e., you cannot expect good advice if you do not pay for it

FOOL

If I gave them all my living I'd keep my coxcombs myself. There's   90
mine; beg another off thy daughters.

LEAR

Take heed, sirrah—the whip.

FOOL

Truth is a dog that must to kennel. He must be whipped out when
Lady the brach may stand by the fire and stink.

LEAR

A pestilent gall to me!   95

FOOL

[*To KENT*] Sirrah, I'll teach thee a speech.

LEAR

Do.

FOOL

Mark it, nuncle.
    [*Sings*]
        Have more than thou showest,
        Speak less than thou knowest,   100
        Lend less than thou owest,
        Ride more than thou goest,
        Learn more than thou trowest,
        Set less than thou throwest;
        Leave thy drink and thy whore,   105
        And keep in-a-door,
        And thou shalt have more
        Than two tens to a score.

LEAR

This is nothing, fool.

FOOL

Then, like the breath of an unfee'd lawyer, you gave me nothing   110
for't. Can you make no use of nothing, uncle?

113: **so...to**: i.e., nothing, because Lear has given away his land and cannot therefore collect money for it

115: **bitter**: satirical

118: Scene: **No, lad. Teach me**: The Fool is more than a mere entertainer; he uses word-play and song to remarkably philosophical ends. In director Joseph Papp's New York City production, 1974, the Fool (Tom Aldridge) was a pointedly caustic politician, rather than a court entertainer. When the King confessed that he had "done her [Cordelia] wrong", he said so not to his own conscience but as an admission to the Fool. In Adrian Noble's 1982 RSC production, Michael Gambon's Lear played opposite Antony Sher's Fool, the latter dressed as if he were a clown who had just tumbled out of a three-ring circus. In Richard Eyre's 1998 TV production, the Fool (Michael Bryant) scolded Lear for giving away his crown and promised to train the King in the art of courtly jesting.

119-133: **That lord...nuncle**: appears only in the First Quarto

125: **motley**: traditional dress of court jesters

126: **The other**: referring to Lear as one of two fools

LEAR
Why no, boy. Nothing can be made out of nothing.

FOOL
[*To KENT*] Prithee, tell him so much the rent of his land comes to.
He will not believe a fool.

LEAR
A bitter fool.   115

FOOL
Dost know the difference, my boy, between a bitter fool and a
sweet fool?

LEAR
No, lad. Teach me.

FOOL
   [*Sings*]
   That lord that counseled thee
   To give away thy land,   120
   Come place him here by me;
   Do thou for him stand.
   The sweet and bitter fool
   Will presently appear,
   The one in motley here,   125
   The other found out there.

LEAR
Dost thou call me fool, boy?

FOOL
All thy other titles thou hast given away. That thou wast born with.

KENT
[*To LEAR*] This is not altogether fool, my lord.

130: lords...me: i.e., important people at court compete with me for the title of "Fool"

131: a **monopoly out**: exclusive control of foolish wisdom

132: snatching: grasping for their part

135: meat: edible part

136: clovest: divided, a reference to Lear's recent division of the kingdom

137-138: thou...dirt: i.e., you carried the mule, rather than letting it carry you

142: foppish: foolish, like a fop, or courtier

144: apish: like an ape, i.e., primitive

145: Scene: **so full of songs**: Tommaso Salvini (1829-1915) reacted to the Fool's jibes with laughter, Sir John Gielgud (1904-2000) with fondness, William C. Macready (1773-1873) with curiosity, and Michael Redgrave (1908-1985) with rage.

146: have used: have been doing

147-148: gavest...breeches: invited them to punish you

151: bo-peep: a game played by mother and child, now commonly referred to as "peekaboo"

FOOL

No, faith; lords and great men will not let me. If I had a   130
monopoly out, they would have part on't, and ladies too, they will
not let me have all the fool to myself—they'll be snatching. Give
me an egg, nuncle, and I'll give thee two crowns.

LEAR

What two crowns shall they be?

FOOL

Why, after I have cut the egg in the middle and eat up the meat,   135
the two crowns of the egg. When thou clovest thy crown i' th'
middle and gavest away both parts, thou borest thy ass o' th'
back o'er the dirt. Thou hadst little wit in thy bald crown when
thou gavest thy golden one away. If I speak like myself in this, let
him be whipped that first finds it so.   140
      [*Sings*]
      Fools had ne'er less wit in a year,
      For wise men are grown foppish.
      They know not how their wits do wear,
      Their manners are so apish.

LEAR

When were you wont to be so full of songs, sirrah?   145

FOOL

I have used it, nuncle, ever since thou madest thy daughters thy
mother; for when thou gavest them the rod and puttest down
thine own breeches,
      [*Sings*]
      Then they for sudden joy did weep,
      And I for sorrow sung,   150
      That such a king should play bo-peep
      And go the fools among.
Prithee, nuncle, keep a schoolmaster that can teach thy fool to lie.
I would fain learn to lie.

LEAR

An you lie, sirrah, we'll have you whipped.   155

162: **one of the parings**: i.e., one of the two daughters who now control the kingdom

163: **frontlet**: cloth or bandage worn on the forehead (to smooth away wrinkles)

163: **What makes that frontlet on?**: Why are you wearing that frown on your forehead?

163: "What makes that frontlet on": Engraving by John Byam Shaw, ca. 1900
Courtesy of the Folger Shakespeare Library

166: **O without a figure**: a number with no value, literally a zero

171-172: **He...some**: he who gives everything away will regret it (proverbial)

173: **shelled peascod**: a peapod without the peas, an expression of meaninglessness

174: **all-licensed**: free to do whatever he wants

175: **retinue**: followers

177: **rank**: excessive

179: **safe redress**: sure resolution

180: **too late**: in the recent past

181: **put it on**: facilitate or encourage

183: **censure**: reprimand; **nor...sleep**: nor would we fail to punish

184: **in...weal**: out of concern for the commonwealth

185: **Might...offense**: could have a negative impact on you

186-197: **That...proceedings**: i.e., Measures that in previous times might have embarrassed you now seem necessary in these precarious times.

FOOL

I marvel what kin thou and thy daughters are. They'll have me
whipped for speaking true, thou wilt have me whipped for lying,
and sometime I am whipped for holding my peace. I had rather
be any kind of thing than a fool; and yet I would not be thee,
nuncle. Thou hast pared thy wit o' both sides and left nothing in   160
the middle.

Enter GONORIL

Here comes one of the parings.

LEAR

How now, daughter, what makes that frontlet on?
Methinks you are too much o' late i' th' frown.

FOOL

Thou wast a pretty fellow when thou hadst no need to care for her   165
frown. Now thou art an O without a figure. I am better than thou
art, now. I am a fool; thou art nothing. [*To* GONORIL] Yes, for-
sooth, I will hold my tongue; so your face bids me, though you say
nothing.

[*Sings*]
Mum, mum.   170
He that keeps neither crust nor crumb,
Weary of all, shall want some.
That's a shelled peascod.

GONORIL

[*To LEAR*] Not only, sir, this your all-licensed fool,
But other of your insolent retinue   175
Do hourly carp and quarrel, breaking forth
In rank and not-to-be-endurèd riots.
Sir, I had thought by making this well known unto you
To have found a safe redress, but now grow fearful,
By what yourself too late have spoke and done,   180
That you protect this course, and put it on
By your allowance; which if you should, the fault
Would not scape censure, nor the redresses sleep
Which in the tender of a wholesome weal
Might in their working do you that offense,   185
That else were shame, that then necessity
Must call discreet proceedings.

189-190: hedge-sparrow...young: The cuckoo lays its eggs in the sparrow's nest; the sparrow feeds the young until the cuckoos are big enough to eat the sparrow. The Fool is inferring that Gonoril is an unnatural child who is at once consuming and ridding herself of her father.

191: darkling: in the dark

194: fraught: supplied

195: dispositions: inclinations or moods

197: May...horse?: i.e., Even a fool can see when things are so out of step that a daughter tells her father what to do.

Kalamandalam Padmanabhan Nair as Lear, Kalamandalam MPS Namboodiri as Gonoril, and Kalamandalam Manoj Kumar as the Fool in the 1999 Shakespeare's Globe production "Kathakali King Lear" directed by Annete Leday, adapted by David McRuvie

Photo: Donald Cooper

198: Jug: Steevens (1773) suggests a lost song; G.L. Kittredge (1940) suggests a nickname for Joan. Foakes (1997) suggests an evasive response. Orgel (2000) suggests a generic name for whore. "Jugge," a deep vessel for carrying liquids, dates to 1538.

201: notion: intellectual abilities

201-202: his...lethargied: i.e., his mental faculties have atrophied

205-208: Lear's shadow...obedient father: appears only in the First Quarto

205: Lear's shadow: a shadow of his former self, but also perhaps playing on the word "shade", meaning "ghost". Lear could be intimating that he is close to death.

205-206: marks of sovereignty: superficial indications of kingship, such as a crown or a sceptor

205-207: I would learn...I had daughters: All of the evidence would falsely indicate that I have loving and respectful daughters.

208: Which: whom

FOOL

    [*To LEAR*] For, you trow, nuncle,
        [*Sings*]
        The hedge-sparrow fed the cuckoo so long
        That it had it head bit off by it young;   190
    So out went the candle, and we were left darkling.

LEAR

    [*To GONORIL*] Are you our daughter?

GONORIL

    Come, sir, I would you would make use of that good wisdom,
    Whereof I know you are fraught, and put away
    These dispositions that of late transform you   195
    From what you rightly are.

FOOL

    May not an ass know when the cart draws the horse?
        [*Sings*]
        Whoop, Jug, I love thee!

LEAR

    Doth any here know me? Why, this is not Lear.
    Doth Lear walk thus, speak thus? Where are his eyes?   200
    Either his notion weakens, or his discernings
    Are lethargied. Sleeping or waking, ha?
    Sure, 'tis not so.
    Who is it that can tell me who I am?
    Lear's shadow? I would learn that, for by the marks   205
    Of sovereignty, knowledge, and reason
    I should be false persuaded I had daughters.

FOOL

    Which they will make an obedient father.

LEAR

    [*To GONORIL*] Your name, fair gentlewoman?

210: **admiration**: phony sense of wonder or disbelief; **much of the savor**: consistent with

213: **reverend**: worthy of reverence

215: **disordered**: disorderly; **debauched**: depraved; **bold**: impudent

217: **Shows**: presents itself; **epicurism**: excessive, hedonistic behavior

222: **disquantity your train**: reduce the number of those who attend you

224: **besort**: be appropriate for

225: **That...you**: who are self-aware enough to serve you in an appropriate way

226: **train**: retinue

227: **Degenerate bastard**: ungrateful daughter who acts as if she were fathered by someone else

229: "You strike my people, and your disordered rabble / Make servants of their betters": Rosalind Cash as Gonoril in the 1973 Public Theater production directed by Edwin Sherin

Photo: George E. Joseph

231: **O sir, are you come?**: appears only in the First Quarto

233: **marble-hearted**: hard-hearted, unfeeling

GONORIL

                                        Come, sir,
This admiration, sir, is much of the savor   210
Of other your new pranks. I do beseech you
To understand my purposes aright,
As you are old and reverend, should be wise.
Here do you keep a hundred knights and squires,
Men so disordered, so debauched and bold   215
That this our court, infected with their manners,
Shows like a riotous inn, epicurism
And lust make it more like to a tavern, or a brothel,
Than a great palace. The shame itself doth speak
For instant remedy. Be thou desired,   220
By her that else will take the thing she begs,
A little to disquantity your train,
And the remainder that shall still depend
To be such men as may besort your age,
That know themselves and you.

LEAR

                                Darkness and devils!   225
Saddle my horses, call my train together!—

                                        [Exit one or more]

Degenerate bastard, I'll not trouble thee.
Yet have I left a daughter.

GONORIL
You strike my people, and your disordered rabble
Make servants of their betters.   230
                                Enter Duke [of ALBANY]

LEAR
We that too late repents—O sir, are you come?
Is it your will that we—prepare my horses.

                                        [Exit one or more]

Ingratitude, thou marble-hearted fiend,
More hideous when thou show'st thee in a child
Than the sea-monster—   235

249–264:
Laurence Olivier as Lear

235: **Pray sir, be patient.**: appears only in the First Quarto

236: **kite**: bird of prey

237: **rarest parts**: finest qualities

239-240: **support...name**: act in a way that does honor to their reputations

242-243: **That...place**: which, like a powerful tool, cut away my natural feelings of love (i.e., his fatherly love for Cordelia) from where they should be

244: **gall**: bitterness

248: **Of what hath moved you.**: from the First Folio

249-264: Scene: David Garrick's (1717-1779) curses took on the aura of holy prayer; Edmund Kean (1787-1833) threw himself on his knees, exhausted and breathless. Henry Irving (1838-1905) spoke his curses as if they had been torn from his heart.

254: **derogate**: corrupt

255: **teem**: give birth

256: **spleen**: anger and bad temper

257: **thwart disnatured torment**: stubborn, unnatural source of difficulty

259: **cadent**: cascading; **fret**: erode

260: **benefits**: joys of motherhood

263: **serpent's tooth**: fangs; see also 2.2.297 (**sharp-tooth'd**), 2.2.322-323 (**struck me...serpent-like**), 5.1.57-58 (**stung...adder**), 5.3.83 (**gilded serpent**)

264: **Go, go, my people!**: appears only in the First Quarto

ALBANY

                   Pray sir, be patient.   235

LEAR

   [*To GONORIL*] Detested kite, thou liest.
   My train are men of choice and rarest parts,
   That all particulars of duty know,
   And in the most exact regard support
   The worships of their name. O most small fault,   240
   How ugly didst thou in Cordelia show,
   That, like an engine, wrenched my frame of nature
   From the fixed place, drew from heart all love,
   And added to the gall! O Lear, Lear, Lear!
   Beat at this gate that let thy folly in,   245
   And thy dear judgment out.—Go, go, my people!

ALBANY

   My lord, I am guiltless as I am ignorant.
   Of what hath moved you.

LEAR

   It may be so, my lord. Hark, Nature, hear.
   Dear goddess, hear. Suspend thy purpose if   250
   Thou didst intend to make this creature fruitful.
   Into her womb convey sterility.
   Dry up in her the organs of increase,
   And from her derogate body never spring
   A babe to honor her. If she must teem,   255
   Create her child of spleen, that it may live
   And be a thwart disnatured torment to her.
   Let it stamp wrinkles in her brow of youth,
   With cadent tears fret channels in her cheeks,
   Turn all her mother's pains and benefits   260
   To laughter and contempt, that she may feel—
   That she may feel
   How sharper than a serpent's tooth it is
   To have a thankless child.—Go, go, my people!
               Exeunt LEAR, KENT, FOOL, and servants

Costume rendering for Lear's men by Susan Tsu from the 2004 Oregon
Shakespeare Festival production directed by James Edmondson
Courtesy of the Oregon Shakespeare Festival

266: **Never...know:** do not bother trying to figure out
267: **disposition:** mood
268: **dotage:** senility
273: **hot tears:** womanly tears
274: **should make thee:** should be worthy of a king; **worst blasts and fogs:** terrible
afflictions and plague-bearing fogs
275: **untented:** deep and infected
276: **fond:** ridiculous
277: **Beweep:** if you cry over
279: **temper clay:** mix with dirt (a threat to gouge out his eyes and stomp them
into the ground)
279: **Yea...Whom:** appears only in the First Quarto
281: **comfortable:** comforting
283: **flay:** strip off the skin
284: **resume the shape:** take back the kingship
288: **To:** because of

ALBANY
  Now, gods that we adore, whereof comes this?   265

GONORIL
  Never afflict yourself to know the cause,
  But let his disposition have that scope
  That dotage gives it.

                                        Enter LEAR and FOOL

LEAR
  What, fifty of my followers at a clap?
  Within a fortnight?

ALBANY
                        What is the matter, sir?   270

LEAR
  I'll tell thee. [*To GONORIL*] Life and death! I am ashamed
  That thou hast power to shake my manhood thus,
  That these hot tears, that break from me perforce
  And should make thee—worst blasts and fogs upon thee!
  Untented woundings of a father's curse   275
  Pierce every sense about thee! Old fond eyes,
  Beweep this cause again I'll pluck you out
  And cast you, with the waters that you make,
  To temper clay. Yea,
  Is't come to this? Yet have I left a daughter   280
  Whom, I am sure, is kind and comfortable.
  When she shall hear this of thee, with her nails
  She'll flay thy wolvish visage. Thou shalt find
  That I'll resume the shape which thou dost think
  I have cast off forever; thou shalt, I warrant thee.   285
                                                      [Exit]

GONORIL
  Do you mark that, my lord?

ALBANY
  I cannot be so partial, Gonoril,
  To the great love I bear you—

288: **Come, sir, no more.**: appears only in the First Quarto

293: **Should sure**: should certainly be sent

294: **halter**: leash for leading an animal to slaughter or hangman's noose

296-307: **This man...th' unfitness**: from the First Folio

296: **This...counsel**: Gonoril says this sarcastically

297: **politic**: wise (also said sarcastically)

298: **At point**: prepared for war; **dream**: imaginary grievance

299: **buzz**: rumor; **fancy**: whim

300: **enguard**: protect

301: **in mercy**: at his mercy

302: **fear too far**: exaggerate the risks

304: **Not...taken**: i.e., instead of living in fear of what could happen

307: **th' unfitness**: the impropriety of doing so

308-309: **What...madam**: appears only in the First Quarto

GONORIL
                        Come, sir, no more.—
You, sir, more knave than fool, after your master!

FOOL
Nuncle Lear, nuncle Lear, tarry, and take the fool with thee.   290
    [*Sings*]
        A fox when one has caught her,
        And such a daughter,
        Should sure to the slaughter,
        If my cap would buy a halter.
        So, the fool follows after.   295
                                      [*Exit*]

GONORIL
This man hath had good counsel—a hundred knights?
'Tis politic and safe to let him keep
At point a hundred knights, yes, that on every dream,
Each buzz, each fancy, each complaint, dislike,
He may enguard his dotage with their powers   300
And hold our lives in mercy.—Oswald, I say!

ALBANY
Well, you may fear too far.

GONORIL
                  Safer than trust too far.
Let me still take away the harms I fear,
Not fear still to be taken. I know his heart.
What he hath uttered I have writ my sister.   305
If she sustain him and his hundred knights
When I have showed th' unfitness—
What, Oswald, ho!

                                [*Enter OSWALD*]

OSWALD
Here, madam.

GONORIL
What, have you writ this letter to my sister?   310

315: **compact**: further prove

317: **Milky gentleness**: motherly or effeminate manner

318: **under pardon**: if you will forgive me for saying so

319: **ataxed**: penalized

320: **harmful mildness**: dangerous gentleness

324: **the event**: i..e.,time will tell how things turn out

OSWALD
Ay, madam.

GONORIL
Take you some company, and away to horse.
Inform her full of my particular fears,
And thereto add such reasons of your own
As may compact it more. Get you gone,   315
And after, your retinue.

                              [Exit OSWALD]

                    Now, my lord,
This milky gentleness and course of yours,
Though I dislike not, yet under pardon
You're much more ataxed for want of wisdom
Than praised for harmful mildness.   320

ALBANY
How far your eyes may pierce I can not tell.
Striving to better aught, we mar what's well.

GONORIL
Nay, then—

ALBANY
Well, well, the event.

                                        Exeunt

0: Location: Before Albany's Palace

Watercolor scene sketch from the promptbook for Charles Kean's 1858 production

Courtesy of the Folger Shakespeare Library

0: Scene: ***Enter...and FOOL***: In Nahum Tate's 1687 adaptation, Shakespeare's Fool was cut altogether. Tate's version was so popular that Shakespeare's Fool was not restored to theatrical productions until 1838 (see "In Production," pages 2-9)

tracks 13-15

2-3: **than...letter**: than what the letter compels her to ask you about
6: **kibes**: chapped or inflamed skin, especially on the heel, caused by exposure to the cold
8: **thy wit...slipshod**: i.e., you need not wear slippers to avoid kibes, since you have no brains
10: **Shalt**: thou shalt; **kindly**: befitting a family member
11: **crab**: crab apple

Act 1, Scene 5]

Enter LEAR, [KENT, disguised, and FOOL]

LEAR

[*To KENT*] Go you before to Gloucester with these letters. Acquaint my daughter no further with anything you know than comes from her demand out of the letter. If your diligence be not speedy, I shall be there before you.

KENT

I will not sleep, my lord, till I have delivered your letter.   5

Exit

FOOL

If a man's brains were in his heels, were't not in danger of kibes?

LEAR

Ay, boy.

FOOL

Then, I prithee, be merry; thy wit shall ne'er go slipshod.

LEAR

Ha, ha, ha!

FOOL

Shalt see thy other daughter will use thee kindly, for though she's   10
as like this as a crab is like an apple, yet I can what I can tell.

LEAR

Why, what canst thou tell, my boy?

FOOL

She'll taste as like this as a crab doth to a crab. Thou canst not tell why one's nose stands in the middle of his face?

6–36:
Paul Scofield as Lear, David Burke as Kent, and Kenneth Branagh as the Fool
Laurence Olivier as Lear, Colin Blakely as Kent, and John Hurt as the Fool

Costume rendering for Kent in disguise from the 1959 production at the Shakespeare Memorial Theatre in Stratford-upon-Avon directed by Glen Byam Shaw

Rare Book and Special Collection Library, University of Illinois at Urbana-Champaign

16: **side's**: side of his; **that**: so that
18: **her**: i.e., Cordelia
23-24 **Why...case**: The Fool is suggesting that a snail is smarter than Lear because a snail builds a house to protect itself, while the King has given his house away and thus is vulnerable.
24: **horns**: 1) snails horns, but also 2) possibly a suggestion that Lear has been cuckolded, betrayed sexually by his daughters. (A man whose wife strayed was thought to grow horns on his forehead.)
25: **nature**: natural paternal love
26: **Thy...them**: i.e., Your servants, who work like mules for you, are getting the horses ready. **seven stars**: the constellation known as the Pleiades

LEAR
No.   15

FOOL
Why, to keep his eyes on either side's nose, that what a man cannot smell out, a may spy into.

LEAR
I did her wrong.

FOOL
Canst tell how an oyster makes his shell?

LEAR
No.   20

FOOL
Nor I neither; but I can tell why a snail has a house.

LEAR
Why?

FOOL
Why, to put his head in, not to give it away to his daughter and
leave his horns without a case.

LEAR
I will forget my nature. So kind a father! Be my horses ready?   25

FOOL
Thy asses are gone about them. The reason why the seven stars
are no more than seven is a pretty reason.

LEAR
Because they are not eight?

FOOL
Yes, indeed. Thou wouldst make a good fool.

tracks 13-15

6–36:
Paul Scofield as Lear, David Burke as Kent, and Kenneth Branagh as the Fool
Laurence Olivier as Lear, Colin Blakely as Kent, and John Hurt as the Fool

30: **To...perforce**: Lear is contemplating 1) the possibility that Gonoril would use force to take back all that she has promised him, and 2) using his army to reclaim his throne.; **monster**: monstrous

36: **in temper**: mentally stable

41: **maid**: virgin; **things**: i.e., penises; **cut shorter**: castrated

LEAR

  To take't again perforce—monster ingratitude!   30

FOOL

  If thou wert my fool, nuncle, I'd have thee beaten for being old
  before thy time.

LEAR

  How's that?

FOOL

  Thou shouldst not have been old before thou hadst been wise.

LEAR

  O, let me not be mad, not mad, sweet heaven! I would not be mad.   35
  Keep me in temper. I would not be mad.

                                                    [Enter SERVANT]

  How now, are the horses ready?

SERVANT

  Ready, my lord.

LEAR

  [*To* FOOL] Come, boy.

                                          Exeunt [LEAR and SERVANT]

FOOL

  She that is a maid now, and laughs at my departure,   40
  Shall not be a maid long, except things be cut shorter.

                                                              Exit

[King Lear

Act 2

0: Location: The Earl of Gloucester's house

Costume rendering for Curan from the 1959 production at the Shakespeare
Memorial Theatre in Stratford-upon-Avon directed by Glen Byam Shaw
Rare Book and Special Collection Library, University of Illinois at Urbana-Champaign

1: **Save**: God save
6: **abroad**: during your travels
7: **ear-bussing arguments**: whispered topics
9: **towards 'twixt**: impending between

tracks 16-18

13–36:
Gerard Murphy as Edmund and David Tennant as Edgar
Toby Stephens as Edmund and Richard McCabe as Edgar

13: **The better, best**: all the better
14: **perforce**: inevitably

Act 2, Scene 1]

Enter Bastard [EDMUND] and CURAN, meeting

EDMUND
Save thee, Curan.

CURAN
And you, sir. I have been with your father, and given him notice
that the Duke of Cornwall and Regan his duchess will be here
with him tonight.

EDMUND
How comes that?   5

CURAN
Nay, I know not. You have heard of the news abroad?—I mean
the whispered ones, for they are yet but ear-bussing arguments.

EDMUND
Not. I pray you, what are they?

CURAN
Have you heard of no likely wars towards 'twixt the two Dukes
of Cornwall and Albany?   10

EDMUND
Not a word.

CURAN
You may do then in time. Fare you well, sir.

Exit

EDMUND
The duke be here tonight! The better, best.
This weaves itself perforce into my business.
Enter EDGAR [at a window above]

tracks 16-18

13–36:
Gerard Murphy as Edmund and David Tennant as Edgar
Toby Stephens as Edmund and Richard McCabe as Edgar

15: **take**: capture
16: **queasy**: question
17: **Which**: for which; **briefness**: quickness
20: **Intelligence**: report, information
23: **i' th' haste**: in great haste
26: **Advise you**: think about your situation; **on't**: of it
28: **In cunning** : i.e., I intend to act as if
29: **quit you**: defend yourself

29: "Now, quit you well": Andrew Long as Edmund and Cameron Folmar as Edgar in the 2000 Shakespeare Theatre Company production directed by Michael Kahn
Photo: Carol Rosegg

31: **Fly**: run away
33-34: **beget...endeavor**: give the impression that I had fought fiercely
35: **in sport**: for fun, in jest
38: **wicked charms**: offers of money
39: **stand 's**: stand for his, act as if he were his; **auspicious mistress**: i.e., the goddess Fortune. See also the following references to Fortune 1.1.274, 2.2.155-156, 4.6.211, 5.3.6, and 5.3.173

My father hath set guard to take my brother;   15
And I have one thing of a queasy question
Which I must ask briefness. Wit and Fortune help!—
Brother, a word. Descend, brother, I say.

[EDGAR climbs down]

My father watches. O sir, fly this place.
Intelligence is given where you are hid.   20
You have now the good advantage of the night.
Have you not spoken 'gainst the Duke of Cornwall aught?
He's coming hither now, in the night, i' th' haste,
And Regan with him. Have you nothing said
Upon his party against the Duke of Albany?   25
Advise you—

EDGAR

                    I am sure on't, not a word.

EDMUND

I hear my father coming. Pardon me.
In cunning I must draw my sword upon you.
Draw. Seem to defend yourself. Now, quit you well.
[Calling] Yield, come before my father. Light here, here!   30
[To EDGAR] Fly, brother, fly! *[Calling]* Torches, torches!
[To EDGAR] So, farewell.

                              [Exit EDGAR]

Some blood drawn on me would beget opinion
Of my more fierce endeavor.

                              [EDMUND wounds his arm]
                    I have seen
Drunkards do more than this in sport. *[Calling]* Father, father!   35
Stop, stop! Ho, help!

                              Enter GLOUCESTER [and others]

GLOUCESTER

                    Now, Edmund, where is the villain?

EDMUND

Here stood he in the dark, his sharp sword out,
Warbling of wicked charms, conjuring the moon
To stand 's auspicious mistress.

44: **that**: when; **revengive gods**: revenging. In Greek mythology, the god of revenge was Nemesis.
45: **bend**: aim

44-45: "But I told him the revengive gods / 'Gainst parricides did all their thunders bend": Andrew Long as Edmund and David Sabin as Gloucester in the 2000 Shakespeare Theatre Company production directed by Michael Kahn
Photo: Carol Rosegg

46: **manifold**: many
47: **in fine**: in conclusion
48: **loathly opposite**: hatefully opposed
49: **fell motion**: deadly thrust
50: **preparèd**: drawn and ready; **home**: straight to the heart
51: **unprovided**: armorless
52: **best alarumed**: thoroughly alarmed and ready
53: **quarrel's rights**: justice on my side
54: **ghasted**: shocked, frightened (from "aghast")
55: **[ ]**: some words may be missing here in the Quarto
58: **dispatch**: dispensed with, taken care of
59: **My worthy arch and patron**: chief architect and supporter of my success

GLOUCESTER

But where is he?

EDMUND
Look, sir, I bleed.

GLOUCESTER

Where is the villain, Edmund?   40

EDMUND
Fled this way, sir, when by no means he could—

GLOUCESTER
Pursue him, ho! go after.

[Exeunt others]

By no means what?

EDMUND
Persuade me to the murder of your lordship,
But that I told him the revengive gods
'Gainst parricides did all their thunders bend,   45
Spoke with how manifold and strong a bond
The child was bound to the father. Sir, in fine,
Seeing how loathly opposite I stood
To his unnatural purpose, with fell motion,
With his preparèd sword, he charges home   50
My unprovided body, lanced mine arm;
But when he saw my best alarumed spirits
Bold in the quarrel's rights, roused to the encounter,
Or whether ghasted by the noise I made,
Or [   ] I know not,   55
But suddenly he fled.

GLOUCESTER

Let him fly far.
Not in this land shall he remain uncaught,
And found, dispatch. The noble duke my master,
My worthy arch and patron, comes tonight.
By his authority I will proclaim it   60

62: **to the stake**: to the appropriate punishment

65: **pitched**: determined; **curst**: angry

66: **discover**: expose

67: **unpossessing bastard**: ineligible to inherit property (because of his illegitimacy)

68: **reposure**: bestowal

70: **faithed**: trusted, believed; **what**: that which

72: **very character**: actual handwritten testimony; **turn**: attribute

73: **suggestion**: instigation

74: **dullard**: idiot

76: **pregnant and potential spurs**: meaningful and potent motivations

77: **fastened villain**: hardened criminal

78: **got**: begot, fathered

80 **ports**: seaports and other exits

81: **picture**: description

84: **natural**: 1) natural love for one's father, and 2) a reference to illegitimacy, as in a child of nature whose birth is not legally sanctioned by marriage

85: **capable**: i.e., legally able to inherit property

That he which finds him shall deserve our thanks,
Bringing the murderous caitiff to the stake;
He that conceals him, death.

EDMUND
When I dissuaded him from his intent
And found him pitched to do it, with curst speech   65
I threatened to discover him. He replied,
"Thou unpossessing bastard, dost thou think
If I would stand against thee, could the reposure
Of any trust, virtue, or worth in thee
Make thy words faithed? No, what I should deny—   70
As this I would, ay, though thou didst produce
My very character—I'd turn it all
To thy suggestion, plot, and damned pretense,
And thou must make a dullard of the world
If they not thought the profits of my death   75
Were very pregnant and potential spurs
To make thee seek it."

GLOUCESTER
                    Strong and fastened villain!
Would he deny his letter? I never got him.

                              [Trumpet within]

Hark, the duke's trumpets. I know not why he comes.
All ports I'll bar. The villain shall not scape.   80
The Duke must grant me that; besides, his picture
I will send far and near, that all the kingdom
May have the due note of him—and of my land,
Loyal and natural boy, I'll work the means
To make thee capable.   85
                    Enter the Duke of CORNWALL [and REGAN]

CORNWALL
How now, my noble friend? Since I came hither,
Which I can call but now, I have heard strange news.

REGAN
If it be true, all vengeance comes too short
Which can pursue the offender. How dost, my lord?

90: **cracked**: broken

Costume rendering for Regan by Susan Tsu from the 2004 Oregon Shakespeare
Festival production directed by James Edmondson

Courtesy of the Oregon Shakespeare Festival

97: **consort**: group
98: **though**: if; **ill affected**: disloyal
99: **put him on**: encouraged him to bring on
100: **the spoil and waste**: the squandering
106: **childlike**: dutiful
107: **betray his practice**: i.e., reveal Edgar's plot
108: **apprehend**: arrest

GLOUCESTER
  O Madam, my old heart is cracked, is cracked.   90

REGAN
  What, did my father's godson seek your life?
  He whom my father named, your Edgar?

GLOUCESTER
  Ay, lady, lady; shame would have it hid!

REGAN
  Was he not companion with the riotous knights
  That tend upon my father?   95

GLOUCESTER
  I know not, madam. 'Tis too bad, too bad.

EDMUND
  Yes, madam, he was of that consort.

REGAN
  No marvel, then, though he were ill affected.
  'Tis they have put him on the old man's death,
  To have the spoil and waste of his revenues.   100
  I have this present evening from my sister
  Been well informed of them, and with such cautions
  That if they come to sojourn at my house
  I'll not be there.

CORNWALL
                  Nor I, assure thee, Regan.
  Edmund, I heard that you have shown your father   105
  A childlike office.

EDMUND
                  'Twas my duty, sir.

GLOUCESTER
  [To CORNWALL] He did betray his practice, and received
  This hurt you see striving to apprehend him.

111-112: **Make...please**: i.e., use my resources in whatever way you see fit to accomplish your goal

112: **For**: as for

117: **However else**: above everything else

120: **poise**: significance

123: **differences**: quarrels

125: **attend dispatch**: are waiting to be sent

128: **instant use**: immediate attention

CORNWALL
   Is he pursued?

GLOUCESTER
              Ay, my good lord.

CORNWALL
   If he be taken, he shall never more   110
   Be feared of doing harm. Make your own purpose
   How in my strength you please. For you, Edmund,
   Whose virtue and obedience doth this instant
   So much commend itself, you shall be ours.
   Natures of such deep trust we shall much need.   115
   You we first seize on.

EDMUND
              I shall serve you truly,
   However else.

GLOUCESTER
            [To CORNWALL] For him I thank your grace.

CORNWALL
   You know not why we came to visit you—

REGAN
   Thus out-of-season threat'ning dark-eyed night—
   Occasions, noble Gloucester, of some poise,   120
   Wherein we must have use of your advice.
   Our father he hath writ, so hath our sister,
   Of differences which I best thought it fit
   To answer from our home. The several messengers
   From hence attend dispatch. Our good old friend,   125
   Lay comforts to your bosom, and bestow
   Your needful counsel to our business,
   Which craves the instant use.

GLOUCESTER
                 I serve you, madam.
   Your Graces are right welcome.

                                     Exeunt

0: **Location**: Before Gloucester's house

1: **even**: evening; **Art**: are you not

4: **mire**: swamp

5: **love me**: honor and respect me (not a romantic question)

6: **I love thee not**: Kent deliberately misinterprets the phrase and answers in more romantic terms.

8: **pinfold**: a place where stray animals are kept; **If...pinfold**: if I had you clenched between my teeth; **care for**: be afraid of

10: **I know thee**: I am on to you

Act 2, Scene 2]

Enter KENT, [disguised, at one door,] and Steward
[OSWALD, at another door]

OSWALD
Good even to thee, friend. Art of the house?

KENT
Ay.

OSWALD
Where may we set our horses?

KENT
I' th' mire.

OSWALD
Prithee, if thou love me, tell me.   5

KENT
I love thee not.

OSWALD
Why then, I care not for thee.

KENT
If I had thee in Lipsbury pinfold I would make thee care for me.

OSWALD
Why dost thou use me thus? I know thee not.

KENT
Fellow, I know thee.   10

OSWALD
What dost thou know me for?

12: broken meats: scraps of food often handed out to the poor

13-14: three-suited...knave: the custodian of a house who is allotted three suits and a salary of one-hundred pounds but dresses like a lowly servant in dirty wool stockings

14: lily-livered: cowardly; **action-taking**: spending a lot of time in the courts filing frivolous lawsuits; **glass gazing**: narcissistic, as in one who constantly looks in the mirror

15: superfinical: finicky, insufferable; **one-trunk-inheriting**: owning so few possessions that they all fit in one suitcase

16: bawd...service: pimp who provides his clients with whatever they want; **composition**: combination

17: pander: pimp

18-19: if thou...addition: i.e., if you try to refute any of the things I have just said about you

24: Draw: draw your sword

25: I'll make...moonshine: i.e., I will give you so many wounds that you will soak up the moonlight the way a piece of toast soaks up brot.h

26: cullionly barber-monger: low-class person who loiters in barbershops

27: have nothing: want nothing

29: Vanity the puppet's part: an allusion the figure of Vanity in Renaissance morality plays, used here in reference to Gonoril's recent actions

30: carbonado your shanks: cut up your legs like meat for grilling

31: come your ways: come on

33 neat: ridiculous

KENT

A knave, a rascal, an eater of broken meats, a base, proud, shallow, beggarly, three-suited, hundred-pound, filthy worsted-stocking knave; a lily-livered, action-taking knave; a whoreson, glass-gazing, superfinical rogue; one-trunk-inheriting slave; one that wouldst be a   15
bawd in way of good service, and art nothing but the composition of a knave, beggar, coward, pander, and the son and heir of a mongrel bitch, one whom I will beat into clamorous whining if thou deny the least syllable of the addition.

OSWALD

Why, what a monstrous fellow art thou, thus to rail on one   20
that's neither known of thee nor knows thee!

KENT

What a brazen-faced varlet art thou, to deny thou knowest me! Is it two days ago since I beat thee and tripped up thy heels before the King? Draw, you rogue; for though it be night, yet the moon shines. [*Draws his sword*] I'll make a sop of the moonshine o' you.   25
Draw, you whoreson, cullionly barber-monger, draw!

OSWALD

Away. I have nothing to do with thee.

KENT

Draw, you rascal. You bring letters against the King, and take Vanity the puppet's part against the royalty of her father. Draw, you rogue, or I'll so carbonado your shanks—draw, you rascal,   30
come your ways!

OSWALD

Help, ho, murder, help!

KENT

Strike, you slave! Stand, rogue! Stand, you neat slave, strike!

OSWALD

Help, ho, murder, help!
          Enter EDMUND with his rapier drawn, [then] GLOUCESTER,
          [then the] Duke [of CORNWALL] and Duchess [REGAN]

35: **matter**: problem

36: **With you**: i.e., my problem is with you; **goodman boy**: an expression of contempt directed at Edmund; **flesh you**: cut you

42: **difference**: 1) quarrel, and 2) reason for fighting

43: **scarce in breath**: winded

45: **disclaims**: disowns; **a tailor made thee**: an insult suggesting that there is nothing to him but the clothes he is wearing

EDMUND
  [*Parting them*] How now, what's the matter?   35

KENT
  With you, goodman boy. An you please come, I'll flesh you. Come
  on, young master.

GLOUCESTER
  Weapons? Arms? What's the matter here?

CORNWALL
  Keep peace, upon your lives. He dies that strikes again. What's
  the matter?   40

REGAN
  The messengers from our sister and the King.

CORNWALL
  [*To KENT and OSWALD*] What's your difference? Speak.

OSWALD
  I am scarce in breath, my lord.

KENT
  No marvel, you have so bestirred your valor, you cowardly rascal.
  Nature disclaims in thee; a tailor made thee.   45

CORNWALL
  Thou art a strange fellow—a tailor make a man?

KENT
  Ay, a tailor, sir. A stone-cutter or painter could not have made him
  so ill though he had been but two hours at the trade.

CORNWALL
  Speak yet; how grew your quarrel?

OSWALD
  This ancient ruffian, sir, whose life I have spared at suit of his   50
  gray beard—

52: **Z**: often interchangeable with S in spelling, hence, an unnecessary letter of the alphabet; **unbolted**: crude, unsophisticated

54: **daub**: plaster; **jakes**: bathroom

55: **wagtail**: a bird like a peacock that wags its tail feathers

60: **rogues**: villains

61: **cords**: family ties or allegiances that keep the peace

62: **too entrench'd to unloose**: too tightly knotted to be undone; **smooth**: flatter

63: **rebel**: go against reason

65: **Renege, affirm**: disagree one minute, agree the next

65-66: **turn...masters**: The kingfisher, whose magical powers included charming the winds and waves, would supposedly turn its beak into the wind if suspended by a rope. Oswald responds similarly to whatever his master tells him; he is like a puppet with no will of his own.

66: **gale and vary**: change in the direction of the wind

67: **following**: flattering and fawning

68: **epileptic visage**: face trembling with fear

69: **Smile you**: do you smile at

70: **Sarum plain**: a plain near Stonehenge; see note for 1.1.0:Scene

71: **Camelot**: ;egendary capitol of Arthur's Britain. Kent presents himself as a man of chivalry, and sees Oswald as a man without honor.

70-71: **Goose...Camelot**: If allowed to, Kent would send Oswald on his way, cackling like a goose.

KENT

Thou whoreson Z, thou unnecessary letter—[*To CORNWALL*] my
lord, if you'll give me leave I will tread this unbolted villain into
mortar, and daub the wall of a jakes with him. [*To OSWALD*]
Spare my gray beard, you wagtail?   55

CORNWALL

Peace, sir. You beastly knave, have you no reverence?

KENT

Yes, sir, but anger has a privilege.

CORNWALL

Why art thou angry?

KENT

That such a slave as this should wear a sword,
That wears no honesty. Such smiling rogues   60
As these, like rats, oft bite those cords in twain
Which are too entrenched to unloose, smooth every passion
That in the natures of their lords rebel,
Bring oil to fire, snow to their colder moods,
Renege, affirm, and turn their halcyon beaks   65
With every gale and vary of their masters,
Knowing naught, like dogs, but following.
[*To OSWALD*] A plague upon your epileptic visage!
Smile you my speeches as I were a fool?
Goose, if I had you upon Sarum Plain   70
I'd send you cackling home to Camelot.

CORNWALL

Why, art thou mad, old fellow?

GLOUCESTER

                               [*To KENT*] How fell you out?
Say that.

KENT

No contraries hold more antipathy
Than I and such a knave.   75

76: **likes**: pleases

82: **affect**: imitate the style of

83-84: **constrains...nature**: pushes plain-speaking, or the absence of flattery, to the point that it becomes a form of deception

84: **He cannot flatter, he.**: a sarcastic reference to Kent as a man who makes grand claims about his hatred for flattering speech

86: **An...plain**: i.e., if people tolerate his bluntness, great; if not, he is just justifying himself by claiming to speak only the truth.

89: **silly-ducking observants**: constantly bowing, ridiculously fawning , obsequious courtiers

90: **That...nicely**: those courtiers who go out of their way to perform their duties as flattering courtiers

91-94: **Sir...front**: Kent here is imitating the words and mannerisms of a fawning courtier

92: **allowance**: approval; **aspect**: 1) countenance, and 2) astrological position

93: **influence**: astrological power

94: **Phoebus' front**: the forehead of the sun

CORNWALL

Why dost thou call him knave?   75
What's his offense?

KENT

His countenance likes me not.

CORNWALL

No more perchance does mine, or his, or hers.

KENT

Sir, 'tis my occupation to be plain:
I have seen better faces in my time
Than stands on any shoulder that I see   80
Before me at this instant.

CORNWALL

This is a fellow,
Who, having been praised for bluntness, doth affect
A saucy roughness, and constrains the garb
Quite from his nature. He cannot flatter, he.
He must be plain, he must speak truth.   85
An they will take't, so; if not, he's plain.
These kind of knaves I know, which in this plainness
Harbor more craft and more corrupter ends
Than twenty silly-ducking observants
That stretch their duties nicely.   90

KENT

Sir, in good sooth, or in sincere verity,
Under the allowance of your grand aspect,
Whose influence, like the wreath of radiant fire
In flickering Phoebus' front—

CORNWALL

What mean'st thou by this?

95: dialect: normal manner of speaking; **discommend**: criticize

96-98: He that...to't: i.e., He who strategically used plain speech to make you suspicious of plain speakers, was in fact nothing but a plain rascal. I refuse to play that role even though it would make me happy, if, in doing so, it displeased you.

100: late: recently

101: upon his misconstruction: as a result of the King's misinterpretation of me

103: When...displeasure: i.e., when he (Kent), conspiring with the King and his men, and seeking to ingratiate himself with the King, who is angry with me

104: being down: already in a disadvantaged position; **railed**: insulted

104-105: And put...him: and acted so passionately that it made him look good in the King's eyes

106: For him...self-subdued: for attacking me even though I chose not to defend myself

107: And...exploit: and he was so thrilled by his first success at carrying out this act of bravery (said ironically)

109: Ajax: In Homer's *Illiad*, the warrior Ajax was tripped by the clever Ulysses in the funeral games for Achilles' armor. He is depicted as a dullard in Shakespeare's *Troilus and Cressida*. **stocks**: device used for punishment that locked either hands or feet, or sometimes both, in place. Stocks were often placed in a public setting for further social rebuke.

108-109: None...fool: One never encounters such rogues and cowards who do not try to be more boastful than Ajax.

110: reverend: revered because of age

115: grace: sovereignty

KENT

To go out of my dialect, which you discommend so much. I know,   95
sir, I am no flatterer. He that beguiled you in a plain accent was a
plain knave, which for my part I will not be, though I should win
your displeasure to entreat me to't.

CORNWALL

[*To OSWALD*] What's the offense you gave him?

OSWALD

I never gave him any.
It pleased the King his master very late   100
To strike at me upon his misconstruction,
When he, conjunct, and flattering his displeasure,
Tripped me behind; being down, insulted, railed,
And put upon him such a deal of man
That worthied him, got praises of the King   105
For him attempting who was self-subdued,
And in the fleshment of this dread exploit
Drew on me here again.

KENT

None of these rogues and cowards
But Ajax is their fool.

CORNWALL

[*Calling*] Bring forth the stocks, ho!
                              [*Exeunt some servants*]
You stubborn, ancient knave, you reverend braggart,   110
We'll teach you.

KENT

Sir, I am too old to learn.
Call not your stocks for me. I serve the King,
On whose employments I was sent to you.
You shall do small respect, show too bold malice
Against the grace and person of my master,   115
Stocking his messenger.

120: **being**: because you are

121: **nature**: character

122: **away**: along

123-128: **Let me...punish'd with**: appears only in the First Quarto

125: **check**: correct; **low correction**: punishment unworthy of Kent's rank

126: **contemnèd**: 1) condemned, and 2) despised

127: **pilf'rings**: thefts

130: **I'll answer that**: I will answer for that (i.e., I will answer to the King for punishing him.)

133: **For following...his legs**: appears only in the First Quarto

133: Stage Direction: *[They put KENT in the stocks.]*: appears only in the First Quarto

134: Stage Direction: *Manet*: Latin for "He (or she) remains," *manet* is used as a stage direction preceding the names of characters who are to remain on stage for the ensuing action while others leave.

CORNWALL

                    [Calling] Fetch forth the stocks!—
As I have life and honor, there shall he sit till noon.

REGAN

Till noon? Till night, my lord, and all night too.

KENT

Why, madam, if I were your father's dog
You could not use me so.

REGAN

                  Sir, being his knave, I will.   120
                          Stocks brought out

CORNWALL

This is a fellow of the selfsame nature
Our sister speaks of.—Come, bring away the stocks.

GLOUCESTER

Let me beseech your grace not to do so.
His fault is much, and the good King his master
Will check him for't. Your purposed low correction   125
Is such as basest and contemnèd wretches
For pilf'rings and most common trespasses
Are punish'd with. The King must take it ill
That he's so slightly valued in his messenger,
Should have him thus restrained.

CORNWALL

                    I'll answer that.   130

REGAN

My sister may receive it much more worse
To have her gentleman abused, assaulted,
For following her affairs. Put in his legs.
                 [They put KENT in the stocks.]
Come, my good lord, away.
            [Exeunt. Manet GLOUCESTER and KENT.]

137: **rubbed**: hindered; **entreat**: intercede

138: **watched**: kept the watch at night instead of sleeping

140: **A good...heels**: Even good men suffer major setbacks sometimes. Literally, the phrase means "to become so poor that one's feet come through the holes in their threadbare stockings".

141: **Give you**: may God give you

143: **Approve...say**: prove the proverb true

146: **Approach, thou beacon**: sun, spread your light (i.e., rise)

147: **comfortable**: comforting

148-149 **Nothing...misery**: i.e., How much more dear miracles are when one is miserable.

151: **obscurèd**: Kent is in disguise and thus, obscured.

153: **remedies**: i.e., cures for what ails the kingdom; **overwatched**: exhausted from not sleeping

154: **Take vantage , heavy eyes**: take advantage of your tiredness

155: **shameful lodging**: i.e., the stocks in which he has been placed

155-156 **Fortune...wheel**: Since Kent is at the bottom of the wheel of Fortune, he's hoping it will turn for him while he sleeps (see also 1.1.274, 2.1.39, 4.6.211, 5.3.6 and 5.3.173).

156: Stage Direction: **Sleeps**: Most editions introduce a new scene division here. This edition does not because Kent remains on stage throughout and the location, before Gloucester's house, remains unchanged.

156: Stage Direction: **Enter Edgar**: In Joseph Papp's 1974 New York City production, Edgar (played by Rene Auberjonois, later of *Deep Space Nine* and *Boston Legal*), was easy-going, open, and, like Cordeila, a little naïve. However, by the time he put on his Poor Tom disguise, he had learned just how profoundly he was deceived. His brother, Edmund, was a lot like Iago in *Othello*: playful and confident, but never jovial.

157: **proclaimed**: declared a wanted man

158: **happy**: luckily or fortunately found

160: **That**: in which

GLOUCESTER
    I am sorry for thee, friend. 'Tis the Duke's pleasure,   135
    Whose disposition, all the world well knows,
    Will not be rubbed nor stopped. I'll entreat for thee.

KENT
    Pray you, do not, sir. I have watched and traveled hard.
    Some time I shall sleep out; the rest I'll whistle.
    A good man's fortune may grow out at heels.   140
    Give you good morrow.

GLOUCESTER
    The duke's to blame in this; 'twill be ill took.

                                              Exit

KENT
    Good King, that must approve the common say,
    Thou out of heaven's benediction com'st
    To the warm sun.   145
                               [He takes out a letter]
    Approach, thou beacon to this under globe,
    That by thy comfortable beams I may
    Peruse this letter. Nothing almost sees miracles
    But misery. I know 'tis from Cordelia,
    Who hath most fortunately been informed   150
    Of my obscurèd course, and shall find time
    For this enormous state, seeking to give
    Losses their remedies. All weary and overwatched,
    Take vantage, heavy eyes, not to behold
    This shameful lodging. Fortune, good night;   155
    Smile; once more; turn thy wheel.

                                            Sleeps
                                  [Enter EDGAR]

EDGAR
    I heard myself proclaimed,
    And by the happy hollow of a tree
    Escaped the hunt. No port is free, no place
    That guard and most unusual vigilance   160

161: **attend my taking**: wait to capture me

162: **bethought**: determined

164: **penury**: poverty

165: **grime**: cover

166: **elf**: tangle (elves were thought to mess up one's hair during sleep)

167: **presented**: uncovered, fully displayed; **outface**: confront

169: **proof**: example

170: **Bedlam beggars**: beggars from Bedlam, a lunatic asylum in London

171: **strike**: stick; **numbed and mortified**: cold and deadened

173: **object**: spectacle; **low**: lowly

174: **pelting**: paltry

175: **lunatic bans**: insane curses

176: **Enforce their charity**: persuade them to give me something; **Tuelygod**: meaning unknown, but the term may suggest the meaningless babble of Edgar's adopted persona as a beggar

176: **Poor...Tom!**: Edgar seems to be practicing his new identity as a beggar. Beggars were known as "poor Toms".

177: **That's...am**: As poor Tom I can make a life for myself. My life as Edgar has ceased to be.

177: Stage Direction: *Exit*: Most editions introduce a new scene division here. Again, this edition does not because Kent remains on stage throughout, and the location, before Gloucester's house, remains unchanged.

178: **they**: i.e., Regan and Cornwall

181: **remove**: move to a different location

182: **shame**: i.e., being in the stocks

Does not attend my taking. While I may scape
I will preserve myself, and am bethought
To take the basest and most poorest shape
That ever penury in contempt of man
Brought near to beast. My face I'll grime with filth,   165
Blanket my loins, elf all my hair with knots,
And with presented nakedness outface
The wind and persecution of the sky.
The country gives me proof and precedent
Of Bedlam beggars who with roaring voices   170
Strike in their numbed and mortified bare arms
Pins, wooden pricks, nails, sprigs of rosemary,
And with this horrible object from low farms,
Poor pelting villages, sheep-cotes and mills,
Sometime with lunatic bans, sometime with prayers   175
Enforce their charity. "Poor Tuelygod, Poor Tom!"
That's something yet. Edgar I nothing am.

                                                                        Exit
                            Enter [King] LEAR, [FOOL, and a KNIGHT]

LEAR
    'Tis strange that they should so depart from home
    And not send back my messenger.

KNIGHT
                            As I learned,
    The night before there was no purpose in them   180
    Of his remove.

KENT
                    [*Waking*] Hail to thee, noble master.

LEAR
    How! Mak'st thou this shame thy pastime?

KENT
                                        No, my lord.

183: **cruel garters**: a joke: garters cover legs, hence the stocks are garters

183: "Ha, ha, look, he wears cruel garters!": Henry Woronicz as Kent and Floyd King as the Fool in the 2000 Shakespeare Theatre Company production directed by Michael Kahn

Photo: Carol Rosegg

185: **over-lusty at legs**: 1) prone to running, or 2) sexually hyperactive

186: **nether-stocks**: stockings

188: **To**: as to

190: **No, no...they have**: appears only in the First Quarto

192: **By Juno, I swear ay**: from the First Folio

192: **Juno**: wife of Jupiter (Kent may be laying the blame with Regan more than with Cornwall.)

FOOL

Ha, ha, look, he wears cruel garters! Horses are tied by the heads,
dogs and bears by th' neck, monkeys by th' loins, and men by th'
legs. When a man's over-lusty at legs, then he wears wooden   185
nether-stocks.

LEAR

[*To KENT*] What's he that hath so much thy place mistook
To set thee here?

KENT

                It is both he and she:
Your son and daughter.

LEAR

           No.

KENT

              Yes.

LEAR

                    No, I say.

KENT

I say, yea.

LEAR

      No, no, they would not.

KENT

                  Yes, they have.   190

LEAR

By Jupiter, I swear, no.

KENT

By Juno, I swear ay.

194: **upon respect**: in spite of my officers, who deserve to be obeyed; **outrage**: insult to the King

195: **Resolve**: inform; **modest**: moderate

198: **commend**: deliver

199-200: **from...kneeling**: from the kneeling position (an indication of my duty)

200: **reeking post**: mail carrier who is hot, sweaty and smelling from his journey

201: **Stewed**: soaked in sweat

203: **spite of intermission**: without concern for interrupting me

205: **meiny**: servants

211: **Displayed so saucily**: behaved in such an impudent manner

212: **Having...wit**: being more manly or fierce than sensible

214: **trespass**: uncivil behavior

216-224: **Winter's not...a year**: from the First Folio

216: **Winter's...way**: if the geese are still flying south, then harsh winter weather is still on its way; i.e., things could still get worse

218: **blind**: indifferent to their fathers' needs

219: **bags**: bags of money

222: **turns the key**: unlocks the door

223: **dolors**: 1) pains, but also 2) a pun on "dollars", a foreign coin at the time

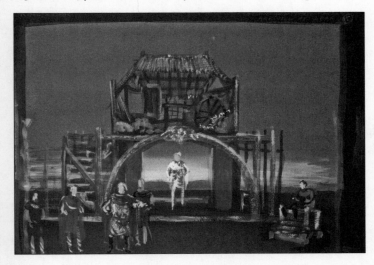

Set design for the 1959 production at the Shakespeare Memorial Theatre in Stratford-upon-Avon directed by Glen Byam Shaw

LEAR

                  They durst not do't,
They would not, could not do't. 'Tis worse than murder,
To do upon respect such violent outrage.
Resolve me, with all modest haste which way   195
Thou may'st deserve or they propose this usage,
Coming from us.

KENT

               My lord, when at their home
I did commend your Highness' letters to them,
Ere I was risen from the place that showed
My duty kneeling, came there a reeking post   200
Stewed in his haste, half breathless, panting forth
From Gonoril, his mistress, salutations,
Delivered letters spite of intermission,
Which presently they read, on whose contents
They summoned up their meiny, straight took horse,   205
Commanded me to follow and attend
The leisure of their answer, gave me cold looks;
And meeting here the other messenger,
Whose welcome I perceived, had poisoned mine—
Being the very fellow that of late   210
Displayed so saucily against your Highness—
Having more man than wit about me, drew.
He raised the house with loud and coward cries.
Your son and daughter found this trespass worth
This shame which here it suffers.   215

FOOL

Winter's not gone yet if the wild geese fly that way.
    [*Sings*]
        Fathers that wear rags
        Do make their children blind,
        But fathers that bear bags
        Shall see their children kind.   220
        Fortune, that arrant whore,
        Ne'er turns the key to th' poor.
But for all this thou shalt have as many dolors for thy daughters
as thou canst tell in a year.

225-226 O, how...*passio*: Based on ancient Greek medical traditions, it was thought in the Renaissance that the womb moved around in the body. When a woman remained a virgin too long, the womb was thought to move upward in the body, thus making breathing difficult. Lear feels as if he is suffocating.

226 *Hysterica passio*: Literally, hysterical passion or passion of the womb. Lear is afraid that he will go mad from grief and that he is reacting in an unmanly way be being so emotional (see 1.4.271-274 for an expression of Lear's fear of feminine emotion).

227: Thy element's below: The womb belongs lower in the body, where it will not interfere with one's breathing.

230: How...King: why does Lear risk

231: An: if

234-235 We'll...winter: If an ant knows not to work in the winter, then a wise man knows not to work on behalf of someone who is down on his luck.

235-237 All that...stinking: A person who has fallen on hard times may be easily avoided by those who can smell (detect) his misfortune.

244: pack: depart

LEAR
    O, how this mother swells up toward my heart!   225
    Hysterica passio, down, thou climbing sorrow;
    Thy element's below.—Where is this daughter?

KENT
    With the Earl, sir, here within.

LEAR
                            Follow me not; stay there.
                                                            [Exit]

KNIGHT
    [*To KENT*] Made you no more offense than what you speak of?

KENT
    No. How chance the King comes with so small a train?   230

FOOL
    An thou hadst been set in the stocks for that question, thou hadst
    well deserved it.

KENT
    Why, fool?

FOOL
    We'll set thee to school to an ant, to teach thee there's no laboring
    in the winter. All that follow their noses are led by their eyes but   235
    blind men, and there's not a nose among a hundred but can smell
    him that's stinking. Let go thy hold when a great wheel runs
    down a hill, lest it break thy neck with following it; but the great
    one that goes up the hill, let him draw thee after. When a wise
    man gives thee better counsel, give me mine again. I would have   240
    none but knaves follow it, since a fool gives it.
        [*Sings*]
        That sir that serves and seeks for gain
        And follows but for form,
        Will pack when it begins to rain,
        And leave thee in the storm,   245

246: "But I will tarry, the fool will stay": Henry Woronicz as Kent and Floyd King as the Fool in the 2000 Shakespeare Theatre Company production directed by Michael Kahn
Photo: Carol Rosegg

248: **The knave...away**: a servant who leaves his master is a fool

249: **pardie**: from the French, "*par Dieu*," for "by God"

254: **images**: signs; **flying off**: desertion

261-262: **Well...man?**: from the First Folio

But I will tarry, the fool will stay,
And let the wise man fly.
The knave turns fool that runs away,
The fool no knave, pardie.

KENT

Where learnt you this, fool?   250

FOOL

Not in the stocks, fool.

Enter LEAR and GLOUCESTER

LEAR

Deny to speak with me? They're sick, they're weary?
They have traveled hard tonight?—mere insolence,
Ay, the images of revolt and flying off.
Fetch me a better answer.

GLOUCESTER

My dear lord,   255
You know the fiery quality of the Duke,
How unremoveable and fixed he is
In his own course.

LEAR

Vengeance, death, plague, confusion!
What "fiery quality"? Why, Gloucester, Gloucester, I'd
Speak with the Duke of Cornwall and his wife.   260

GLOUCESTER

Well, my good lord, I have informed them so.

LEAR

"Informed them"! Dost thou understand me, man?

GLOUCESTER

Ay, my good lord.

265: **tends**: waits for

266: **Are...blood**: from the First Folio

266: **My breath and blood**: by my very life (an oath)

269-270: **Infirmity...bound**: i.e., Illness compels us to neglect those duties we would be obligated to perform if we were well.

272: **forbear**: hold off my condemnation

273: **am fallen out**: now disapprove of; **headier**: impetuous

274: **to take**: to have initially assumed

275: **sound man**: those who are in good health; **Death...state**: a common oath, relevant here given the status of Lear's kingship

277: **remotion**: removal from the King's sight

278: **practice**: deception; **Give...forth**: Release my servant from the stocks.

282: **cry sleep to death**: make so much noise that sleep will become extinct

284: **cockney**: a woman from London who does not know how to cook eels

285: **paste**: pie crust; **coxcombs**: heads

286: **wantons**: 1) playful creatures, but also 2) a sexual reference because eels are phallic. The fool is making an analogy between a cockney wife's unsuccessful efforts to persuade eels to lie still so she can bake them in a pie and Lear's comparably unsuccessful effort to keep his emotions under control.

286-287: **'Twas...hay**: A man who butters hay in order to give his horses a treat is foolish because horses do not like greasy hay (i.e., good intentions cannot compensate for ignorance). This expression is another analogy aimed at depicting the foolishness of Lear's "womanly" emotions and tender-heartedness.

LEAR
>   The King would speak with Cornwall; the dear father
>   Would with his daughter speak, commands, tends service.   265
>   Are they "informed" of this? My breath and blood—
>   "Fiery?" The "fiery" Duke?—tell the hot Duke that Lear—
>   No, but not yet. Maybe he is not well.
>   Infirmity doth still neglect all office
>   Whereto our health is bound. We are not ourselves   270
>   When nature, being oppressed, commands the mind
>   To suffer with the body. I'll forbear,
>   And am fallen out with my more headier will,
>   To take the indisposed and sickly fit
>   For the sound man.—Death on my state,   275
>   Wherefore should he sit here? This act persuades me
>   That this remotion of the Duke and her
>   Is practice only. Give me my servant forth.
>   Go tell the Duke and 's wife I'll speak with them,
>   Now, presently. Bid them come forth and hear me,   280
>   Or at their chamber door I'll beat the drum
>   Till it cry sleep to death.

GLOUCESTER
>   I would have all well
>   Betwixt you.

>   *[Exit]*

LEAR
>   O me, my heart, my heart!

FOOL
>   Cry to it, nuncle, as the cockney did to the eels when she put 'em
>   i' th' paste alive. She rapped 'em o' th' coxcombs with a stick,   285
>   and cried "Down, wantons, down!" 'Twas her brother that, in
>   pure kindness to his horse, buttered his hay.
>   *Enter [Duke of] CORNWALL and REGAN,*
>   *[GLOUCESTER, and others]*

LEAR
>   Good morrow to you both.

293-294: **I would...adultress**: i.e., I would refuse to honor your mother's tomb because an adulteress is buried there.

296: **naught**: evil

297: **Sharp-tooth'd**: as a serpent (see also 1.4.263, 2.2.322-323, 5.1.57-58 and 5.3.83); **here**: in his heart

299: **quality**: disposition

300-302: **I have...duty**: i.e., I must believe that she is better at fulfilling her obligations to you than you are at evaluating her.

302-307: **Say, how...all blame**: from the First Folio

Costume rendering for Gloucester from the 1959 production at the Shakespeare Memorial Theatre in Stratford-upon-Avon directed by Glen Byam Shaw
Rare Book and Special Collection Library, University of Illinois at Urbana-Champaign

CORNWALL
  Hail to your Grace!

                                    [KENT here set at liberty]

REGAN
  I am glad to see your Highness.   290

LEAR
  Regan, I think you are. I know what reason
  I have to think so. If thou shouldst not be glad
  I would divorce me from thy mother's shrine,
  Sepulch'ring an adultress. [*To KENT*] Yea, are you free?
  Some other time for that.—Belovèd Regan,   295
  Thy sister is naught. O, Regan, she hath tied
  Sharp-tooth'd unkindness like a vulture here.
  I can scarce speak to thee. Thou'lt not believe
  Of how deplored a quality—O, Regan!

REGAN
  I pray you, sir, take patience. I have hope.   300
  You less know how to value her desert
  Than she to slack her duty.

LEAR
                        Say, how is that?

REGAN
  I cannot think my sister in the least
  Would fail her obligation. If, sir, perchance
  She have restrained the riots of your followers,   305
  'Tis on such ground and to such wholesome end
  As clears her from all blame.

LEAR
  My curses on her.

309-310: Nature...confine: you have one foot in the grave

311: By...state: by someone who is astute enough to understand your present condition

315: becomes the house: is appropriate behavior for the royal family (said sarcastically)

318: raiment: clothing

319: unsightly: distasteful, unendurable

321: abated: deprived

322: black: disparagingly

322-323: struck me...serpent-like: see also 1.4.263, 2.2.297, 5.1.57-58, 5.2.83

325: ungrateful top: ungrateful head

326: taking: infectious

326: Fie, fie, sir.: appears only in the First Quarto

329: fen-sucked fogs: infectious vapors from marshes (it was thought that the sun sucked up poisonous gasses from marshes)

330: blast her pride: destroy her vanity by causing blisters to form on her (appears only in the First Quarto)

REGAN

               O sir, you are old.
Nature in you stands on the very verge
Of her confine. You should be ruled and led   310
By some discretion that discerns your state
Better than you yourself. Therefore I pray you
That to our sister you do make return;
Say you have wronged her, sir.

LEAR

                    Ask her forgiveness?
Do you but mark how this becomes the house?   315
[*Kneeling*] "Dear daughter, I confess that I am old.
Age is unnecessary. On my knees I beg
That you'll vouchsafe me raiment, bed, and food."

REGAN

Good sir, no more. These are unsightly tricks.
Return you to my sister.

LEAR

              [*Rising*] No, Regan.   320
She hath abated me of half my train,
Looked black upon me, struck me with her tongue
Most serpent-like upon the very heart.
All the stored vengeances of heaven fall
On her ungrateful top! Strike her young bones,   325
You taking airs, with lameness!

CORNWALL

                Fie, fie, sir.

LEAR

You nimble lightnings, dart your blinding flames
Into her scornful eyes. Infect her beauty,
You fen-sucked fogs drawn by the pow'rful sun
To fall and blast her pride.   330

333: **tender-hefted**: gentle, sensitive

337: **bandy**: exchange; **scant my sizes**: reduce my monetary allotments

339: **oppose the bolt**: lock the door

340: **The offices...childhood**: those duties and obligations that are natural between parent and child

341: **effects**: standard practices

343: **to th' purpose**: get to the point

345: **approves**: confirms

347: **easy-borrowed**: easily assumed

348: **fickle grace**: unpredictable favor

349: **varlet**: worthless person

REGAN

O, the blest gods!   330
So will you wish on me when the rash mood—

LEAR
No, Regan. Thou shalt never have my curse.
Thy tender-hefted nature shall not give
Thee o'er to harshness. Her eyes are fierce, but thine
Do comfort and not burn. 'Tis not in thee   335
To grudge my pleasures, to cut off my train,
To bandy hasty words, to scant my sizes,
And, in conclusion, to oppose the bolt
Against my coming in. Thou better know'st
The offices of nature, bond of childhood,   340
Effects of courtesy, dues of gratitude.
Thy half of the kingdom hast thou not forgot,
Wherein I thee endowed.

REGAN

Good sir, to th' purpose.

LEAR
Who put my man i' th' stocks?

[Trumpet within]

CORNWALL

What trumpet's that?
Enter Steward [OSWALD]

REGAN
I know't, my sister's. This approves her letters   345
That she would soon be here. [*To OSWALD*] Is your lady come?

LEAR
This is a slave, whose easy-borrowed pride
Dwells in the fickle grace of her a follows.

[He strikes OSWALD]

Out, varlet, from my sight!

353: **Allow**: approve

358: **indiscretion**: lack of good judgment

359: **sides**: i.e., the sides of his chest, which can hardly contain his bursting sorrow

362: **much less advancement**: to be treated much more harshly

363: **seem so**: act accordingly

363: "I pray you, father, being weak, seem so": Angela Pierce as Gonoril and Laura Odeh as Regan in the 2007 Public Theater production directed by James Lapine
Photo: Michal Daniel

365: **sojourn**: stay with

367: **from**: away from

368: **entertainment**: appropriate care

CORNWALL

What means your grace?

Enter GONORIL

GONORIL

Who struck my servant? Regan, I have good hope   350
Thou didst not know on't.

LEAR

Who comes here? O heavens,
If you do love old men, if your sweet sway
Allow obedience, if yourselves are old,
Make it your cause! Send down and take my part.
[*To GONORIL*] Art not ashamed to look upon this beard?   355
O Regan, wilt thou take her by the hand?

GONORIL

Why not by the hand, sir? How have I offended?
All's not offense that indiscretion finds
And dotage terms so.

LEAR

O sides, you are too tough!
Will you yet hold?—How came my man i' th' stocks?   360

CORNWALL

I set him there, sir; but his own disorders
Deserved much less advancement.

LEAR

You? Did you?

REGAN

I pray you, father, being weak, seem so.
If till the expiration of your month
You will return and sojourn with my sister,   365
Dismissing half your train, come then to me.
I am now from home, and out of that provision
Which shall be needful for your entertainment.

370: **abjure**: do without

372: **wage**: do battle

373: **Necessity's sharp pinch**: hunger's discomfort

374: **hot-blood**: youthful and spirited; **in France**: (referring to the King of France)

376: **knee**: kneel down before

378: **sumpter**: packhorse (a beast of burden)

386: **embossèd carbuncle**: swollen tumor

388: **call**: summon

389: **thunder-bearer**: i.e., Jove (Jupiter, in Roman mythology), the god of the sky and thunder (see also 1.1.173)

390: **high-judging**: judging from on high

394: **look not for you**: was not expecting you

395: **Give ear**: listen

396: **For...passion**: for those who rationally interpret your temper tantrums

LEAR

    Return to her, and fifty men dismissed?
    No, rather I abjure all roofs, and choose   370
    To be a comrade with the wolf and owl,
    To wage against the enmity of the air
    Necessity's sharp pinch. Return with her?
    Why, the hot-blood in France that dowerless took
    Our youngest born—I could as well be brought   375
    To knee his throne and, squire-like, pension beg
    To keep base life afoot. Return with her?
    Persuade me rather to be slave and sumpter
    To this detested groom.

GONORIL

                        At your choice, sir.

LEAR

    Now I prithee, daughter, do not make me mad.   380
    I will not trouble thee, my child. Farewell.
    We'll no more meet, no more see one another.
    But yet thou art my flesh, my blood, my daughter –
    Or rather a disease that lies within my flesh,
    Which I must needs call mine. Thou art a boil,   385
    A plague-sore, an embossèd carbuncle
    In my corrupted blood. But I'll not chide thee.
    Let shame come when it will, I do not call it.
    I do not bid the thunder-bearer shoot,
    Nor tell tales of thee to high-judging Jove.   390
    Mend when thou canst; be better at thy leisure.
    I can be patient, I can stay with Regan,
    I and my hundred knights.

REGAN

                    Not altogether so, sir.
    I look not for you yet, nor am provided
    For your fit welcome. Give ear, sir, to my sister;   395
    For those that mingle reason with your passion
    Must be content to think you are old, and so—
    But she knows what she does.

399: **avouch**: vouch for

401: **sith that**: since; **charge**: expense

407: **slack**: neglect

408: **control**: discipline

410: **five-and-twenty**: appears only in the First Quarto (see also lines 416 and 423)

411: **place or notice**: residence or hospitality

413: **depositaries**: trustees of royal power

414: **kept a reservation**: reserved the right

416: **five-and-twenty**: appears only in the First Quarto (see also lines 410 and 423)

LEAR

                         Is this well spoken now?

REGAN
  I dare avouch it, sir. What, fifty followers?
  Is it not well? What should you need of more,   400
  Yea, or so many, sith that both charge and danger
  Speaks 'gainst so great a number? How in a house
  Should many people under two commands
  Hold amity? 'Tis hard, almost impossible.

GONORIL
  Why might not you, my lord, receive attendance   405
  From those that she calls servants, or from mine?

REGAN
  Why not, my lord? If then they chanced to slack you,
  We could control them. If you will come to me—
  For now I spy a danger—I entreat you
  To bring but five-and-twenty; to no more   410
  Will I give place or notice.

LEAR
  I gave you all.

REGAN
                And in good time you gave it.

LEAR
  Made you my guardians, my depositaries,
  But kept a reservation to be followed
  With such a number. What, must I come to you   415
  With five-and-twenty, Regan? Said you so?

REGAN
  And speak't again, my lord. No more with me.

418: **well favored**: attractive

420: **Stands...praise**: is, by comparison, deserving of praise

423: **five-and-twenty**: appears only in the First Quarto (see also lines 410 and 416)

424: **follow**: wait on you

426: **reason not**: do not interpret rationally

427-428: **Our...superfluous**: Even the most impoverished among us have some small thing beyond what they absolutely need to survive.

437-438: **fool me...tamely**: do not make me so foolish as to tolerate this calmly

439: **woman's weapons**: tears

441: "I will have such revenges on you both": Ted van Griethuysen as Lear and Jennifer Harmon as Regan in the 2000 Shakespeare Theatre Company production directed by Michael Kahn

Photo: Carol Rosegg

LEAR
    Those wicked creatures yet do seem well favored
    When others are more wicked. Not being the worst
    Stands in some rank of praise. [*To GONORIL*] I'll go with thee.   420
    Thy fifty yet doth double five-and-twenty,
    And thou art twice her love.

GONORIL
                            Hear me, my lord
    What need you five-and-twenty, ten, or five,
    To follow in a house where twice so many
    Have a command to tend you?

REGAN
                            What needs one?   425

LEAR
    O, reason not the need! Our basest beggars
    Are in the poorest thing superfluous.
    Allow not nature more than nature needs,
    Man's life's as cheap as beast's. Thou art a lady.
    If only to go warm were gorgeous,   430
    Why, nature needs not what thou, gorgeous, wearest,
    Which scarcely keeps thee warm. But for true need—
    You heavens, give me that patience, patience I need.
    You see me here, you gods, a poor old fellow,
    As full of grief as age, wretchèd in both.   435
    If it be you that stir these daughters' hearts
    Against their father, fool me not so much
    To bear it tamely. Touch me with noble anger.
    O, let not women's weapons, water-drops,
    Stain my man's cheeks! No, you unnatural hags,   440
    I will have such revenges on you both
    That all the world shall—I will do such things—
    What they are, yet I know not; but they shall be
    The terrors of the earth. You think I'll weep.
    No, I'll not weep.   445
                            [Storm within]

447: **flaws**: pieces

448: **Or ere**: before

451: **bestowed**: accommodated; **blame**: fault

452: **Hath**: that he has; **put...rest**: 1)made himself homeless, 2) lost his sense of security; **taste**: suffer the consequences of

453: **For his particular**: with regard for him individually

457: **high**: extreme

457-458: **Whither...horse**: from the First Folio

458: **calls to horse**: call for his horse

459: **give him way**: let him go where he pleases; **He leads himself**: he follows his own stubborn path

I have full cause of weeping, but this heart
Shall break into a hundred thousand flaws
Or ere I'll weep.—O fool, I shall go mad!
Exeunt LEAR, GLOUCESTER, KENT, [KNIGHT] and FOOL

CORNWALL
Let us withdraw. 'Twill be a storm.

REGAN
This house is little. The old man and his people   450
Cannot be well bestowed.

GONORIL
　　　　　　'Tis his own blame;
Hath put himself from rest, and must needs taste his folly.

REGAN
For his particular I'll receive him gladly,
But not one follower.

GONORIL
So am I purposed. Where is my Lord of Gloucester?   455

CORNWALL
Followed the old man forth.

　　　　　　　　　　　　　　Enter GLOUCESTER
　　　　　　　　He is returned.

GLOUCESTER
The king is in high rage.

CORNWALL
　　　　　　Whither is he going?

GLOUCESTER
He calls to horse, and will I know not whither.

REGAN
'Tis good to give him way. He leads himself.

460: **entreat...means**: do not ask him under any circumstances

462: **rustle**: blow

467-468: **being...abused**: predisposed to take bad advice

GONORIL
    [*To GLOUCESTER*] My lord, entreat him by no means to stay.   460

GLOUCESTER
    Alack, the night comes on, and the bleak winds
    Do sorely rustle. For many miles a bout
    There's not a bush.

REGAN
             O, sir, to willful men
    The injuries that they themselves procure
    Must be their schoolmasters. Shut up your doors.   465
    He is attended with a desperate train,
    And what they may incense him to, being apt
    To have his ear abused, wisdom bids fear.

CORNWALL
    Shut up your doors, my lord. 'Tis a wild night.
    My Regan counsels well. Come out o' th' storm.   470
                                   Exeunt

[King Lear

Act 3

0: Location: a clearing in Gloucestershire

3: **fretful element**: agitated earth

5: **main**: mainland

6-14: **tears his...take all**: appears only in the First Quarto

7: **eyeless rage**: rage that is blind (to Lear's royal status)

8: **make nothing of**: toss about disrespectfully

11: **cub-drawn bear**: mother bear who is weak and weary from starving herself to feed her cubs; **couch**: crouch, hide inside the den

13: **keep their fur dry**: i.e., remain inside; **unbonneted**: hatless, uncovered

14: **bids what will take all**: goes all in (from gambling, signalling desperate defiance, when a gambler defiantly bets everything on one last hand)

15-16: **outjest...injuries**: rid the body of illness with humor

Act 3, Scene 1]

*[Storm.] Enter KENT [disguised] and FIRST
GENTLEMAN, at several doors.*

KENT
What's here, besides foul weather?

FIRST GENTLEMAN
                                                One minded like the weather,
    Most unquietly.

KENT
                        I know you. Where's the king?

FIRST GENTLEMAN
    Contending with the fretful element;
    Bids the winds blow the earth into the sea
    Or swell the curlèd water 'bove the main,   5
    That things might change or cease; tears his white hair,
    Which the impetuous blasts, with eyeless rage,
    Catch in their fury, and make nothing of;
    Strives in his little world of man to outstorm
    The to-and-fro-conflicting wind and rain.   10
    This night, wherein the cub-drawn bear would couch,
    The lion and the belly-pinchèd wolf
    Keep their fur dry, unbonneted he runs,
    And bids what will take all.

KENT
                        But who is with him?

FIRST GENTLEMAN
    None but the Fool, who labors to outjest   15
    His heart-struck injuries.

Costume rendering for Kent from the 1959 production at the Shakespeare
Memorial Theatre in Stratford-upon-Avon directed by Glen Byam Shaw

Rare Book and Special Collection Library, University of Illinois at Urbana-Champaign

17-18: **And dare...you**: and risk, on the basis of what kind of person I know you to
be, to entrust you with a secret mission

20: **mutual cunning**: seeming goodwill on both sides

21-28: **Who have...furnishings**: from the First Folio

21-22: **as who...high**: as all who have achieved greatness do

22: **no less**: nothing more than servants

23: **speculations**: secret agents

24: **Intelligent of**: providing information pertinent to

25: **snuffs and packings**: resentments and plots

26-27: **Or the...King**: or the harsh restrictions the two of them have imposed on Lear

28: **furnishings**: outward shows

29-41: **But true...to you**: appears only in the First Quarto

29: **power**: army

30: **scattered**: fragmented, divided

31: **wise in**: capitalizing upon; **feet**: footholds

32: **at point**: prepared for battle

33: **open banner**: unfurled flag (here implying true intentions)

34: **credit**: trustworthiness; **so far**: so far as

35: **make your speed**: make haste, go quickly

36: **just**: accurate

38: **plain**: complain

39: **of blood and breeding**: of noble birth

40: **assurance**: confidence

41: **office**: assignment

44: **out-wall**: outer wall; i.e., external appearance

46: **fear not but**: be assured that

47: **fellow**: i.e., Kent

KENT

                  Sir, I do know you,
And dare, upon the warrant of my art
Commend a dear thing to you. There is division,
Although as yet the face of it be covered
With mutual cunning, 'twixt Albany and Cornwall;   20
Who have—as who have not that their great stars
Throned and set high—servants, who seem no less,
Which are to France the spies and speculations
Intelligent of our state. What hath been seen,
Either in snuffs and packings of the Dukes,   25
Or the hard rein which both of them have borne
Against the old kind King; or something deeper,
Whereof perchance these are but furnishings—
But true it is. From France there comes a power
Into this scattered kingdom, who already,   30
Wise in our negligence, have secret feet
In some of our best ports, and are at point
To show their open banner. Now to you:
If on my credit you dare build so far
To make your speed to Dover, you shall find   35
Some that will thank you, making just report
Of how unnatural and bemadding sorrow
The King hath cause to plain.
I am a gentleman of blood and breeding,
And, from some knowledge and assurance offer   40
This office to you.

FIRST GENTLEMAN

I will talk further with you.

KENT

                  No, do not.
For confirmation that I am much more
Than my out-wall, open this purse, and take
What it contains. If you shall see Cordelia—   45
As fear not but you shall—show her this ring
And she will tell you who your fellow is,
That yet you do not know. Fie on this storm!
I will go seek the King.

50: **to effect**: in their consequences

50-51: **Few words...yet**: I have but a few words to say, but they are of greater consequence than all I have said so far.

52: **in which...that**: in which effort, I'll go my way and you'll go yours

53: **lights on him**: comes upon him

FIRST GENTLEMAN
                        Give me your hand.
    Have you no more to say?

KENT
                        Few words, but to effect,   50
    More than all yet: that, when we have found the King—
    In which endeavor I'll this way, you that—
    He that first lights on him holla the other.

                                                    [Exeunt]

0: Location: a clearing in Gloucestershire

0: Scene: Edmund Kean (1787-1833) experimented with a wind machine, but the noise was such that audiences had difficulty hearing his lines. The productions of his son, Charles Kean (1811-1868), included masses of black clouds drifting across the sky, glimpses of moonlight, howling winds, thunderclaps, and even rain pattering on the stage. Laurence Olivier (1907-1989) "moved like a tall ship driven before the storm," while in Peter Brook's 1971 film, Paul Scofield seemed detached, as if speaking from another world.

tracks 19-21

1–24:
Donald Wolfit as Lear and Job Stewart as the Fool
Paul Scofield as Lear and Kenneth Branagh as the Fool

1: **Blow, wind, and crack your cheeks**: Maps in Shakespeare's day often depicted Aeolus, god of the wind, with puffed cheeks, blowing ships upon the sea.
2: **cataracts**: heavy downpours; **hurricanoes**: waterspouts
3: **drenched**: drowned; **steeples**: churches; **cocks**: weathervanes
4: **thought-executing fires**: lightning that acts with the quickness of thought
5: **Vaunt-couriers**: forerunners
8: **Crack nature's mould**: break apart the mold from which all life is made;
all germens spill: damage all the seeds
10: **court holy water**: courtly flattery
14: **Nor**: neither
15: **tax**: accuse
17: **subscription**: allegiance
20: **ministers**: agents
21: **pernicious**: evil
22: **high-engendered battles**: regiments of troops created in heaven

Act 3, Scene 2]

[Storm.] Enter LEAR and FOOL.

LEAR

    Blow, wind, and crack your cheeks! Rage, blow,
    You cataracts and hurricanoes, spout
    Till you have drenched the steeples, drowned the cocks!
    You sulphurous and thought-executing fires,
    Vaunt-couriers to oak-cleaving thunderbolts,   5
    Singe my white head; and thou all-shaking thunder,
    Smite flat the thick rotundity of the world,
    Crack nature's mould, all germens spill at once
    That make ingrateful man.

FOOL

    O nuncle, court holy water in a dry house is better than this   10
    rainwater out o' door. Good nuncle, in, and ask thy daughter's
    blessing. Here's a night pities neither wise man nor fool.

LEAR

    Rumble thy bellyful; spit, fire; spout, rain.
    Nor rain, wind, thunder, fire are my daughters.
    I tax not you, you elements, with unkindness.   15
    I never gave you kingdom, called you children.
    You owe me no subscription. Why then, let fall
    Your horrible pleasure. Here I stand your slave,
    A poor, infirm, weak and despised old man,
    But yet I call you servile ministers,   20
    That have with two pernicious daughters joined
    Your high-engendered battles 'gainst a head
    So old and white as this. O, ho, 'tis foul!

1–24:
Donald Wolfit as Lear and Job Stewart as the Fool
Paul Scofield as Lear and Kenneth Branagh as the Fool

Alan Howard as Lear and Alan Dobie as the Fool in the 1997 production at the Old Vic directed by Peter Hall

Photo: Donald Cooper

24: **head piece**: 1) helmet, and 2) a head for common sense

25: **codpiece**: an ornamental covering for the male genitals worn over the pants (here, a house for the penis)

25-26: **The codpiece...any**: the man who busies himself finding a woman in which to put his genitals before he has found a place to live

27: **The head...louse**: will wind up, as many penniless married, couples do, in lice-infested poverty

29-30: **The man...make**: the man who foolishly prioritizes the baser things in life over matters of the heart

31-32: **Shall have...wake**: will suffer sadness and sleeplessness

33: **made mouths in a glass**: made faces in a mirror

37: **Marry**: an oath, contracted form of "by the Virgin Mary"; **grace**: royal grace

40: **Gallow**: frighten or terrify; **wanderers of the dark**: wild beasts of the night

41: **keep**: remain inside

46: **pother**: hubbub; i.e., the noise of the storm

FOOL

He that has a house to put his head in has a good head piece.

[*Sings*]

The codpiece that will house   25
Before the head has any,
The head and he shall louse,
So beggars marry many.
The man that makes his toe
What he his heart should make   30
Shall have a corn cry woe,
And turn his sleep to wake—

For there was never yet fair woman but she made mouths in a glass.

LEAR

No, I will be the pattern of all patience.

                        [He sits.] Enter KENT, [disguisèd].

I will say nothing.   35

KENT

Who's there?

FOOL

Marry, here's grace and a codpiece—that's a wise man and a fool.

KENT

[*To LEAR*] Alas, sir, sit you here? Things that love night
Love not such nights as these. The wrathful skies
Gallow the very wanderers of the dark   40
And makes them keep their caves. Since I was man
Such sheets of fire, such bursts of horrid thunder,
Such groans of roaring wind and rain I ne'er
Remember to have heard. Man's nature cannot carry
The affliction nor the force.

LEAR

                    Let the great gods,   45
That keep this dreadful pother o'er our heads,
Find out their enemies now. Tremble, thou wretch
That hast within thee undivulgèd crimes

50: **simular**: phony
51: **caitiff**: wretch
52: **convenient seeming**: opportune deception
53: **practiced on**: plotted against
54: **Close...centers**: O, you secret and repressed feelings of guilt, tear open those hiding places that conceal you.
55: **And cry...grace**: And pray for mercy; **summoners**: officers who served offenders with warrants to appear before ecclesiastical courts
62: **Which**: the occupants of which; **demanding**: inquiring
64: **scanted**: withheld, meager

"King Lear and the Fool in the Storm"; Painting ca. 1851
William Dyce (1806-1864)

68-69: **The art...precious**: Poverty (necessity) performs the work of alchemy, transforming worthless objects into precious ones. (Lear is mocking the alchemists' practice by ascribing such skills to himself. Like these practitioners, Lear and the Fool's need for shelter have transformed straw into a bed, a hovel into a palace.)
72-75: **He that...day**: part of a popular song sung by Feste in *Twelfth Night* (5.1)

Unwhipped of justice; hide thee, thou bloody hand,
Thou perjured and thou simular man of virtue   50
That art incestuous; caitiff, in pieces shake,
That under covert and convenient seeming
Hast practiced on man's life;
Close pent-up guilts, rive your concealèd centers
And cry these dreadful summoners grace.   55
I am a man more sinned against than sinning.

KENT
Alack, bare-headed?
Gracious my lord, hard by here is a hovel.
Some friendship will it lend you 'gainst the tempest.
Repose you there whilst I to this hard house—   60
More hard than is the stone whereof 'tis raised,
Which even but now, demanding after you,
Denied me to come in—return, and force
Their scanted courtesy.

LEAR
My wit begins to turn.   65
[To FOOL] Come on, my boy. How dost, my boy? Art cold?
I am cold myself.—Where is this straw, my fellow?
The art of our necessities is strange,
That can make vile things precious. Come, your hovel—
Poor fool and knave, I have one part of my heart   70
That sorrows yet for thee.

FOOL
        [Sings]
        He that has and a little tiny wit,
        With heigh-ho, the wind and the rain,
        Must make content with his fortunes fit,
        For the rain it raineth every day.   75

LEAR
True, my good boy. [To KENT] Come, bring us to this hovel.
                                        Exit LEAR and KENT

77-92: This is...his time: from the First Folio

77: brave: excellent

77: This is...courtesan: this night is so stormy it could cool down the lust of a courtesan (prostitute)

78: When...matter: when priests do not practice what they preach

79: mar: dilute

80: When...tailors: when aristocrats try to teach their tailors about fashions

81: No heretics...suitors: when heretics are no longer burned at the stake for violating religious truths; instead, practitioners of lechery, the new heresy, are punished, not by burning but by contracting venereal disease

82: realm of Albion: Kingdom of England. "Albion" is from the Latin *albus*, meaning "white", an allusion to the white cliffs of Dover.

84: right: just

86: When slanders...tongues: when tongues cease to speak slanders

87: cutpurses: pickpockets

88: tell: count

90: who: whoever

91: That going...feet: that walking will be accomplished by use of the feet (an anti-climatic, rather pessimistic conclusion suggesting that in the end, nothing will have changed because none of the reforms mentioned before will ever come to pass)

92: Merlin: the legendary wizard at the court of King Arthur, who lived and ruled after the time of Lear's reign

FOOL

    This is a brave night to cool a courtesan. I'll speak a prophecy ere I go:

        When priests are more in word than matter;
        When brewers mar their malt with water;
        When nobles are their tailors' tutors,   80
        No heretics burned, but wenches' suitors,
        Then shall the realm of Albion
        Come to great confusion.
        When every case in law is right;
        No squire in debt nor no poor knight;   85
        When slanders do not live in tongues,
        Nor cutpurses come not to throngs;
        When usurers tell their gold i' th' field,
        And bawds and whores do churches build,
        Then comes the time, who lives to see't,   90
        That going shall be used with feet.

    This prophecy Merlin shall make; for I live before his time.

                                                Exit

0: Location: Gloucester's house

Set design for the 1959 production at the Shakespeare Memorial Theatre in Stratford-upon-Avon directed by Glen Byam Shaw

Rare Book and Special Collection Library, University of Illinois at Urbana-Champaign

3: **pity**: take mercy on
6: **entreat**: intervene or speak on his behalf
10: **closet**: private chamber
11: **revenged home**: revenged thoroughly
12: **power**: armed force; **incline to**: side with
13: **privily**: privately
17: **toward**: impending
18: **courtesy**: i.e., compassion for Lear; **forbid thee**: forbidden (to be shown by) thee
20-21: **This seems...all**: My betrayal of my father is something he has brought on himself. As such, it will surely put me in line to become the Earl of Gloucester and to receive all of Gloucester's wealth.

Enter GLOUCESTER and the Bastard [EDMUND], with lights

GLOUCESTER
Alack, alack, Edmund, I like not this
Unnatural dealing. When I desired their leave
That I might pity him, they took from me
The use of mine own house, charged me on pain
Of their displeasure neither to speak of him,   5
Entreat for him, nor any way sustain him.

EDMUND
Most savage and unnatural!

GLOUCESTER
Go to, say you nothing. There's a division betwixt the dukes, and
a worse matter than that. I have received a letter this night—'tis
dangerous to be spoken—I have locked the letter in my closet.   10
These injuries the King now bears will be revenged home. There's
part of a power already landed. We must incline to the King. I will
seek him and privily relieve him. Go you and maintain talk with
the Duke, that my charity be not of him perceived. If he ask for
me, I am ill and gone to bed. Though I die for't—as no less is   15
threatened me—the King my old master must be relieved. There
is some strange thing toward. Edmund, pray you be careful.

Exit

EDMUND
This courtesy, forbid thee, shall the Duke
Instantly know, and of that letter too.
This seems a fair deserving, and must draw me   20
That which my father loses: no less than all.
The younger rises when the old do fall.

Exit

0: Location: A clearing before a hovel

Watercolor scene sketch from the promptbook for Charles Kean's 1858 production
Courtesy of the Folger Shakespeare Library

2: **tyranny**: harshness

3: **nature**: human nature

4: **Will't...heart?**: By taking shelter from the storm, Lear will be free to focus on what his daughters have done to him, and it will break his heart (see lines 3.4.11–14).

8: **fixed**: lodged

11: **i' th' mouth**: head on; **free**: i.e., free of anxiety

12: **The body's delicate**: i.e., The body's needs become more pressing.

15: **as**: as if

16: **sure**: fully

Act 3, Scene 4]

Storm. Enter LEAR, KENT [disguised] and FOOL.

KENT
    Here is the place, my lord. Good my lord, enter.
    The tyranny of the open night's too rough
    For nature to endure.

                                                          [Storm still]

LEAR
                            Let me alone.

KENT
    Good my lord, enter here.

LEAR
                          Will't break my heart?

KENT
    I had rather break mine own. Good my lord, enter.   5

LEAR
    Thou think'st 'tis much that this contentious storm
    Invades us to the skin. So 'tis to thee;
    But where the greater malady is fixed,
    The lesser is scarce felt. Thou'dst shun a bear,
    But if thy flight lay toward the roaring sea   10
    Thou'dst meet the bear i' th' mouth. When the mind's free,
    The body's delicate. This tempest in my mind
    Doth from my senses take all feeling else
    Save what beats there: filial ingratitude.
    Is it not as this mouth should tear this hand   15
    For lifting food to't? But I will punish sure.
    No, I will weep no more.—In such a night
    To shut me out? Pour on, I will endure.

20: **frank**: generous

24: **will not give me leave to ponder**: keeps me from thinking

25: **things**: things such as my daughter's ingratitude

30: **unfed sides**: bodies so thin from hunger that their ribs are visible

31: **looped and windowed raggedness**: ragged clothes full of holes like windows and loopholes

32-33: **I have...this**: When I was King, I did not concern myself enough with the welfare of the impoverished subjects in my kingdom

33: **Take physic, pomp**: fix this problem, you pompous fools who care so little for others; **pomp**: 1) pompous fools, and also 2) a reference to himself, the formerly pompous, meaning "stately" or "splendid"

35: **shake...them**: share the wealth of the kingdom with the poor

37: **Fathom and half**: a nautical cry exclaimed by sailors when measuring the depth of water; here, a playful reference to the heavy rains (from the First Folio)

37–69:
*David Tennant as Edgar, John Rogan as the Fool, Anton Lesser as Kent,
and Trevor Peacock as Lear*
*Richard McCabe as Edgar, Kenneth Branagh as the Fool, David Burke as Kent,
and Paul Scofield as Lear*

In such a night as this! O Regan, Gonoril,
Your old kind father, whose frank heart gave you all—   20
O, that way madness lies. Let me shun that.
No more of that.

KENT

                          Good my lord, enter here.

LEAR

  Prithee, go in thyself. Seek thy own ease.
  This tempest will not give me leave to ponder
  On things would hurt me more; but I'll go in.   25
  [*To FOOL*] In, boy; go first. [*Kneeling*] You houseless poverty—
  Nay, get thee in. I'll pray, and then I'll sleep.

                                                    [Exit FOOL]

  Poor naked wretches, whereso'er you are,
  That bide the pelting of this pitiless night,
  How shall your houseless heads and unfed sides,   30
  Your looped and windowed raggedness, defend you
  From seasons such as these? O, I have ta'en
  Too little care of this. Take physic, pomp,
  Expose thyself to feel what wretches feel,
  That thou may'st shake the superflux to them   35
  And show the heavens more just.

                                                    [Enter FOOL]

EDGAR

  Fathom and half! Fathom and half! Poor Tom!

FOOL

  Come not in here, nuncle; here's a spirit. Help me, help me!

KENT

  Give me thy hand. Who's there?

FOOL

  A spirit, a spirit. He says his name's Poor Tom.   40

tracks 22-24

37–69:
David Tennant as Edgar, John Rogan as the Fool, Anton Lesser as Kent, and Trevor Peacock as Lear
Richard McCabe as Edgar, Kenneth Branagh as the Fool, David Burke as Kent, and Paul Scofield as Lear

45-46: "Hast thou given all to thy two daughters, / And art thou come to this?": James Earl Jones as Lear, Rene Auberjonois as Edgar, and Tom Aldredge as Fool in the 1973 Public Theater production directed by Edwin Sherin
Photo: George E. Joseph

49-50: **has laid...potage:** According to Poor Tom, these are all the things that the devil has done to tempt him to commit suicide and damn him to hell: stowed knives under his pillow while he was asleep, placed a hangman's noose in his church pew, and set rat poison next to his soup.

50-52: **made him...traitor:** Here the devil tempts him to sin by encouraging him to commit flashy, prideful acts such as, in this case, trying to ride a horse over bridges that are only four inches wide in order to chase his own shadow.

52: **five wits:** a reference either to the five senses, or to the Renaissance notion of the five mental faculties: common wit, imagination, fantasy, estimation, and memory

53: **star-blasting and taking:** afflictions caused by stars and evil spirits

54-55: **There could...there:** Edgar is swatting at head lice and other insects as if they were devils.

56: **pass:** wretched situation (Lear is projecting his own troubles onto Poor Tom)

58: **reserved a blanket:** kept a piece of cloth to cover himself; **shamed:** naked

59: **pendulous:** 1) thick, heavy, fog-like, and 2) hanging, suspended

KENT

What art thou that dost grumble there in the straw?
Come forth.

[Enter EDGAR as a Bedlam beggar]

EDGAR

Away, the foul fiend follows me. Through the sharp hawthorn
blows the cold wind. Go to thy cold bed and warm thee.

LEAR

Hast thou given all to thy two daughters,   45
And art thou come to this?

EDGAR

Who gives any thing to Poor Tom, whom the foul fiend hath led
through fire and through flame, through ford and whirlypool, o'er
bog and quagmire; that has laid knives under his pillow and halters
in his pew, set ratsbane by his potage, made him proud of heart to   50
ride on a bay trotting-horse over four-inched bridges, to course his
own shadow for a traitor. Bless thy five wits, Tom's a-cold! Bless
thee from whirlwinds, star-blasting and taking. Do Poor Tom some
charity, whom the foul fiend vexes. There could I have him, now,
and there, and there again, and there.   55

[Storm still]

LEAR

What, has his daughters brought him to this pass?
[To EDGAR] Couldst thou save nothing? Didst thou give them all?

FOOL

Nay, he reserved a blanket, else we had been all shamed.

LEAR

[To EDGAR] Now all the plagues that in the pendulous air
Hang fated o'er men's faults fall on thy daughters!   60

KENT

He hath no daughters, sir.

37–69:
David Tennant as Edgar, John Rogan as the Fool, Anton Lesser as Kent, and Trevor Peacock as Lear
Richard McCabe as Edgar, Kenneth Branagh as the Fool, David Burke as Kent, and Paul Scofield as Lear

65: should have thus...flesh: should mutilate themselves by sticking pins into their flesh, as Edgar has done

67: pelican: greedy, parasitic (young pelicans were thought to kill their parents and then feed on their mother's blood)

68: Pillicock: similar in sound to pelican, this word appears in nursery rhymes of the time and may have been a euphemism for penis

69: "This cold night...fools and madmen": Christopher Benjamin as Kent, Michael Maloney as Edgar, Nigel Hawthorne as Lear, and Hiroyuki Sanada as the Fool in the 1999 Royal Shakespeare Company production directed by Yukio Ninagawa
Photo: Donald Cooper

71: commit...spouse: i.e., do not commit adultery. Edgar is mimicking the Ten Commandments in this speech.

75: gloves: gloves given by one's mistress as a token of her love

80: light of ear: attentive for useful gossip; **bloody of hand:** murderous

81-82: creaking...silks: referring to noises made by lovers who sneak around to be with each other

83: placket: opening in a woman's skirt or petticoat

85: Heigh no...boy: random fragments of lyrics from songs

LEAR

Death, traitor! Nothing could have subdued nature
To such a lowness but his unkind daughters.
[*To EDGAR*] Is it the fashion that discarded fathers
Should have thus little mercy on their flesh?   65
Judicious punishment. 'Twas this flesh begot
Those pelican daughters.

EDGAR

Pillicock sat on pillicock's hill; a lo, lo, lo.

FOOL

This cold night will turn us all to fools and madmen.

EDGAR

Take heed o' th' foul fiend; obey thy parents; keep thy word   70
justly; swear not; commit not with man's sworn spouse; set not
thy sweet heart on proud array. Tom's a-cold.

LEAR

What hast thou been?

EDGAR

A servingman, proud in heart and mind, that curled my hair,
wore gloves in my cap, served the lust of my mistress' heart, and   75
did the act of darkness with her; swore as many oaths as I spake
words, and broke them in the sweet face of heaven; one that slept
in the contriving of lust, and waked to do it. Wine loved I deeply,
dice dearly, and in woman out-paramoured the Turk. False of
heart, light of ear, bloody of hand; hog in sloth, fox in stealth, wolf 80
in greediness, dog in madness, lion in prey. Let not the creaking of
shoes nor the rustlings of silks betray thy poor heart to women.
Keep thy foot out of brothel, thy hand out of placket, thy pen from
lenders' books, and defy the foul fiend. Still through the hawthorn
blows the cold wind. Heigh no nonny. Dolphin, my boy, my boy!   85
Cease, let him trot by.

[Storm still]

89-90: Thou owest...perfume: Out here, naked to the elements, one is freed from debts to animals who provide materials for making elegant clothes worn at court.

90: the cat no perfume: Musky perfume was derived from the anal glands of the civet cat, a small African or Asian mammal that looks like a cat.

90-91: Here's three...itself: Lear is contrasting Kent, the Fool, and himself, all still dressed in the fineries of the royal court, with Edgar, who is nearly naked and thus close to nature.

91: Unaccommodated: animal-like, stripped of the trappings of society such as clothes

93: Scene: Off, off, you lendings!: Lear begins to take off his clothes here.

94: This is...swim in: the weather is much too nasty to act as if one is about to go for a swim

95: wild field: uncultivated land, like Edgar, who is uncivilized

96: on 's: of his

97: *Flibbertigibbet*: the name of a devil in English folklore who is mentioned in Samuel Harsnett's *Declaration of Egregious Popish Impostures* (1603)

97: "This is the foul fiend": Ted van Griethuysen as Lear, Henry Woronicz as Kent, Floyd King as the Fool, and Cameron Folmar as Edgar in the 2000 Shakespeare Theatre Company production directed by Michael Kahn

Photo: Carol Rosegg

97-98: He...cock: He roams the earth from sundown to sunup (the first crowing of the cock)

98: web and the pin: cataract of the eye; **squinies**: squints

99: white wheat: wheat that is ready to be harvested

101: footed thrice the wold: walked around the earth three times

105: aroint thee: begone

LEAR

Why, thou wert better in thy grave than to answer with thy
uncovered body this extremity of the skies. Is man no more but
this? Consider him well. Thou owest the worm no silk, the beast
no hide, the sheep no wool, the cat no perfume. Ha, here's three   90
on 's are sophisticated; thou art the thing itself. Unaccommodated
man is no more but such a poor, bare, forked animal as thou art.
Off, off, you lendings! Come on, be true.

FOOL

Prithee, nuncle, be content. This is a naughty night to swim in. Now
a little fire in a wild field were like an old lecher's heart—a small   95
spark, all the rest on 's body cold. Look, here comes a walking fire.

                              Enter GLOUCESTER [with a torch]

EDGAR

This is the foul fiend, *Flibbertigibbet*. He begins at curfew, and
walks till the first cock. He gives the web and the pin, squinies the
eye, and makes the harelip; mildews the white wheat, and hurts
the poor creature of earth.   100
        [*Sings*]
        Swithin footed thrice the wold,
        A met the night mare and her nine foal;
        Bid her alight
        And her troth plight,
        And aroint thee, witch, aroint thee!   105

KENT

[*To LEAR*] How fares your Grace?

LEAR

                              What's he?

KENT

[*To GLOUCESTER*] Who's there? What is't you seek?

GLOUCESTER

What are you there? Your names?

110: **wall-newt**: lizard; **water**: frog or water newt

112: **ditch-dog**: a dead dog in a ditch; **green mantle**: pond scum

112: **standing**: stagnant

113: **tithing to tithing**: from one hospital ward to another (see note 1.2.114); **stock-punished**: placed in the stocks

116: **deer**: creatures

118: **Smolking**: a familiar demon that appears in Harsnett's *Declaration* (see note 3.4.97)

120: **The Prince of Darkness**: i.e., the devil

121: **Modo, Mahu**: both are names for the Devil in Harsnett's *Declaration* (see note 3.4.97)

122-23: **Our flesh...it**: 1) children are now so sinful that they hate their parents, or 2) life has become so utterly wretched that people regret being born

124: **suffer**: allow me

125: **hard**: merciless

EDGAR
> Poor Tom, that eats the swimming frog, the toad, the tadpole, the
> wall-newt and the water; that in the fury of his heart, when the foul   110
> fiend rages, eats cow-dung for salads, swallows the old rat and the
> ditch-dog, drinks the green mantle of the standing pool; who is
> whipped from tithing to tithing, and stock-punished, and impris-
> oned; who hath had three suits to his back, six shirts to his body,
> > Horse to ride, and weapon to wear.   115
> > But mice and rats and such small deer
> > Have been Tom's food for seven long year—
> Beware my follower. Peace, Smolking; peace, thou fiend!

GLOUCESTER
> [*To LEAR*] What, hath your grace no better company?

EDGAR
> The Prince of Darkness is a gentleman;   120
> Modo he's called, and Mahu—

GLOUCESTER
> [*To LEAR*] Our flesh and blood is grown so vile, my lord,
> That it doth hate what gets it.

EDGAR
> > > Poor Tom's a-cold.

GLOUCESTER
> [*To LEAR*] Go in with me. My duty cannot suffer
> To obey in all your daughters' hard commands.   125
> Though their injunction be to bar my doors
> And let this tyrannous night take hold upon you,
> Yet have I ventured to come seek you out
> And bring you where both food and fire is ready.

LEAR
> First let me talk with this philosopher.   130
> [*To EDGAR*] What is the cause of thunder?

133: **Theban**: Perhaps a reference to Crates of Thebes (ca. 368–288 BCE), a Hellenistic philosopher; here, used generally to refer someone who has studied philosophy

134: **study**: area of expertise

135: **prevent**: thwart

138: **His wits...unsettle**: he is going insane

143: **outlawed...blood**: disowned; a fugitive from the law

147: **cry your mercy**: I beg your pardon

148: "Tom's a-cold": Simon Russell Beale as Edgar in the 1993 Royal Shakespeare Company production directed by Adrian Noble

Photo: Donald Cooper

KENT
                              My good lord,
     Take his offer; go into the house.

LEAR
     I'll talk a word with this most learnèd Theban.
     [*To EDGAR*] What is your study?

EDGAR
     How to prevent the fiend, and to kill vermin.   135

LEAR
     Let me ask you one word in private.

                                        [*They converse apart*]

KENT
     [*To GLOUCESTER*] Importune him once more to go, my lord.
     His wits begin to unsettle.

GLOUCESTER
                         Canst thou blame him?

                                             [*Storm still*]
     His daughters seek his death. O, that good Kent,
     He said it would be thus, poor banished man!   140
     Thou sayst the King grows mad; I'll tell thee, friend,
     I am almost mad myself. I had a son,
     Now outlawed from my blood; a sought my life
     But lately, very late. I loved him, friend;
     No father his son dearer. True to tell thee,   145
     The grief hath crazed my wits. What a night's this!
     [*To LEAR*] I do beseech your grace—

LEAR
                              O, cry your mercy.
     [*To EDGAR*] Noble philosopher, your company.

EDGAR
                              Tom's a-cold.

152: **soothe**: humor

153: **Take him you on**: he can go ahead with you

155: **Athenian**: philosopher, perhaps Lear is thinking of Socrates (ca. 470–399 BCE)

156: **Child Roland...come**: line perhaps from a ballad of medieval origin, now lost

157: **Fie, fo, and fum**: similar to what appears in the English fairy tale, Jack and the Beanstalk

GLOUCESTER
In, fellow, there in t' hovel; keep thee warm.

LEAR
Come, let's in all.

KENT
                    This way, my lord.

LEAR
                              With him!   150
I will keep still with my philosopher.

KENT
[*To GLOUCESTER*] Good my lord, soothe him; let him take the fellow.

GLOUCESTER
Take him you on.

KENT
[*To EDGAR*] Sirrah, come on. Go along with us.

LEAR
[*To EDGAR*] Come, good Athenian.

GLOUCESTER
                    No words, no words. Hush.   155

EDGAR
Child Roland to the dark tower come,
His word was still "Fie, fo, and fum;
I smell the blood of a British man."

                                        Exeunt

0: Location: Gloucester's house

Watercolor scene sketch from the promptbook for Charles Kean's 1858 production
Courtesy of the Folger Shakespeare Library

2: **censured**: judged; **nature**: familial devotion

3: **something fears**: somewhat frightens

5: **his**: i.e., his father's

5-6: **but a...himself**: rather it was brought on by self-esteem generated by the Earl of Gloucester's reprehensible badness

7: **that...just**: that I must betray my own father to be deemed loyal and honest

8-9: **which approves...of France**: which proves he is a spy working for France

10: **detector**: discoverer

15: **for our apprehension**: for us to arrest him

Act 3, Scene 5]

Enter CORNWALL and Bastard [EDMUND]

CORNWALL
I will have my revenge ere I depart the house.

EDMUND
How, my lord, I may be censured, that nature thus gives way to
loyalty, something fears me to think of.

CORNWALL
I now perceive, it was not altogether your brother's evil disposition made him seek his death, but a provoking merit set a-work   5
by a reprovable badness in himself.

EDMUND
How malicious is my fortune that I must repent to be just! This is
the letter which he spoke of, which approves him an intelligent
party to the advantages of France. O heavens, that his treason
were not, or not I the detector!   10

CORNWALL
Go with me to the duchess.

EDMUND
If the matter of this paper be certain, you have mighty business in
hand.

CORNWALL
True or false, it hath made thee Earl of Gloucester. Seek out
where thy father is, that he may be ready for our apprehension.   15

16: him: i.e., Gloucester; **comforting**: giving aid and comfort to

16-17: it will...fully: it will make him even more suspicious

18: sore...blood: painful between my loyalty to you (Cornwall) and to my family

EDMUND

[*Aside*] If I find him comforting the King, it will stuff his suspicion
more fully. [*To CORNWALL*] I will persever in my course of loyalty,
though the conflict be sore between that and my blood.

CORNWALL

I will lay trust upon thee, and thou shalt find a dearer father in
my love.   20

Exeunt

0: Location: inside a building on Gloucester's estate
1-2: **piece out the comfort**: make it more comfortable
3: **impatience**: unwillingness to endure anything else
5: **Frateretto**: another devil identified by Harsnett (see note 3.4.97); **Nero**: brutal Roman emperor who ruled from 54-68 CE; **Nero is an angler**: Rome burned during Nero's reign, and he blamed the Christians, whose symbol was the fish. Nero tortured some, crucified others. Edgar may be saying that Nero was selecting or fishing for Christians.
6: **innocent**: simpleton

7-8: "Whether a madman be a gentleman": Engraving by John Byam Shaw, ca. 1900
Courtesy of the Folger Shakespeare Library

8: **yeoman**: property owner of lower status than a gentleman
10-11: **he's a...him**: it drives a father to madness when he sees his son advance to a higher status before he does (from the First Folio)
12-13: **To have...them**: Lear fantasizes that Gonoril and Regan will someday be painfully tortured, either by their enemies or in hell; inserting red-hot pokers into an advesary's anus was a common form of torture
14-49: **The foul fiend...let her 'scape**: appears only in the First Quarto
15-16: **tameness...health**: wolves cannot be tamed, and horses are very vulnerable to disease

Act 3, Scene 6]

Enter GLOUCESTER and KENT[, disguised]

GLOUCESTER

Here is better than the open air; take it thankfully. I will piece out
the comfort with what addition I can. I will not be long from you.

KENT

All the power of his wits have given way to his impatience; the
gods discern your kindness!

[Exit GLOUCESTER]
[Enter LEAR, EDGAR as a Bedlam beggar, and FOOL]

EDGAR

Frateretto calls me, and tells me Nero is an angler in the lake of   5
darkness. Pray, innocent; and beware the foul fiend.

FOOL

[To LEAR] Prithee, nuncle, tell me whether a madman be a gentleman or a yeoman.

LEAR

A king, a king!

FOOL

No, he's a yeoman that has a gentleman to his son; for he's a mad   10
yeoman that sees his son a gentleman before him.

LEAR

To have a thousand with red burning spits
Come hissing in upon them!

EDGAR

The foul fiend bites my back.

FOOL

[To LEAR] He's mad that trusts in the tameness of a wolf, a   15

17: arraign them straight: immediately put his daughters on trial
18: justicer: judge, justice; Lear implies that Edgar is to serve as the judge in the trial
19: sapient: learned, all-knowing
20: he: i.e., Lear, who by this point, has had mental breakdown; **want'st thou...madam?**: are you in need of more spectators at your trial, your Majesty?
21: burn: brook; **Come...me**: the first line of a well-known ballad by William Birche (1558)
22: Her...leak: she is a promiscuous woman, or she's menstruating
25: Poor Tom...nightingale: Edgar asserts that Poor Tom has been possessed by a demon disguised as a bird.
26: Hoppedance: Harsnett's *Declaration* (see note 3.4.97) refers to a devil named Hoberdidance; **white herring**: herring that have not been smoked (as opposed to the black angel, a demon darkened by the fires of hell)
26-27: croak not: telling his growling, hungry stomach to be quiet
30: the evidence: the witnesses (who will testify against his daughters)

30: "I'll see their trial first. Bring in the evidence": Pal Aron as Edgar, Leo Wringer as the Fool, Louis Hilyer as Kent, and Corin Redgrave as Lear in the 2005 Royal Shakespeare Company production directed by Bill Alexander
Photo: Donald Cooper

31: robèd man: referring to Edgar, who is dressed in his blanket
32: yokefellow in equity: legal partner
33: Bench: be seated on the bench; **o' th' commission**: the person hired to be the judge
36-39: Sleepest...harm: perhaps an Elizabethan nursery rhyme

horse's health, a boy's love, or a whore's oath.

LEAR
    It shall be done. I will arraign them straight.
    [*To EDGAR*] Come, sit thou here, most learnèd justicer.
    [*To FOOL*] Thou sapient sir, sit here.—No, you she-foxes –

EDGAR
    Look where he stands and glares. Want'st thou eyes at troll-madam?   20
    [*Sings*]
        Come o'er the burn, Bessy, to me.

FOOL
    [*Sings*]
        Her boat hath a leak,
        And she must not speak
        Why she dares not come over to thee.

EDGAR
    The foul fiend haunts Poor Tom in the voice of a nightingale.   25
    Hoppedance cries in Tom's belly for two white herring. Croak
    not, black angel: I have no food for thee.

KENT
    [*To LEAR*] How do you, sir? Stand you not so amazed.
    Will you lie down and rest upon the cushions?

LEAR
    I'll see their trial first. Bring in the evidence.   30
    [*To EDGAR*] Thou robèd man of justice, take thy place;
    [*To FOOL*] And thou, his yokefellow of equity,
    Bench by his side. [*To KENT*] You are o' th' commission,
    Sit you too.

EDGAR
    Let us deal justly.   35
    [*Sings*]
        Sleepest or wakest thou, jolly shepherd?
        Thy sheep be in the corn,

38-39: And for...harm: should you utter but one scream from your small mouth, your sheep shall return from the field safely

40: Purr, the cat: Purr is identified as a devil in Harsnett's *Declaration* (see note 3.4.97).

41-74: Scene: Garrick (1717-1779) played Lear as distracted and alienated; William C. Macready (1773-1873) wrestled to hold onto sanity; and Edmund Kean (1787-1833) maintained a dream-like state . Tommaso Salvini (1829-1915) played the role as if Lear had become completely unhinged while John Gielgud (1904-2000) doddered and twitched.

45: joint-stool: low stool; **Cry you...joint-stool**: i.e., I beg your pardon for not noticing you.

46: another: i.e., Regan

46: warped looks: twisted or evil countenance

47: store: stored materials; **on**: of

49: let her 'scape: permitted Regan to leave the courtroom

54: They'll mar my counterfeiting: i.e., His tears will wash off the dirt he has rubbed on his face as part of his disguise.

And for one blast of thy minikin mouth
Thy sheep shall take no harm.
Purr, the cat is gray.   40

LEAR

Arraign her first. 'Tis Gonoril. I here take my oath before this
honorable assembly she kicked the poor King her father.

FOOL

Come hither, mistress. Is your name Gonoril?

LEAR

She cannot deny it.

FOOL

Cry you mercy, I took you for a joint-stool.   45

LEAR

And here's another, whose warped looks proclaim
What store her heart is made on. Stop her there.
Arms, arms, sword, fire, corruption in the place!
False justicer, why hast thou let her 'scape?

EDGAR

Bless thy five wits.   50

KENT

[*To LEAR*] O pity! Sir, where is the patience now
That thou so oft have boasted to retain?

EDGAR

[*Aside*] My tears begin to take his part so much
They'll mar my counterfeiting.

LEAR

                                The little dogs and all,
Tray, Blanch, and Sweetheart—see, they bark at me.   55

56: throw his head at them: bark back, i.e., threaten the dogs so that they'll be quiet

57: or black: either black

60: brach: a type of dog, probably a bloodhound or other kind of hunting dog

61: Bobtail tike or trundle-tail: a mixed-species dog with a docked tail or a curly tail

64: hatch: the lower half of a Dutch door

65: wakes: parish festivals

66: horn: container used by beggars as a cup for both drinking and panhandling

67: anatomize: dissect

69: entertain...hundred: hire you to be one of my hundred knights

70-71: Persian attire: rich, handmade robes from Persia

73: curtains: bed curtains; Lear, hallucinating from madness, thinks he is in a proper bed

75: And I'll go to bed at noon: from the First Folio

79: upon: against

EDGAR

Tom will throw his head at them.—Avaunt, you curs!
Be thy mouth or black or white,
Tooth that poisons if it bite,
Mastiff, greyhound, mongrel grim,
Hound or spaniel, brach or him,   60
Bobtail tike or trundle-tail,
Tom will make them weep and wail;
For with throwing thus my head,
Dogs leap the hatch, and all are fled.
Loudla, doodla! Come, march to wakes and fairs   65
And market towns. Poor Tom, thy horn is dry.

LEAR

Then let them anatomize Regan; see what breeds about her heart.
Is there any cause in nature that makes this hardness? [*To
EDGAR*] You, sir, I entertain you for one of my hundred, only I do
not like the fashion of your garments. You'll say they are Persian   70
attire, but let them be changed.

KENT

Now, good my lord, lie here and rest awhile.

LEAR

Make no noise, make no noise. Draw the curtains. So, so, so. We'll
go to supper i' th' morning. So, so, so.

[He sleeps.] Enter GLOUCESTER.

FOOL

And I'll go to bed at noon.   75

GLOUCESTER

[*To KENT*] Come hither, friend. Where is the King my master?

KENT

Here, sir, but trouble him not; his wits are gone.

GLOUCESTER

Good friend, I prithee take him in thy arms.
I have o'erheard a plot of death upon him.

80: **litter**: portable bed

83: **dally**: delay

86-87: **to some...conduct**: to safety quickly take you

87-91: **Oppressèd nature...stay behind**: appears only in the First Quarto

88: **balmed...sinews**: soothed, healed your damaged nerves

89: **convenience**: circumstances

90: **Stand...cure**: will be hard to cure

92: **our woes**: similar problems

92-105: **When we...Lurk, lurk.**: appears only in the First Quarto

93: **We scarcely...foes**: we almost stop thinking about our own miseries

94: **Who alone suffers**: He who suffers alone

95: **free...shows**: carefree ways and happy times

96-97: **But then...fellowship**: Whereas the mind can overcome great suffering when one has companionship

98: **portable**: bearable

100: **He...fathered**: he has been treated as badly by his children as I have by my father

101-102: **Mark...thee**: Pay attention to what is said about important people or events, then keep your identity hidden until those who have slandered you, when convinced of innocence, invite you to return and restore you to favor

104: **What...King!**: whatever else may happen tonight, let us hope the king escapes to safety

105: **Lurk**: Stay out of sight

There is a litter ready. Lay him in't   80
And drive towards Dover, friend, where thou shalt meet
Both welcome and protection. Take up thy master.
If thou shouldst dally half an hour, his life,
With thine and all that offer to defend him,
Stand in assurèd loss. Take up, take up,   85
And follow me, that will to some provision
Give thee quick conduct.

KENT
                    [*To LEAR*] Oppressèd nature sleeps.
This rest might yet have balmed thy broken sinews
Which, if convenience will not allow,
Stand in hard cure. [*To FOOL*] Come, help to bear thy master.   90
Thou must not stay behind.

GLOUCESTER
                    Come, come, away.
                                          Exeunt. [Manet EDGAR.]

EDGAR
When we our betters see bearing our woes,
We scarcely think our miseries our foes.
Who alone suffers, suffers most i' th' mind,
Leaving free things and happy shows behind.   95
But then the mind much sufferance doth o'erskip
When grief hath mates, and bearing fellowship.
How light and portable my pain seems now,
When that which makes me bend, makes the King bow.
He childed as I fathered. Tom, away.   100
Mark the high noises, and thyself bewray
When false opinion, whose wrong thoughts defiles thee,
In thy just proof repeals and reconciles thee.
What will hap more tonight, safe scape the King!
Lurk, lurk.   105

                                          Exit

0: Location: Gloucester's house

Set design for the 1959 production at the Shakespeare Memorial Theatre in Stratford-upon-Avon directed by Glen Byam Shaw

Rare Book and Special Collection Library, University of Illinois at Urbana-Champaign

1: **Post speedily**: hurry
6: **sister**: i.e., sister-in-law, Gonoril
7: **bound**: obliged, obligated
8: **Duke**: i.e., the Duke of Albany
9: **festinate**: hasty
9: **are bound**: are committed
10: **posts**: messengers; **intelligence**: information
14: **his**: i.e., Lear's
15: **questants after him**: searchers for Lear
16: **the lord's dependants**: servants belonging to Gloucester

Enter CORNWALL and REGAN, GONORIL and
Bastard [EDMUND, and SERVANTS]

CORNWALL

[*To GONORIL*] Post speedily to my lord your husband.Show him
this letter. The army of France is landed. [*To SERVANTS*] Seek
out the villain Gloucester.

[Exeunt some]

REGAN

Hang him instantly.

GONORIL

Pluck out his eyes.   5

CORNWALL

Leave him to my displeasure.—Edmund, keep you our sister company. The revenges we are bound to take upon your traitorous
father are not fit for your beholding. Advise the Duke where you
are going, to a most festinate preparation; we are bound to the like.
Our posts shall be swift, and intelligence betwixt us.—Farewell,   10
dear sister. Farewell, my lord of Gloucester.

Enter Steward [OSWALD]

How now, where's the King?

OSWALD

My lord of Gloucester hath conveyed him hence.
Some five- or six-and-thirty of his knights,
Hot questants after him, met him at gate,   15
Who, with some other of the lord's dependants,
Are gone with him towards Dover, where they boast
To have well-armèd friends.

CORNWALL

Get horses for your mistress.

[Exit OSWALD]

21: **Pinion him**: bind his hands

22: **pass upon his life**: sentence him to death

23: **form of justice**: a proper trial

24: **do a curtsy**: do a courtesy to, yield to

26: **corky**: dried and withered from age

31: Stage Direction: *[REGAN plucks his beard]*: Ellen Holly as Regan, Paul Sorvino as Gloucester, and the Ensemble in the 1973 Public Theater production directed by Edwin Sherin
Photo: George E. Joseph

32: Stage Direction: *Plucks*: pulls out at the root

GONORIL

    Farewell, sweet lord, and sister.

CORNWALL
 Edmund, farewell.

      Exeunt GONORIL and Bastard [EDMUND]
   [To Servants] Go seek the traitor Gloucester.   20
 Pinion him like a thief; bring him before us.

        [Exeunt other SERVANTS]

 Though well we may not pass upon his life
 Without the form of justice, yet our power
 Shall do a curtsy to our wrath, which men
 May blame but not control. Who's there—the traitor? 25

   Enter GLOUCESTER brought in by two or three

REGAN
 Ingrateful fox, 'tis he.

CORNWALL

    [To Servants] Bind fast his corky arms.

GLOUCESTER
 What means your graces? Good my friends, consider
 You are my guests. Do me no foul play, friends.

CORNWALL
 [To Servants] Bind him, I say—

REGAN

      Hard, hard! O filthy traitor!

GLOUCESTER
 Unmerciful lady as you are, I am true.   30

CORNWALL
 [To Servants] To this chair bind him. *[To GLOUCESTER]* Villain, thou
  shalt find—

        [REGAN plucks his beard]

34: white: white-haired, esteemed; **Naughty**: wicked

36: quicken: come to life

37-38: With robbers'...thus: You should not abuse my hospitality by handling my face as if you were you thieves trying to rob me.

39: late: lately

41: confederacy: understanding, allegiance

42: Late footed: having recently arrived

42-43: "To whose hands / You have send the lunatic King": Ralph Cosham as Cornwall, Jennifer Harmon as Regan, and the Ensemble in the 2000 Shakespeare Theatre Company production directed by Michael Kahn
Photo: Carol Rosegg

44: guessingly set down: conjecturally written

GLOUCESTER
  By the kind gods, 'tis most ignobly done,
  To pluck me by the beard.

REGAN
  So white, and such a traitor!

GLOUCESTER
                    Naughty lady,
  These hairs, which thou dost ravish from my chin   35
  Will quicken, and accuse thee. I am your host.
  With robbers' hands my hospitable favors
  You should not ruffle thus. What will you do?

CORNWALL
  Come, sir, what letters had you late from France?

REGAN
  Be simple, answerer, for we know the truth.   40

CORNWALL
  And what confederacy have you with the traitors
  Late footed in the kingdom?

REGAN
                    To whose hands
  You have sent the lunatic King. Speak.

GLOUCESTER
  I have a letter guessingly set down,
  Which came from one that's of a neutral heart,   45
  And not from one opposed.

CORNWALL
                    Cunning.

REGAN
                              And false.

tracks 25-27

47–90:
Samantha Bond as Regan, Rob Edwards as Cornwall, and
Clive Merrison as Gloucester
Sara Kestelman as Regan, Jack Klaff as Cornwall, and
Alec McCowen as Gloucester

48: **charged at peril**: ordered at risk of death
50: **tied to th' stake**: powerless and surrounded by danger; **stand the course**: suffer
the attacks
54: **anointed**: sanctified, holy; sovereigns were anointed with holy oil at coronation;
rash: slash violently (the First Folio reads "stick")
56-57: **would have quenched the fires**: would have risen high enough to drench the
stars in the sky with water
58: **holped**: helped
58: **holped...rage**: appears only in the First Quarto, the First Folio reads "help the
heavens to rain"
59: **stern**: dire
60: **turn the key**: unlock the gate and let them in
61: **All...subscribe**: I acknowledge and support all cruel creatures
62: **The wingèd vengeance**: God's divine revenge carried out by one of his winged
angels, sweeping down from heaven like birds of prey
65: **will think**: wants, aspires

66: Stage Direction: *CORNWALL pulls out one of GLOUCESTER's eyes*: Brendan O'Hea
as Cornwall and Richard O'Callaghan as Gloucester in the 2005 Chichester Festival
Theatre production directed by Steven Pimlott
Photo: Donald Cooper

CORNWALL
Where hast thou sent the King?

GLOUCESTER
To Dover.

REGAN
Wherefore to Dover? Wast thou not charged at peril—

CORNWALL
Wherefore to Dover?—Let him first answer that.

GLOUCESTER
I am tied to th' stake, and I must stand the course.   50

REGAN
Wherefore to Dover, sir?

GLOUCESTER
Because I would not see thy cruel nails
Pluck out his poor old eyes, nor thy fierce sister
In his anointed flesh rash boarish fangs.
The sea, with such a storm as his buoyed head   55
In hell-black night endured, would have buoyed up
And quenched the stellèd fires. Yet, poor old heart,
He holped the heavens to rage.
If wolves had at thy gate howled that stern time,
Thou shouldst have said "Good porter, turn the key;   60
All cruels I'll subscribe." But I shall see
The wingèd vengeance overtake such children.

CORNWALL
See't shalt thou never.—Fellows, hold the chair.—
Upon those eyes of thine I'll set my foot.

GLOUCESTER
He that will think to live till he be old,   65
Give me some help!—O cruel! O ye gods!
    [CORNWALL pulls out one of GLOUCESTER's eyes and stamps on it]

tracks 25-27

47–90:
*Samantha Bond as Regan, Rob Edwards as Cornwall,
and Clive Merrison as Gloucester*
*Sara Kestelman as Regan, Jack Klaff as Cornwall,
and Alec McCowen as Gloucester*

67: One side...too: One eye will remind you of the other's loss; i.e., best to take them both out.

72-73: If you...quarrel: Even if you were old and venerable (wise old men wore beards) I'd still challenge your authority in these actions.

73: What do you mean?: What on earth do you think you are doing or intend to do? (The First Quarto assigns the question to the servant.)

68-78: Scene: Peter Brook's 1962 RSC production cut the part of the servant who attempts to save Gloucester after his blinding altogether.

74: villein: servant

75: take the chance of anger: take the risks of an angry fight that could lead to bloodshed

76: stand up thus: behave so impudently

76: Stage Direction: *She...behind*: This stage direction appears only in the First Quarto.

77-78: Yet...him: Nevertheless, my death will have not been in vain, since you still have one eye left to see to it that Cornwall suffers for my death.

REGAN
    [*To CORNWALL*] One side will mock another; t'other, too.

CORNWALL
    [*To GLOUCESTER*] If you see vengeance—

SERVANT
                                        Hold your hand, my lord.
    I have served you ever since I was a child,
    But better service have I never done you   70
    Than now to bid you hold.

REGAN
                        How now, you dog!

SERVANT
    If you did wear a beard upon your chin
    I'd shake it on this quarrel. [*To CORNWALL*] What do you mean?

CORNWALL
    My villein!

SERVANT
    Why then, come on, and take the chance of anger.   75
                                [They draw and fight]

REGAN
    [*To another servant*] Give me thy sword. A peasant stand up thus!
                    She takes a sword and runs at him behind

SERVANT
    [*To GLOUCESTER*] O, I am slain, my lord! Yet have you one eye left
    To see some mischief on him.
                                [REGAN stabs him again]
                    O!
                                        [He dies]

47–90:
Samantha Bond as Regan, Rob Edwards as Cornwall,
and Clive Merrison as Gloucester
Sara Kestelman as Regan, Jack Klaff as Cornwall,
and Alec McCowen as Gloucester

79: Scene: Some directors have staged this scene with Gloucester lying on the ground during the blinding; others have him tied to a chair. In certain productions, the cruelty of this scene has been amplified by having Cornwall or Regan do ghoulish things with Gloucester's eyes once they've been gouged out, such as playing catch with them or smashing them in their hands. In Brook's 1962 RSC production, Cornwall (Tony Church) brought a kind of fascistic sadism to the role, calmly grinding his shining boot spur into Gloucester's eyes, as if he were merely putting out a cigarette underfoot.

80: **luster**: the glimmer in your eyes
82: **nature**: filial love
83: **quit**: requite, revenge yourself

83: "Out, treacherous villain!": Sally Dexter as Regan and Norman Rodway as Gloucester in the 1990 Royal Shakespeare Company production directed by Nicholas Hytner
Photo: Donald Cooper

95-103: **I'll never care...heaven help him**: These last nine lines, showing the servants not only expressing sympathy for Gloucester but also deciding to follow him, appear only in the First Quarto.

CORNWALL
　Lest it see more, prevent it. Out, vile jelly!
　　　　　　　　　　[He pulls out GLOUCESTER's other eye]
　Where is thy luster now?

GLOUCESTER
　All dark and comfortless. Where's my son Edmund?
　Edmund, enkindle all the sparks of nature
　To quit this horrid act.

REGAN
　　　　　　　　　　　　Out, treacherous villain!
　Thou call'st on him that hates thee. It was he
　That made the overture of thy treasons to us,　　　　　　85
　Who is too good to pity thee.

GLOUCESTER
　O, my follies! Then Edgar was abused.
　Kind gods, forgive me that, and prosper him!

REGAN
　[To SERVANTS] Go thrust him out at gates, and let him smell
　His way to Dover. *[To CORNWALL]* How is't, my lord? How look you?　90

CORNWALL
　I have received a hurt. Follow me, lady.
　[To SERVANTS] Turn out that eyeless villain. Throw this slave
　Upon the dunghill.
　　　　　　　　　Exit [one or more with GLOUCESTER
　　　　　　　　　　　　　　and the body]
　　　　　　　Regan, I bleed apace.
　Untimely comes this hurt. Give me your arm.
　　　　　　　　　Exeunt [CORNWALL and REGAN]

SECOND SERVANT
　I'll never care what wickedness I do　　　　　　　　95
　If this man come to good.

97: **old course of death**: die of natural causes

99: **Bedlam**: the lunatic released from the insane asylum, i.e., poor Tom

100-101: **His...thing**: He is a rogue and a lunatic, and therefore has the freedom to do what ever we ask of him.

THIRD SERVANT

                    If she live long
And in the end meet the old course of death,
Women will all turn monsters.

SECOND SERVANT
Let's follow the old Earl and get the Bedlam
To lead him where he would. His roguish madness   100
Allows itself to any thing.

THIRD SERVANT
Go thou. I'll fetch some flax and whites of eggs
To apply to his bleeding face. Now heaven help him!

                                      Exeunt

[King Lear

Act 4

0: Location: A clearing

Watercolor scene sketch from the promptbook for Charles Kean's 1858 production
Courtesy of the Folger Shakespeare Library

1-2: Yet...flattered: It is better to be openly reviled for being a beggar, than to be constantly reviled behind one's back and flattered to one's face—an indictment of the manner in which many people behave at court
2: worst: at one's worst; at the very bottom
3: dejected: disconsolate
4: Stands...fear: stands in hope and has no fear that things will get worse
5-6: The lamentable...laughter: i.e., A change from the best brings sadness; a change from the worst brings joy.
6-9: Welcome...thy blasts: from the First Folio
9: Owes...blasts: has no obligation to your strong winds
10: poorly led: guided by someone who is feeble and poor
11-12: But that...age: i.e., Were it not that life's unpredictable changes of fortune compelled us to hate life, none of us would ever acquiesce to old age and death.
20: I stumbled when I saw: i.e., I was blind to the truth (of Edgar's love) when I could see.
21-22: Our...commodities: i.e., Our wealth may give us a sense of security, but it is our insignificant flaws that turn out to be the most valuable.

Act 4, Scene 1]

Enter EDGAR [as a Bedlam beggar]

EDGAR
Yet better thus, and known to be contemned
Than still contemned and flattered. To be worst,
The low'st and most dejected thing of Fortune,
Stands still in esperance, lives not in fear.
The lamentable change is from the best;   5
The worst returns to laughter. Welcome, then,
Thou unsubstantial air that I embrace.
The wretch that thou hast blown unto the worst
Owes nothing to thy blasts.
                              Enter GLOUCESTER led by an OLD MAN
Who's here? My father, poorly led? World, world, O world!   10
But that thy strange mutations make us hate thee,
Life would not yield to age.

                                        [EDGAR stands aside]

OLD MAN
[*To GLOUCESTER*] O my good lord, I have been your tenant
And your father's tenant this fourscore—

GLOUCESTER
Away, get thee away, good friend, be gone.   15
Thy comforts can do me no good at all;
Thee they may hurt.

OLD MAN
Alack, sir, you cannot see your way.

GLOUCESTER
I have no way, and therefore want no eyes.
I stumbled when I saw. Full oft 'tis seen   20
Our means secure us, and our mere defects

23: The...wrath: the one who nourished your deceived father's anger

Costume rendering for the Old Man from the 1959 production at the Shakespeare Memorial Theatre in Stratford-upon-Avon directed by Glen Byam Shaw
Rare Book and Special Collection Library, University of Illinois at Urbana-Champaign

28-29: The worst...worst: i.e., As long as we are able to say how bad things are, they can get even worse.

33: A has some reason: i.e., he is not completely insane

38: wanton: recklessly cruel

Prove our commodities. Ah dear son Edgar,
The food of thy abusèd father's wrath—
Might I but live to see thee in my touch
I'd say I had eyes again!

OLD MAN

How now? Who's there?   25

EDGAR
[*Aside*] O gods! Who is't can say "I am at the worst"?
I am worse than e'er I was.

OLD MAN

'Tis poor mad Tom.

EDGAR
[*Aside*] And worse I may be yet. The worst is not
As long as we can say "This is the worst."

OLD MAN
[*To EDGAR*] Fellow, where goest?   30

GLOUCESTER
Is it a beggarman?

OLD MAN
Madman and beggar too.

GLOUCESTER
A has some reason, else he could not beg
In the last night's storm I such a fellow saw,
Which made me think a man a worm. My son   35
Came then into my mind, and yet my mind
Was then scarce friends with him. I have heard more since.
As flies to wanton boys are we to th' gods;
They kill us for their sport.

39: How...be?: i.e., How is it possible that he has been so transformed?

40-41: Bad is...others: i.e., What an awful business it is that I must continue to deceive my grief-stricken father, even though doing so is rather irritating for all of us.

43: Then prithee, get thee gone.: appears only in the First Quarto

44: wilt o'ertake us: catch up to us

45: for ancient love: i.e., out of respect for the longstanding landlord/tenant relationship from which you and I have both benefited

48: 'Tis the time's plague: i.e., it is indicative of the sickness of our state

50: Above the rest: most importantly; above all

52: Come on't what will: regardless of what I get out of it

53: dance it farther: maintain this disguise any longer (the First Folio reads "daub")

EDGAR

          [Aside] How should this be?
Bad is the trade that must play fool to sorrow,   40
Ang'ring itself and others.

                            [He comes forward]
          Bless thee, master!

GLOUCESTER
  Is that the naked fellow?

OLD MAN
          Ay, my lord.

GLOUCESTER
  Then prithee, get thee gone. If for my sake
  Thou wilt o'ertake us hence a mile or twain
  I' th' way toward Dover, do it for ancient love,   45
  And bring some covering for this naked soul,
  Who I'll entreat to lead me.

OLD MAN
          Alack, sir, he is mad.

GLOUCESTER
  'Tis the time's plague when madmen lead the blind.
  Do as I bid thee; or rather do thy pleasure.
  Above the rest, be gone.   50

OLD MAN
  I'll bring him the best 'parel that I have,
  Come on't what will.

                                [Exit]

GLOUCESTER
          Sirrah, naked fellow!

EDGAR
  Poor Tom's a-cold. *[Aside]* I cannot dance it farther.

GLOUCESTER
  Come hither, fellow.

59-62: Five fiends...master.: appears only in the First Quarto

59-61: Obidicut...mowing: the names of devils and their traits as listed in Harnsett's *Declaration* (see note 3.4.97)

61: mowing: mouthing; **since:** ever since then

64: Have...strokes: have weakened us to the point that we are vulnerable to each of Fortune's punches

66: superfluous and lust-dieted: excessive and luxuriously fed

67: That...ordinance: who opposes your divine laws

67-68: that...feel: who refuses to see the truth because he has not suffered enough to feel anything

69: distribution: equal allocation of all wealth

72: bending: overhanging

73: confinèd: 1) obscure; perhaps a sea so deep it will never reveal its secrets, and 2) enclosed; the Straits of Dover are surrounded by its cliffs and the shores of France; **looks in the confinèd deep:** peers into the secretive depths of the sea below (the English Channel)

76: about me: around me, in my possession

EDGAR

                   [Aside] And yet I must.
[*To GLOUCESTER*] Bless thy sweet eyes, they bleed.   55

GLOUCESTER
  Know'st thou the way to Dover?

EDGAR
  Both stile and gate, horseway and footpath. Poor Tom hath been
  scared out of his good wits. Bless thee, goodman, from the foul
  fiend. Five fiends have been in Poor Tom at once, as Obidicut of
  lust, Hobbididence prince of dumbness, Mahu of stealing, Modo of   60
  murder, Flibbertigibbet of mocking and mowing, who since possesses chambermaids and waiting-women. So bless thee, master.

GLOUCESTER
  Here, take this purse, thou whom the heavens' plagues
  Have humbled to all strokes. That I am wretched
  Makes thee the happier. Heavens deal so still.   65
  Let the superfluous and lust-dieted man
  That stands your ordinance, that will not see
  Because he does not feel, feel your power quickly.
  So distribution should undo excess,
  And each man have enough. Dost thou know Dover?   70

EDGAR
  Ay, master.

GLOUCESTER
  There is a cliff whose high and bending head
  Looks saucily in the confinèd deep.
  Bring me but to the very brim of it
  And I'll repair the misery thou dost bear   75
  With something rich about me. From that place
  I shall no leading need.

EDGAR
  Give me thy arm. Poor Tom shall lead thee.
                           [Exit EDGAR guiding GLOUCESTER]

0: Location: Before the Duke of Albany's Palace

Set design for the 1959 production at the Shakespeare Memorial Theatre in Stratford-upon-Avon directed by Glen Byam Shaw

Rare Book and Special Collection Library, University of Illinois at Urbana-Champaign

2: **Not met**: has not met

8: **sot**: fool

13: **cowish**: cow-like, cowardly

14: **undertake**: hazard, take responsibility (for)

14-15: **He'll...answer**: i.e., He will not seriously take insults that would compel him to defend himself

15-16: **Our...effects**: i.e., The plot we hatched during our journey (to have Edmund supplant Albany) may come to fruition.

16: **brother**: brother-in-law, i.e., Cornwall

17: **musters**: gathering of the troops; **powers**: soldiers

18; **change arms at home**: exchange weapons, i.e. give up women's work and become the master of the house; **distaff**: staff used for spinning thread, i.e., woman's work

20: **like**: likely

24: **Would...air**: would give you an erection

25: **Conceive**: comprehend what I'm saying, with sexual implications (impregnate)

Act 4, Scene 2]

Enter at one door GONORIL and Bastard [EDMUND]

GONORIL
  Welcome, my lord. I marvel our mild husband
  Not met us on the way.

  [Enter at another door Steward OSWALD]
  Now, where's your master?

OSWALD
  Madam, within; but never man so changed.
  I told him of the army that was landed;
  He smiled at it. I told him you were coming;   5
  His answer was, "The worse." Of Gloucester's treachery
  And of the loyal service of his son
  When I informed him, then he called me sot,
  And told me I had turned the wrong side out.
  What he should most defy seems pleasant to him;   10
  What like, offensive.

GONORIL
  [To EDMUND] Then shall you go no further.
  It is the cowish terror of his spirit
  That dares not undertake. He'll not feel wrongs
  Which tie him to an answer. Our wishes on the way   15
  May prove effects. Back, Edmund, to my brother.
  Hasten his musters and conduct his powers.
  I must change arms at home, and give the distaff
  Into my husband's hands. This trusty servant
  Shall pass between us. Ere long you are like to hear,   20
  If you dare venture in your own behalf,
  A mistress's command. Wear this. Spare speech.
  Decline your head. This kiss, if it durst speak,
  Would stretch thy spirits up into the air.

  [She kisses him]
  Conceive, and fare you well.   25

26: **Yours in the ranks of death**: i.e., I will remain true to you even in death.

27: **man and man**: i.e., Albany, her husband, and Edmund, her lover

29: **My fool...body**: 1) my husband, who is a fool, controls my body, or 2) my foolish lust for Edmund now controls my body

30: **worth the whistling**: deserving of men's sexual attraction

32-59: **I fear...why does he so?"**: appears only in the First Quarto

32: **fear your disposition**: mistrust your nature

33: **contemns**: despises, disdains

34: **bordered certain**: securely kept in bounds

35: **sliver and disbranch**: tear off and break from

36: **material sap**: the stock from which she was nurtured

37: **to deadly use**: to a destructive end; **The text**: this sermon you are preaching

39: **savor but themselves**: relish only filthy things

42: **head-lugged bear**: an angry bear dragged by a chain around his neck

43: **madded**: made mad, driven insane

44: **brother**: brother-in-law, i.e., Cornwall

EDMUND
    Yours in the ranks of death.

GONORIL
                    My most dear Gloucester.
                                        [Exit EDMUND]
    O, the difference of man and man!
    To thee a woman's services are due;
    My fool usurps my body.

OSWALD
                    Madam, here comes my lord.

                                        Exit
                                [Enter ALBANY]

GONORIL
    I have been worth the whistling.

ALBANY
                        O Gonoril,   30
    You are not worth the dust which the rude wind
    Blows in your face. I fear your disposition.
    That nature which contemns its origin
    Cannot be bordered certain in itself.
    She that herself will sliver and disbranch   35
    From her material sap perforce must wither,
    And come to deadly use.

GONORIL
                    No more. The text is foolish.

ALBANY
    Wisdom and goodness to the vile seem vile;
    Filths savor but themselves. What have you done?
    Tigers, not daughters, what have you performed?   40
    A father, and a gracious agèd man,
    Whose reverence even the head-lugged bear would lick,
    Most barbarous, most degenerate, have you madded.
    Could my good-brother suffer you to do it—

46: **If that**: If; **visible spirits**: angels

Costume rendering for Gonoril by Susan Tsu from the 2004 Oregon Shakespeare Festival production directed by James Edmondson
Courtesy of the Oregon Shakespeare Festival

50: **Milk-livered**: white-livered, i.e., spineless, cowardly (cowardice was believed to have come from the whiteness or lack of blood in the liver)
52-53: **discerning...suffering**: able to distinguish between insults that should be refuted and those that should be tolerated
53-59: **that not...does he so**: appears only in the First Quarto
55: **Where's thy drum?**: i.e., Why have you not prepared yourself for battle?
56: **noiseless**: without martial sounds, i.e., peaceful, unprepared for war
57: **plumèd helm**: feather-topped helmet; **flaxen biggins**: white linen nightcap
60-61: **Proper...woman**: i.e., Those deformities that commonly distort the facial features of the devil are even more hideous looking when they distort a woman's face.
62-69: **Thou changèd...SECOND GENTLEMAN**: appears only in the First Quarto
62: **self-covered**: disguised or hidden under a fiendish exterior
63: **Bemonster**: make monstrous or hideous; **Were't my fitness**: i.e., if it were suitable for me
67: **doth shield thee**: protects you (Albany cannot attack her because she is female)
68: **mew**: an exclamation of disgust, here aimed at mocking Albany's masculinity

A man, a prince by him so benefacted?   45
If that the heavens do not their visible spirits
Send quickly down to tame these vile offenses,
It will come,
Humanity must perforce prey on itself,
Like monsters of the deep.

GONORIL
                              Milk-livered man,   50
That bear'st a cheek for blows, a head for wrongs;
Who hast not in thy brows an eye discerning
Thine honor from thy suffering; that not know'st
Fools do those villains pity who are punished
Ere they have done their mischief. Where's thy drum?   55
France spreads his banners in our noiseless land,
With plumèd helm thy flaxen biggins threats,
Whiles thou, a moral fool, sits still and cries
"Alack, why does he so?"

ALBANY
                              See thyself, devil.
Proper deformity seems not in the fiend   60
So horrid as in woman.

GONORIL
                              O vain fool!

ALBANY
Thou changèd and self-covered thing, for shame
Bemonster not thy feature. Were't my fitness
To let these hands obey my blood,
They are apt enough to dislocate and tear   65
Thy flesh and bones. Howe'er thou art a fiend,
A woman's shape doth shield thee.

GONORIL
Marry, your manhood mew—

                              Enter SECOND GENTLEMAN

73: bred: employed in his household; **thralled with remorse**: enthralled, deeply moved by regret

74: Opposed against: objecting to; **bending his sword**: directing his sword

76: Flew on him: attacked him

78: plucked him after: sent him to his death

79: above: i.e., in heaven

80: justicers: (heavenly) judges; **nether**: earthly

84: One way: in one way; i.e., now that Cornwall is dead, Edmund can claim the throne as Duke of Gloucester

85: my Gloucester: Edmund

86-87: May all...life: i.e., my fantasies of having the whole kingdom and Edmund to myself may come crashing down on me

88: tart: bitter

ALBANY
  What news?

SECOND GENTLEMAN
  O my good lord, the Duke of Cornwall's dead,   70
  Slain by his servant going to put out
  The other eye of Gloucester.

ALBANY
                    Gloucester's eyes?

SECOND GENTLEMAN
  A servant that he bred, thralled with remorse,
  Opposed against the act, bending his sword
  To his great master who, thereat enraged,   75
  Flew on him, and amongst them felled him dead,
  But not without that harmful stroke which since
  Hath plucked him after.

ALBANY
  This shows you are above,
  You justicers, that these our nether crimes
  So speedily can venge. But O, poor Gloucester!   80
  Lost he his other eye?

SECOND GENTLEMAN
                    Both, both, my lord.
  [*To GONORIL*] This letter, madam, craves a speedy answer.
  'Tis from your sister.

GONORIL
                    [*Aside*] One way I like this well;
  But being widow, and my Gloucester with her,   85
  May all the building in my fancy pluck
  Upon my hateful life. Another way
  The news is not so tart.—I'll read and answer.

                                                      [Exit]

89: **his son**: i.e., Edmund; **his**: i.e., Gloucester's

90: **hither**: to Albany's castle

91: **back again**: on the way back from (Albany's palace)

ALBANY
Where was his son when they did take his eyes?

SECOND GENTLEMAN
Come with my lady hither.

ALBANY
       He is not here.   90

SECOND GENTLEMAN
No, my good lord; I met him back again.

ALBANY
Knows he the wickedness?

SECOND GENTLEMAN
Ay, my good lord; 'twas he informed against him,
And quit the house on purpose that their punishment
Might have the freer course.

ALBANY
       Gloucester, I live   95
To thank thee for the love thou showd'st the King,
And to revenge thy eyes.—Come hither, friend.
Tell me what more thou knowest.

                 Exeunt

0: Location: The French camp near Dover

0-54: The entire scene appears only in the First Quarto.

Set design for the 1959 production at the Shakespeare Memorial Theatre in Stratford-upon-Avon directed by Glen Byam Shaw
Rare Book and Special Collection Library, University of Illinois at Urbana-Champaign

1: **gone back**: returned to France

3: **imperfect in the state**: unsettled in state matters

5: **imports**: foreshadows

10: **pierce**: move

12: **trilled**: trickled

14: **who**: which

Act 4, Scene 3]

Enter KENT [disguised] and FIRST GENTLEMAN

KENT
  Why the King of France is so suddenly gone back; know you the
  reason?

FIRST GENTLEMAN
  Something he left imperfect in the state
  Which, since his coming forth, is thought of, which
  Imports to the kingdom so much fear and danger   5
  That his personal return was most required
  And necessary.

KENT
  Who hath he left behind him general?

FIRST GENTLEMAN
  The Maréchal of France, Monsieur la Far.

KENT
  Did your letters pierce the Queen to any demonstration of grief?   10

FIRST GENTLEMAN
  Ay, sir. She took them, read them in my presence,
  And now and then an ample tear trilled down
  Her delicate cheek. It seemed she was a queen
  Over her passion who, most rebel-like,
  Sought to be king o'er her.

KENT
                        O, then it moved her.   15

17: **express her goodliest**: cast her in the best light

19: **like, a better way**: similar to that, but better

20-21: **seemed...eyes**: seemed unaware that she was crying

23: **a rarity**: something precious, like a jewel

24: **become it**: be so attractive (when grief-stricken)

25: **heaved**: breathed with great difficulty

31: **clamor mastered**: having gotten control over her cries of grief

33: **conditions**: characters

34: **one self**: the same; **mate and make**: i.e., father and mother

35: **issues**: children

36: **King**: the King of France; **returned**: returned to his kingdom

FIRST GENTLEMAN
Not to a rage. Patience and sorrow strove
Who should express her goodliest. You have seen
Sunshine and rain at once; her smiles and tears
Were like, a better way. Those happy smilets
That played on her ripe lip seemed not to know 20
What guests were in her eyes, which parted thence
As pearls from diamonds dropped. In brief,
Sorrow would be a rarity most beloved
If all could so become it.

KENT
Made she no verbal question?

FIRST GENTLEMAN
Faith, once or twice she heaved the name of "father" 25
Pantingly forth as if it pressed her heart,
Cried "Sisters, sisters, shame of ladies, sisters,
Kent, father, sisters, what, i' th' storm, i' th' night?
Let piety not be believed!" There she shook
The holy water from her heavenly eyes 30
And clamor mastered, then away she started
To deal with grief alone.

KENT
It is the stars,
The stars above us, govern our conditions,
Else one self mate and make could not beget
Such different issues. You spoke not with her since? 35

FIRST GENTLEMAN
No.

KENT
Was this before the King returned?

FIRST GENTLEMAN
No, since.

38: **better tune**: more stable state of mind

40: **yield**: agree, consent

41: **sovereign**: overpowering, like a king; **elbows him**: prods or compels him (to remember)

42: **turned her**: forced her (to seek)

43: **foreign casualties**: chances or opportunities abroad

46: **Detains him from**: keeps him from (seeing)

47: **powers**: armies

48: **afoot**: on the march

50: **dear cause**: important objective

51: **wrap me up**: occupy me

52-53: **grieve...acquaintance**: regret having talked with me

KENT

    Well, sir, the poor distressèd Lear's i' th' town,
    Who sometime in his better tune remembers
    What we are come about, and by no means
    Will yield to see his daughter.

FIRST GENTLEMAN

                    Why, good sir?   40

KENT

    A sovereign shame so elbows him. His own unkindness,
    That stripped her from his benediction, turned her
    To foreign casualties, gave her dear rights
    To his dog-hearted daughters—these things sting
    His mind so venomously that burning shame   45
    Detains him from Cordelia.

FIRST GENTLEMAN

                Alack, poor gentleman!

KENT

    Of Albany's and Cornwall's powers you heard not?

FIRST GENTLEMAN

    'Tis so; they are afoot.

KENT

    Well, sir, I'll bring you to our master Lear,
    And leave you to attend him. Some dear cause   50
    Will in concealment wrap me up a while.
    When I am known aright you shall not grieve
    Lending me this acquaintance. I pray you go
    Along with me.

                                  Exeunt

0: **Location**: The French Camp

0: Stage Direction: ***DOCTOR***: the First Quarto specifies "Doctor" here and at line 11
3: **fumitor**: fumitory, a poisonous herb
3: **furrow-weeds**: weeds that grow in the furrows of a plowed field
4: **burdocks**: weed-like plant; **cuckoo-flowers**: flowers that bloom in the late spring when the cuckoo sings
5: **Darnel**: grass-like weed; **idle**: useless
6: **sustaining corn**: life-giving grain; **centuries**: troops of one hundred soldiers
8: **man's wisdom**: medical knowledge
9: **his**: of his, i.e., Lear's
10: **outward**: visible, material

10: "He that can help him take all my outward worth": Kristen Bush as Cordelia in the 2007 Public Theater production directed by James Lapine
Photo: Michal Daniel

12: **foster-nurse**: most effective or promising treatment
13: **That to provoke in him**: to induce that in him, i.e., to help him sleep
14: **simples operative**: effective treatments
16: **unpublished virtues**: secret cures
17: **Spring**: grow; **aidant and remediate**: helpful and curative
19: **rage**: madness
20: **wants**: lacks; **means**: i.e., sanity

Act 4, Scene 4]

Enter [Queen] CORDELIA, DOCTOR, and others

CORDELIA

   Alack, 'tis he! Why, he was met even now,
   As mad as the racked sea, singing aloud,
   Crowned with rank fumitor and furrow-weeds,
   With burdocks, hemlock, nettles, cuckoo-flowers,
   Darnel, and all the idle weeds that grow   5
   In our sustaining corn. The centuries send forth.
   Search every acre in the high-grown field,
   And bring him to our eye.

                                           [Exit one or more]

                    What can man's wisdom
   In the restoring his bereavèd sense,
   He that can help him take all my outward worth.   10

DOCTOR

   There is means, madam.
   Our foster-nurse of nature is repose,
   The which he lacks. That to provoke in him
   Are many simples operative, whose power
   Will close the eye of anguish.

CORDELIA

                 All blest secrets,   15
   All you unpublished virtues of the earth,
   Spring with my tears, be aidant and remediate
   In the good man's distress!—Seek, seek for him,
   Lest his ungoverned rage dissolve the life
   That wants the means to lead it.   20

               Enter MESSENGER

22: preparation: army

23-24: Scene: O dear father...I go about: Jonathan Miller, director of the BBC-TV 1982 production, sought to emphasize some of the play's spiritual themes. When Cordelia says that she is tending to her father's business, there is a sense in which she's also referring to God the Father. The actress, Brenda Blethyn, crosses herself reverently while saying it. Also, Edgar, disguised as Poor Tom, wears a crown of thorns, an allusion to Jesus Christ.

Costume rendering for Cordelia by Susan Tsu from the 2004 Oregon Shakespeare Festival production directed by James Edmondson
Courtesy of the Oregon Shakespeare Festival

26: importuant: importunate, pleading

27: blown: swollen, prideful

MESSENGER

News, madam.   20
    The British powers are marching hitherward.

CORDELIA
    'Tis known before; our preparation stands
    In expectation of them.—O dear father,
    It is thy business that I go about;
    Therefore great France   25
    My mourning and importuant tears hath pitied.
    No blown ambition doth our arms incite,
    But love, dear love, and our aged father's right.
    Soon may I hear and see him!

Exeunt

0: Location: Gloucester's house

Set design for the 1959 production at the Shakespeare Memorial Theatre in Stratford-upon-Avon directed by Glen Byam Shaw

Rare Book and Special Collection Library, University of Illinois at Urbana-Champaign

1: **my brother's powers**: i.e., Albany's armies

4: **spake**: spoke

6: **What might...to him**: i.e., What do my sister's letters impart to him?

8: **is posted**: has gone quickly

9: **ignorance**: stupidity

12: **his**: i.e., Gloucester's

13: **nighted**: dark, blinded to; **descry**: find out

Act 4, Scene 5]

Enter REGAN and Steward [OSWALD]

REGAN
But are my brother's powers set forth?

OSWALD
                    Ay, madam.

REGAN
Himself in person there?

OSWALD
                Madam, with much ado.
Your sister is the better soldier.

REGAN
Lord Edmund spake not with your lord at home?

OSWALD
No, madam.   5

REGAN
What might import my sister's letters to him?

OSWALD
I know not, lady.

REGAN
Faith, he is posted hence on serious matter.
It was great ignorance, Gloucester's eyes being out,
To let him live. Where he arrives he moves   10
All hearts against us. Edmund, I think, is gone,
In pity of his misery, to dispatch
His nighted life, moreover to descry
The strength o' th' army.

15: **must needs after**: need to follow

18: **charged my duty**: emphasized the importance of obeying her

20: **Transport**: tell me; **Belike**: perhaps

24: **late being**: recent presence

25: **oeillades**: amorous glances

26: **of her bosom**: in her confidence

29: **take this note**: take note of this

30: **have talked**: are in agreement

31: **convenient**: suitable

32: **gather more**: read into or infer

33: **this**: i.e., information, letter, or token of her affection

OSWALD
  I must needs after with my letters, madam.   15

REGAN
  Our troop sets forth tomorrow. Stay with us.
  The ways are dangerous.

OSWALD
                    I may not, madam.
  My lady charged my duty in this business.

REGAN
  Why should she write to Edmund? Might not you
  Transport her purposes by word? Belike   20
  Something, I know not what. I'll love thee much:
  Let me unseal the letter.

OSWALD
                  Madam, I'd rather—

REGAN
  I know your lady does not love her husband.
  I am sure of that, and at her late being here
  She gave strange oeillades and most speaking looks   25
  To noble Edmund. I know you are of her bosom.

OSWALD
  I, madam?

REGAN
  I speak in understanding, for I know't.
  Therefore I do advise you take this note.
  My lord is dead. Edmund and I have talked,   30
  And more convenient is he for my hand
  Than for your lady's. You may gather more.
  If you do find him, pray you give him this,
  And when your mistress hears thus much from you,
  I pray desire her call her wisdom to her.   35
  So, farewell.

38: **Preferment**: reward, promotion

40: **what lady**: The First Folio prints "what party", meaning "which sister".

If you do chance to hear of that blind traitor,
Preferment falls on him that cuts him off.

OSWALD
Would I could meet him, madam. I should show
What lady I do follow.

REGAN

                     Fare thee well.   40
                                                  Exeunt

1: **that same hill**: the hill we discussed earlier (see 4.1.72-74)

Pal Aron as Edgar and David Hargreaves as Gloucester in the 2005 Royal
Shakespeare Company production directed by Bill Alexander
Photo: Donald Cooper

Act 4, Scene 6]

Enter EDGAR [disguised as a peasant, with a staff,
guiding the blind] GLOUCESTER

GLOUCESTER
When shall we come to th' top of that same hill?

EDGAR
You do climb up it now. Look, how we labor.

GLOUCESTER
Methinks the ground is even.

EDGAR
        Horrible steep.
Hark, do you hear the sea?

GLOUCESTER
       No, truly.

EDGAR
Why, then your other senses grow imperfect   5
By your eyes' anguish.

GLOUCESTER
      So may it be indeed.
Methinks thy voice is altered, and thou speak'st
With better phrase and matter than thou didst.

EDGAR
You're much deceived. In nothing am I changed
But in my garments.

GLOUCESTER
     Methinks you're better spoken.   10

13: **choughs**: crow-like birds; **midway air**: the air halfway between the top of the cliff and the sea below

14: **so gross**: as large

15: **samphire**: herb used for pickling

18: **barque**: bark, a small sailing ship

19: **diminished...cock**: shrunk to the size of a cockboat, a small boat that accompanies a large ship

23: **my brain turn**: i.e., I get dizzy

26: **all beneath the moon**: i.e., everything on earth

27: **upright**: up and down

30: **Prosper it**: increase its value

33: **trifle**: play with

EDGAR
Come on, sir, here's the place. Stand still. How fearful
And dizzy 'tis to cast one's eyes so low!
The crows and choughs that wing the midway air
Show scarce so gross as beetles. Halfway down
Hangs one that gathers samphire, dreadful trade!   15
Methinks he seems no bigger than his head.
The fishermen that walk upon the beach
Appear like mice, and yon tall anchoring barque
Diminished to her cock, her cock a buoy
Almost too small for sight. The murmuring surge   20
That on the unnumbered idle pebbles chafes
Cannot be heard, it's so high. I'll look no more,
Lest my brain turn and the deficient sight
Topple down headlong.

GLOUCESTER
                    Set me where you stand.

EDGAR
Give me your hand. You are now within a foot   25
Of th' extreme verge. For all beneath the moon
Would I not leap upright.

GLOUCESTER
                    Let go my hand.
Here, friend, 's another purse; in it a jewel
Well worth a poor man's taking. Fairies and gods
Prosper it with thee! Go thou farther off.   30
Bid me farewell, and let me hear thee going.

EDGAR
Now fare you well, good sir.

                                        [He stands aside]

GLOUCESTER
                    With all my heart.

EDGAR
[Aside] Why I do trifle thus with his despair
Is done to cure it.

38: **To quarrel with**: in rebellion against; **opposeless**: irrefutable

39: **snuff**: useless; **of nature**: of my life

42: **conceit**: imagination

44: **Yields**: consents

45: **by this**: by this time

47: **pass**: expire, die

48: **What**: who

50: **precipitating**: falling

51: **shivered**: shattered or cracked

53: **a-length**: in length

57: **chalky bourn**: white cliff (part of the White Cliffs of Dover)

58: **a-height**: on high; **shrill-gorged**: shrill-throated

GLOUCESTER
                    O you mighty gods,

                                                   [He kneels]
This world I do renounce, and in your sights   35
Shake patiently my great affliction off!
If I could bear it longer, and not fall
To quarrel with your great opposeless wills,
My snuff and loathèd part of nature should
Burn itself out. If Edgar live, O bless him!—   40
Now, fellow, fare thee well.

EDGAR
                         Gone, sir. Farewell.
                              [GLOUCESTER falls forward]
[Aside] And yet I know not how conceit may rob
The treasury of life, when life itself
Yields to the theft. Had he been where he thought,
By this had thought been past.—Alive or dead?   45
[To GLOUCESTER] Ho, you, sir, friend; hear you, sir? Speak.
[Aside] Thus might he pass indeed. Yet he revives.
[To GLOUCESTER] What are you, sir?

GLOUCESTER
                              Away, and let me die.

EDGAR
Hadst thou been aught but gossamer, feathers, air,
So many fathom down precipitating   50
Thou hadst shivered like an egg. But thou dost breathe,
Hast heavy substance, bleed'st not, speak'st, art sound.
Ten masts a-length make not the altitude
Which thou hast perpendicularly fell.
Thy life's a miracle. Speak yet again.   55

GLOUCESTER
But have I fallen, or no?

EDGAR
From the dread summit of this chalky bourn.
Look up a-height. The shrill-gorged lark so far
Cannot be seen or heard. Do but look up.

61: **benefit**: consolation

63: **beguile**: charm

71: **whelked**: twisted

72: **happy father**: fortunate old man

73: **clearest**: purest, most righteous

73-74: **who...impossibilities**: who achieved their fame by doing things humans cannot do

76-77: **till...“Enough, enough”**: i.e., until the sources of my suffering cease of their own accord

GLOUCESTER
    Alack, I have no eyes. 60
    Is wretchedness deprived that benefit
    To end itself by death? 'Twas yet some comfort
    When misery could beguile the tyrant's rage
    And frustrate his proud will.

EDGAR
                  Give me your arm.
    Up. So, how now? Feel you your legs? You stand. 65

GLOUCESTER
    Too well, too well.

EDGAR
             This is above all strangeness.
    Upon the crown of the cliff what thing was that
    Which parted from you?

GLOUCESTER
             A poor unfortunate beggar.

EDGAR
    As I stood here below, methoughts his eyes
    Were two full moons. A had a thousand noses, 70
    Horns whelked and wavèd like the enridgèd sea.
    It was some fiend. Therefore, thou happy father,
    Think that the clearest gods, who made their honors
    Of men's impossibilities, have preserved thee.

GLOUCESTER
    I do remember now. Henceforth I'll bear 75
    Affliction till it do cry out itself
    "Enough, enough," and die. That thing you speak of,
    I took it for a man. Often would it say
    "The fiend, the fiend!" He led me to that place.

80: Stage Direction: *Enter LEAR mad [crowned with weeds and flowers]*: Kevin Kline as Lear in the 2007 Public Theater production directed by James Lapine
Photo: Michal Daniel

81-82: **The safer...thus**: i.e., No one in his right mind would dress himself in such a way.

83: **touch**: arrest; **coining**: minting coins

84: **side-piercing**: heart-rending, an allusion to the suffering of Christ

85: **Nature...respect**: Life offers more examples of human tragedy than art; **press-money**: payment for enlisting

86: **crow-keeper**: laborer hired to keep the crows from eating the grain

86-87: **Draw...yard**: i.e., Draw your bow to the full length of the arrow for me.

88: **do it**: do the trick (to capture the mouse); **gauntlet**: glove thrown down as a challenge; **prove it**: use it to challenge

89: **brown bills**: spears or soldiers carrying spears; **word**: password

90: **Sweet marjoram**: herb thought to ease mental disease

93: **Ha, Gonoril! Ha, Regan!**: appears only in the First Quarto

93: **like a dog**: as a dog fawns on his master, hoping for food

94: **I had...there**: i.e., I had the wisdom of an old man before I could even grow a beard (when I was still young)

94-96: **To say...divinity**: i.e., It goes against the Bible for them to flatter me by agreeing with everything I said. See James 5:12: "let your yea be yea and your nay, nay."

100: **ague-proof**: immune from sickness

EDGAR
    Bear free and patient thoughts.
                    Enter LEAR mad, [crowned with weeds and flowers]
                            But who comes here?   80
    The safer sense will ne'er accommodate
    His master thus.

LEAR
    No, they cannot touch me for coining. I am the King himself.

EDGAR
    O thou side-piercing sight!

LEAR
    Nature is above art in that respect. There's your press-money. That   85
    fellow handles his bow like a crow-keeper. Draw me a clothier's
    yard. Look, look, a mouse! Peace, peace, this piece of toasted cheese
    will do it. There's my gauntlet. I'll prove it on a giant. Bring up the
    brown bills. O, well flown, bird, in the air. Ha! Give the word.

EDGAR
    Sweet marjoram.   90

LEAR
    Pass.

GLOUCESTER
    I know that voice.

LEAR
    Ha, Gonoril! Ha, Regan! They flattered me like a dog, and told me
    I had white hairs in my beard ere the black ones were there. To say
    "ay" and "no" to every thing that I said "ay" and "no" to was no   95
    good divinity. When the rain came to wet me once, and the wind to
    make me chatter, when the thunder would not peace at my bidding,
    there I found them, there I smelt them out. Go to, they are not men
    of their words. They told me I was everything; 'tis a lie, I am not
    ague-proof.   100

101: **trick**: peculiarity

AY EVERY INCH A KING   ACT IV SCENE IV

102: "Ay, every inch a king": Engraving by John Byam Shaw, ca. 1900

Courtesy of the Folger Shakespeare Library

104: **cause**: offense

106: **goes to't**: copulates

107: **Does lecher**: copulates promiscuously

110: **Got...sheets**: begotten lawfully, i.e., by a married couple; **To't, luxury, pell mell**: have sex, lechery, quickly

112: **Whose...snow**: whose icy countenance suggests she is frigid between her legs

113: **That minces**: who acts as if she has; **does shake the head**: moves the head from side to side (showing scorn)

115: **The fitchew...to't**: neither the polecat nor the well-pastured horse has sex

116: **Down from the waist**: from the waist down

117: **centaurs**: mythical creatures whose upper halves are human and whose lower halves are equine

118: **to the girdle**: only from the waist up; **inherit**: possess

122: **civet**: musk perfume (see note 3.4.90)

126: **piece**: 1) masterpiece, and 2) fragment

126-127: **This...naught**: i.e., This great universe shall exhaust itself out of existence.

GLOUCESTER
　The trick of that voice I do well remember.
　Is't not the King?

LEAR
　　　　　　Ay, every inch a king.

　　　　　　　　　　　　　　　[GLOUCESTER kneels]

　When I do stare, see how the subject quakes!
　I pardon that man's life. What was thy cause?
　Adultery? Thou shalt not die. Die for adultery.　　　　　　105
　No, the wren goes to't, and the small gilded fly
　Does lecher in my sight.
　Let copulation thrive, for Gloucester's bastard son
　Was kinder to his father than my daughters
　Got 'tween the lawful sheets. To't, luxury, pell-mell,　　110
　For I lack soldiers. Behold yon simp'ring dame,
　Whose face between her forks presageth snow,
　That minces virtue, and does shake the head
　To hear of pleasure's name:
　The fitchew, nor the soilèd horse goes to't　　　　　　115
　With a more riotous appetite. Down from the waist
　They're centaurs, though women all above.
　But to the girdle do the gods inherit;
　Beneath is all the fiends. There's hell, there's darkness,
　There's the sulphury pit, burning, scalding,　　　　　　120
　Stench, consummation. Fie, fie, fie; pah, pah!
　Give me an ounce of civet, good apothecary,
　To sweeten my imagination.
　There's money for thee.

GLOUCESTER
　　　　　　　O, let me kiss that hand!

LEAR
　Here, wipe it first; it smells of mortality.　　　　　　125

GLOUCESTER
　O ruined piece of nature! This great world
　Shall so wear out to naught. Do you know me?

128: **squiny on**: squint at
132: **I would not take this from report**: i.e., I would not have believed this if it had been reported to me; **it is**: and yet, here it is, incredibly enough
135: **case of eyes**: i.e., eye sockets
137: **heavy case**: sad state; **light**: i.e., empty

136-137: "No eyes in your head, nor no money in your purse?": David Hargreaves as Gloucester and Corin Redgrave as Lear in the 2005 Royal Shakespeare Company production directed by Bill Alexander
Photo: Donald Cooper

139: **feelingly**: 1) by means of touch, and 2) painfully
141: **simple**: humble, ordinary
142: **handy-dandy**: i.e., choose whichever hand you like (from a popular children's game)
145: **creature**: poor fellow; **cur**: dog, mongrel
147: **A dog's obeyed in office**: i.e., Even a dog commands obedience when it is in a position of power.

LEAR

I remember thy eyes well enough. Dost thou squiny on me?
No, do thy worst, blind Cupid! I'll not love.
Read thou this challenge. Mark but the penning of't.   130

GLOUCESTER

Were all the letters suns, I could not see one.

EDGAR

[*Aside*] I would not take this from report; it is,
And my heart breaks at it.

LEAR

[*To GLOUCESTER*] Read.

GLOUCESTER

What—with the case of eyes?   135

LEAR

O ho, are you there with me? No eyes in your head, nor no money
in your purse? Your eyes are in a heavy case, your purse in a light;
yet you see how this world goes.

GLOUCESTER

I see it feelingly.

LEAR

What, art mad? A man may see how this world goes with no eyes;   140
look with thy ears. See how yon justice rails upon yon simple
thief. Hark, in thy ear: handy-dandy, which is the thief, which is
the justice? Thou hast seen a farmer's dog bark at a beggar?

GLOUCESTER

Ay, sir.

LEAR

And the creature run from the cur, there thou mightst   145
Behold the great image of authority.
A dog's obeyed in office.

148: **beadle**: parish officer whose duty it was to whip beggars and whores

151: **The usurer hangs the cozener**: i.e., The money lender (who can bribe the judge) hangs the con man.

153-158: **Plate sin...accuser's lips.**: from the First Folio

154: **hurtless breaks**: cracks without injury

158: **glass eyes**: 1) spectacles, and 2) eyes made of glass (to replace his)

159: **scurvy**: corrupt, hypocritical

160: **No tears, now.**: appears only in the First Quarto

162: **matter and impertinency**: profundity and insanity

164: **weep**: cry over

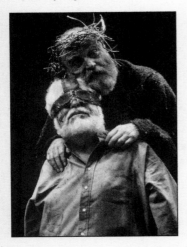

164: "If thou wilt weep my fortune, take my eyes": Ted van Griethuysen as Lear and David Sabin as Gloucester in the 2000 Shakespeare Theatre Company production directed by Michael Kahn

Photo: Carol Rosegg

171: **This' a good block**: this (head) is a good mold for a hat. Here, Lear may be referring to the crown of flowers he has just removed from his head (as one removes a hat before entering a church)

172-173: **to shoe...felt**: to use felt padding instead of metal horseshoes (a tactic employed by armies to surprise their enemies)

173: **in proof**: to the test

Thou rascal beadle, hold thy bloody hand.
Why dost thou lash that whore? Strip thine own back.
Thy blood as hotly lusts to use her in that kind   150
For which thou whip'st her. The usurer hangs the cozener.
Through tattered rags small vices do appear;
Robes and furred gowns hides all. Plate sin with gold,
And the strong lance of justice hurtless breaks;
Arm it in rags, a pigmy's straw does pierce it.   155
None does offend, none, I say none. I'll able 'em.
Take that of me, my friend, who have the power
To seal th' accuser's lips. Get thee glass eyes,
And, like a scurvy politician, seem
To see the things thou dost not. No tears, now.   160
Pull off my boots. Harder, harder! So.

EDGAR
  [*Aside*] O, matter and impertinency mixed—
  Reason in madness!

LEAR
  If thou wilt weep my fortune, take my eyes.
  I know thee well enough: thy name is Gloucester.   165
  Thou must be patient. We came crying hither.
  Thou know'st, the first time that we smell the air
  We wail and cry. I will preach to thee. Mark me.

GLOUCESTER
  Alack, alack, the day!

LEAR
  [*Removing his crown of weeds*] When we are born, we cry that we
      are come   170
  To this great stage of fools. This' a good block.
  It were a delicate stratagem to shoe
  A troop of horse with felt; I'll put 't in proof,
  And when I have stol'n upon these son-in-laws,
  Then kill, kill, kill, kill, kill, kill!   175
                                    Enter three GENTLEMEN

Edwin Forrest as Lear: Photogravure by Gebbie & Co., ca. 1897
Courtesy of the Library of Congress

179: **natural fool of Fortune**: born to be a source of amusement to Fortune
181: **cut to the brains**: mentally ill
183: **seconds**: supporters
184: **of salt**: of salty tears
186: **Ay...Good sir**: appears only in the First Quarto
186: **laying**: keeping down
187: **die bravely**: 1) die courageously, or 2) die in royal finery, but also, 3) copulate vigorously, hence the following reference to bridegroom; **smug**: 1) elegantly dressed, but also, 2) satisfied with himself as a lover
188: **jovial**: 1) majestic like Jove, and 2) jolly
189: **masters**: good sirs
191: **life**: cause for optimism; **an**: if
192: **Sa, sa, sa, sa**: cry used by hunters in pursuit of game
195: **general curse**: i.e., Eve's primordial sin
196: **twain**: 1) Regan and Gonoril, and 2) Adam and Eve; i.e., the two halves of the divided

FIRST GENTLEMAN
> O, here he is. Lay hands upon him, sirs.
> [*To LEAR*] Your most dear daughter—

LEAR
> No rescue? What, a prisoner? I am e'en
> The natural fool of Fortune. Use me well.
> You shall have ransom. Let me have a surgeon;   180
> I am cut to the brains.

FIRST GENTLEMAN
> You shall have anything.

LEAR
> No seconds? All myself?
> Why, this would make a man a man of salt,
> To use his eyes for garden water-pots,   185
> Ay, and laying autumn's dust.

FIRST GENTLEMAN
>   Good sir—

LEAR
> I will die bravely, like a smug bridegroom.
> What, I will be jovial. Come, come,
> I am a king, my masters, know you that?

FIRST GENTLEMAN
> You are a royal one, and we obey you.   190

LEAR
> Then there's life in't. Nay, an you get it, you shall get it with
> running. Sa, sa, sa, sa!
>   *Exit running [pursued by two GENTLEMEN.]*

FIRST GENTLEMAN
> A sight most pitiful in the meanest wretch,
> Past speaking in a king. Thou hast one daughter
> Who redeems nature from the general curse   195
> Which twain hath brought her to.

197: **gentle**: noble

198: **speed you**: Godspeed, may God bless you

199: **aught**: anything; **toward**: on the horizon

200: **vulgar**: widely spoken of

203: **on speedy foot**: on horseback; **the main**: the majority of the troops

203-204: **descriers...thoughts**: i.e., lookouts expect the army's arrival within hours

208: **worser spirit**: depressive thoughts

210: **father**: honorific term used for older men, but ironic here because Edgar is speaking to his father (see also lines 4.6.72, 242, and 271)

EDGAR
  Hail, gentle sir.

FIRST GENTLEMAN
  Sir, speed you. What's your will?

EDGAR
  Do you hear aught, sir, of a battle toward?

FIRST GENTLEMAN
  Most sure and vulgar, everyone hears that,   200
  That can distinguish sense.

EDGAR
  But, by your favor, how near's the other army?

FIRST GENTLEMAN
  Near and on speedy foot, the main; descriers
  Stands on the hourly thoughts.

EDGAR
                                      I thank you, sir. That's all.

FIRST GENTLEMAN
  Though that the Queen on special cause is here,   205
  Her army is moved on.

EDGAR
                                      I thank you, sir.

                                      Exit [GENTLEMAN]

GLOUCESTER
  You ever gentle gods, take my breath from me.
  Let not my worser spirit tempt me again
  To die before you please.

EDGAR
  Well pray you, father.   210

210: what: who

211: tame: weak, vulnerable

212: known: personally experienced; **feeling**: heartfelt

213: Am pregnant to: have the capacity to offer

214: 'biding: nearby dwelling

215: benison: blessing

216: boot: reward; **to boot**: in addition; **proclaimed prize**: one who has been publicly declared to have a price on his head; **happy**: fortunate

217: framed flesh: born

219: thyself remember: pray for yourself

220: friendly: welcome, longed for

222: published: proclaimed

224: Like: the same

225: Ch'ill: "I will" (Edgar speaks in a rustic dialect to represent peasant speech); **vurther 'cagion**: further occasion, more cause than this

GLOUCESTER

Now, good sir, what are you?   210

EDGAR

A most poor man, made tame to Fortune's blows,
Who by the art of known and feeling sorrows
Am pregnant to good pity. Give me your hand,
I'll lead you to some 'biding.

GLOUCESTER

[*Rising*] Hearty thanks.
The bounty and the benison of heaven   215
To send thee boot to boot.

Enter Steward [OSWALD]

OSWALD

A proclaimed prize! Most happy!
That eyeless head of thine was first framed flesh
To raise my fortunes. Thou most unhappy traitor,
Briefly thyself remember. The sword is out
That must destroy thee.

GLOUCESTER

Now let thy friendly hand   220
Put strength enough to't.

OSWALD

[*To EDGAR*] Wherefore, bold peasant,
Darest thou support a published traitor? Hence,
Lest the infection of his fortune take
Like hold on thee. Let go his arm.

EDGAR

Ch'ill not let go, sir, without vurther 'cagion.   225

OSWALD

Let go, slave, or thou diest.

227: **go your gate**: go your own way; **An chud**: if I could

228: **swaggered**: intimidated, bullied

228-229: **it would...vortnight**: i.e., I would not have survived more than a fortnight (a few weeks, though "fortnight" means two weeks).

229-230: **che vor' ye**: I warrant you

230: **costard**: head (literally, apple)

233: **no...foins**: i.e., your thrusts mean nothing to me

234: **Villain**: serf

236: **about me**: on my person

238: **Upon...party**: on the British side (of the conflict)

239: **serviceable**: officious

244: **sorrow**: sorrowful

245: **deathsman**: executioner

246: **Leave**: by your leave, with your permission; **wax**: wax seal on the letter

247: **rip**: 1) rip open, or 2) rip out

EDGAR

Good gentleman, go your gate. Let poor volk pass. An chud have
been swaggered out of my life, it would not have been so long as
'tis by a vortnight. Nay, come not near the old man. Keep out, che
vor' ye, or I'll try whether your costard or my baton be the   230
harder; I'll be plain with you.

OSWALD

Out, dunghill!

They fight

EDGAR

Chill pick your teeth, sir. Come, no matter for your foins.

[EDGAR knocks him down]

OSWALD

Slave, thou hast slain me. Villain, take my purse.
If ever thou wilt thrive, bury my body,   235
And give the letters which thou find'st about me
To Edmund, Earl of Gloucester. Seek him out
Upon the British party. O, untimely death! Death!

He dies

EDGAR

I know thee well—a serviceable villain,
As duteous to the vices of thy mistress   240
As badness would desire.

GLOUCESTER

What, is he dead?

EDGAR

Sit you down, father. Rest you.

[GLOUCESTER sits]

Let's see his pockets. These letters that he speaks of
May be my friends. He's dead; I am only sorrow
He had no other deathsman. Let us see.   245
Leave, gentle wax; and manners, blame us not.
To know our enemies' minds, we'd rip their hearts;
Their papers is more lawful.

250: **him**: i.e., Albany; **want not**: is not lacking

251: **fruitfully**: plentifully, successfully; **There is nothing done**: i.e., nothing will have been accomplished

253: **supply the place**: take his place; **for your labor**: 1) as payment for your efforts, and 2) as the place for your sexual labors

255: **and for...venture**: i.e., and willing to risk her own fortune for you

256: **O indistinguished...wit**: i.e., how indiscriminate women are in choosing who they bring to their bed to sate their appetites. (Given Edgar's disgust with Gonoril's adulterous plans, "space" is clearly intended here to refer to the vagina.)

259: **Thee I'll rake up**: i.e., I'll merely cover your body (a burial in an unmarked grave suitable for a felon or someone of low status); **post unsanctified**: sinful messenger

260: **in...time**: at the right moment

261: **ungracious**: depraved; **strike the sight**: amaze the eyes

262: **Of the...Duke**: of Albany, the target of this murderous plot; **For him 'tis well**: i.e., it is fortunate for him

264: **How...sense**: how resilient my loathsome mental faculties must be

265: **stand up**: am still standing; **ingenious feeling**: conscious awareness

267: **fencèd**: fenced off

268: **wrong imaginations lose**: delusional thoughts should forget

271: **bestow**: safely lodge

[Reads the letter]
Let our reciprocal vows be remembered. You have many opportu-
nities to cut him off. If your will want not, time and place will be   250
fruitfully offered. There is nothing done if he return the conqueror;
then am I the prisoner, and his bed my jail, from the loathed
warmth whereof, deliver me, and supply the place for your labor.
      Your—wife, so I would say—your affectionate
      servant, and for you her own for venture, Gonoril.   255
O indistinguished space of woman's wit –
A plot upon her virtuous husband's life,
And the exchange my brother!—Here in the sands,
Thee I'll rake up, the post unsanctified
Of murderous lechers, and in the mature time   260
With this ungracious paper strike the sight
Of the death-practiced Duke. For him 'tis well
That of thy death and business I can tell.

        [Exit with the body]

GLOUCESTER
  The King is mad. How stiff is my vile sense,
  That I stand up and have ingenious feeling   265
  Of my huge sorrows! Better I were distraught;
  So should my thoughts be fencèd from my griefs,
  And woes by wrong imaginations lose
  The knowledge of themselves.

      A drum afar off. [Enter EDGAR.]

EDGAR
          Give me your hand.
  Far off methinks I hear the beaten drum.   270
  Come, father, I'll bestow you with a friend.

      Exit [EDGAR, guiding GLOUCESTER]

0: Location: The French camp

Set design for the 1959 production at the Shakespeare Memorial Theatre in Stratford-upon-Avon directed by Glen Byam Shaw

Rare Book and Special Collection Library, University of Illinois at Urbana-Champaign

3: **every measure fail me**: all my efforts (to match your goodness) will fail

5: **my reports**: reports of my service to Lear

6: **Nor more, nor clipped**: i.e., neither more nor less; **suited**: dressed

7: **weeds**: ragged cloths

9: **Yet...intent**: were I to reveal my true identity now, my well-made plan would be cut short

10: **My boon**: the favor I seek from you; **know**: acknowledge

11: **meet**: suitable

Act 4, Scene 7]

[*Soft music.*] *Enter CORDELIA, and KENT* [*disguised*].

CORDELIA
O thou good Kent,
How shall I live and work to match thy goodness?
My life will be too short, and every measure fail me.

KENT
To be acknowledged, madam, is o'erpaid.
All my reports go with the modest truth,   5
Nor more, nor clipped, but so.

CORDELIA
                      Be better suited.
These weeds are memories of those worser hours.
I prithee put them off.

KENT
               Pardon me, dear madam.
Yet to be known shortens my made intent.
My boon I make it that you know me not   10
Till time and I think meet.

CORDELIA
               Then be't so, my good lord.
             [*Enter DOCTOR and FIRST GENTLEMAN*]
How does the King?

DOCTOR
           Mad'm, sleeps still.

14: **untuned**: discordant; **wind up**: tune up, as in the tightening of a string on a lute
15: **child-changèd**: changed by (the cruelty of) his children
18: **I' th' sway**: under the control; **arrayed**: arranged comfortably
22: **temperance**: self-control, tranquility
22-23: **Very well...music there!**: appears only in the First Quarto

23: "Louder the music there!": Engraving by John Byam Shaw, ca. 1900
Courtesy of the Folger Shakespeare Library

24: **restoration**: recuperation
27: **reverence**: wisdom, venerable condition

CORDELIA

                    O you kind gods,
Cure this great breach in his abusèd nature;
The untuned and hurrying senses, O wind up
Of this child-changèd father!

DOCTOR

                  So please your Majesty   15
That we may wake the King? He hath slept long.

CORDELIA

Be governed by your knowledge, and proceed
I' th' sway of your own will. Is he arrayed?

FIRST GENTLEMAN

Ay, madam. In the heaviness of his sleep
We put fresh garments on him.   20

DOCTOR

Good madam, be by when we do awake him.
I doubt not of his temperance.

CORDELIA

                  Very well.

DOCTOR

Please you draw near. Louder the music there!

                [LEAR is discovered asleep.]

CORDELIA

O my dear father, restoration hang
Thy medicine on my lips, and let this kiss   25
Repair those violent harms that my two sisters
Have in thy reverence made!

KENT

                Kind and dear princess!

28: **Had you**: Even if you had; **white flakes**: locks of gray hair

29: **Had challenged**: would have demanded

31-34: **To stand...thin helm?**: appears only in the First Quarto

31: **deep**: deep-sounding; **dread-bolted**: dreadful and filled with lightning bolts

33: **cross-lightning**: zigzag lightning; **watch**: keep the watch; go sleepless; *perdu*: *sentinel perdu* (French), an isolated sentinel in a dangerous area

34: **thin helm**: thin helmet, i.e., balding head

36: **Against**: in front of; **fain**: compelled

37: **rogues forlorn**: forsaken beggars

40: **concluded all**: come to an end all at once

42–73
Rosalind Iden as Cordelia and Donald Wolfit as Lear
Julia Ford as Cordelia and Trevor Peacock as Lear

45: **wheel of fire**: a hellish torment for the sinful (from the myth of Ixion, a murderer condemned to have his crime purged by a fire); **that**: so that

48: **far wide**: 1) wide of the mark, and 2) lost and wandering afar

48: "You're a spirit, I know. Where did you die?": Ted van Griethuysen as Lear, Monique Holt as Cordelia, and the Ensemble in the 2000 Shakespeare Theatre Company production directed by Michael Kahn

Photo: Carol Rosegg

CORDELIA
  Had you not been their father, these white flakes
  Had challenged pity of them. Was this a face
  To be exposed against the warring winds,   30
  To stand against the deep dread-bolted thunder
  In the most terrible and nimble stroke
  Of quick cross-lightning, to watch—poor *perdu*—
  With this thin helm? Mine injurer's mean'st dog,
  Though he had bit me, should have stood that night   35
  Against my fire. And wast thou fain, poor father,
  To hovel thee with swine and rogues forlorn
  In short and musty straw? Alack, alack,
  'Tis wonder that thy life and wits at once
  Had not concluded all! [*To DOCTOR*] He wakes. Speak to him.   40

DOCTOR
  Madam, do you; 'tis fittest.

CORDELIA
  [*To LEAR*] How does my royal lord? How fares your Majesty?

LEAR
  You do me wrong to take me out o' th' grave.
  Thou art a soul in bliss, but I am bound
  Upon a wheel of fire, that mine own tears   45
  Do scald like molten lead.

CORDELIA
                Sir, do you know me.

LEAR
  You're a spirit, I know. Where did you die?

CORDELIA
  [*To DOCTOR*] Still, still far wide!

DOCTOR
  He's scarce awake. Let him alone a while.

tracks 28–30

42–73
Rosalind Iden as Cordelia and Donald Wolfit as Lear
Julia Ford as Cordelia and Trevor Peacock as Lear

51: **abused**: confused, ill treated by my own senses

52: **another thus**: another person so bewildered

55: Scene: **O look upon me, sir**: Edwin Forrest's (1806-1872) Lear begged for salvation, and Tommaso Salvini (1829-1915) played Lear as humiliated and self-reproachful. In Peter Brook's 1971 film, Paul Scofield appeared to be shrunken, broken, and older, and John Gielguid's (1904-2000) Lear appeared bewildered and sullen.

58: **fond**: senile

60: **Not an hour more nor less**: from the First Folio

63: **mainly**: completely

64: **skill**: mental acuity

LEAR

 Where have I been? Where am I? Fair daylight?   50
 I am mightily abused. I should e'en die with pity
 To see another thus. I know not what to say.
 I will not swear these are my hands. Let's see;
 I feel this pin prick. Would I were assured
 Of my condition.

CORDELIA

         [*Keeling*] O look upon me, sir,   55
 And hold your hands in benediction o'er me.
 No, sir, you must not kneel.

LEAR

          Pray do not mock.
 I am a very foolish, fond old man,
 Fourscore and upward,
 Not an hour more nor less, and to deal plainly,   60
 I fear I am not in my perfect mind.
 Methinks I should know you, and know this man;
 Yet I am doubtful, for I am mainly ignorant
 What place this is, and all the skill I have
 Remembers not these garments, nor I know not   65
 Where I did lodge last night. Do not laugh at me,
 For, as I am a man, I think this lady
 To be my child, Cordelia.

CORDELIA

         And so I am, I am.

LEAR

 Be your tears wet? Yes, faith. I pray, weep not.
 If you have poison for me, I will drink it.   70
 I know you do not love me, for your sisters
 Have, as I do remember, done me wrong.
 You have some cause; they have not.

CORDELIA

         No cause, no cause.

75: **abuse me**: 1) deceive me, and also 2) hurt me (by reminding me that I gave away my kingdom)
76: **rage**: frenzy, distemper

Costume rendering for the Doctor from the 1959 production at the Shakespeare Memorial Theatre in Stratford-upon-Avon directed by Glen Byam Shaw

Rare Book and Special Collection Library, University of Illinois at Urbana-Champaign

77-78: **and yet...he has lost**: appears only in the First Quarto

78: **even o'er**: go over in his memory

80: **further settling**: he is further settled

85-95: **Holds it...battle's fought**: appears only in the First Quarto

85: **Holds it true**: i.e., does it still hold true

87: **conductor**: leader

LEAR
  Am I in France?

KENT
  In your own kingdom, sir.

LEAR
                    Do not abuse me.   75

DOCTOR
  Be comforted, good madam. The great rage
  You see is cured in him, and yet it is danger
  To make him even o'er the time he has lost.
  Desire him to go in; trouble him no more
  Till further settling.   80

CORDELIA
  [*To LEAR*] Will't please your Highness walk?

LEAR
  You must bear with me.
  Pray you now, forget and forgive. I am old
  And foolish.
                    Exeunt. Manet KENT and [FIRST] GENTLEMAN.

FIRST GENTLEMAN
  Holds it true, sir, that the Duke   85
  Of Cornwall was so slain?

KENT
                    Most certain, sir.

FIRST GENTLEMAN
  Who is conductor of his people?

KENT
                              As 'tis said,
  The bastard son of Gloucester.

91: **look about**: assess the situation carefully; **powers of the kingdom**: i.e., British armies

93: **arbitrement**: arbitration by force of arms; **like**: likely

94: **My point...wrought**: my fate (literally, the period at the end of my life's sentence) will be thoroughly determined

95: **Or**: Either; **as**: according to how

FIRST GENTLEMAN

                          They say Edgar,
His banished son, is with the Earl of Kent
In Germany.

KENT

                   Report is changeable.   90
'Tis time to look about. The powers of the kingdom
Approach apace.

FIRST GENTLEMAN

The arbitrement is like to be bloody. Fare you well, sir.

                                        [Exit]

KENT

My point and period will be throughly wrought,
Or well or ill, as this day's battle's fought.   95
                                       Exit

[King Lear

Act 5

0: Location: The British camp near Dover

Watercolor scene sketch from the promptbook for Charles Kean's 1858 production
Courtesy of the Folger Shakespeare Library

1: **Know**: Inquire; **last purpose hold**: most recent plan (to fight) remains firm
2: **since**: since then; **advised by aught**: influenced by anything
3: **abdication**: resignation
4: **self-reproving**: self-recrimination; **his constant pleasure**: the decision he has settled on
5: **man**: i.e., Oswald; **miscarried**: gone amiss
6: **doubted**: feared
9: **honored**: honorable
11: **forfended place**: forbidden place, i.e., the place on her body forbidden to him by injunctions against adultery
12-14: **That thought...call hers**: appears only in the First Quarto
12: **abuses**: degrades
13: **conjunct and bosomed**: sexually intimate
14: **As far as we call hers**: as fully as a man can be with a woman

Act 5, Scene 1]

Enter EDMUND, REGAN, and their powers

EDMUND
Know of the Duke if his last purpose hold,
Or whether since he is advised by aught
To change the course. He's full of abdication
And self-reproving. Bring his constant pleasure.

[Exit one or more]

REGAN
Our sister's man is certainly miscarried.   5

EDMUND
'Tis to be doubted, madam.

REGAN
                  Now, sweet lord,
You know the goodness I intend upon you.
Tell me but truly—but then speak the truth—
Do you not love my sister?

EDMUND
               Ay, honored love.

REGAN
But have you never found my brother's way   10
To the forfended place?

EDMUND
That thought abuses you.

REGAN
            I am doubtful
That you have been conjunct and bosomed with her,
As far as we call hers.

15: **endure**: tolerate

16: **familiar**: intimate

17: **Fear me not**: you need not worry about me in such matters

18-19: [*Aside*]**...and me**: appears only in the First Quarto

20: **bemet**: met

22: **rigor of our state**: i.e., harshness of our governance

23-28: **Where I...speak nobly**: appears only in the First Quarto

23: **cry out**: rebel; **Where**: when; **honest**: honorable

24: **For**: as for

25: **touches us as**: concerns us insomuch as

26: **Yet bolds...fear**: i.e., Not only does it embolden the King, but I fear it encourages others as well.

27: **make oppose**: stir up opposition

28: **Why...reasoned**: i.e., Why are we reasoning about why we should fight, when we should be fighting?

30: **domestic poor particulars**: petty household squabbles

32: **ensign of war**: commissioned officers

EDMUND
> No, by mine honor, madam.

REGAN
> I never shall endure her. Dear my lord, 15
> Be not familiar with her.

EDMUND
> Fear me not. She and the duke her husband!
>> *Enter ALBANY and GONORIL with troops*

GONORIL
> [*Aside*] I had rather lose the battle than that sister
> Should loosen him and me.

ALBANY
> [*To REGAN*] Our very loving sister, well bemet, 20
> For this I hear: the King is come to his daughter,
> With others whom the rigor of our state
> Forced to cry out. Where I could not be honest
> I never yet was valiant. For this business,
> It touches us as France invades our land; 25
> Yet bold's the King, with others whom I fear.
> Most just and heavy causes make oppose.

EDMUND
> Sir, you speak nobly.

REGAN
> Why is this reasoned?

GONORIL
> Combine together 'gainst the enemy;
> For these domestic poor particulars
> Are not to question here. 30

ALBANY
> Let us then determine with the ensign of war
> On our proceedings.

33-34: **I shall...your tent**: appears only in the First Quarto

36: **convenient**: appropriate

37: **I know the riddle**: i.e., I see all too clearly why she insists that I accompany her: she doesn't want me to be alone with Edmund.

40: **this letter**: Gonoril's letter to Edmund (removed from Oswald after he was killed; see line 4.6.236)

43: **prove**: demonstrate in combat

44: **avouchèd**: acknowledged; **miscarry**: die in battle

46: **machination**: plotting (to kill you)

EDMUND
                    I shall attend you
Presently at your tent.

                                        [Exit with his powers]

REGAN
                    Sister, you'll go with us?

GONORIL
    No.   35

REGAN
    'Tis most convenient. Pray you go with us.

GONORIL
    [Aside] O ho, I know the riddle! *[To REGAN]* I will go.
                        Enter EDGAR [disguised as a peasant]

EDGAR
    [To ALBANY] If e'er your grace had speech with man so poor,
    Hear me one word.

ALBANY
                    [To the others] I'll overtake you.
                        [Exeunt. Manet ALBANY and EDGAR]

                                        Speak.

EDGAR
    Before you fight the battle, ope this letter.   40
    If you have victory, let the trumpet sound
    For him that brought it. Wretched though I seem,
    I can produce a champion that will prove
    What is avouchèd there. If you miscarry,
    Your business of the world hath so an end,   45
    And machination ceases. Fortune love you—

ALBANY
    Stay till I have read the letter.

51: **o'erlook**: glance at

53: **guess**: assessment

54: **discovery**: reconnoitering

55: **We...time**: i.e., We will be prepared for whatever happens.

57: **jealous**: wary

58: **adder**: poisonous snake

62: **hardly**: with difficulty; **carry...side**: fulfill my half of our reciprocal vows of love

64: **countenance**: support, authority

66: **taking off**: killing

69: **Shall**: they shall

69-70: **my state...debate**: i.e., I must maintain my position with force not with words

EDGAR
    I was forbid it.
    When time shall serve, let but the herald cry,
    And I'll appear again.   50

ALBANY
    Why, fare thee well. I will o'erlook the paper.

[Exit EDGAR]
Enter EDMUND

EDMUND
    The enemy's in view; draw up your powers.

[EDMUND offers ALBANY a paper]

    Here is the guess of their great strength and forces
    By diligent discovery; but your haste
    Is now urged on you.

ALBANY
                      We will greet the time.   55

[Exit]

EDMUND
    To both these sisters have I sworn my love,
    Each jealous of the other as the stung
    Are of the adder. Which of them shall I take?—
    Both?—one?—or neither? Neither can be enjoyed,
    If both remain alive. To take the widow   60
    Exasperates, makes mad, her sister Gonoril,
    And hardly shall I carry out my side,
    Her husband being alive. Now then, we'll use
    His countenance for the battle, which being done,
    Let her that would be rid of him devise   65
    His speedy taking off. As for the mercy
    Which he intends to Lear and to Cordelia,
    The battle done, and they within our power,
    Shall never see his pardon; for my state
    Stands on me to defend, not to debate.   70

Exit

0: Location: The battlefield

6: "King Lear hath lost, he and his daughter ta'en:" John Wood as Lear and Alex
Kingston as Cordelia in the 1991 Royal Shakespeare Company production directed
by Nicholas Hytner
Photo: Donald Cooper

0: Stage Direction: *Alarum*: trumpet call to arms
1: **father**: venerated old man (see note 4.6.210)
2: **host**: source of shelter
4: Stage Direction: *Alarum and retreat*: trumpet call for withdrawal
11: **Ripeness is all**: i.e., Timing is everything (we do not leave this world till it is our
time).
12: **And that's true too**: from the First Folio

*Alarum. Enter the powers of France over the stage led by
CORDELIA with her father in her hand. Then enter EDGAR
[disguised as a peasant, guiding] GLOUCESTER.*

EDGAR
Here, father, take the shadow of this bush
For your good host; pray that the right may thrive.
If ever I return to you again
I'll bring you comfort.

Exit

GLOUCESTER
Grace go with you, sir.
Alarum and retreat. [Enter EDGAR.]

EDGAR
Away, old man. Give me thy hand. Away.   5
King Lear hath lost, he and his daughter ta'en.
Give me thy hand. Come on.

GLOUCESTER
No farther, sir. A man may rot even here.

EDGAR
What, in ill thoughts again? Men must endure
Their going hence even as their coming hither.   10
Ripeness is all. Come on.

GLOUCESTER
And that's true too.

[Exit EDGAR, guiding GLOUCESTER]

0: Location: The British Camp

1: **Good guard**: guard them well
2: **their greater pleasures**: the desires of those in command
3: **That are**: to those who are; **censure**: judge

3-4: "We are not the first / Who with best meaning have incurred the worst":
Corin Redgrave as Lear and Sîan Brooke as Cordelia in the 2005 Royal Shakespeare
Company production directed by Bill Alexander
Photo: Donald Cooper

6: **Fortune**: the goddess of luck; see also lines 1.1.274, 2.1.39, 2.2.155-56, 4.6.211, and
5.3.173
7: **Shall...sisters**: i.e., Are we not even allowed to talk to Gonoril and Reagan before
they put us in jail?
13: **gilded butterflies**: beautifully attired courtiers
16: **take upon 's**: try to solve, assume responsibility for
17: **God's spies**: divine observers of the world who watch events unfold from
heaven; **wear out**: live longer than
18-19: **pacts...moon**: i.e., alliances and cliques that are aligned with those who are
in power and constantly in a state of flux

Act 5, Scene 3]

Enter EDMUND with LEAR and CORDELIA prisoners,
[a CAPTAIN, and soldiers]

EDMUND
  Some officers take them away. Good guard
  Until their greater pleasures best be known
  That are to censure them.

CORDELIA
               [To LEAR] We are not the first
  Who with best meaning have incurred the worst.
  For thee, oppressèd King, am I cast down,   5
  Myself could else outfrown false Fortune's frown.
  Shall we not see these daughters and these sisters?

LEAR
  No, no, no, no. Come, let's away to prison.
  We two alone will sing like birds i' th' cage.
  When thou dost ask me blessing, I'll kneel down   10
  And ask of thee forgiveness; so we'll live,
  And pray, and sing, and tell old tales, and laugh
  At gilded butterflies, and hear poor rogues
  Talk of court news, and we'll talk with them too—
  Who loses and who wins, who's in, who's out,   15
  And take upon 's the mystery of things
  As if we were God's spies; and we'll wear out
  In a walled prison pacts and sects of great ones
  That ebb and flow by th' moon.

EDMUND
               [To Soldiers] Take them away.

Set design for the 1959 production at the Shakespeare Memorial Theatre in Stratford-upon-Avon directed by Glen Byam Shaw

Rare Book and Special Collection Library, University of Illinois at Urbana-Champaign

21: The gods...incense: i.e., The gods themselves will not accept Cordelia's sacrificial rites, but will perform them for her.

22-23: He that...foxes: i.e., Only someone from heaven, bringing a firebrand (a burning stick used to break up a lead of foxes), can separate us from each other again.

24-25: The goodyear...weep: i.e., The years to follow will be kind to us and will destroy our enemies before they have had a chance cause us any more pain

28: advanced: promoted

31: Are as the time is: must adapt to the rigors of the times

32: a sword: i.e., a warrior

32: great employment: important task

32-33: Thy...bear question: there is no room for debate within the important task

35: write "happy": i.e., consider yourself fortunate

37-38: I cannot...I'll do't.: appears only in the First Quarto

39: strain: lineage

41: opposites: enemies

LEAR

    [To CORDELIA] Upon such sacrifices, my Cordelia,   20
    The gods themselves throw incense. Have I caught thee?
    He that parts us shall bring a brand from heaven
    And fire us hence like foxes. Wipe thine eyes.
    The goodyear shall devour 'em, flesh and fell,
    Ere they shall make us weep. We'll see 'em starve first. Come.   25
    [Exeunt. Manet EDMUND and CAPTAIN]

EDMUND

    Come hither, captain. Hark.
    Take thou this note. Go follow them to prison.
    One step I have advanced thee; if thou dost
    As this instructs thee, thou dost make thy way
    To noble fortunes. Know thou this: that men   30
    Are as the time is. To be tender-minded
    Does not become a sword. Thy great employment
    Will not bear question. Either say thou'lt do't,
    Or thrive by other means.

CAPTAIN

    I'll do't, my lord.

EDMUND

    About it, and write "happy" when thou hast done.   35
    Mark, I say, instantly, and carry it so
    As I have set it down.

CAPTAIN

    I cannot draw a cart,
    Nor eat dried oats. If it be man's work, I'll do't.

    Exit.
    Enter Duke [of ALBANY], the two ladies [GONORIL
    and REGAN, another CAPTAIN and] others.

ALBANY

    [To EDMUND] Sir, you have showed today your valiant strain,
    And fortune led you well. You have the captives   40
    That were the opposites of this day's strife.

46: **retention**: imprisonment

47: **age**: advanced age; **title**: royal status

48: **pluck the common bosom**: appeal to the sympathy of the common people

49: **impressed lances**: lancers (soldiers) whom we have recruited

50: **Queen**: i.e., Cordelia, now Queen of France

52: **further space**: a later date

53: **session**: interrogation, trial

53-58: **At this time...fitter place**: appears only in the First Quarto

55-56: **And...sharpness**: i.e., and even the most virtuous of conflicts are reviled by those who have suffered their dire consequences

59: **subject of**: subordinate in

60: **list**: please

61: **pleasure**: desire, objective; **demanded**: taken up, asked about

62: **powers**: troops

64: **immediate**: most pressing

65: **hot**: fast

66-67:"In his own grace he doth exalt himself / More than in your advancement": Rosalind Cash as Gonoril, Ellen Holly as Regan, and the Ensemble in the 1973 Public Theater production directed by Edwin Sherin

Photo: George E. Joseph

67: **your advancement**: the promotions you confer

We do require then of you, so to use them
As we shall find their merits and our safety
May equally determine.

EDMUND

                    Sir, I thought it fit
To send the old and miserable King   45
To some retention and appointed guard,
Whose age has charms in it, whose title more,
To pluck the common bosom on his side
And turn our impressed lances in our eyes
Which do command them. With him I sent the Queen,   50
My reason all the same, and they are ready
Tomorrow, or at further space, to appear
Where you shall hold your session. At this time
We sweat and bleed. The friend hath lost his friend,
And the best quarrels in the heat are cursed   55
By those that feel their sharpness.
The question of Cordelia and her father
Requires a fitter place.

ALBANY

                    Sir, by your patience,
I hold you but a subject of this war,
Not as a brother.

REGAN

               That's as we list to grace him.   60
Methinks our pleasure should have been demanded
Ere you had spoke so far. He led our powers,
Bore the commission of my place and person,
The which immediate may well stand up
And call itself your brother.

GONORIL

                  Not so hot.   65
In his own grace he doth exalt himself
More than in your advancement.

68: **me invested**: myself appointed; **compeers**: compares favorably to
69: **the most**: the most with which you could invest him
70: **prove**: prove to be
71: **asquint**: with a squint, i.e., furtively, suspiciously
73: **From...stomach**: i.e., with tremendous anger
74: **patrimony**: inheritance
75: **Dispose...thine**: from the First Folio
75: **The walls is thine**: I surrender all of me, body and soul, to you. (Given the sexualized banter between the two sisters, and Gonoril's subsequent question in line 77, Regan is literally offering Edmund her walls, i.e., her vaginal walls.)
77: **enjoy**: have sex with

Costume rendering for Gonoril from the 1959 production at the Shakespeare Memorial Theatre in Stratford-upon-Avon directed by Glen Byam Shaw
Rare Book and Special Collection Library, University of Illinois at Urbana-Champaign

78: **The...will**: i.e., You have no say in this matter.
79: **Half-blooded fellow**: illegitimate bastard

REGAN
                                    In my right
  By me invested, he compeers the best.

GONORIL
  That were the most if he should husband you.

REGAN
  Jesters do oft prove prophets.

GONORIL
                                    Holla, holla—   70
  That eye that told you so looked but asquint.

REGAN
  Lady, I am not well, else I should answer
  From a full-flowing stomach. [*To EDMUND*] General,
  Take thou my soldiers, prisoners, patrimony.
  Dispose of them, of me. The walls is thine.   75
  Witness the world that I create thee here
  My lord and master.

GONORIL
                          Mean you to enjoy him, then?

ALBANY
  The let-alone lies not in your goodwill.

EDMUND
  Nor in thine, lord.

ALBANY
                      Half-blooded fellow, yes.

EDMUND
  Let the drum strike and prove my title good.   80

82: in thine attaint: 1) as your companion in corruption, and 2) as an accuser in this effort to attaint you (i.e., to strip you of your civil rights)

83: subcontracted: contracted, engaged

86: contradict: oppose; **banns**: public announcement of a proposed marriage

87: make your love to me: i.e., petition me for permission

88: An interlude: a play, i.e., what a farce this is, how melodramatic you all are (from the First Folio)

89: Let the trumpet sound: from the First Folio

92: prove it on thy heart: i.e., kill you

93: in nothing less: in no respect less guilty

96: What: whoever

97: villain-like he lies: 1) lie dead like a villain (in an unmarked grave), and 2) tell lies like a villain

100: firmly: violently

ALBANY
    Stay yet, hear reason. Edmund, I arrest thee
    On capital treason, and in thine attaint
    This gilded serpent. [*To REGAN*] For your claim, fair sister,
    I bar it in the interest of my wife.
    'Tis she is subcontracted to this lord,   85
    And I, her husband, contradict the banns.
    If you will marry, make your love to me.
    My lady is bespoke.—

GONORIL
                An interlude!

ALBANY
    Thou art armed, Gloucester. Let the trumpet sound.
    If none appear to prove upon thy head   90
    Thy heinous, manifest, and many treasons,

                                  [He throws down a glove]

    There is my pledge. I'll prove it on thy heart,
    Ere I taste bread, thou art in nothing less
    Than I have here proclaimed thee.

REGAN
    Sick, O sick!

GONORIL
           [*Aside*] If not, I'll ne'er trust poison.   95

EDMUND [*To ALBANY, throwing down a glove*]
    There's my exchange. What in the world he is
    That names me traitor, villain-like he lies.
    Call by thy trumpet. He that dares, approach;
    On him, on you—who not?—I will maintain
    My truth and honor firmly.   100

ALBANY
    A herald, ho!

102: **A herald, ho, a herald!**: appears only in the First Quarto

103: **Trust to thy single virtue**: i.e., rely on your own strength alone

104: **levied**: financed

110: **Sound, trumpet!**: appears only in the First Quarto

111: **quality or degree**: noble birth or rank; **host**: roster

114-115: **Sound...Again!**: appears only in the First Quarto

Costume rendering for the Herald from the 1959 production at the Shakespeare Memorial Theatre in Stratford-upon-Avon directed by Glen Byam Shaw

Rare Book and Special Collection Library, University of Illinois at Urbana-Champaign

EDMUND
  A herald, ho, a herald!

                                              [Enter HERALD]

ALBANY
  [To EDMUND] Trust to thy single virtue, for thy soldiers,
  All levied in my name, have in my name
  Took their discharge.   105

REGAN
  This sickness grows upon me.

ALBANY
  She is not well. Convey her to my tent.
                          [Exit one or more with REGAN]
                          [Enter a HERALD and a trumpeter]
  Come hither, herald. Let the trumpet sound,
  And read out this.

SECOND CAPTAIN
  Sound, trumpet!   110
                                        [Trumpeter sounds]

HERALD
  *[Reads] If any man of quality or degree in the host of the army will
  maintain upon Edmund, supposed Earl of Gloucester, that he's a
  manifold traitor, let him appear at the third sound of the trumpet.
  He is bold in his defense.*

EDMUND
  Sound!
                                        [Trumpeter sounds]
                  Again!   115
    Enter EDGAR, [armed,] at the third sound, a trumpet before him.

ALBANY
  [To HERALD] Ask him his purposes, why he appears
  Upon this call o' th' trumpet.

117: **What**: who

120: **canker-bit**: chewed full of holes, as caterpillars do to the leaves of plants

122: **cope**: confront

128: **profession**: rank as a knight

129: **Maugre**: in spite of

130: **victor-sword and fire-new fortune**: victory in battle and newly-minted fortune

131: **heart**: courage

134: **upward**: top

135: **descent**: lowest extreme

136: **toad-spotted**: 1) venomous, and 2) having a spotty or checkered past; **Say thou no**: if you deny it

137: **bent**: inclined, prepared

HERALD

                                    [*To EDGAR*] What are you?
Your name and quality, and why you answer
This present summons?

EDGAR

                            O, know, my name is lost,
By treason's tooth bare-gnawn and canker-bit.   120
Yet ere I move't, where is the adversary
I come to cope withal?

ALBANY

                        Which is that adversary?

EDGAR

What's he that speaks for Edmund, Earl of Gloucester?

EDMUND

Himself. What sayst thou to him?

EDGAR

                           Draw thy sword,
That if my speech offend a noble heart   125
Thy arm may do thee justice. Here is mine.

                               [He draws his sword]

Behold, it is the privilege of my tongue,
My oath, and my profession. I protest,
Maugre thy strength, youth, place, and eminence,
Despite thy victor-sword and fire-new fortune,   130
Thy valour and thy heart, thou art a traitor,
False to thy gods, thy brother, and thy father,
Conspirant 'gainst this high illustrious prince,
And from the extremest upward of thy head
To the descent and dust beneath thy feet   135
A most toad-spotted traitor. Say thou no,
This sword, this arm, and my best spirits are bent
To prove upon thy heart, whereto I speak,
Thou liest.

139: **wisdom**: prudence

141: **tongue some say**: speech somewhat indicates

142: **What safe...demand**: from the First Folio

143: **right of knighthood**: chivalric right to refuse combat with an unknown person of uncertain rank

144: **toss...head**: confront you directly with those crimes of which you accuse me

145: **hell-hated**: hated as much as hell is hated

147: **give...way**: deliver them directly to your heart

148: **Where...ever**: they (the charges of treason you have leveled at me) will forever be applied to you (after I defeat you); **speak**: sound

149: **Save**: spare (Albany wants Edmund to live to be put on trial for his crimes); **practice**: trickery

151: **opposite**: opponent

152: **cozened and beguiled**: deceived and misled

153: **stopple it**: stop it up

155: **no tearing**: i.e., do not destroy the evidence (the letter plotting Albany's death)

EDMUND

               In wisdom I should ask thy name,
But since thy outside looks so fair and warlike,   140
And that thy tongue some say of breeding breathes,
What safe and nicely I might well demand
My right of knighthood I disdain and spurn.
Here do I toss those treasons to thy head,
With the hell-hated lie o'erturn thy heart,   145
Which, for they yet glance by and scarcely bruise,
This sword of mine shall give them instant way
Where they shall rest forever. Trumpets, speak!
         [Flourish. They fight. EDMUND is vanquished.]

ALBANY

Save him, save him!

GONORIL

             This is mere practice, Gloucester.
By the law of arms thou art not bound to answer   150
An unknown opposite. Thou art not vanquished,
But cozened and beguiled.

ALBANY

                 Stop your mouth, dame,
Or with this paper shall I stopple it.
[To EDMUND] Hold, sir, thou worse than anything, read thine
    own evil.
[To GONORIL] Nay, no tearing, lady. I perceive you know't.   155

GONORIL

Say if I do, the laws are mine, not thine.
Who shall arraign me for't.

ALBANY

               Most monstrous!
O, Know'st thou this paper?

GONORIL

             Ask me not what I know.

                                           Exit

159: **Govern**: restrain

163: **fortune on**: victory over

164: **charity**: forgiveness

168: **pleasant vices**: sins of pleasure

170: **got**: begot you

173: **The wheel...circle**: 1) Everything has come around to where it began, 2) my crimes have received their appropriate punishment, and 3) the wheel of fortune has turned. See also 1.1.274, 2.1.39, 2.2.155-56, 4.6.211, and 5.3.6.

174: **gait**: bearing

Costume rendering for Albany from the 1959 production at the Shakespeare Memorial Theatre in Stratford-upon-Avon directed by Glen Byam Shaw

ALBANY
> Go after her. She's desperate. Govern her.

> *[Exit one or more]*

EDMUND
> What you have charged me with, that have I done, 160
> And more, much more. The time will bring it out.
> 'Tis past, and so am I. [*To EDGAR*] But what art thou,
> That hast this fortune on me? If thou beest noble,
> I do forgive thee.

EDGAR
>   Let's exchange charity.
> I am no less in blood than thou art, Edmund. 165
> If more, the more ignobly thou hast wronged me.
> My name is Edgar, and thy father's son.
> The gods are just, and of our pleasant vices
> Make instruments to scourge us.
> The dark and vicious place where thee he got 170
> Cost him his eyes.

EDMUND
> Thou hast spoken truth.
> The wheel is come full circle. I am here.

ALBANY
> [*To EDGAR*] Methought thy very gait did prophesy
> A royal nobleness. I must embrace thee. 175
> Let sorrow split my heart if I did ever hate
> Thee or thy father!

EDGAR
> Worthy prince, I know't.

ALBANY
>   Where have you hid yourself?
> How have you known the miseries of your father?

180: **List**: listen to

182: **The bloody proclamation to escape**: i.e., the proclamation (my death sentence) that caused me to escape

183: **followed me so near**: was never very far from thoughts

185: **shift**: change

187: **habit**: disguise

188: **rings**: i.e., eye sockets

189: **precious stones**: i.e., sparkling, jewel-like eyes

193: **success**: outcome

195: **my pilgrimage**: the story of my disguised exile; **flawed**: weakened, broken

202: **dissolve**: i.e., dissolve into tears

203-220: **This would...a slave**: appears only in the First Quarto

203: **a period**: the limit

204: **such as**: those who

204-206: **but another...extremity**: i.e., yet one more sad circumstance remains to be elaborated which, adding as it does more sorrow to what was already too much, brought much more and exceeded the limit

207: **big in clamor**: loud in lamenting (all that had happened)

EDGAR

By nursing them, my lord. List a brief tale, 180
And when 'tis told, O that my heart would burst!
The bloody proclamation to escape
That followed me so near—O, our lives' sweetness,
That with the pain of death would hourly die
Rather than die at once!—taught me to shift 185
Into a madman's rags, to assume a semblance
That very dogs disdained; and in this habit
Met I my father with his bleeding rings,
The precious stones new-lost; became his guide,
Led him, begged for him, saved him from despair; 190
Never—O father!—revealed myself unto him
Until some half hour past, when I was armed.
Not sure, though hoping, of this good success,
I asked his blessing, and from first to last
Told him my pilgrimage; but his flawed heart— 195
Alack, too weak the conflict to support—
'Twixt two extremes of passion, joy and grief,
Burst smilingly.

EDMUND

                    This speech of yours hath moved me,
And shall perchance do good. But speak you on—
You look as you had something more to say. 200

ALBANY

If there be more, more woeful, hold it in,
For I am almost ready to dissolve,
Hearing of this.

EDGAR

                    This would have seemed a period
To such as love not sorrow; but another
To amplify, too much would make much more, 205
And top extremity.
Whilst I was big in clamor came there in a man
Who, having seen me in my worst estate,
Shunned my abhorred society; but then, finding

212: **As**: as if; **threw...father**: threw himself on my father Gloucester's corpse

215: **puissant**: powerful; **strings of life**: heartstrings

217: **tranced**: entranced, dazed

219: **enemy king**: i.e., Lear, the king who had banished him (and thus could be thought of as Kent's enemy)

221-222: **What kind...bloody knife**: appears only in the First Quarto

222: **smokes**: steams (as with the heat of fresh blood)

223: **O, she's dead!**: from the First Folio

224: **Who, man?**: appears only in the First Quarto

227: **contracted**: betrothed

Who 'twas that so endured, with his strong arms   210
He fastened on my neck and bellowed out
As he'd burst heaven; threw him on my father,
Told the most piteous tale of Lear and him
That ever ear received, which in recounting
His grief grew puissant and the strings of life   215
Began to crack. Twice then the trumpets sounded,
And there I left him tranced.

ALBANY

                      But who was this?

EDGAR
  Kent, sir, the banished Kent, who in disguise
Followed his enemy king, and did him service
Improper for a slave.   220
Enter [SECOND GENTLEMAN] with a bloody knife.

SECOND GENTLEMAN
  Help, help, O, help!

ALBANY

                What kind of help?
What means that bloody knife?

SECOND GENTLEMAN

                      It's hot, it smokes.
It came even from the heart of—O, she's dead!

ALBANY
  Who, man? Speak.

SECOND GENTLEMAN
  Your lady, sir, your lady; and her sister   225
By her is poisoned—she hath confessed it.

EDMUND
  I was contracted to them both; all three
Now marry in an instant.

229-234: Produce...urges: appears only in the First Quarto

234: The compliment...urges: i.e., the ceremonial reception demanded by common courtesy

236: Aye good night: farewell forever

237: Scene: Great thing of us forgot!: Audiences have often found something darkly humorous about this line in performance.

239: object: horrific sight (of all the dead)

245: Despite: in spite; **Quickly send**: quickly send a messenger

246: writ: written order of execution

ALBANY
     Produce their bodies, be they alive or dead.
     This justice of the heavens, that makes us tremble,   230
     Touches us not with pity.

                                   Enter KENT [as himself]

EDGAR
     Here comes Kent, sir.

ALBANY
     O, 'tis he; the time will not allow
     The compliment that very manners urges.

KENT
     I am come to bid my king and master   235
     Aye good night. Is he not here?

ALBANY
     Great thing of us forgot!—
     Speak, Edmund; where's the King, and where's Cordelia?
               The bodies of GONORIL and REGAN are brought in.
     Seest thou this object, Kent?

KENT
     Alack, why thus?

EDMUND
                         Yet Edmund was beloved.   240
     The one the other poisoned for my sake,
     And after slew herself.

ALBANY
     Even so.—Cover their faces.

EDMUND
     I pant for life. Some good I mean to do,
     Despite of my own nature. Quickly send,   245
     Be brief in it, to th' castle; for my writ
     Is on the life of Lear and on Cordelia.
     Nay, send in time.

tracks 31-33

258–279
Paul Scofield as Lear, David Burke as Kent, Richard McCabe as Edgar,
and Peter Blythe as Albany
Sir John Gielgud as Lear

249: **office**: duty (to carry out the execution)
256: **fordid herself**: undid or destroyed herself, i.e., committed suicide

257: Scene: *Enter LEAR*: Edmund Kean (1787-1833) staggered in carrying Cordeila; John Gielgud (1904-2000) carried her vigorously over one shoulder. In Peter Brook's 1971 film, Paul Scofield appeared to be strong physically but seemed broken emotionally and spiritually. Tommaso Salvini (1829-1915) and Orson Welles (1915-1985) dragged Cordelia's body behind them.

257: Stage Direction: *Enter LEAR with CORDELIA in his arms*: Ted van Griethuysen as Lear and Monique Holt as Cordelia, in the 2000 Shakespeare Theatre Company production directed by Michael Kahn
Photo: Carol Rosegg

260: **heaven's...crack**: i.e., the skies would open up and rain down tears
263: **stone**: i.e., the mirror's surface
264: **Is...end**: i.e., Is this all that comes of our efforts and hopes in life?

ALBANY
            Run, run, O run!

EDGAR
  To who, my lord?—Who hath the office? Send
  Thy token of reprieve.   250

EDMUND
  Well thought on! Take my sword. The captain,
  Give it the captain.

ALBANY
                Haste thee for thy life.
                              [Exit SECOND CAPTAIN]

EDMUND
  He hath commission from thy wife and me
  To hang Cordelia in the prison, and
  To lay the blame upon her own despair,   255
  That she fordid herself.

ALBANY
  The gods defend her!—Bear him hence a while.
                              [Exeunt some with EDMUND.]
                         [Enter LEAR with CORDELIA in his arms,
                              followed by the SECOND CAPTAIN.]

LEAR
  Howl, howl, howl, howl! O, you are men of stones.
  Had I your tongues and eyes, I would use them so
  That heaven's vault should crack. She's gone forever.   260
  I know when one is dead and when one lives.
  She's dead as earth.
                                        [He lays her down.]
                Lend me a looking-glass.
  If that her breath will mist or stain the stone,
  Why, then she lives.

KENT
                Is this the promised end?

258–279
Paul Scofield as Lear, David Burke as Kent, Richard McCabe as Edgar, and Peter Blythe as Albany
Sir John Gielgud as Lear

265: **horror**: i.e., the Apocalypse
265: **Fall and cease**: i.e., We sin and we die. Given the religious context, Albany could be describing human history in biblical terms: the Fall (from Eden) and the resulting end (the Apocalypse).

"King Lear Weeping over the Dead Body of Cordelia": Painting (1786-1788)
James Barry (1741-1806)

277: **falchion**: light sword
278: **skip**: run in terror
279: **same crosses spoil me**: i.e., comparable adversities exhaust me (also a reference to Christ bearing the cross)
280: **I'll...straight**: i.e., I'll be able to recognize you momentarily

EDGAR
Or image of that horror?

ALBANY
Fall and cease.   265

LEAR
This feather stirs. She lives. If it be so,
It is a chance which does redeem all sorrows
That ever I have felt.

KENT
[*Kneeling*] Ah, my good master!

LEAR
Prithee, away.

EDGAR
'Tis noble Kent, your friend.

LEAR
A plague upon you, murderous traitors all.   270
I might have saved her; now she's gone forever.—
Cordelia, Cordelia, stay a little. Ha?
What is't thou sayst?—Her voice was ever soft,
Gentle, and low, an excellent thing in women.—
I killed the slave that was a-hanging thee.   275

SECOND CAPTAIN
'Tis true, my lords, he did.

LEAR
Did I not, fellow?
I have seen the day with my good biting falchion
I would have made them skip. I am old now,
And these same crosses spoil me. [*To KENT*] Who are you?
Mine eyes are not o' the best, I'll tell you straight.   280

281-282: **If Fortune...behold**: i.e., If the goddess Fortune were to celebrate the lives of two people who had suffered the greatest fall from good luck to bad, Lear would be one of them.

283: **This...sight**: 1) my eyes are failing me, and 2) I can barely recognize you

284: **Caius**: the name Kent used when he disguised himself (this is its only mention in the play)

288: **I'll...straight**: i.e., I'll process that information momentarily

289: **difference**: i.e., the initial conflict between Lear and Cordelia; **decay**: the current deterioration of Lear's health and fortune

292: **So think I, too**: appears only in the First Quarto

293: **desperately**: in despair

KENT
    If Fortune bragged of two she loved or hated,
    One of them we behold.

LEAR
    This is a dull sight. Are not you Kent?

KENT
    The same, your servant Kent. Where is your servant Caius?

LEAR
    He's a good fellow, I can tell you that.   285
    He'll strike, and quickly too. He's dead and rotten.

KENT
    No, my good lord, I am the very man—

LEAR
    I'll see that straight.

KENT
    That from your first of difference and decay
    Have followed your sad steps.

LEAR
                                   You're welcome hither.   290

KENT
    Nor no man else. All's cheerless, dark, and deadly.
    Your eldest daughters have fordone themselves,
    And desperately are dead.

LEAR
                        So think I, too.

ALBANY
    He knows not what he sees; and vain it is
    That we present us to him.   295

295: **very bootless**: in vain
296: **trifle**: small matter
298: **decay**: 1) decay of Lear, and 2) decay of the kingdom (from the ravages of war)
299: **for**: as for
302: **With...honors**: with whatever benefit and such further distinctions as your honorable conduct in this conflict
306: **poor fool**: Lear is using the word "fool" here as a term of endearment to refer to Cordelia.

306: Scene: **And my poor fool is hanged**: Akira Kurosawa's *Ran* (1984) follows the fortunes of King Hidetora, who has three sons. At the film's climax, Hidetora and his loyal son, Saburo, are ambushed. The father cradles his bleeding son's corpse in his arms:

310: **O...O!**: appears only in the First Quarto
311-312: **Do you...there**: from the First Folio

314: "Look up, my lord": the Ensemble in the 2000 Shakespeare Theatre Company production directed by Michael Kahn
Photo: Carol Rosegg

EDGAR

                        Very bootless.   295
                           Enter another CAPTAIN

THIRD CAPTAIN
   [*To ALBANY*] Edmund is dead, my lord.

ALBANY
                       That's but a trifle here. –
   You lords and noble friends, know our intent.
   What comfort to this great decay may come
   Shall be applied; for us, we will resign
   During the life of this old Majesty   300
   To him our absolute power; [*To EDGAR and KENT*] you to your rights
   With boot and such addition as your honors
   Have more than merited. All friends shall taste
   The wages of their virtue, and all foes
   The cup of their deservings.—O see, see!   305

LEAR
   And my poor fool is hanged. No, no, no life.
   Why should a dog, a horse, a rat have life,
   And thou no breath at all? O, thou wilt come no more,
   Never, never, never, never, never.—Pray you, undo
   This button. Thank you, sir. O, O, O, O!   310
   Do you see this? Look on her. Look, her lips,
   Look there, look there.

EDGAR
   He faints. [*To LEAR*] My lord, my lord!

KENT
   [*To LEAR*] Break, heart, I prithee break.

EDGAR
                      [*To LEAR*] Look up, my lord.

315: **Vex...ghost**: i.e., Disturb not his spirit as it moves on to the afterlife.

316: **rack**: 1) torture device, and 2) perhaps a pun on wreck, as in shipwreck, referring to the disastrous wreck of Lear's life

317: Scene: *[LEAR dies]*: In Peter Brook's 1962 RSC production, Paul Scofield played Lear's final dying moments as if acknowledging the stark truth that there was no God. Half-smiling, half-weeping, Scofield's Lear seemed keenly aware of the cosmic farce in which he had been accorded the lead role.

At least some cues for performing Lear's final moments are to be found in the two extant versions of the play themselves. In the Quarto, for example, Lear's last utterance begins with his dying groan, "O, o, o, o," and is followed by the following final words: "Break heart, I prithee break." Lear, on the verge of death here, seems to be hastening his own heart to bring the suffering of his life to an end. In the Folio version of the play, published some fifteen years later, Kent is given the line, "Break heart, I prithee break," and Lear's final words are: "Do you see this? Look on her. Look, her lips, / Look there, look there." As such, Lear in this later version dies in a sort of ecstasy, thinking that Cordelia's lips are moving and that she is still alive. In Nahum Tate's famous Restoration adaptation of the play, the Folio's version of Lear's dying words authorized Tate to rewrite the play's ending altogether so that both Lear and Cordelia live happily ever after.

319: **but usurped his life**: only forcibly borrowed his existence from God

321: **general woe**: official mourning period and funeral ceremonies

322: **the gored state**: our country, which has been maimed and bloodied by war

323: **journey**: journey to the afterlife

KENT

Vex not his ghost. O, let him pass. He hates him   315
That would upon the rack of this tough world
Stretch him out longer.

[LEAR dies]

EDGAR

O, he is gone, indeed.

KENT

The wonder is he hath endured so long.
He but usurped his life.

ALBANY

[To Attendants] Bear them from hence. Our present business   320
Is general woe. *[To KENT and EDGAR]* Friends of my soul, you twain
Rule in this kingdom, and the gored state sustain.

KENT

I have a journey, sir, shortly to go:
My master calls, and I must not say no.

ALBANY

The weight of this sad time we must obey,   325
Speak what we feel, not what we ought to say.
The oldest hath borne most. We that are young
Shall never see so much, nor live so long.

[Exeunt carrying the bodies]

A Voice Coach's Perspective on Speaking Shakespeare

KEEPING SHAKESPEARE PRACTICAL

Andrew Wade

tracks 34-35

Introduction to Speaking Shakespeare: Derek Jacobi
Speaking Shakespeare: Andrew Wade with Myra Lucretia Taylor

Why, you might be wondering, is it so important to keep Shakespeare practical? What do I mean by practical? Why is this the way to discover how to speak the text and understand it?

Plays themselves are not simply literary events—they demand interpreters in the deepest sense of the word, and the language of Shakespeare requires, therefore, not a vocal demonstration of writing techniques but an imaginative response to that writing. The key word here is imagination. The task of the voice coach is to offer relevant choices to the actor so that the actor's imagination is titillated, excited by the language, which he or she can then share with an audience, playing on that audience's imagination. Take the word "IF"—it is only composed of two letters when written, but if you say it aloud and listen to what it implies, then your reaction, the way the word plays through you, can change the perception of meaning. "Iffffffff"... you might hear and feel it implying "possibilities," "choices," "questioning," "trying to work something out." The saying of this word provokes active investigation of thought. What an apt word to launch a play: "If music be the food of love, play on" (Act 1, Scene 1 in *Twelfth Night, or What You Will*). How this word engages the listener and immediately sets up an involvement is about more than audibility. How we verbalize sounds has a direct link to meaning and understanding. In the words of Touchstone in *As You Like It*, "Much virtue in if."

I was working with a company in Vancouver on *Macbeth,* and at the end of the first week's rehearsal—after having explored our voices and opening out different pieces of text to hear the possibilities of the rhythm, feeling how the meter affects the thinking and feeling, looking at structure and form— one of the actors admitted he was also a writer of soap operas and that I had completely changed his way of writing. Specifically, in saying a line like, "The multitudinous seas incarnadine / Making the green one red" he heard the complexity of meaning revealed in the use of polysyllabic words becom- ing monosyllabic, layered upon the words' individual dictionary definitions. The writer was reminded that merely reproducing the speech of everyday life was nowhere near as powerful and effective as language that is shaped.

Do you think soap operas would benefit from rhyming couplets? Somehow this is difficult to imagine! But, the writer's comments set me thinking. As I am constantly trying to find ways of exploring the acting process, of opening out actors' connection with language that isn't their own, I thought it would be a good idea to involve writers and actors in some practical work on language. After talking to Cicely Berry (Voice Director, the Royal Shakespeare Company) and Colin Chambers (the then RSC Production Adviser), we put together a group of writers and actors who were interested in taking part. It was a fasci- nating experience all round, and it broke down barriers and misconceptions.

The actors discovered, for instance, that a writer is not coming from a very different place as they are in their creative search; that an idea or an image may result from a struggle to define a gut feeling and not from some crafted, well-formed idea in the head. The physical connection of language to the body was reaffirmed. After working with a group on Yeats' poem *Easter 1916*, Ann Devlin changed the title of the play she was writing for the Royal Shakespeare Company to *After Easter*. She had experienced the poem read aloud by a circle of participants, each voice becoming a realization of the shape of the writing. Thus it made a much fuller impact on her and caused her thinking to shift. Such practical exchanges, through language work and voice, feed and stimulate my work to go beyond making sure the actors' voices are technically sound.

It is, of course, no different when we work on a Shakespeare play. A similar connection with the language is crucial. Playing Shakespeare, in many ways, is crafted instinct. The task is thus to find the best way to tap into someone's imagination. As Peter Brook put it, "People forget that a text is dumb. To make it speak, one must create a communication machine. A living network, like a nervous system, must be made if a text which comes from far away is to touch the sensibility of the present."

This journey is never to be taken for granted. It is the process that every text must undergo every time it is staged. There is no definitive rehearsal that would solve problems or indicate ways of staging a given play. Again, this is where creative, practical work on voice can help forge new meaning by offering areas of exploration and challenge. The central idea behind my work comes back to posing the question, "How does meaning change by speaking out aloud?" It would be unwise to jump hastily to the end process for, as Peter Brook says, "Shakespeare's words are records of the words that he wanted spoken, words issuing from people's mouths, with pitch, pause and rhythm and gesture as part of their meaning. A word does not start as a word—it is the end product which begins as an impulse, stimulated by attitude and behavior which dictates the need for expression" (1).

PRACTICALLY SPEAKING

Something happens when we vocalize, when we isolate sounds, when we start to speak words aloud, when we put them to the test of our physicality, of our anatomy. We expose ourselves in a way that makes taking the language back more difficult. Our body begins a debate with itself, becomes alive with the vibrations of sound produced in the mouth or rooted deep in the muscles that aim at defining sound. In fact, the spoken words bring into play all the senses, before sense and another level of meaning are reached.

"How do I know what I think, until I see what I say," Oscar Wilde once said. A concrete illustration of this phrase was reported to me when I was leading a workshop recently. A grandmother said the work we had done that day reminded her of what her six-year-old grandson had said to his mother while they were driving through Wales: "Look, mummy, sheep! Sheep! Sheep!" "You don't have to keep telling us," the mother replied, but the boy said, "How do I know they're there, if I don't tell you?!"

Therefore, when we speak of ideas, of sense, we slightly take for granted those physical processes which affect and change their meaning. We tend to separate something that is an organic whole. In doing so, we become blind to the fact that it is precisely this physical connection to the words that enables the actors to make the language theirs.

The struggle for meaning is not just impressionistic theater mystique; it is an indispensable aspect of the rehearsal process and carries on during the life of every production. In this struggle, practical work on Shakespeare is vital and may help spark creativity and shed some light on the way meaning is born into language. After a performance of *More Words*, a show devised and directed by Cicely Berry and myself, Katie Mitchell (a former artistic director of The Other Place in Stratford-upon-Avon) gave me an essay by Ted Hughes that echoes with the piece. In it, Ted Hughes compares the writing of a poem—the coming into existence of words—to the capture of a wild animal. You will notice that in the following passage Hughes talks of "spirit" or "living parts" but never of "thought" or "sense." With great care and precaution, he advises, "It is better to call [the poem] an assembly of living parts moved by a single spirit. The living parts are the words, the images, the rhythms. The spirit is the life which inhabits them when they all work together. It is impossible to say which comes first, parts or spirit."

This is also true of life in words, as many are connected directly to one or several of our senses. Here Hughes talks revealingly of "the five senses," of "word," "action," and "muscle," all things which a practical approach to language is more likely to allow one to perceive and do justice to.

Words that live are those which we hear, like "click" or "chuckle," or which we see, like "freckled" or "veined," or which we taste, like "vinegar" or "sugar," or touch, like "prickle" or "oily," or smell, like "tar" or "onion," words which belong to one of the five senses. Or words that act and seem to use their muscles, like "flick" or "balance" (2).

In this way, practically working on Shakespeare to arrive at understanding lends itself rather well, I think, to what Adrian Noble (former artistic director of the RSC) calls "a theater of poetry," a form of art that, rooted deeply in its classical origins, would seek to awaken the imagination of its audiences through love and respect for words while satisfying our eternal craving for myths and twice-told tales.

This can only be achieved at some cost. There is indeed a difficult battle to fight and hopefully to win: "the battle of the word to survive." This phrase was coined by Michael Redgrave at the beginning of the 1950s, a period when theater began to be deeply influenced by more physical forms, such as mime (3). Although the context is obviously different, the fight today is of the same nature.

LISTENING TO SHAKESPEARE

Because of the influence of television, our way of speaking as well as listening has changed. It is crucial to be aware of this. We can get fairly close to the way *Henry V* or *Hamlet* was staged in Shakespeare's time; we can try also to reconstruct the way English was spoken. But somehow, all these fall short of the real and most important goal: the Elizabethan ear. How did one "hear" a Shakespeare play? This is hardest to know. My personal view is that we will probably never know for sure. We are, even when we hear a Shakespeare play or a recording from the past, bound irrevocably to modernity. The Elizabethan ear was no doubt different from our own, as people were not spoken to or entertained in the same way. A modern voice has to engage us in a different way in order to make us truly listen in a society that seems to rely solely on the belief that image is truth, that it is more important to show than to tell.

Sometimes, we say that a speech in Shakespeare, or even an entire production, is not well-spoken, not up to standard. What do we mean by that? Evidently, there are a certain number of "guidelines" that any actor now has to know when working on a classical text. Yet, even when these are known, actors still have to make choices when they speak. A sound is not a sound without somebody to lend an ear to it: rhetoric is nothing without an audience.

There are a certain number of factors that affect the receiver's ear. These can be cultural factors such as the transition between different acting styles or the level of training that our contemporary ear has had. There are also personal and emotional factors. Often we feel the performance was not well-spoken because, somehow, it did not live up to our expectations of how we think it should have been performed. Is it that many of us have a self-conscious model, perhaps our own first experience of Shakespeare, that meant something to us and became our reference point for the future (some treasured performance kept under glass)? Nothing from then on can quite compare with that experience.

Most of the time, however, it is more complex than nostalgia. Take, for example, the thorny area of accent. I remind myself constantly that audibility is not embedded in Received Pronunciation or Standard American. The familiarity that those in power have with speech and the articulate confidence gained from coming from the right quarters can lead us all to hear certain types of voices as outshining others. But, to my mind, the role of theater is at least to question these assumptions so that we do not perpetuate those givens but work towards a broader tolerance.

In Canada on a production of *Twelfth Night*, I was working with an actor who was from Newfoundland. His own natural rhythms in speaking seemed completely at home with Shakespeare's. Is this because his root voice has direct links back to the voice of Shakespeare's time? It does seem that compared to British dialects, which are predominantly about pitch, many North American dialects have a wonderful respect and vibrancy in their use of vowels. Shakespeare's language seems to me very vowel-aware. How useful it is for an actor to isolate the vowels in the spoken words to hear the music they produce, the rich patterns, their direct connection to feelings. North Americans more easily respond to this and allow it to feed their speaking. I can only assume it is closer to how the Elizabethans spoke.

In *Othello* the very names of the characters have a direct connection to one vowel in particular. All the male names, except the Duke, end in the sound OH: Othello, Cassio, Iago, Brabantio, etc. Furthermore, the sound OH ripples through the play both consciously and unconsciously. "Oh" occurs repeatedly and, more interestingly, is contained within other words: "so," "soul," and "know." These words resonate throughout the play, reinforcing another level of meaning. The repetition of the same sounds affects us beyond what we can quite say.

Vowels come from deep within us, from our very core. We speak vowels before we speak consonants. They seem to reveal the feelings that require the consonants to give the shape to what we perceive as making sense.

Working with actors who are bilingual (or ones for whom English is not the native language) is fascinating because of the way it allows the actor to have an awareness of the cadence in Shakespeare. There seems to be an objective perception to the musical patterns in the text, and the use of alliteration and assonance are often more easily heard not just as literary devices, but also as means by which meaning is formed and revealed to an audience.

Every speech pattern (i.e., accent, rhythm) is capable of audibility. Each has its own music, each can become an accent when juxtaposed against another. The point at which a speech pattern becomes audible is in the dynamic of the physical making of those sounds. The speaker must have the desire to get through to a listener and must be confident that every speech pattern has a right to be heard.

SPEAKING SHAKESPEARE

So, the way to speak Shakespeare is not intrinsically tied to a particular sound; rather, it is how a speaker energetically connects to that language. Central to this is how we relate to the form of Shakespeare. Shakespeare employs verse, prose, and rhetorical devices to communicate meaning. For example, in *Romeo and Juliet*, the use of contrasts helps us to quantify Juliet's feelings: "And learn me how to lose a winning match," "Whiter than new snow upon a raven's back." These extreme opposites, "lose" and "winning," "new snow" and "raven's back," are her means to express and make sense of her feelings.

On a more personal note, I am often reminded how much, as an individual, I owe to Shakespeare's spoken word. The rather quiet and inarticulate schoolboy I once was found in the speaking and the acting of those words a means to quench his thirst for expression.

NOTES:
(1) Peter Brook, *The Empty Space* (Harmondsworth: Penguin, 1972)
(2) Ted Hughes, *Winter Pollen* (London: Faber and Faber, 1995)
(3) Michael Redgrave, *The Actor's Ways and Means*
    (London: Heinemann, 1951)

In the Age of Shakespeare

Thomas Garvey

One of the earliest published pictures of Shakespeare's birthplace, from an original watercolor
by Phoebe Dighton (1834)

The works of William Shakespeare have won the love of millions since he
first set pen to paper some four hundred years ago, but at first blush, his
plays can seem difficult to understand, even willfully obscure. There are so
many strange words: not fancy, exactly, but often only half-familiar. And the
very fabric of the language seems to spring from a world of forgotten

assumptions, a vast network of beliefs and superstitions that have long been dispelled from the modern mind.

In fact, when "Gulielmus filius Johannes Shakespeare" (Latin for "William, son of John Shakespeare") was baptized in Stratford-on-Avon in 1564, English itself was only just settling into its current form; no dictionary had yet been written, and Shakespeare coined hundreds of words himself. Astronomy and medicine were entangled with astrology and the occult arts; democracy was waiting to be reborn; and even educated people believed in witches and fairies, and that the sun revolved around the Earth. Yet somehow Shakespeare still speaks to us today, in a voice as fresh and direct as the day his lines were first spoken, and to better understand both their artistic depth and enduring power, we must first understand something of his age.

REVOLUTION AND RELIGION

Shakespeare was born into a nation on the verge of global power, yet torn by religious strife. Henry VIII, the much-married father of Elizabeth I, had

From *The Book of Martyrs* (1563), this woodcut shows the Archbishop of Canterbury being burned at the stake in March 1556

Map of London ca. 1625

defied the Pope by proclaiming a new national church, with himself as its head. After Henry's death, however, his daughter Mary reinstituted Catholicism via a murderous nationwide campaign, going so far as to burn the Archbishop of Canterbury at the stake. But after a mere five years, the childless Mary also died, and when her half-sister Elizabeth was crowned, she declared the Church of England again triumphant.

In the wake of so many religious reversals, it is impossible to know which form of faith lay closest to the English heart, and at first, Elizabeth was content with mere outward deference to the Anglican Church. Once the Pope hinted her assassination would not be a mortal sin, however, the suppression of Catholicism grew more savage, and many Catholics—including some known in Stratford—were hunted down and executed, which meant being hanged, disemboweled, and carved into quarters. Many scholars suspect that Shakespeare himself was raised a Catholic (his father's testament of faith was found hidden in his childhood home). We can speculate about the impact this religious tumult may have had on his plays. Indeed, while explicit Catholic themes, such as the description of Purgatory in *Hamlet*, are rare, the larger themes of disguise and double allegiance are prominent across the canon. Prince Hal offers false friendship to Falstaff in the histories, the heroines of the comedies are forced to disguise themselves as men, and the action of the tragedies is driven by double-dealing villains. "I am not what I am," Iago tells us (and himself) in *Othello*, summing up in a single stroke what may have been Shakespeare's formative social and spiritual experience.

If religious conflict rippled beneath the body politic like some ominous undertow, on its surface the tide of English power was clearly on the rise. The defeat of the Spanish Armada in 1588 had established Britain as a global power; by 1595 Sir Walter Raleigh had founded the colony of Virginia (named for the Virgin Queen), and discovered a new crop, tobacco, which would inspire a burgeoning international trade. After decades of strife and the threat of invasion, England enjoyed a welcome stability. As the national coffers grew, so did London; over the course of Elizabeth's reign, the city would nearly double in size to a population of some 200,000.

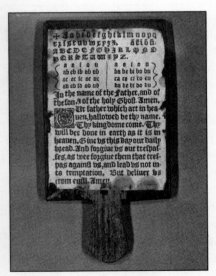

Hornbook from Shakespeare's lifetime

A 1639 engraving of a scene from a royal state visit of Marie de Medici depicts London's packed, closely crowded half-timbered houses.

FROM COUNTRY TO COURT

The urban boom brought a new dimension to British life—the mentality of the metropolis. By contrast, in Stratford-on-Avon, the rhythms of the rural world still held sway. Educated in the local grammar school, Shakespeare was taught to read and write by a schoolmaster called an "abecedarian", and as he grew older, he was introduced to logic, rhetoric, and Latin. Like most schoolboys of his time, he was familiar with Roman mythology and may have learned a little Greek, perhaps by translating passages of the New Testament. Thus while he never attended a university, Shakespeare could confidently refer in his plays to myths and legends that today we associate with the highly educated.

Beyond the classroom, however, he was immersed in the life of the countryside, and his writing all but revels in its flora and fauna, from the wounded deer of *As You Like It* to the herbs and flowers which Ophelia scatters in *Hamlet*. Pagan rituals abounded in the rural villages of Shakespeare's day, where residents danced around maypoles in spring, performed "mummers' plays" in winter, and recited rhymes year-round to ward off witches and fairies.

The custom most pertinent to Shakespeare's art was the medieval "mystery play," in which moral allegories were enacted in country homes and village squares by troupes of traveling actors. These strolling players—usually four men and two boys who played the women's roles—often lightened the moralizing with bawdy interludes in a mix of high and low feeling, which would become a defining feature of Shakespeare's art. Occasionally even a professional troupe, such as Lord Strange's Men, or the Queen's Men, would arrive in town, perhaps coming straight to Shakespeare's door (his father was the town's bailiff) for permission to perform.

Rarely, however, did such troupes stray far from their base in London, the nation's rapidly expanding capital and cultural center. The city itself had existed since the time of the Romans (who built the original London Bridge), but it was not until the Renaissance that its population spilled beyond its ancient walls and began to grow along (and across) the Thames, by whose banks the Tudors had built their glorious palaces. It was these two contradictory worlds—a modern metropolis cheek-by-jowl with a medieval court—that provided the two very different audiences who applauded Shakespeare's plays.

Londoners both high and low craved distraction. Elizabeth's court constantly celebrated her reign with dazzling pageants and performances that required a local pool of professional actors and musicians. Beyond the graceful landscape of the royal parks, however, the general populace was packed into little more than a square mile of cramped and crooked streets where theatrical entertainment was frowned upon as compromising public morals.

Just outside the jurisdiction of the city fathers, however, across the twenty arches of London Bridge on the south bank of the Thames, lay the wilder district of "Southwark." A grim reminder of royal power lay at the end of the bridge—the decapitated heads of traitors stared down from pikes at passersby. Once beyond their baleful gaze, people found the amusements they desired, and their growing numbers meant a market suddenly existed for daily entertainment. Bear-baiting and cockfighting flourished, along with taverns, brothels, and even the new institution of the theater.

Southwark, as depicted in Hollar's long view of London (1647). Blackfriars is on the top right and the labels of Bear-baiting and the Globe were inadvertently reversed.

THE ADVENT OF THE THEATRE

The first building in England designed for the performance of plays—called, straightforwardly enough, "The Theatre"—was built in London when Shakespeare was still a boy. It was owned by James Burbage, father of Richard Burbage, who would become Shakespeare's lead actor in the acting company The Lord Chamberlain's Men. "The Theatre," consciously or unconsciously, resembled the yards in which traveling players had long plied their trade—it was an open-air polygon, with three tiers of galleries surrounding a canopied stage in a flat central yard, which was ideal for the athletic competitions the building also hosted. The innovative arena must have found an appreciative audience, for it was soon joined by the Curtain, and then the Rose, which was the first theater to rise in Southwark among the brothels, bars, and bear-baiting pits.

Even as these new venues were being built, a revolution in the drama itself was taking place. Just as Renaissance artists turned to classical models for inspiration, so English writers looked to Roman verse as a prototype for the new national drama. "Blank verse," or iambic pentameter (that is, a poetic line with five alternating stressed and unstressed syllables), was an adaptation of Latin forms, and first appeared in England in a translation of Virgil's *Aeneid*. Blank verse was first spoken on stage in 1561, in the now-forgotten *Gorboduc*, but it was not until the brilliant Christopher Marlowe (born the same year as Shakespeare) transformed it into the "mighty line" of such plays as *Tamburlaine* (1587) that the power and flexibility of the form made it the baseline of English drama.

Marlowe—who, unlike Shakespeare, had attended college—led the "university wits," a clique of hard-living free thinkers who in between all manner of exploits managed to define a new form of theater. The dates of Shakespeare's arrival in London are unknown—we have no record of him in Stratford after 1585—but by the early 1590s he had already absorbed the essence of Marlowe's invention, and begun producing astonishing innovations of his own.

While the "university wits" had worked with myth and fantasy, however, Shakespeare turned to a grand new theme, English history—penning the three-part saga of *Henry VI* in or around 1590. The trilogy was such a success that Shakespeare became the envy of his circle—one unhappy competitor, Robert Greene, even complained in 1592 of "an upstart crow...beautified with our feathers...[who is] in his own conceit the only Shake-scene in a country."

Such jibes perhaps only confirmed Shakespeare's estimation of himself, for he began to apply his mastery of blank verse in all directions, succeeding at tragedy (*Titus Andronicus*), farce (*The Comedy of Errors*), and romantic comedy (*The Two Gentlemen of Verona*). He drew his plots from everywhere: existing poems, romances, folk tales, even other plays. In fact a number of Shakespeare's dramas (*Hamlet* included) may be revisions of earlier texts owned by his troupe. Since copyright laws did not exist, acting companies usually kept their texts close to their chests, only allowing publication when a play was no longer popular, or, conversely, when a play was *so* popular (as with *Romeo and Juliet*) that unauthorized versions had already been printed.

Demand for new plays and performance venues steadily increased. Soon, new theaters (the Hope and the Swan) joined the Rose in Southwark, followed shortly by the legendary Globe, which opened in 1600. (After some trouble with their lease, Shakespeare's acting troupe, the Lord

pendeſt on ſo meane a ſtay ♦ Baſe minded men all three
of you, if by my miſerie you be not warnd: for vnto none
of you (like mee) ſought thoſe burres to cleaue : thoſe
Puppets (J meane) that ſpake from our mouths, thoſe
Anticks garniſht in our colours. Js it not ſtrange, that
J, to whom they all haue beene beholding: is it not like
that you, to whome they all haue beene beholding, ſhall
(were yee in that caſe as J am now) bee both at once of
them forſaken : Yes truſt them not : for there is an vp-
ſtart Crow, beautified with our feathers, that with his
Tygers hart wrapt in a Players hyde, ſuppoſes he is as
well able to bombaſt out a blanke verſe as the beſt of
you : and beeing an abſolute Iohannes fac totum, is in
his owne conceit the onely Shake-ſcene in a countrey.
O that J might intreat your rare wits to be imploied in
more profitable courſes : & let thoſe Apes imitate your
paſt excellence, and neuer more acquaint them with
your admired inuentions ♦ J knowe the beſt huſband of

Greene's insult, lines 9–14

Chamberlain's Men, had disassembled "The Theatre" and transported its
timbers across the Thames, using them as the structure for the Globe.)
Shakespeare was a shareholder in this new venture, with its motto "All the
world's a stage," and continued to write and perform for it as well. Full-
length plays were now being presented every afternoon but Sunday, and
the public appetite for new material seemed endless.

The only curb on the public's hunger for theater was its fear of the
plague—for popular belief held the disease was easily spread in crowds.
Even worse, the infection was completely beyond the powers of Elizabethan
medicine, which held that health derived from four "humors" or internal
fluids identified as bile, phlegm, blood, and choler. Such articles of faith,
however, were utterly ineffective against a genuine health crisis, and in times
of plague, the authorities' panicked response was to shut down any venue
where large crowds might congregate. The theaters would be closed for
lengthy periods in 1593, 1597, and 1603, during which times Shakespeare

was forced to play at court, tour the provinces, or, as many scholars believe, write what would become his famous cycle of sonnets.

THE NEXT STAGE

Between these catastrophic closings, the theater thrived as the great medium of its day; it functioned as film, television, and radio combined as well as a venue for music and dance (all performances, even tragedies, ended with a dance). Moreover, the theater was the place to see and be seen; for a penny

Famous scale model of the Globe completed by Dr. John Cranford Adams in 1954. Collectively, 25,000 pieces were used in constructing the replica. Dr. Adams used walnut to imitate the timber of the Globe, plaster was placed with a spoon and medicine dropper, and 6,500 tiny "bricks" measured by pencil eraser strips were individually placed on the model.

you could stand through a performance in the yard, a penny more bought you a seat in the galleries, while yet another purchased you a cushion. The wealthy, the poor, the royal, and the common all gathered at the Globe, and Shakespeare designed his plays—with their action, humor, and highly refined poetry—not only to satisfy their divergent tastes but also to respond to their differing points of view. In the crucible of Elizabethan theater, the various classes could briefly see themselves as others saw them, and drama could genuinely show "the age and body of the time his form and pressure," to quote Hamlet himself.

In order to accommodate his expanding art, the simplicity of the Elizabethan stage had developed a startling flexibility. The canopied platform of the Globe had a trap in its floor for sudden disappearances, while an alcove at the rear, between the pillars supporting its roof, allowed for "discoveries" and interior space. Above, a balcony made possible the love scene in *Romeo and Juliet*; while still higher, the thatched roof could double as a tower or rampart. And though the stage was largely free of scenery, the costumes were sumptuous—a theater troupe's clothing was its greatest asset. Patrons were used to real drums banging in battle scenes and real cannons firing overhead (in fact, a misfire would one day set the Globe aflame).

With the death of Elizabeth, and the accession of James I to the throne in 1603, Shakespeare only saw his power and influence grow. James, who considered himself an intellectual and something of a scholar, took over the patronage of the Lord Chamberlain's Men, renaming them the King's Men; the troupe even marched in his celebratory entrance to London. At this pinnacle of both artistic power and prestige, Shakespeare composed *Othello*, *King Lear*, and *Macbeth* in quick succession, and soon the King's Men acquired a new, indoor theater in London, which allowed the integration of more music and spectacle into his work. At this wildly popular venue, Shakespeare developed a new form of drama that scholars have dubbed "the romance," which combined elements of comedy and tragedy in a magnificent vision that would culminate in the playwright's last masterpiece, *The Tempest*. Not long after this final innovation, Shakespeare retired to Stratford a wealthy and prominent gentleman.

BEYOND THE ELIZABETHAN UNIVERSE

This is how Shakespeare fit into his age. But how did he transcend it? The answer lies in the plays themselves. For even as we see in the surface of his drama the belief system of England in the sixteenth century, Shakespeare himself is always questioning his own culture, holding its ideas up to the light and shaking them, sometimes hard. In the case of the Elizabethan faith in astrology, Shakespeare had his villain Edmund sneer, "We make guilty of our disasters the sun, the moon, and stars; as if we were villains on necessity." When pondering the medieval code of chivalry, Falstaff decides, "The better part of valor is discretion." The divine right of kings is questioned in *Richard II*, and the inferior status of women—a belief that survived even the crowning of Elizabeth—appears ridiculous before the brilliant examples of Portia (*The Merchant of Venice*), and Rosalind (*As You Like It*). Perhaps it is through this constant shifting of perspective, this relentless sense of exploration, that the playwright somehow outlived the limits of his own period, and became, in the words of his rival Ben Jonson, "not just for an age, but for all time."

Conclusion of the Sourcebooks Shakespeare **KING LEAR**
Sir Derek Jacobi

track 36

About the Online Teaching Resources

The Sourcebooks Shakespeare is committed to supporting students and educators in the study of Shakespeare. A web site with additional articles and essays, extended audio, a forum for discussions, as well as other resources can be found (starting in August 2006) at www.sourcebooksshakespeare.com. To illustrate how the Sourcebooks Shakespeare may be used in your class, Jeremy Ehrlich, the head of education at the Folger Shakespeare Library, contributed an essay called "Working with Audio in the Classroom." The following is an excerpt:

One possible way of approaching basic audio work in the classroom is shown in the handout [on the site]. It is meant to give some guidance for the first-time user of audio in the classroom. I would urge you to adapt this to the particular circumstances and interests of your own students.

To use it, divide the students into four groups. Assign each group one of the four technical elements of audio – volume, pitch, pace, and pause – to follow as you play them an audio clip or clips. In the first section, have them record what they hear: the range they encounter in the clip and the places where their element changes. In the second section, have them suggest words for the tone of the passage based in part on their answers to the first. Sections three and four deal with tools of the actor. Modern acting theory finds the actor's objective is his single most important acting choice; an actor may then choose from a variety of tactics in order to achieve that objective. Thus, if a character's objective on stage is to get sympathy from his scene partner, he may start out by complaining, then shift to another tactic (asking for sympathy directly? throwing a tantrum?) if the first tactic fails. Asking your students to try to explain what they think a character is trying to get, and how she is trying to do it, is a way for them to follow this process through closely. Finally, the handout asks students to think about the meaning (theme) of the passage, concluding with a traditional and important tool of text analysis.

As you can see, this activity is more interesting and, probably, easier for students when it's used with multiple versions of the same piece of text. While defining an actor's motivation is difficult in a vacuum, doing so in relation to another performance may be easier: one Othello may be more

concerned with gaining respect, while another Othello may be more concerned with obtaining love, for instance. This activity may be done outside
of a group setting, although for students doing this work for the first time I
suggest group work so they will be able to share answers on some potentially
thought-provoking questions...

For the complete essay, please visit www.sourcebooksshakespeare.com.

Acknowledgments

The series editors wish to give heartfelt thanks to the advisory editors of the series, David Bevington and Peter Holland, for their ongoing support, timely advice, and keen brilliance.

We are incredibly grateful to the community of Shakespeare scholars for their generosity in sharing their talents, collections, and even their address books. We would not have been able to put together such an august list of contributors without their help. Our sincere thanks go to our text editor, Douglas Brooks, for his brilliant work, and to Bradley Ryner, Tom Garvey, Doug Lanier, and Andrew Wade for their marvelous essays. We are also grateful to William Proctor Williams for his continuing guidance.

Our research was aided immensely by the wonderful staff at Shakespeare archives and libraries around the world: the staff at The Shakespeare Birthplace Trust; Jeremy Ehrlich, Bettina Smith, and everyone at the Folger Shakespeare Library; and Gene Rinkel, Bruce Swann, and Tim Cole from the Rare Books and Special Collections Library at the University of Illinois. These individuals were instrumental in helping us gather audio: Justyn Baker, Janet Benson, Barbara Brown, Nelda Gil, Liz Cooper and Josh Flanagan for the Olivier audio. The following are the talented photographers who shared their work with us: Donald Cooper, George Joseph, Michal Daniel, and Carol Rosegg. Thank you to Jessica Talmage at the Mary Evans Picture Library and to Tracey Tomaso at Corbis. We appreciate all your help. Extra appreciation goes to Doug Lanier for all his guidance and the use of his personal Shakespeare collection.

From the world of drama, the following shared their passion with us and helped us develop the series into a true partnership between the artistic and academic communities. We are indebted to: Liza Holtmeier, Lauren Beyea, and the team from the Shakespeare Theatre Company; Amy Richard from the Oregon Shakespeare Festival; Nancy Becker of The Shakespeare Society; and Myra Lucretia Taylor.

With respect to the audio, we extend our heartfelt thanks to our narrating team: our director, John Tydeman, our esteemed narrator, Sir Derek Jacobi, and the staff of Motivation Studios. John has been a wonderful, generous resource to us and we look forward to future collaborations. We owe a debt of gratitude to Nicolas Soames for introducing us and for being unfailingly helpful. Thank you to Joe Plummer for his excellent work on the audio analysis. Thanks also to the "Speaking Shakespeare" team: Andrew Wade and Myra Lucretia Taylor for that wonderful recording, and Steve Alvarado and the team at Dubway Studios. Thank you to Paul Estby for mastering the entire CD.

We would also like to thank Tanya Gough, the proprietor of The Poor Yorick Shakespeare Catalog, for all her efforts on behalf of the series. Our personal thanks for their kindness and unstinting support go to our friends and our extended families.

Finally, thanks to everyone at Sourcebooks who contributed their talents in realizing The Sourcebooks Shakespeare–in particular: Todd Green, Todd Stocke, Megan Dempster, and Melanie Thompson. Special mention to Nikki Braziel and Elizabeth Lhost, assistants extraordinaire for the Sourcebooks Shakespeare.

So, thanks to all at once and to each one (Macbeth, 5.7.104)

Audio Credits

In all cases, we have attempted to provide archival audio in its original form. While we have tried to achieve the best possible quality on the archival audio, some audio quality is the result of source limitations. Archival audio research by Marie Macaisa. Audio analysis by Joe Plummer. Narration script by Marie Macaisa. Narration recording and audio engineering by Motivation Sound Studios, London, UK. Mastering by Paul Estby. Recording for "Speaking Shakespeare" by Dubway Studios, New York City, USA.

Narrated by Sir Derek Jacobi
Directed by John Tydeman
Produced by Marie Macaisa

Photo Credits

Every effort has been made to correctly attribute all the materials reproduced in this book. If any errors have been made, we will be happy to correct them in future editions. Photos are credited on the pages in which they
appear.

Images from the 1959 production at the Shakespeare Memorial Theatre in
Stratford-upon-Avon directed by Glen Byam Shaw are courtesy of the Rare
Book and Special Collections Library, University of Illinois at Urbana-
Champaign.

Photos from the Shakespeare Theatre Company's 2000 production directed
by Michael Kahn are © 2000 Carol Rosegg.

Photos from the Public Theater's 1973 production directed by Edwin Sherin
are © 1973 George E. Joseph; from its 2007 production directed by James
Lapine are © 2007 Michal Daniel.

Photos from the Royal Shakespeare Company's 1991 production directed by
Nicholas Hytner are © 1991 Donald Cooper; from its 1993 production
directed by Adrian Noble are © 1993 Donald Cooper; from its 1999 production directed by Yukio Ninagawa are © 1999 Donald Cooper; from its 2005
production directed by Bill Alexander are © 2005 Donald Cooper; from its
2007 production directed by Trevor Nunn are © 2007 Donald Cooper.

Photos from the Oregon Shakespeare Festival's 2004 production directed by
James Edmondson are courtesy of the Oregon Shakespeare Festival.

Photos from the 1999 Shakespeare's Globe production directed by Annete
Leday are © 1999 Donald Cooper.

Photos from the 1997 Old Vic production directed by Peter Hall are © 1997
Donald Cooper.

Engravings by John Byam Shaw and watercolor sketches from Charles Kean's 1858 promptbook are courtesy of the Folger Shakespeare Library.

William Shakespeare's signature (on the title page) courtesy of Mary Evans Picture Library. Other images from the Mary Evans Picture Library used in the text are credited on the pages in which they appear.

Images from "In the Age of Shakespeare" courtesy of The Folger Shakespeare Library.

About the Contributors

TEXT EDITOR

Douglas A. Brooks is Associate Professor of English at Texas A&M University and the Editor of *Shakespeare Yearbook*. He is the author of *From Playhouse to Printing House: Drama and Authorship in Early Modern England* (Cambridge UP, 2000) and the editor of two collections of essays, *Printing and Parenting in Early Modern England* (Ashgate Publishing Co., 2005) and *Milton and the Jews*, forthcoming Cambridge UP. Brooks has published essays in *Medieval and Renaissance Drama in England*, *Shakespeare Studies*, *ELR*, *Philological Quarterly*, *Genre*, *Renaissance Drama*, *Studies in English Literature*, and *Poetics Today*. He is presently completing a book entitled *The Gutenberg Father in Early Modern England*.

SERIES EDITORS

Marie Macaisa spent twenty years in her first career: high tech. She has a bachelor's degree in computer science from the Massachusetts Institute of Technology, a master's degree in artificial intelligence from the University of Pennsylvania, and worked for many years on the research and development of innovative applications of computer technology. She became the series editor of *The Sourcebooks Shakespeare* in 2003. She contributed the *Cast Speaks* essays for previous volumes and is the producer of the accompanying audio CDs.

Dominique Raccah is the founder, president, and publisher of Sourcebooks. Born in Paris, France, she has a bachelor's degree in psychology and a master's in quantitative psychology from the University of Illinois. She also serves as series editor of *Poetry Speaks* and *Poetry Speaks to Children*.

ADVISORY BOARD

David Bevington is the Phyllis Fay Horton Distinguished Service Professor in the Humanities at the University of Chicago. A renowned text scholar, he has edited several Shakespeare editions including the *Bantam Shakespeare* in individual paperback volumes, *The Complete Works of Shakespeare*

(Longman, 2003), and *Troilus and Cressida* (Arden, 1998). He teaches courses in Shakespeare, renaissance drama, and medieval drama.

Peter Holland is the McMeel Family Chair in Shakespeare Studies at the University of Notre Dame. One of the central figures in performance-oriented Shakespeare criticism, he has also edited many Shakespeare plays, including *A Midsummer Night's Dream* for the Oxford Shakespeare series. He is also general editor of Shakespeare Survey and co-general editor (with Stanley Wells) of Oxford Shakespeare Topics. Currently he is completing a book, *Shakespeare on Film*, and editing *Coriolanus* for the Arden 3rd series.

ESSAYISTS

Thomas Garvey has been acting, directing, or writing about Shakespeare for over two decades. A graduate of the Massachusetts Institute of Technology, he studied acting and directing with the MIT Shakespeare Ensemble, where he played Hamlet, Jacques, Iago, and other roles, and directed *All's Well That Ends Well* and *Twelfth Night*. He has since directed and designed several other Shakespearean productions, as well as works by Chekhov, Ibsen, Sophocles, Beckett, Moliere, and Shaw. Mr. Garvey has written on theatre for the *Boston Globe* and other publications.

Douglas Lanier is an associate professor of English at the University of New Hampshire. He has written many essays on Shakespeare in popular culture, including "Shakescorp Noir" in *Shakespeare Quarterly* 53.2 (Summer 2002) and "Shakespeare on the Record" in *The Blackwell Companion to Shakespeare in Performance* (edited by Barbara Hodgdon and William Worthen, Blackwell, 2005). His book *Shakespeare and Modern Popular Culture* (Oxford University Press) was published in 2002. He is currently working on a book-length study of cultural stratification in early modern British theater.

Bradley D. Ryner is an Assistant Professor of English at Arizona State University. His work has appeared in the journals *English Studies* and *Shakespeare* (both published by Routledge), and *The Oxford Companion to Shakespeare* (edited by Michael Dobson and Stanley Wells). He is working on a book manuscript that examines the conventions for representing economic systems on the English Renaissance stage. An essay on *Cymbeline* derived from this project is scheduled to appear in a collection to be published by Palgrave.

Andrew Wade was head of voice for the Royal Shakespeare Company from 1990 to 2003 and voice assistant director from 1987 to 1990. During this time he worked on 170 productions and with more than 80 directors. Along with Cicely Berry, Andrew recorded *Working Shakespeare* and the DVD series on *Voice and Shakespeare*, and he was the verse consultant for the movie *Shakespeare In Love*. In 2000, he won a Bronze Award from the New York International Radio Festival for the series *Lifespan*, which he co-directed and devised. He works widely teaching, lecturing, and coaching throughout the world.

AUDIO CONTRIBUTORS

Sir Derek Jacobi (Series Narrator) is one of Britain's foremost actors of stage and screen. One of his earliest Shakespearean roles was Cassio to Sir Laurence Olivier's Othello in Stuart Burge's 1965 movie production. More recent roles include Hamlet in the acclaimed BBC Television Shakespeare production in 1980, the Chorus in Kenneth Branagh's 1989 film of *Henry V*, and Claudius in Branagh's 1996 movie *Hamlet*. He has been accorded numerous honors in his distinguished career, including a Tony award for Best Actor in *Much Ado About Nothing* and a BAFTA (British Academy of Film and Television) for his landmark portrayal of Emperor Claudius in the blockbuster television series *I, Claudius*. He was made a Knight of the British Empire in 1994 for his services to the theatre.

John Tydeman (Series Director) was the Head of Drama for BBC Radio for many years and is the director of countless productions, with 15 Shakespeare plays to his credit. Among his numerous awards are the Prix Italia, Prix Europa, UK Broadcasting Guild Best Radio Programme (*When The Wind Blows* by Raymond Briggs), and the Sony Personal Award for services to radio. He has worked with most of Britain's leading actors and dramatists and has directed for the theatre, television, and commercial recordings. He holds an M.A. from Cambridge University.

Joe Plummer (Audio Analyst) is the Director of Education for the Williamstown Theatre Festival and Assistant Professor of Shakespearean Performance with Roger Rees at Fordham University's Lincoln Center Campus. He has taught several Master classes on Shakespeare and performance at Williams College, the National Shakespeare Company and Brandeis University, and also teaches privately. Joe is currently the Artist-In-Residence and Director of Educational Outreach for The Shakespeare Society in New York City and is the founder and Producing Artistic Director of poortom productions, the only all-male Shakespeare Company in the US. He has performed extensively in New York and in regional theaters.

Dictionary of Eponyms

The Wordsworth
Dictionary of Eponyms
—

Martin H. Manser

Wordsworth Reference

First published in Great Britain 1988 by Sphere Books

This edition published 1996 by Wordsworth Editions Ltd
Cumberland House, Crib Street, Ware, Hertfordshire SG12 9ET

ISBN 1 85326 373 7

Typeset by Antony Gray
Printed and bound in Great Britain by
Mackays of Chatham plc, Chatham, Kent

PREFACE

This book explores that part of the rich heritage of the English language that concerns the derivation of words from the names of people. The idea for the book originally arose several years ago, after an evening meal with my mother. We quite simply tried to think of as many objects named after people as we could. We quickly exhausted the very familiar **macintosh**, **wellington**, **sandwich**; the scientific **ampere**, **watt**, **volt** and so on. The concept of compiling a list of such words remained at the back of my mind, so when Sphere Books suggested putting together a book on the subject I welcomed the task enthusiastically, since the project was close to my heart.

Eponyms are the people who give their names to words. Most eponymous words derive from a person's surname: **boycott**, for instance, from the Irish landlord Captain Charles Cunningham Boycott; **dahlia**, from the Swedish botanist Anders Dahl; the **sousaphone**, from the American bandmaster John Philip Sousa; and **volt**, from the Italian physicist Count Alessandro Volta. Many eponymous words come from literary, biblical or mythological sources: **malapropism**, from Mrs Malaprop in Sheridan's *The Rivals*; **Dickensian** – for example, 'a really old-fashioned Dickensian Christmas' – from the English writer Charles Dickens; **as old as Methuselah**, from the age of the Old Testament patriarch; and **aphrodisiac**, from the Greek goddess of love and beauty Aphrodite. In this book, I have concentrated on the more well-known eponymous words in general use and have sought to give background detail on interesting aspects of an individual's life.

The entries are listed according to the name of the thing referred to, not the name the thing derives from. So the entry **spoonerism** is followed by an explanation of its derivation from the Reverend William Archibald Spooner. Note that when the name of the thing is itself a person's name, this is listed in alphabetical order thus: an **Aunt Sally** is listed at **Aunt**, **Mrs Grundy** at **Mrs** and a **smart alec** at **smart**.

I would like to thank my family and friends, particularly Friedemann

Lux, for their helpful advice on numerous points of detail; Christopher Potter of Sphere Books for his encouragement; and my secretary, Mrs Rosalind Desmond, for her painstaking research and typing work.

MARTIN H. MANSER

TRADEMARKS

A

Aaron's beard; Aaron's rod

Aaron, the brother of Moses, has given his name to two plants.

Aaron's beard is another name for rose of Sharon (also called St John's Wort) – a creeping shrub, *Hypericum calycinum*, which has large yellow flowers. The term derives from the Bible: 'It is like the precious ointment upon the head, that ran down the beard, even Aaron's beard: that went down to the skirts of his garments' (Psalm 133:2).

Aaron's rod is a mullein, *Verbascum trapsus*, a plant that has tall spikes of yellow flowers and broad hairy leaves. The name Aaron's rod comes from one of the rods that were placed in the tabernacle. Aaron's rod had the next day budded, blossomed and produced almonds (Numbers 17:1–13).

abigail

Abigail is an archaic word for a lady's maid. The name comes originally from Nabal's wife, Abigail, in the Bible (1 Samuel 25). Abigail apologised for her husband's meanness in refusing to give food to David's followers. She herself provided food for them, waylaying David even as he planned to attack Nabal and his people. In the space of seventeen verses of the Bible text, Abigail refers to herself as 'thine handmaid' six times. Later, after Nabal's death, Abigail became David's wife.

The name and occupation came into more general use from the 'waiting gentlewoman' in the play *The Scornful Lady* by Sir Francis Beaumont and John Fletcher, first performed in 1610.

Swift, Fielding and other novelists of the period used the name further and it became popularised by the notoriety of Abigail Hill, lady-in-waiting to Queen Anne, 1704–14, who used her friendship with the queen to try to secure personal favours.

Abraham's bosom

Abraham's bosom refers to the sleeping-place of the blessed in death. It is well known from Shakespeare's *Richard III*: 'The sons of Edward sleep in Abraham's bosom' (Act 4, Scene 3), but originally it was a figure of speech used by Jesus in the parable of Lazarus and the rich man (Luke 16:19–31): 'The beggar [Lazarus] died, and was carried by the angels into Abraham's bosom' (verse 22). In the language of the Talmud to sit in Abraham's bosom meant to enter paradise.

academy

Nowadays an academy is a school that gives a particular training – for example, a military academy, or, as in Scotland, a secondary school. An academy is also an association of learned people organised to promote literature, art or science: the Royal Academy, the French Academy, etc.

The word academy comes from the Academeia, a pleasure garden in the suburbs of Athens where the philosopher Plato taught in the late fourth century BC. The garden itself was named after the Greek mythological hero Academos.

Achilles' heel; Achilles tendon

To mention an Achilles' heel is to refer to a weakness, fault or vulnerable spot in a person or thing that is otherwise strong: 'The party knows that its group of political extremists might well be its Achilles' heel.'

The expression derives from Greek mythology. Thetis, the mother of Achilles, is said to have dipped him into the River Styx to make him invulnerable. His one weak spot was the heel by which Thetis held him during the dipping and which therefore was not touched by the water. It was during the siege of Troy that Achilles was mortally wounded by a poisoned arrow that was shot into his heel.

The fibrous cord connecting the heel-bone to the muscles of the calf is known as the Achilles tendon.

Adam's apple; Adam's ale; the old Adam; not to know someone from Adam

The visible projection at the front of the neck formed by the thyroid cartilage is called the Adam's apple. It is traditionally thought that this name derives from the belief that a piece of apple from the forbidden tree became stuck in Adam's throat. It is however interesting to note that the Bible nowhere mentions that the fruit was in fact an apple.

Adam's ale is water: the first human would have had nothing else to drink.

The 'old Adam' refers to the sinful nature of all human beings.

If you don't know someone from Adam, you don't recognise him or her – you have no idea who he or she is: 'I think you'd better explain to Mr Chadwick who I am – he won't know me from Adam.' The expression derives from the fact that Adam, as the first man, is someone whom one could not know.

adonis

Adonis, 'a handsome young man', was a youth in Greek mythology who was renowned for his great beauty. Loved by Aphrodite, he was killed by a boar while hunting but resurrected by Persephone. He was celebrated in many festivals as a vegetation god, his death and restoration to life symbolising the seasonal decay and rebirth of nature.

Aladdin's cave

'With everything from children's games to computer software, the shop's a real Aladdin's cave for bargain hunters!' The expression, referring to a source or place of great riches, comes originally from the oriental story *Aladdin or the Wonderful Lamp*. Aladdin, the poor son of a Chinese tailor, is used by a Moorish magician to fetch from an underground cave a lamp with magical powers.

albert

An albert is a kind of watch chain usually attached to a waistcoat. The name comes from Prince Albert (1819–61), Prince Consort of Queen Victoria. When he visited Birmingham in 1849, the jewellers of that city presented him with such a chain. Very satisfied with their gift, he wore it from that time onwards and created a fashion.

alexandrine

An alexandrine is a verse metre made up of a line of twelve syllables, usually with major stresses on the sixth and final syllables. The name comes from twelfth-century French poems about Alexander the Great (356–323BC), king of Macedonia. The alexandrine has been the dominant metre of French poetry since the sixteenth century, and was much used by Racine and Corneille.

algorithm

An algorithm is a step-by-step method of solving mathematical problems. The word algorithm is an alteration of the Middle English *algorisme* and comes from Old French and Medieval Latin. Ultimately it comes from the name of the ninth-century Arab mathematician Mohammed ibn Musa al-Khuwarizmi. He introduced the Indian decimal system and the use of zero into Arabic mathematics.

Alice in Wonderland

'Alice in Wonderland' is sometimes used to describe a strange, fantastic world in which the normal laws of logic and reason have been suspended. The phrase comes from *Alice's Adventures in Wonderland*, a story for children by Lewis Carroll, published in 1865. The story was in fact originally titled 'Alice's Adventures Under Ground'. The model for the character Alice was Alice Liddell, daughter of Dean Henry George Liddell, co-author of the standard Greek-English Dictionary, Liddell & Scott's Greek Lexicon.

amazon

An amazon is a tall, strong and athletic woman. In Greek mythology, Amazons were a nation of female warriors who lived on the shores of the Black Sea. The word *amazon* itself means 'without breast', because the Amazons were said to remove their right breasts to enable them to draw bows more easily. It is thought that the South American River Amazon was so called because the Spanish explorer Francisco de Orellana thought he saw female warriors there in 1541.

America

America is named after the Italian navigator Amerigo Vespucci (1454–1512). He was a merchant who worked for a firm that fitted out ships for, among others, the explorer Christopher Columbus. Vespucci may well have gone on the voyages of some other explorers, but in 1499 he himself explored the north-east coast of South America. In 1507 an inaccurate record of his explorations was published, in which it was claimed that in 1497 he had discovered a new world, 'a continent more densely peopled and abounding in animals than our Europe or Asia or Africa'.

The two continents were therefore named in his honour – *Americus* being the Latin form of Amerigo.

ammonia

Ammonia is a colourless, poisonous, highly soluble gas that is used in making fertilisers, explosives, etc. The word comes from Latin *sal ammoniacus* – 'sal ammoniac'. Ammoniac is a salt or gum resin thought to have been obtained from a district in Libya near the temple of the Egyptian god Ammon.

ampere

Ampere – often shortened to amp – is a common domestic word: we are familiar with 13-amp plugs, a 5-amp fuse, etc. The ampere is the basic metric unit of electric current. The word comes from the name of the French physicist André Marie Ampère (1775–1836), noted for his discoveries about the nature of electricity and magnetism. Three other familiar electrical terms named after scientists are: **ohm, volt, watt.**

Although Ampère enjoyed a brilliant career, his private life was tragically unhappy. When he was only eighteen, he saw his father guillotined during the Reign of Terror; he was so shocked that he was unable to speak for over a year. He married at twenty-four, but his wife died a year later. These personal tragedies led him to immerse himself in his work.

Anderson shelter; Morrison shelter

An Anderson shelter was a partly prefabricated air-raid shelter. It was named after John Anderson, 1st Viscount Waverley (1882–1958), a civil servant who entered parliament. As home secretary and minister of home security (1939–40) he was faced with the urgent need to supply air-raid shelters to protect the civilian population. Designed by the engineer William, later Sir William, Paterson, the Anderson shelter could easily be erected by a non-specialist. About three-million Anderson shelters were distributed. Anderson later became chancellor of the exchequer (1943–5).

A further eponymous air-raid shelter used in the Second World War was the Morrison shelter – an indoor shelter with a steel table-top and wired sides – named after the British statesman Herbert Stanley Morrison (1888–1965), later Baron Morrison of Lambeth. Morrison was home secretary and minister for home security in Churchill's war cabinet (1942–5).

ångström

An ångström is a unit of length formerly in technical use to measure the wavelengths of electromagnetic radiations. It is named after the Swedish physicist and astronomer Anders Jonas Ångström (1814–74). He was a student and later professor at the University of Uppsala; he founded the science of spectroscopy, his studies of the sun's spectra resulting in the discovery, in 1862, of hydrogen in the sun.

Annie Oakley

In theatrical (especially American) slang, an Annie Oakley is a free ticket. The name is the shortened name of the American markswoman Phoebe Anne Oakley Mozee (1860–1926). She was the star rifle-shooter of Buffalo Bill's Wild West Show.

The complimentary tickets have a hole punched in them to ensure that they are not exchanged for cash at the box office. The tickets are probably so called because of Annie's most famous trick: tossing a playing-card – especially the five of hearts – into the air and shooting holes through all the card's pips.

aphrodisiac

An aphrodisiac is a substance that stimulates sexual desire. The word comes from the name of Aphrodite, the goddess of love and beauty in Greek mythology. According to one of the earliest of Greek poets, Hesiod, she was born from the foam (*aphros*) of the sea. According to Homer, she was the daughter of Dione and Zeus.

Appleton layer

The Appleton layer is the former name of the F-layer of the earth's atmosphere – the layer in the ionosphere about 150–1000 km above the earth. Of all the three different layers in the ionosphere, the F-layer contains the highest proportion of free electrons and is the most useful for long-range radio transmission.

The Appleton layer was so called because it was discovered by the British physicist Sir Edward Appleton (1892–1963).

See also **Heaviside layer**.

arachnid

An arachnid is an invertebrate insect-like animal with eight legs that belongs to the order Arachnida, which includes spiders, scorpions, ticks and mites. The word arachnid comes ultimately from Arachne, in Greek mythology a girl from Lydia who presumptuously challenged the goddess Athena to a weaving contest. Jealous, Athena tore Arachne's attractive tapestry to pieces, whereupon Arachne tried to hang herself. Not content with this outcome, Athena changed Arachne into a spider (in Greek, *arachne*).

Archimedes' principle; Archimedes' screw

The Greek mathematician and scientist Archimedes (*c.*287–*c.*212BC) is noted for his work in geometry, mechanics and hydrostatics. He is well known for his discovery, that when a body is immersed in a liquid its apparent loss of weight equals the weight of the water that is displaced (Archimedes' principle). It is alleged that he discovered this while taking a bath; on noticing that his body displaced the water in his bath, he is said to have exclaimed, '*Eureka!*' ('I have found it!')

His discovery enabled him to give a response to King Hiero II. The king had asked Archimedes to find out the amount of gold in a crown that had been made for him, since he suspected that it was not made of pure gold. Archimedes' discovery led him to realise that since gold was heavier than silver, a floating vessel holding a pure-gold crown would displace more water than one holding a crown made of mixed metals. His tests proved that the king had in fact been supplied with a crown made of gold and base metal.

Archimedes is also remembered for a device for raising water (the Archimedes' screw). He reputedly invented it, but it was probably already known to the Egyptians.

assassin

The word assassin, meaning a person who kills someone prominent, especially for political motives, derives from the name of a secret fanatical sect of Muslims, the Assassins, that operated in Persia and Syria in the eleventh and twelfth centuries. The sect was infamous for its campaign of terror in attempting to dominate the Muslim world. The name of the sect itself derives from the Arabic *hashshashin*, meaning 'hashish eaters', as it is commonly believed that they ate or smoked hashish before being sent to carry out their evil deeds.

atlas

In Greek mythology Atlas was one of the Titans who, as a punishment for his part in the attempt to overthrow Zeus, was condemned to hold up the heavens on his shoulders for the rest of his life. Atlas came to be used to refer to a book of maps after a drawing of Atlas was included on the title-page of a collection of maps by the mapmaker Mercator, published in the late sixteenth century.

See also **Mercator projection**.

attic

It is surprising to think that attic, the word for the room in the space below the roof of a house, is eponymous, but this is so. Attic comes from the Attic, or Athenian, architectural style. A feature of this style was a wall that decorated the façade of the highest storey. In time, the space behind the decorative wall came to be referred to as an attic.

The expression Attic salt (meaning elegant and pointed wit) derives from Attica, the ancient Greek state whose capital was Athens. Salt was a common term for wit in both Latin and Greek, and Athenian men were famous for their wit and elegant expression.

aubrietia

The trailing perennial plant bearing small purple flowers that is widely grown in rock gardens is known as aubrietia or aubretia. It was named in 1763 by the French naturalist Michel Adamson after the French painter of flowers and animals Claude Aubnet (1665–1742).

Augean – to clean the Augean stables

It is difficult to think of a worse mess than stables for 3000 oxen would be in if they had not been cleaned out for thirty years. The stables of King Augeas in Greek mythology were, however, in this condition. The cleansing of these stables was one of the twelve labours of Hercules: he caused the River Alpheus to flow through them, cleansing them in a day. (Incidentally, when Hercules had successfully completed the task, Augeas meanly refused him a reward.) The phrase 'to clean the Augean stables' has come to refer to the task of removing the accumulation of different sorts of corruption.

August

The first Roman emperor, Octavian (63BC–AD14), was the great-nephew and adopted son of Julius Caesar. After Caesar's assassination in 44BC, Octavian ruled Rome jointly with Mark Antony and Lepidus. Octavian defeated Mark Antony at Actium in 31BC to become, two years later, the first emperor, the Senate later awarding him the title Augustus ('venerable') for his distinguished service to the state.

In 46BC Caesar had established the so-called Julian calendar, adding the months January and February to the previous calendar. Caesar decided to rename one of the old months, formerly called Quintilis because it was the fifth (the first month being March), and chose to name it after himself: July. Not wishing to be outdone, Augustus wanted to have a month named after himself as well. His birth month was September, but he chose the sixth month Sextilis, as this had been the month in which he had achieved his greatest civil and military triumphs. Furthermore, as Augustus did not want Julius Caesar's month to have more days than his own month, he took a day from February to give both August and July thirty-one days.

Aunt Sally

Originally, an Aunt Sally was an effigy of an old woman at which one threw objects at a fair. This sense has broadened and the expression is now applied to any easy target for insults or criticism: 'In times of peace, a large part of a dictator's role would be as a sort of national Aunt Sally, a symbol on which citizens could vent their frustration.' (*Punch*)

The explanation of this expression is not certain: the elderly fairground figure resembles an aunt, but it has not been satisfactorily explained why the name Sally was chosen to stand for the unfortunate target.

B

bacchanalia

Bacchanalia is used to refer to a drunken orgy. It derives from *Bacchanalia*, ancient mysteries or orgies in honour of Bacchus (the Roman name of the Greek god Dionysus), the god of wine. Coming from southern Italy, the cult reached Rome in the second century BC. The Roman festival of Bacchus, celebrated with dancing, song and revelry, was marked by drunkenness, debauchery and sexual immorality. A decree from the Senate in 186 BC prohibited Bacchanalia in Rome.

Baedeker

A Baedeker at one time referred only to a travel guidebook published by the German Karl Baedeker (1801–59), but it is now sometimes used to refer to any authoritative travel guide. Baedeker's publishing firm was established in 1827. The fame of Baedeker's guides developed during the first three editions of J. A. Klein's *Rhineland Journey* (1833, second edition 1835, third edition 1839). By 1872, he had published guides to the whole of Europe, the guides being published in German, English and French. His guides were well known for being authoritative and comprehensive – even Chekhov was to write from Venice, 'Here I am alone with my thoughts and my Baedeker.'

During the Second World War, German air raids (1941–2) on places of cultural or historical importance, such as Canterbury and York, in England were known as Baedeker raids, because the German Luftwaffe used the Baedeker to determine the targets.

Baffin Bay; Baffin Island

Baffin Island is the largest island in the Canadian Arctic and is situated between Greenland and Hudson Bay. Baffin Bay is the name of the part of the Northwest Passage between Baffin Island and Greenland. The bay and the island are named after the English navigator William Baffin (*c.*1584–1622). In 1615–16 he was the pilot on *Discovery* on expeditions with Captain Robert Bylot attempting to find the sea route along the north coast of North America linking the Atlantic and Pacific

Oceans (the Northwest Passage). Failing to find such a route, he explored the Hudson Strait and Baffin Island.

Bailey bridge

A Bailey bridge is a kind of temporary military bridge. Named after its inventor, the English engineer Sir Donald Bailey (1901–85), the Bailey bridge played a crucial role in the Allied victory in the Second World War. As Field Marshal Montgomery put it, 'Without the Bailey bridge we should not have won the war.' Bailey bridges were quickly assembled from prefabricated lattice-steel welded panels linked by pinned joints; they were capable of supporting heavy vehicles such as tanks and trains. Bailey bridges are still used in flood and disaster areas throughout the world.

Bakelite

Bakelite is the trademark for a kind of synthetic thermosetting resin and plastic used to make electrical insulating material and plastic fittings. Bakelite is named after the Belgian-born American chemist Leo Hendrik Baekeland (1863–1944). He discovered that the sticky resin formed by heating phenols and aldehydes under pressure had a number of useful properties: it was hard and strong, yet light; it could be moulded and coloured. In 1909 he announced the invention of Bakelite and, as president of the Bakelite Corporation (1910–39), he saw his product find many applications throughout the world.

banting

Banting is a method of slimming by eating high amounts of protein and avoiding sugar, starch and fat. It is named after a London undertaker William Banting (1797–1878). Grossly overweight himself, Banting tried various slimming methods with no success, so he resorted to a strict diet. He lost 46 pounds (21 kg), reducing his waist measurement by 12 inches (32 cm). His efforts attracted some publicity, and he wrote a book about his experience, *Letter on Corpulence* (1863), outlining his methods of slimming. Banting's diet undoubtedly helped him: he was in his sixties when he started slimming and he lived to be eighty-one.

baroque

The highly ornate style of architecture and art that flourished in Europe from the late sixteenth to the early eighteenth centuries is known as baroque. There are different theories as to the word's origin: it may have come via French from the Portuguese *barroco*, 'irregular pearl'. Alternatively, the word may perhaps derive via French from the name Federigo Barocci (c.1535–1612), an Italian artist who painted in this style.

Bartlett pear

A Bartlett pear (also known as a Williams pear) is a kind of pear tree with a large juicy yellow sweet fruit. It is named after Enoch Bartlett (1779–1860), a merchant in Massachusetts, USA, but Bartlett was not the first to develop the fruit. It was a Captain Thomas Brewer who imported the trees from England; Bartlett, who bought up Brewer's farm, distributed the pears using his own name in the early 1800s.

Baskerville

The style of type known as Baskerville derives its name from its designer, the English printer John Baskerville (1706–75). At first a writing-master in Birmingham, Baskerville had by 1754 established a printing office and type-foundry in that city. His first work, a Latin Virgil, was printed in 1757. As printer to Cambridge University, he later produced editions of the Book of Common Prayer and the Bible. His books are notable for their high quality of presswork and type, and he was the first to use original high-gloss paper. The typeface that is named after him, Baskerville, is of a traditional style, with exaggerated serifs and open curves.

Other designers of type who have given their names to typestyles include: Christophe Plantin (c.1520–89), a French printer; (Arthur) Eric (Rowton) Gill (1882–1940), a British sculptor, engraver and typographer; and Claude Garamond (c.1800–61), a French type founder.

batiste

Batiste is a fine, soft, sheer fabric of plain weave, used especially in shirts, lingerie, dresses and handkerchiefs. The word derives from French *toile de baptiste*, baptist cloth, and probably comes ultimately from the thirteenth-century French weaver, Baptiste of Cambrai, as he is reputed to have been its first manufacturer.

The town of Cambrai in north-east France was known from the sixteenth century for its cambric linen cloth; it seems that the English merchants, wanting a different name for the new Cambrai fabric, called it after the French weaver, but misspelt his name in the process.

baud

A baud is a unit of measuring the speed of electronic data transmission, one baud equaling one unit of information per second. It is named after the French inventor and pioneer of telegraphic communication Jean

M. E. Baudot (1845–1903).

A baud was originally equivalent to twice the number of **Morse code** dots transmitted continuously per second. With the development of electronics, the term has been used to describe any of several different units.

BCG

This abbreviation is well known amongst schoolchildren who are having their BCG vaccine. The initials stand for *bacille* (or bacillus) Calmette–Guérin, after the French bacteriologists who developed the vaccine – Albert Léon Charles Calmette (1863–1933) and Camille Guérin (1872–1961). The vaccine stimulates the body's defence system against tuberculosis.

Beau Brummel

George Bryan Brummel (1778–1840) was known as Beau Brummel and this latter name has come to be used to refer to a dandy, fop or leader of male fashion. For almost twenty years a prominent member of English fashionable society and a friend of the Prince of Wales (later King George IV), Beau Brummel is remembered for the extravagance of his dress. It is said that he spent an entire day preparing himself and his attire for a royal ball. Eventually, however, he quarrelled with the prince, and the wealth that he had inherited being exhausted, he was forced to flee to France in 1816 to escape his creditors. His final years he spent in poverty, suffering from periodic attacks of paralysis.

Beaufort scale

The Beaufort scale is a measure of wind speed. The scale was devised in 1805 by the surveyor Sir Francis Beaufort (1774–1857), who later became a rear-admiral and official hydrographer to the Royal Navy. The scale is based on easily observable features such as the movement of trees and smoke. It has the numbers 0 to 12, 0 being 'calm' and 12 'hurricane', or as Beaufort described it, 'that which no canvas could withstand'.

béchamel sauce

A béchamel sauce is a white sauce made from flour, butter and milk and flavoured with vegetables and seasonings. It comes from the French sauce *béchamel* and is named after the French financier Marquis Louis de Béchamel (*d.*1703), the steward of Louis XIV of France, who is reputed to have invented it. It seems that the original béchamel sauce was a more elaborate mixture; it included in its ingredients old hens and old partridges.

becquerel

A becquerel is the basic metric unit of radiation activity, equal to one disintegration per second. It is named after the discoverer of radioactivity, the French physicist Antoine-Henri Becquerel (1852–1908).

The becquerel has now displaced the curie – itself an eponymous word, named after the French physicist and chemist Marie Curie (1867–1934) – as the basic measure of radioactivity. The curie is a much larger unit; it is equal to 3.7×10^{10} becquerel.

begonia

Begonia is a genus of succulent herbaceous plants, originally found in the tropics. The genus contains about 1000 species, grown as pot or bedding plants and having showy, often brightly coloured, flowers with asymmetrical leaves.

Begonias are named after the French patron of science Michel Bégon (1638–1710). While working as Royal Commissioner in Santo Domingo, his enthusiastic amateur interest in botany led him to direct a study of the island's plant life. Among the plants found was the one that is now named after him. He later took species of the plant back to France, introducing them to his fellow European botanists. Species of the plant were brought to England in 1777 – sixty-seven years after Bégon's death – and it was here that the genus of plant was named *Begonia* in his memory.

Belisha beacon

The Belisha beacon, a flashing light in an amber ball that is mounted on a post to mark a pedestrian crossing, is named after the British politician, 1st Baron (Isaac) Leslie Hore-Belisha (1893–1957). Hore-Belisha was National Liberal minister of transport from 1934–7, and later secretary of state for war 1937–40. His introduction of Belisha beacons as a road-safety measure to reduce the number of accidents was successful.

Benedictine

The name of a wine or spirit is often taken from the region where it was developed. Examples include champagne from Champagne, the former province in north-east France, and cognac from Cognac, the town in south-west France. The brandy-based liqueur known as Benedictine is, however, named after a person, St Benedict (c.480–c.547). St Benedict does not seem to have considered establishing a monastic order himself although the rule of St Benedict (c.540) became the basis of the rule of Western Christian monastic orders.

It was in a Benedictine monastery at Fécamp, northern France, in about 1510 that a monk, Don Bernando Vincelli, first made the liqueur. His fellow monks declared it 'refreshing and recuperative'. During the French Revolution the monastery was destroyed. The secret formula for making the liqueur was kept safe, however, and some fifty years later Benedictine was manufactured by a Frenchman, Le Grand, his distillery standing on the site of the former abbey.

Bessemer process

The Bessemer process is a method for converting pig iron into steel, invented in 1856 by the British engineer Sir Henry Bessemer (1813–98). Molten pig iron is loaded into a refractory-lined furnace (Bessemer converter) at about 1250°C. In the original version, air was blown into the furnace and the impurities removed. The result was that the quality of steel was improved and the costs of production were reduced. The modern version of the process has oxygen and steam blown into the furnace instead of air.

An identical process was developed at almost the same time by the American inventor William Kelly (1811–88), and a long legal battle followed over which company, Kelly's or the one using the Bessemer process, should produce the steel in the USA. The dispute was finally resolved when the rival companies merged.

Betty Martin – all my eye and Betty Martin

The idiomatic expression 'all my eye and Betty Martin' is used as a response to state that something is untrue or utter nonsense. The expression is often shortened to 'all my eye' or 'my eye'. The expression is traditionally seen as a garbled version of the Latin prayer: *O mihi, beate Martini* (O grant me, blessed Martin), but since there is no fixed prayer resembling this, the explanation seems unlikely.

Eric Partridge (*A Dictionary of Catch Phrases*) suggests an alternative theory of the origin of the expression: in the late eighteenth century, 'an abandoned woman . . . named Grace . . . induced a Mr Martin to marry her. She became notorious as Betty Martin: and favourite expressions of hers were "my eye!" and "all my eye!".'

Biedermeier

Biedermeier is used as a noun or an adjective to describe a style of German decoration and furniture of the mid-nineteenth century. The style, marked by simple, solid and conventional features, is named after the unimaginative and bourgeois author Gottlieb Biedermeier, an

Big Bertha was the name given to one of the three large German guns (with a range of some 75 miles) that were used to bombard Paris in the last months of the First World War. The name is a translation of the German *dicke Bertha*, 'fat Bertha', the uncomplimentary reference being to Bertha Krupp von Bohlen und Halbach (1886–1957), whose husband owned the Krupp armaments factory at Essen. The Germans originally used the name *die dicke Bertha* to refer to their 42-cm howitzer, it being wrongly believed that it was made at the Krupp factory. The name was later used to refer to the gun of a larger range.

bignonia

Bignonia – not to be confused with begonia – is a tropical American flowering shrub, grown for its trumpet-shaped yellow or red flowers. (It is sometimes also called cross vine.) The species is named after Abbé Jean-Paul Bignon (1662–1743), who was court librarian to Louis XIV, the name being given about 1700 by the French botanist Joseph Pitton de Tournefort (1656–1708) to honour the abbé.

billy goat see nancy

billycock see bowler

Biro

Biro is a trademark used to describe a kind of ballpoint pen. It is named after its Hungarian-born inventor László Jozsef Biró (1900–85). Biro patented his ballpoint pen, containing quick-drying ink, in Hungary in 1938. The rise of Nazism meant that Biro left Hungary, and settled in Argentina.

Biro's pen soon proved popular: for instance, Royal Air Force navigators found that it wrote better at high altitudes than a conventional fountain pen. Towards the end of the Second World War, Biro found an English company who backed his product, but the company was soon taken over by the French firm Bic. So it is that the ballpoint pen is known in France as a bic and in the UK as a biro.

Black Maria

A Black Maria is a police van for transporting prisoners and suspects. It is traditionally thought that the expression originally referred to Maria Lee, a strong, powerfully built American negro woman who, in about 1800, kept a boarding-house for sailors in Boston. She was also known for the help she gave to the police: the expression, 'Send for the Black Maria', it is supposed, became common when there was trouble and the drunk and disorderly needed to be removed. When the first police horse vans were introduced in Britain in 1938 they may well have been named in honour of this awesome lady.

blimp

A blimp (or Colonel Blimp) is a pompous, reactionary person with extremely conservative views. The origin of the word is the cartoon character Colonel Blimp invented by the New Zealand-born political cartoonist Sir David Low (1891–1963) in daily papers, particularly the *London Evening Standard*, of the 1930s and 1940s. Blimp was depicted as an elderly, unimaginative, unprogressive character. The adjective blimpish, derived from blimp, means 'reactionary or very conservative'.

The word blimp probably gained greater currency because it also referred to a small, non-rigid airship used in the First World War. This blimp probably owes its origin to the fact that it was also described as a limp airship: this was the successful type B version (hence B-limp), type A not having been a success.

Bloody Mary

A Bloody Mary is a cocktail drink that consists mainly of vodka and tomato juice. The expression was originally the nickname of Queen Mary I of England (1516–58). As queen (1553–8), Mary's aim was to restore Roman Catholicism to England: earlier Protestant legislation was repealed and heresy laws were reintroduced. Nearly 300 men and women were burnt at the stake, including the bishops Hugh Latimer and Nicholas Ridley, and the Archbishop of Canterbury, Thomas Cranmer. It was as Latimer was burnt at the stake with Ridley that he encouraged his fellow sufferer with the famous words, 'Be of good comfort, Master Ridley, and play the man. We shall this day light such a candle by God's grace in England as I trust shall never be put out.'

Mary's cruel actions earned her the nickname 'Bloody Mary' and so it is that she has been remembered by the red of the cocktail.

bloomers

The word bloomers nowadays refers to the women's undergarment that has full, loose legs gathered at the knee. The word owes its origin to the American feminist Amelia Jenks Bloomer (1818–94), but the garment Bloomer introduced into American society was not the garment known as bloomers today. The original garment was an entire costume consisting of a loose-fitting tunic, a short knee-length skirt, and billowing Turkish-style trousers gathered by elastic at the ankle. The costume, made originally from a design by Elizabeth Smith Miller, was worn by Mrs Bloomer and introduced at a ball in Lowell, Massachusetts, in July 1851. The outfit aroused considerable controversy at the time, largely because it was thought that trousers were a garment to be worn only by men.

Later, bloomers came to refer to just the trousers in the outfit, then, towards the end of the nineteenth century, to knee-length knickerbockers worn by cyclists, and today, in somewhat informal and wry usage, to the variety of women's underwear.

See also **Knickerbockers**.

blue peter see Jolly Roger

bluebeard

Bluebeard, referring to a man who marries and then kills one wife after another, was originally a character in European folklore. The earliest literary form of the fairytale is that of Charles Perrault (1628–1703), published in 1697, in which six wives are the victims of the seductive yet evil desires of the husband and the seventh is rescued by the opportune arrival of her brothers, who then kill the murderer. The original Bluebeard is thought by some to have been Gilles de Retz, Marquis de Laval, who lived in Brittany and who was accused of murdering six of his seven wives; in 1440 he was burnt at the stake for his crimes. Other sources, however, assign the original Bluebeard to an earlier date.

blurb

A blurb is a short publicity notice on the jacket or cover of a book. The word was coined in 1907 by the American humorist and illustrator Gelett Burgess (1866–1951) to promote his book *Are you a Bromide?*

In the early years of the twentieth century, American novels commonly had a picture of an attractive young woman on the cover. In an effort to parody this practice, Burgess produced a picture of a sickly sweet girl, Miss Belinda Blurb – for the purpose, he hoped, of 'blurbing a blurb to end all blurbs'. The outstanding success of this example meant that the word became associated with all such publicity copy.

bobby

The name for a policeman in British informal usage is a bobby: your friendly neighbourhood bobby. Bobby is the familiar form of Robert, coming from, as is well known, the British statesman Sir Robert Peel (1788–1850). In 1812 Peel was appointed chief secretary for Ireland; in 1814 he founded the Irish Constabulary, members of which were nicknamed peelers. As home secretary, Peel passed the Metropolitan Police Act, which founded the Metropolitan Police (1829). The word bobby was then used to describe the new London police force, later passing into general use to refer to all British policemen.

Bob's your uncle

'Bob's your uncle' is a slang expression meaning everything is or will be fine; there'll be no difficulties. The phrase became current in the 1880s, but its origin is uncertain. A possible explanation is the allusion to the appointments of Arthur Balfour (1848–1930) to various posts such as secretary for Ireland, first lord of the treasury and leader of the House of Commons. The appointments were made by Balfour's uncle, the prime minister Robert (hence Bob) Gascoyne Cecil, 3rd Marquess of Salisbury (1830–1903). The apparently nepotistic choice meant that with Prime Minister Bob as his uncle, Arthur Balfour had no problem obtaining whatever he wanted.

bogus

There are a number of different theories as to the origin of the word bogus meaning 'counterfeit; sham'. Some sources suggest that the word is an alteration of the name Borghese, an Italian man who in the 1830s supplied counterfeit banknotes to the American West. The Boston *Courier* reported that in about 1837 the people shortened Borghese's name to bogus, his banknotes being called bogus currency.

Other sources suggest that the word bogus referred originally to a device used for making counterfeit coins. The first citation of the word used in this way is in 1827, some ten years earlier than the usage described above. Still others suggest that bogus is derived from the French *bagasse*, 'rubbish'. The origin of bogus remains unproven; it may well be that all the sources mentioned have exercised an influence on the word's acceptance.

Bolivia

The South American country Bolivia owes its name to the soldier and statesman Simón Bolívar (1783–1830), known as the Liberator for his unremitting struggle to free Venezuela, Colombia, Ecuador and Peru from Spanish rule. He succeeded in liberating these countries, but failed to join them in one united republican confederation. In 1825 Upper Peru became a separate state, taking the name Bolivia in honour of Bolívar, who later became its president. He is one of the very few men in history who not only has had a country named after him but also drew up that country's constitution.

Boolean algebra

George Boole (1815–64) was a British mathematician who applied the methods of algebra to logic, in the same way that conventional algebra is used to express relationships in mathematics. In Boolean algebra, variables express not numbers but logical statements and the relationships between them. Boole's work was developed further by such philosopher-mathematicians as Frege, Russell and Whitehead and is important in the logic of computers.

bougainvillaea; Bougainville

Bougainvillaea is the name given to a genus of tropical South American woody climbing shrub bearing bright purple or red bracts that cover the flowers. The genus is named after the French navigator Louis Antoine de Bougainville (1729–1811). On an expedition round the world under his leadership (1766–9), the Solomon Islands were sighted. The largest island in the Solomon Islands archipelago is named after him, and is part of Papua New Guinea. Naturalists on Bougainville's expedition named the shrub in his honour.

bowdlerise

To bowdlerise a book means that all the words or passages considered indecent are removed. The word is traditionally thought to have come from the name of the British doctor Thomas Bowdler (1734–1825). Having retired from medicine, Bowdler published his *Family Shakespeare* in 1818; it excluded or modified words and expressions and even characters and plots that he found objectionable. The title page explains that, 'Nothing is added to the text; but those expressions are omitted which cannot with propriety be read aloud in a family.' Inspired by his success in this venture, Bowdler then published his expurgated version of Gibbon's *History of the Decline and Fall of the Roman Empire* in 1823.

Some recent research has, however, suggested that it was not Thomas Bowdler but his sister, Henrietta Maria, known as Harriet, who edited the original *Family Shakespeare*, first published in 1807. This, it seems, was followed by the revised and second edition of 1818, with Thomas Bowdler as editor.

bowie knife

A bowie knife is a stout hunting knife, with a long, one-edged blade curving to a point. It is named after the American soldier and adventurer James Bowie (1799–1836). It was James Bowie who popularised the knife, but he did not invent it. It seems it was originally designed by his father or by his older brother Rezin Pleasant Bowie (1793–1841).

Bowie's exploits made him something of an American folk hero. He is said to have used the knife to kill six men and wound fifteen others in the course of a duel at Natchez, Mississippi, in about 1827. James later became a colonel in the Texan army in the war of independence against Mexico. In 1836, fewer than 200 Texans, including James Bowie and the legendary Davy Crockett, held out against some 4000 Mexicans for thirteen days at the Alamo, but the Texans were eventually all slaughtered, James Bowie being slain on his sickbed.

bowler

There are various theories as to the origin of the word bowler, the stiff felt hat that has a rounded crown and a narrow brim. The word may well be derived from the name Bowler, a family of nineteenth-century London hatters. Some sources suggest that the name of the hatmaker was Beaulieu; others suppose that the hat is so named because of its shape – it resembles a bowl or basin, and since it is round and stiff, it could be bowled along.

It is also interesting to note that a bowler hat was probably originally called a billycock. There are two theories as to the origin of this word. On the one hand billycock could be derived from bullycocked hat, a hat tilted at an aggressive angle. On the other hand, billycock could come from the name William (Billy) Coke, an English sportsman. In about 1850 the London hatters Lock's of St James's made a hat for Billy Coke. It is said that he wanted a hat that was more practical than a traditional 'topper', as the tall topper kept being knocked off by branches when Coke rode to the hounds.

Box and Cox

The origin of the expression 'Box and Cox' lies in the farce *Box and Cox* by the English dramatist J. M. Morton (1811–91), published in 1847. In the farce, two men, one named Box and the other Cox lived in the same room, the one occupying the room by day and the other by night and neither knowing of the other's existence. In 1867 the play was adapted as a comic opera with music by Sir Arthur Sullivan and text by Sir Francis Cowley Burnand. The expression 'Box and Cox' means alternating or in turn.

boycott

Boycott is one of the most well-known eponyms in the English language. To boycott a person, organisation, etc., means that you refuse to deal with them, as an expression of disapproval and often as a means of trying to force them to accept certain conditions. The word comes from the name of the Irish landlord Captain Charles Cunningham Boycott (1832–97).

After retiring from the British army, Boycott was hired to look after the Earl of Erne's estates in County Mayo, Ireland. In 1880 the Irish Land League, wanting land reform, proposed a reduction in rents, stating that landlords who refused to accept such rents should be ostracised. Boycott refused and was promptly ostracised. His workers were forced to leave him, tradesmen refused to supply him, and his wife was threatened – indeed he was persecuted to such a degree that he and his wife were forced to flee to England, in so doing making the first boycott a success. The word quickly passed into other European languages, e.g. German *boykottieren*.

Boyle's law

Boyle's law states that at a constant temperature, the pressure of a gas is inversely proportionate to its volume. This law is named after the Irish-born British physicist and chemist Robert Boyle (1627–91). In fact, Boyle's law is only roughly true for real gases; a gas that obeys Boyle's law completely (which would exist only in hypothetical instances) is called an ideal gas or a perfect gas.

In France and other countries on the continent of Europe, the law is known as Mariotte's law, after the French physicist Edmé Mariotte (1620–84). Mariotte discovered the law independently of Boyle in 1676, thirteen years after the publication of Boyle's law.

boysenberry see loganberry

Bradshaw

Bradshaw was the informal name for the British railway passenger timetable *Bradshaw's Railway Guide*. First issued in 1839, it is named after its original publisher George Bradshaw (1801–53). It was discontinued in 1961.

braggadocio

The word braggadocio, meaning 'empty boasting' comes from the character Braggadocchio in the poem *The Faerie Queene* by the English poet Edmund Spenser (*c.*1552–99). The character personified boasting and the poem records his adventures and ultimate exposure. Spenser probably coined the name from the English word braggart and the Italian suffix *-occhio* meaning 'great'. He may have had in mind the Duke d'Alençon, one of the many suitors of Queen Elizabeth I.

Braille

The name of the system of raised dots by which blind people can read comes from the Frenchman Louis Braille (1809–52). Blinded at the age of three by an accident with an awl in his father's workshop, Braille went, at the age of ten, to study at the National Institute for the Blind in Paris. The Institute then possessed only three books, each in twenty parts and weighing 400 pounds (180 kg). The cumbersome text was written in large embossed letters to be felt by hand, yet Braille learned to read using this means.

At that same time an artillery captain, Charles Barbier, invented a primitive method of 'night writing'. Combinations of raised dots and dashes were used to communicate messages that could be understood by touch – that is, without the need for illumination. Barbier demonstrated his invention at the institute and Braille was inspired to refine it for use by the blind.

At the age of twenty, Braille published his first book in his new system, soon applying his skill as a musician – he enjoyed organ playing – to adapt his system for use in music. He remained a teacher at the institute until his death in 1852.

Bramley

The word referring to the variety of cooking apple known as a Bramley probably comes from the name Matthew Bramley, an English butcher who is said to have first grown it around 1850. Bramley lived in

Southwell, Nottinghamshire, and it is thought that the first Bramley was the result of a bud mutation: a variation in which only part of the tree was affected.

brougham

The name of the light, closed, four-wheeled, horse-drawn carriage with an open seat in front for the driver, honours the Scottish lawyer and statesman Henry Peter Brougham, Baron Brougham and Vaux (1778–1868). Brougham (both the name and the carriage are pronounced broom or brooerm) designed the carriage in about 1850, originally describing it as a 'garden chair on wheels'. The brougham remained a popular form of public transport until it was surpassed by the hansom cab.

Brougham's achievements include his advocacy, along with William Wilberforce, of the abolition of slavery; his defence in the House of Lords of Caroline of Brunswick against the charges of adultery brought by her husband, the Regent and later King George IV; and, as lord chancellor, his speech in the House of Lords that contributed to the passing of the Reform Bill of 1832.

Browning automatic rifle

The Browning automatic rifle (BAR), a portable gas-operated, air-cooled rifle, is named after its designer, the American John Moses Browning (1834–1926). Capable of firing 200–350 rounds a minute, the BAR was used widely in the Second World War and was the standard automatic weapon in the US army until about 1950. A prolific firearm designer, Browning also designed machine-guns, pistols and shotguns.

Buckley's chance

'Buckley's chance' is an Australian expression which means a very remote chance. Two chances, Buckley's and none, amounts in reality to next to no chance at all. The expression may derive from William Buckley (d. 1856), who against all odds lived with Aborigines for thirty years; perhaps, more likely, a Melbourne store named Buckley and Nunn has become linked with the phrase.

Buddhism; Buddhist

The founder of Buddhism was the Hindu Prince Gautama Siddharta (c. 563–c. 483 BC). At the age of sixteen he married his cousin, the Princess Yasodharma, who later bore him a son, Rahula. In his late twenties, he became dissatisfied with their life of luxury, so he left his family in order to try to find answers to the problems of human suffering and existence. Six years of asceticism followed, but these convinced him that self-mortification did not provide the solutions he was searching for. So, keeping himself from the extremes of self-mortification and indulgence, he turned to enlightenment alone, meditating within himself. He is traditionally said to have reached enlightenment while sitting under a fig tree in what is now called Buddh Gaya, a village in Bihar, in northeast India. He then took the title Buddha, meaning in Sanskrit 'the Awakened One'. The next forty-five years of his life were devoted to teaching the principles of enlightenment.

buddleia

Buddleia is a genus of trees and shrubs that have showy clusters of yellow or mauve flowers. Native to tropical or warmer regions in Asia and America, the first specimens were collected in the early eighteenth century by the Scottish-born botanist William Houstoun (*c.*1695–1733). He wished to name the plant after the Essex rector and botanist Adam Buddle (*c.*1660–1715). This desire was later honoured by Linnaeus in his plant classification.

One particular species of buddleia, *Buddleia davidii*, was introduced into Britain from China in the late nineteenth century. This species is also known as the butterfly bush because its flowers are very attractive to butterflies. The word *davidii* is also eponymous – it comes from the French missionary and explorer of China Père Armand David (1826–1900). The rare Chinese deer, Père David's deer, is also named in his honour.

Bunsen burner

The Bunsen burner, the gas burner with an adjustable air valve used widely in chemistry laboratories, is named after the German chemist Robert Wilhelm Bunsen (1811–99). Bunsen is generally credited with the invention of the Bunsen burner, although some authorities point out that similar designs had been developed earlier by such scientists as Michael Faraday. Even if this is true, it was certainly Bunsen who popularised the use of the burner.

Bunsen is also famous for his discovery, with the German physicist Gustav Robert Kirchoff (1824–87), of the two chemical elements caesium and rubidium in 1860.

Buridan's ass

Buridan's ass is an illustration of a philosophical position. In the example, a hungry ass stands an equal distance between two identical bales of hay. He starves to death, however, because there is no reason why he should choose to eat one bale rather than the other. The dilemma is said to show the indecisiveness of the will when faced with two equal alternatives. The philosophical example is associated with the French philosopher Jean Buridan (c.1295–1356), although it was first found in the philosophy of Aristotle.

burke

'To burke' means to murder someone in such a way that no marks are left on the body. The word comes from the name of the notorious murderer William Burke (1792–1829). Originally an Irish labourer, Burke moved to Scotland in about 1818, renting a room in Edinburgh from a fellow countryman William Hare. When one of Hare's lodgers died owing him money, Hare and Burke took the body to an Edinburgh anatomist, Dr Robert Knox, who gave them seven pounds and ten shillings for it.

Quickly realising what profit there was to be made, Hare and his wife together with Burke and his mistress disposed of between fifteen and thirty other unfortunates in a similar way. They were careful to suffocate their victims, leaving no marks of violence, so that it would appear that the bodies had been taken from graves. The murderers became careless, however, killing an attractive eighteen-year-old woman, Mary Peterson, whose corpse was recognised by the students at Knox's anatomy school. Other murders followed, and Burke and Hare were eventually caught with the body of a missing woman. Hare turned king's evidence, however, testifying against his accomplice. Hare was set free, but Burke was hanged in January 1829, before a crowd of about 30,000 people. On the way to the gallows the crowd shouted, 'Burke him! Burke him!' wanting him to suffer the same fate as his victims.

With all the publicity, Burke's name came to stand for the murderous act, and figuratively to mean 'hush up' or 'stifle'.

Burnham scale

The name of the former salary scale for teachers in state schools in England and Wales, the Burnham scale, comes from Harry Lawson, 1st Viscount Burnham (1862–1933). A member of parliament, Burnham chaired the committee that in 1919–20 originally established the salary scale.

busby

A busby is the name for the tall bearskin fur hat worn by soldiers, especially hussars and members of certain British army regiments. In the eighteenth century a busby was a large, bushy wig.

The word is traditionally thought to come from the name of the disciplinarian headmaster Dr Richard Busby (1606–95). Headmaster of Westminster School, Busby had among his pupils Dryden, Locke and Christopher Wren. It is not certain, however, that Busby himself wore a bushy wig. It may be that his hair naturally stood on end, thus suggesting the wig that became fashionable.

Byronic

The adjective 'Byronic' is sometimes used to mean wildly romantic yet melancholy and despairing. The word alludes to characteristics of the life and writings of George Gordon, Lord Byron (1788–1824). A significant romantic poet, whose writings included *Childe Harold's Pilgrimage* (1812–18) and *Don Juan* (1819–24), Byron is noted for his physical lameness, his attractive appearance, his many romantic liaisons and his journeyings on the European continent. Towards the end of his life, Byron became involved in the Greek struggle for independence. He died of malaria at Missolonghi in western Greece in 1824.

C

Cabal

A cabal is a small group of people who meet secretly or unofficially, especially for the purpose of political intrigue. The word derives ultimately from Hebrew *qabbālāh* (what is received or tradition). It is popularly believed, however, that the word cabal originated with the initials of the names of King Charles II's ministers from 1667 to 1673: Sir Thomas Clifford (1630–73), Lord Ashley (later 1st Earl of Shaftesbury) (1621–73), the 2nd Duke of Buckingham (1628–87), the 1st Earl of Arlington (1618–85) and the Duke of Lauderdale (1616–82). The political group's powerful scheming and intriguing met with great unpopularity. It was noticed that the ministers' initials made up the word cabal and it seems certain that the existence of this faction made the use of the word more current, adding to it pejorative connotations of reproach.

Cadmean victory see Pyrrhic victory

Caesarean section

A Caesarean section (or Caesarean) is a surgical incision through the walls of the abdomen and womb in order to deliver a baby. The expression is commonly thought to allude to the popular belief that Julius Caesar was born in this manner.

An alternative theory is that Caesarean comes from the Latin *caesus*, the past participle of the verb *caedera* 'to cut'.

Caesar's wife must be above suspicion

The expression 'Caesar's wife must be above suspicion' referred originally to Caesar's second wife Pompeia. According to rumours circulating in about 62BC, it seems that her name was linked with Publius Clodius, a notorious dissolute man of the time. Caesar did not believe such rumours but he made it clear, when divorcing her, that even Caesar's wife must be above suspicion. The expression 'like Caesar's wife' also comes from this account, to refer to someone who is pure and honest in morals.

calamine

Calamine, the pink powder of zinc oxide and ferric oxide that is used in soothing lotions for the skin, is an alteration of the Latin *cadmia*. This Latin word derives ultimately from the Greek name Cadmus, the legendary founder of Thebes, *kadmeia* meaning (Theban) earth. For further discussion of Cadmus and the expression Cadmean victory, see **Pyrrhic victory**.

Calvinist

The name of the theological system known as Calvinism comes from the French theologian John Calvin (1509–64), whose original name was Jean Cauvin (sometimes also spelt Chauvin). Converted in about 1532, Calvin's most famous work is his Institutes, first published in Latin (*Christianae Religionis Institutio*) in 1536.

Calvin has generally been held in low esteem. He himself wrote in 1559 that 'never was a man more assailed, stung, and torn by calumny' than he was. He is known chiefly for his teaching on predestination, yet this was taught earlier by Augustine and is found in the Bible. Calvin himself was careful to keep this teaching in a healthy tension with other biblical doctrines and it is some of his followers who have upset Calvin's balance.

Calvin also sought to reform the behaviour of people in the city of Geneva, to make the whole of Genevan society a model community where every citizen came under a strict religious discipline. A wide range of laws regulated the people's dress and morals. It is this rigorous and austere aspect of Calvin's work that is recalled in the present-day connotation of the word Calvinist, seen for example in the phrase a strict Calvinist upbringing.

camellia

Camellia refers to a genus of ornamental shrubs, of which perhaps the best known is *Camellia japonica*. This has shiny evergreen leaves and showy, rose-like flowers. The word camellia comes from the name of the Moravian Jesuit missionary George Josef Kamel (1661–1706), also known by the Latinised form of his name, Camellus. Kamel lived in Manila in the Philippine Islands and there he ran a pharmacy, which was supplied by his herb garden. He published reports on the plants he grew in the *Philosophical Transactions of the Royal Society*. He was certainly the first to describe the shrub and some sources suggest that he may also have been the first to send specimens of it to Europe. In any event, it was the Swedish botanist Linnaeus who read of Kamel's accounts in *Philosophical Transactions* and later named the plant in his honour.

cannibal

A cannibal, referring to someone who eats the flesh of other human beings, comes from the Spanish *Canibales*. This was the name given by Christopher Columbus to the Caribs, the American Indian people of the Lesser Antilles and northern South America. Before the conquest by the Spaniards, the Caribs expelled the Arawak Indians from the Lesser Antilles, enslaving the women and killing and eating the men. The Spanish word *Canibal* is derived from the Arawak term *Caniba* for the Caribs. The Caribbean Sea is also named after the Carib people.

cant

The word cant, meaning insincere or hypocritical talk; repeated or specialised language, comes from the verb to cant, to talk whiningly like a beggar, and ultimately from the Latin *cantare*, to sing or chant. It is quite possible, however, that the meaning of the word and the frequency of its usage were influenced by the name of a Scottish minister Andrew Cant (1590–1663). Cant was a Presbyterian minister in Aberdeen; it was said of him that he talked 'in the pulpit in such a dialect that . . . he was understood by none but his own Congregation, and not by all of them', though how true this was is uncertain since many churches have said the same of their preachers! Andrew Cant and his brother Alexander were zealous leaders of the Covenanters – the Scottish Presbyterians who bound themselves on oath to defend their church. Some authorities describe the bigotry and hypocrisy of the Cant brothers, persecuting their religious opponents, yet also praying for them. So while the ultimate derivation of cant certainly is Latin *cantare*, it appears that the actions of the Cant brothers may well have supported the meaning of the word.

cardigan

The cardigan, the knitted jacket or sweater fastened with buttons, is named after the British cavalry officer James Thomas Brudenell, 7th Earl of Cardigan (1797–1868). The garment was first worn by British soldiers in the intense cold of the Crimean winter. See also **Raglan**.

It was the Earl of Cardigan who led the Charge of the Light Brigade in the most famous battle of the Crimean War, near the village of Balaclava, on 25 October 1854. (Interestingly, the word for the woollen hood-like head-covering takes its name from this village.)

Casanova

A Casanova is a man noted for his, often unscrupulous, amorous adventures. The word comes from the name of the Italian adventurer Giovanni Jacopo Casanova (1725–98). Born in Venice, the son of an actor, Casanova was expelled at the age of sixteen from a seminary for monks for his immoral behaviour. He went on to live in many European cities, working at different times as, amongst other things, a preacher, a philosopher, a diplomat, a gambler and a violinist. He mixed with the wealthy aristocracy, engaging in many romantic liaisons, making and losing riches and friends wherever he went. He finally settled down as librarian to the Count von Waldstein in Bohemia, and it was here that he wrote his memoirs – about one and a half million words in twelve volumes – which were published posthumously between 1826 and 1838.

Cassandra

A Cassandra is a person whose prophecies of misfortune are ignored. The original Cassandra was a daughter of Priam, king of Troy in Greek legend. She was endowed with the gift of prophecy, but after she rejected the advances of Apollo, she suffered the punishment of her prophecies being eternally disbelieved.

Cassandra prophesied the sacking of Troy. When Troy was captured, she fell by lot to Agamemnon, who took her back to Greece and although she prophesied the doom that awaited him. Cassandra Agamemnon were subsequently murdered by Clytemnestra. Thus it is that a modern-day Cassandra is someone whose predictions of doom are fated to go unheeded.

Castor and Pollux

The names of Castor and Pollux are used to mean two faithful friends. They were twin brothers in Greek mythology, known jointly as the Dioscuri. Pollux was immortal, the son of Leda and Zeus; Castor was mortal, the son of Leda and Tyndareus. After Castor's death, Pollux asked Zeus that he might be allowed to die too, in order that the two should be together, and this wish was granted.

The twins' names are used for two stars. The brightest star in the Gemini constellation is Pollux, and the second brightest, Castor.

Catherine wheel

The kind of firework which spins as it burns is known as a Catherine wheel and is named after a princess, St Catherine of Alexandria.

A martyr for her Christian faith, she is said to have been sentenced to death in about AD 307 by being broken on a spiked wheel. Legend has it that she survived this torture as it was the wheel, not her body, that was miraculously broken. Catherine was then beheaded, her body, it is thought, being carried by angels to Mount Sinai where it was found in about the year 800. On the site of the discovery a monastery was built to honour her resting-place. In 1969 the Roman Catholic Church ceased to recognise St Catherine because of doubts about her existence. St Catherine's symbol is a spiked wheel.

A Catherine wheel is the name given also to a circular window that has spokes radiating from its centre, and to the sideways handspring more commonly known as a cartwheel.

cattleya

Cattleya is the name of a genus of tropical American orchids that are grown for their showy hooded flowers. The orchids are named after the English botanist and horticultural patron William Cattley (*d.*1832). The Cattleya fly and the subtropical fruit Cattley guava also honour this patron of botany.

Celsius

Celsius is the name of the temperature scale for which 0° is the freezing point of water and 100° the boiling point. The scale is named after the Swedish astronomer and scientist Anders Celsius (1701–44), who devised it in 1742. The new scale simplified the earlier Fahrenheit scale by dividing the temperature between boiling point and freezing point into a hundred equal parts.

Originally, Celsius set 0° as the boiling point of water, and 100° as the freezing-point; later the designations were reversed.

The Celsius scale was formerly called centigrade, but this name was officially changed in 1948 to avoid confusion with centigrade meaning 'a hundredth part of a grade'. Centigrade is, however, still used in a few non-technical contexts.

cereal

It may seem unlikely, but the origin of cereal, for many people a familiar sight on the breakfast table, lies ultimately in the name of a Roman goddess. Originally an adjective meaning 'of edible grain', cereal comes from Latin *cerealis*, 'relating to the cultivation of grain', which in turn derives from Ceres the goddess of grain and agriculture. Originally a Roman goddess, Ceres, became identified with the Greek goddess Demeter.

Charles's law

Charles's law states that the volume of a gas at constant pressure expands by 1/273 of its volume at 0°C for each degree Celsius increase in temperature. The law is named after the French scientist Jacques Alexandre César Charles (1746–1823). His law was the result of experiments that began in about 1787.

Charles's law is sometimes known as Gay-Lussac's law after the French scientist Joseph Louis Gay-Lussac (1778–1850). In 1802 Gay-Lussac published findings that were more accurate than Charles's.

Charles is also famous as the inventor of the hydrogen balloon, in which he made the first ascent in 1783.

charlotte – apple charlotte; charlotte russe

A charlotte, the baked dessert made of fruit (commonly apples) layered with bread, sponge, etc., is thought to come originally from the name of Princess Charlotte (1796–1817), the only daughter of King George IV. The French chef Marc-Antoine Carême (1784–1833) is said to have created a sumptuous pastry in honour of the princess.

Carême's culinary preparations were so highly regarded that it is said they were taken from the table of the king's court to the marketplace where they were sold for a lot of money.

While serving Tsar Alexander I in Russia, Carême created the charlotte russe (*russe* being French for 'Russian'): the dessert consisting of a mixture of whipped cream and custard set in a crown of sponge fingers.

chateaubriand

The large, thick, fillet steak known as a chateaubriand comes from the name of the French writer and statesman François René Vicomte de Chateaubriand (1768–1848).

Chateaubriand fought in the Royalist army in France, living in exile in England from 1793 to 1800. On returning to France in 1800, he achieved great fame with his writings, notably *Le Génie du Christianisme* (1802), and is generally considered as one of the significant leaders of early French Romanticism. Under Louis XVIII, he was French ambassador in London.

It is probable that the steak named in Chateaubriand's honour was created by his chef, Montmirel, and was first prepared at the French embassy in London.

chauvinism

The word chauvinism, referring to an excessive unthinking devotion to

one's country, comes from the name of the French soldier Nicolas
Chauvin of Rochefort.

A soldier in Napoleon's army and wounded many times, Chauvin
was ridiculed by his fellow-soldiers for his fanatical devotion to
Napoleon. Even when Chauvin was pensioned off with a medal, a
ceremonial sabre, and a meagre pension of 200 francs a year, his
patriotic zeal continued unabated.

It was the dramatists Charles and Jean Cogniard who made the name
Chauvin famous in their comedy *Le Cocarde Tricolore* (1831). In this,
Chauvin is a young recruit who sings several songs with the chorus that
includes the lines, *Je suis français, je suis Chauvin*. The character of
Chauvin later featured in a number of other French comedies and as a
result became widely known. The word chauvinism soon became
familiar in English to describe fanatical patriotism. In more recent
years, the sense of the word has widened to include an unreasoned and
prejudiced belief in the superiority of one's group or cause, as in the
expression male chauvinism.

Chesterfield

Chesterfield is used to refer to two items: a padded, often leather, sofa
with upright armrests which are the same height as the back, and a
man's overcoat with concealed buttons and a velvet collar. Both the
sofa and the coat are generally thought to be named after a nineteenth-
century Earl of Chesterfield (probably not the famous eighteenth-
century 4th Earl of Chesterfield, Philip Dormer Stanhope), but it is
uncertain which.

Chippendale

The gracefully decorative English furniture style known as Chippendale takes its name from its originator, the English cabinet-maker and
furniture designer Thomas Chippendale (*c.*1718–79).

The son of a Yorkshire picture-frame maker, Chippendale set up a
furniture factory in London in 1749, five years later publishing *The
Gentleman and Cabinet Maker's Director*. Illustrating some 160 designs in
Louis XV, Chinese and Gothic styles, this was the first extensive
furniture catalogue and was significant in furniture design in both
England and America. Chippendale's son, also Thomas (1749–1822),
continued his father's business.

Christian; Christmas; christen

The word Christian occurs in the New Testament in Acts 11:26: 'And
the disciples were called Christians first in Antioch.' From this, its two

other occurrences in the New Testament and a reference in the writings of the Roman historian Tacitus, it can be inferred that Christian was a generally recognised title for a follower of Jesus Christ in the time of the New Testament.

The word Christ itself comes from the Greek *christos*, meaning 'the anointed one', translated from the Hebrew *Mashsah* (Messiah). The name of Christ is also used in other words such as christen, Christianity and Christendom. The name of the festival of Christmas comes from the Old English *Cristes maesse* (Christ's mass).

Christopher Columbus

Christopher Columbus is an expression used to show great surprise: 'Christopher Columbus! What on earth are you doing here? I thought you were still in Germany!' The name is, of course, that of the Italian navigator and explorer (1451–1506), who landed on what he named San Salvador island on 12 October 1492.

Also named after Columbus is the Republic of Columbia and numerous cities in the USA.

churrigueresque

The word churrigueresque (pronounced chure-rig-a-resk) is used to describe a Spanish style of baroque architecture of the late seventeenth and early eighteenth centuries. Marked by highly detailed ornate surface features, this style takes its name from the Spanish architect and sculptor José Churriguera (1650–1725)

cicerone

A person who acts as a guide to sightseers is sometimes called a cicerone. The word comes from the name of the Roman orator and statesman Marcus Tullius Cicero (106–43BC). Guides take their name from Cicero because he typifies the eloquence and knowledge that is expected of them. In short, they are required to point out items of local interest to visitors in the style of the orator Cicero.

cinchona

Cinchona is the name of a genus of South American trees and shrubs that contains some forty species. One of the most important species is calisaya as its bark produces a drug that can be used in the treatment of malaria.

Cinchona is named after the Spanish vicereine of Peru, Countess Ana de Chinchón (1576–1641). In about 1638 the countess was afflicted by a tropical fever that could not be cured by European doctors. The

powdered bark of a native Peruvian tree restored her to health,
however. The bark was taken back to Spain where it was called
Peruvian bark or Countess bark. The modern name *Cinchona* was given
the genus by Linnaeus in honour of the Countess, but he must have
inadvertently misspelled her name: what should really have been
Chinchona was called *Cinchona*.

Cinderella

A person or thing described as a Cinderella is one that is regarded as
being unjustifiably neglected: 'For too long distribution has been the
Cinderella of the publishing industry.'

The expression comes from the well-known fairytale in which the
heroine Cinderella is cruelly treated by her stepmother and her two
stepsisters but with the help of a fairy godmother finally marries a
prince.

clarence

A clarence was a closed, four-wheeled, horse-drawn carriage for four
passengers, the driver's seat being outside the carriage. It was named
after the Duke of Clarence, later to become King William IV (1765–
1837).

See also **Silly Billy.**

clerihew

A clerihew is a witty four-line verse that consists of two rhymed
couplets, usually biographical in content. The clerihew was invented by
the English writer Edmund Clerihew Bentley (1875–1956).

The first clerihew was composed (according to Bentley's friend
G. K. Chesterton) while Bentley was at school, 'listening to a chemical
exposition, with his rather bored air and a blank sheet of blotting-paper
before him'. On this he wrote:

> Sir Humphry Davy
> Abominated gravy.
> He lived in the odium
> Of having discovered sodium.

Under the name E. Clerihew, Bentley published his first clerihews in
1905. He is also known for his journalistic writings and his detective
novel *Trent's Last Case* (1913), but it is for his clerihews he is chiefly
remembered. Perhaps the best known is:

Sir Christopher Wren
Said, 'I am going to dine with some men.
If anybody calls
Say I am designing St Paul's.'

clever Dick see smart alec

Cocker – according to Cocker

The phrase 'according to Cocker' means in a manner that is correct, accurate, or reliable. The expression honours the English arithmetician Edward Cocker (1631–75). He is the reputed author of a popular book on mathematics titled *Arithmetick*, which went into more than a hundred editions.

The expression was popularised when introduced into the play *The Apprentice* (1756) by the actor and playwright Arthur Murphy (1727–1805)

The American equivalent of 'according to Cocker' is 'according to Hoyle'. This expression honours the British clubman and expert on games Sir Edmund Hoyle (1672–1769). At that time the game of whist was very popular and Hoyle was the first person to prepare an authoritative guide to its rules, *A Short Treatise on the Game of Whist*, published in 1742. He also compiled *Hoyle's Standard Games*, the authoritative book of rules of card games. The expert reputation of Hoyle meant that the expression 'according to Hoyle' was applied not only to a method of play in accordance with the rules but also more generally to correct or honourable behaviour.

Colt

Colt is the trademark for a type of pistol with a revolving magazine.

It has a single barrel with a revolving breech for six bullets. The pistol is named after its inventor, the American engineer Samuel Colt (1814–62). Born in Connecticut, Colt ran away to sea at the age of sixteen. While aboard ship he carved a wooden model of the revolver. On his return home, he established an arms factory, patenting his invention in 1835. The pistol was used notably in the Mexican War (1846–8). In 1854 it was adopted by the Royal Navy, and a modified .45 calibre version was used by the US army and navy until 1945.

comstockery

Comstockery is strict censorship of literary works on the grounds of immorality or obscenity. The term comes from the name of the American moral crusader Anthony Comstock (1844–1915).

Comstock devoted most of his life to suppressing plays and books that he considered immoral. He founded a number of moralistic causes, notably the New York Society for the Suppression of Vice in 1873, the year in which he also secured the passing of the so-called Comstock Laws through Congress to prevent objectionable books and magazines from being sent by the post. As a guardian of the post, he is said to have arrested about 3000 people and destroyed some 50 tons of books that he considered to be immoral. Comstock objected greatly to *Mrs Warren's Profession*, the play by George Bernard Shaw, and it was Shaw who in 1905 coined the word comstockery to describe a narrow moralistic censorship.

Confucianism; Confucius say

Confucianism is the ethical system of the Chinese philosopher Confucius (551–479BC). Born in Lu, a small state in what is now Shandong province, Confucius became a minor official, later rising to prime minister of Lu, being well known for his wise, just government. After his advice was ignored, however, he left Lu, returning only in the last years of his life.

From an early age he gathered a group of disciples round him and continued to teach his ethical ideas. (His name in Chinese is Kong Zi, meaning 'Kong the Master'.) In his final years he edited the books now known as the *Classics*. After his death, his disciples collected his sayings, which became known as the *Analects*. Confucius's ethical system is sometimes summed up in the rule, 'What you do not want others to do to you, do not do to them.'

'Confucius, he say . . . ' is a humorous expression sometimes used to introduce a maxim or thought that is considered wise.

cordoba

The cordoba is the basic money unit of Nicaragua. The word derives ultimately from the name of the Spanish soldier and explorer Francisco Fernandez de Córdoba (*c.*1475–1526). It was Córdoba who in 1522 took possession of Nicaragua for the Spanish.

Couéism

'Every day, in every way, I am getting better and better.' This was the formula advocated by the French psychologist and chemist Emil Coué (1857–1926) in the treatment of his patients. Establishing a clinic at Nancy in 1910, Coué practised his system of psychotherapy. He believed that by means of autosuggestion – summed up in the formula above – ideas that lead to illness could be removed from the realm of the will.

coulomb

A coulomb is the basic metric unit of electric charge. The term honours the name of the French physicist Charles Augustin de Coulomb (1736–1806).

Originally a French military engineer, Coulomb was forced because of bad health to retire from the army; subsequently he developed his interests in electricity and magnetism. Coulomb is remembered for his invention of the torsion balance to measure the force between two charged particles and his formulation of what is now known as Coulomb's law.

cravat

A cravat is a silk or fine-wool scarf worn by men round the neck, often tucked into a shirt. The first cravats were scarves worn by Croatian mercenaries serving in France in the Thirty Years' War (1618–48). Some members of French fashionable society were so impressed with the cravats that they adopted the style, calling the scarf after the name of the people, *Hrvat* (pronounced roughly with an initial k-sound), which means 'native of Croatia'.

cretin

A cretin is someone afflicted with cretinism, the condition that arises from thyroid deficiency and leads to retarded growth and mental impairment. The word was originally applied to people who lived in the Swiss Alps. The Swiss called such a person *crestin*, meaning 'Christian, a Christian being, one who is not an animal', this word deriving from the name Christ.

crisscross

The word crisscross, referring to a pattern of intersecting lines, comes from Christ's cross, the cross of Christ. This word derives in part from the mark of a cross in a children's sixteenth-century hornbook primer, which was a sheet of paper mounted on a wooden tablet and protected by a thin plate of horn. The paper listed the alphabet, the Lord's Prayer, and some numbers. The alphabet that was printed on the top line of the paper was preceded by a small Maltese cross known as the Christ-cross or Christ's cross. The row of letters in the alphabet became known as Christ-cross row, this in time becoming changed to crisscross.

The word crisscross is also usually considered to be a duplication of sounds based on the word cross, with the vowel changing (other examples of such duplication being dilly-dally and ding-dong).

Crockford

Crockford is the name often used to refer to *Crockford's Clerical Directory*, the reference book giving facts about the Church of England and its clergy, first published in 1860. It is called Crockford after John Crockford (1823–65), managing clerk to serjeant-at-law Edward Cox, who first published the directory. It seems that Cox preferred to use his clerk's name because of his own official position.

Croesus – as rich as Croesus

Croesus was the last king of Lydia, a region of Asia Minor, who reigned from 560 to 546BC. As a result of his conquests, Croesus became extremely rich. Indeed, he was considered by the Greeks to be the wealthiest person on earth, hence the contemporary expression 'as rich as Croesus' meaning very rich.

Legend has it that the Athenian statesman Solon once told Croesus that no man should be considered happy, despite his riches, till he died. Later, when Cyrus the Great defeated Croesus, he condemned Croesus to be burnt alive. It is said that Croesus shouted out Solon's words from the stake. Cyrus intervened, demanding an explanation of Croesus' words, and, being so moved by what his prisoner said, reprieved him and became his friend.

Cruft's

Cruft's is the name of the annual British dog show. It takes its name from the British dog breeder and showman Charles Cruft (1852–1938), who in 1886 organised the first dog show.

Cuisenaire rods

'Cuisenaire rods' is the trademark of a set of rods that have different colours and lengths. The rods are named after the Belgian educationalist Emil-Georges Cuisenaire (c.1891–1976). Standing for various numbers, the rods are used to teach arithmetic to young children.

Cupid – to play Cupid; Cupid's bow

The expression 'to play Cupid', meaning to play the role of matchmaker, alludes to the Roman god of love. Identified with the Greek god Eros, Cupid is usually represented as a winged naked boy holding a bow and arrow.

The shape of the bow that Cupid is traditionally shown as carrying is referred to in the expression 'Cupid's bow', used to describe the shape of the upper human lip.

curie see becquerel

curry favour

The expression curry favour, meaning to try to gain favour by flattery or attention, has nothing to do with the spicy oriental dish. The phrase is a corruption of the Middle English expression, 'to curry Favel'. To curry means to groom or stroke down a horse; Favel (or Fauvel) was the name of a chestnut horse in a fourteenth-century French satirical poem, the *Roman de Favel*. Favel symbolised cunning or hypocrisy, so to curry Favel was to try to ingratiate oneself through insincere means.

Curzon line

The Curzon line, marking the border between Poland and the Soviet Union, was confirmed at the Yalta Conference of 1945. The boundary is named after the British politician George Nathaniel, 1st Marquis Curzon of Kedleston (1859–1925). Curzon served the British government in many capacities, among them viceroy of India (1899–1905), lord privy seal (1915–16) and foreign secretary (1919–24).

The Curzon line was proposed in the Russo-Polish War (1919–20); Lord Curzon suggested that the Poles – who had invaded Russia – should retreat to this line while awaiting a peace conference.

Cushing's disease

Cushing's disease is a condition caused by excessive secretion of certain steroid hormones such as cortisone; its symptoms include obesity, muscular weakness and high blood pressure. The disease is named after the American neurosurgeon Harvey Williams Cushing (1869–1939), who was the first to identify and describe the condition.

Custer's last stand

The expression 'Custer's last stand', referring to a great effort that ends in utter defeat, refers to the American cavalry general George Armstrong Custer (1839–76). After distinctive service in the Civil War, Custer commanded the Seventh Cavalry against the Sioux Indian chief Sitting Bull. Custer and his men were massacred by the Indians at the Battle of the Little Bighorn, Montana (25 June 1876) in what became known as Custer's Last Stand.

cynic

The followers of the Greek philosopher Antisthenes (*c.*445–*c.*360BC), notably his later disciples such as Diogenes (411–322BC), were known as Cynics. There are two theories of the origin of this word. One is that the members of the sect were rude and churlish in manner, hence *kunikos*, Greek for 'dog-like'. The other theory is that the sect met in a school called Kunosarges, Greek for 'white dog', as it was supposed that a white dog had once carried off part of a sacrifice being offered to the gods.

Whatever the precise origin of their name, the Cynics were scornful of the accepted values of the rest of society. They tended to live unconventional lives, believing in the self-sufficiency of the individual and that virtue was the highest good, the way to goodness being through self-control. It was, however, the negative aspects of the Cynics' beliefs that came to be emphasised, leading to the contemporary sense of the word, someone who sarcastically doubts others' sincerity, believing that all acts are motivated by selfishness.

Cyrillic

Cyrillic is the name of the alphabet used in writing Slavonic languages such as Russian and Bulgarian. The alphabet is traditionally thought to have been developed by two Greek brothers, St Cyril (hence Cyrillic) (826–69) and St Methodius (*c.*815–85), during the course of translation of the Bible and liturgy into Slavonic. The Cyrillic alphabet is derived from the Greek alphabet and is supplemented by Hebrew letters for non-Greek sounds.

czar see **tsar**

D

daguerrotype

One of the earliest practicable photographic processes was the daguerrotype, named after its inventor, the French painter and pioneering photographer Louis Jaques Mandé Daguerre (1789–1851). In the daguerrotype process, an image is produced on iodine-sensitised silver and developed in mercury vapour.

Daguerre, an officer for the French inland revenue and a landscape and theatrical scenery painter, had been involved in producing the diorama, a method of exhibiting pictures by using special lighting effects. In 1829 Daguerre met the physicist Joseph Niepce (1765–1833), who had been experimenting with different photography methods for some years. Daguerre continued the work after Niepce's death, producing his results in 1839, for which he was awarded the French Legion of Honour.

At about the same time the British botanist and physicist William Henry Fox Talbot (1800–77) was perfecting a photographic process using negatives. Although Fox's system became the basis of modern photography, it was Daguerre's invention that aroused widespread public interest in photography.

dahlia

Dahlia is a genus of herbaceous perennial plants that have showy, brightly coloured flowers and tuberous roots. Originally cultivated as a food crop, dahlias are now grown commonly as ornamental plants.

The dahlia was discovered by the German explorer and naturalist Alexander von Humboldt (1769–1859) in Mexico in 1789. It was sent to the Botanic Garden in Madrid, where Professor Cavanilles named it in honour of the Swedish botanist Anders Dahl (1751–89), who had died that same year.

daltonism; Dalton's law

Daltonism is another word for colour blindness, especially the inability to distinguish red and green. It is named after the English scientist

John Dalton (1766–1844), who himself suffered from this disability. He was the first person to give a detailed description of this condition, in *Extraordinary Facts Relating to the Vision of Colours* (1794).

It is for his work in physics and chemistry that Dalton is better known. He is regarded as the originator of the modern atomic theory of matter and he formulated the law relating to the pressure of gases that is known as Dalton's law.

Dandie Dinmont terrier

Dandie Dinmont is the name of a breed of Scottish terrier character-ised by short legs, a long coat and drooping ears. The breed is named after Dandie Dinmont, a character in the novel *Guy Mannering* (1815) by the Scottish writer Sir Walter Scott (1771–1832). Andrew Dinmont was a sturdy farmer who lived in Liddesdale in the Scottish Lowlands and owned a pack of such dogs.

dandy

There are two theories of the origin of the word dandy, meaning a man who takes excessive care over his dress and appearance. One is that the word is short for Jack-a-dandy, meaning 'a beau'; the other sees dandy as a nickname for Andrew, this name being, it seems, arbitrarily chosen.

Daniel come to judgment; Daniel in the lions' den

The expression 'a Daniel come to judgment' refers to someone who makes a wise decision about something that has puzzled others. It alludes to the biblical Daniel (Daniel 5: 14–16 and, perhaps more specifically, the devout and upright young man of the apocryphal book of Susanna), but the source of the actual quotation is Shakespeare's *Merchant of Venice* (Act 4, Scene 1):

> A Daniel come to judgment! yea a Daniel!
> O wise young judge, how I do honour thee!

The phrase Daniel in the lions' den, referring to someone who is in a place where he or she is exposed to intense personal danger, alludes to the Book of Daniel, chapter 6.

darbies

The word darbies, slang for handcuffs, is a shortening of the phrase 'Father Derby's [or Darby's] bands'. This was a sixteenth-century expression alluding to the rigid agreement binding a debtor to a moneylender. Derby (or Darby) may well have been the name of a notorious usurer of the period.

Darby and Joan

A happily married elderly couple are sometimes known as Darby and Joan: 'One summer afternoon we drove to my aunt and uncle's home for tea. They were a real old Darby and Joan – as much in love at eighty as they were at eighteen.' These names first appeared in a song by Henry Woodfall published in *The Gentlemen's Magazine* (1735).

The original Darby and Joan are thought to have been the London printer John Darby (*d.*1730), to whom Woodfall served as an apprentice, and his wife Joan.

The names are further remembered in the 'Darby and Joan' club, a club for elderly people.

davenport

A davenport is a small compact writing desk with a vertically folding writing surface and side drawers. The word derives from the name Davenport between 1820 and 1840, but sources differ as to whether Davenport was a furniture maker or a captain who first commissioned its manufacture. The sense of the word common in America for a large sofa, especially one that can be converted into a bed, came later.

David and Goliath; David and Jonathan

The David in the expressions David and Goliath and David and Jonathan is the Old Testament king of Israel (*c.*1000–962bc). The youngest son of Jesse, David was anointed by Samuel as the successor to Saul as king of Israel. David's successes against the Philistines included the slaying of Goliath. Goliath, as is well known, was the Philistine giant who was dealt a fatal blow by the seemingly insignificant David – Goliath, the armoured champion, bearing a javelin and a spear; David, the mere shepherd boy, bearing a staff, five smooth stones in his shepherd's bag and a sling. Yet it was David who slung a stone that killed the giant (I Samuel 17). The expression David and Goliath is used, therefore, to refer to a contest between someone who is apparently weak and someone who seems to possess overwhelmingly superior strength.

David became a close friend of Jonathan, Saul's eldest son, and the Bible records their mutual loyalty and affection (I Samuel 20) – hence the expression 'David and Jonathan' to refer to close friends of the same sex.

Davis Cup

The Davis Cup is the annual international lawn tennis championship for men. It is named after the American statesman and sportsman

Dwight Filley Davis (1879–1945), who instituted the competition in 1900 and donated the trophy that was to be presented to the winners.

An excellent tennis player himself – he was one-time US national doubles champion – Davis was also a respected statesman: he served as secretary of war (1925–9) and governor-general of the Philippines (1929–32). See also **Wightman Cup**.

Davy Crockett hat

The American frontiersman, politician and soldier Davy Crockett (1786–1836) is one of the most popular of American heroes. His fearless deeds have been widely described, and his name is still remembered for the Davy Crockett hat, the style of fur hat with a characteristic extended tailpiece that he is said to have worn. Crockett died defending the Alamo during the war for Texan independence.

Davy lamp

The Davy lamp (also known as the safety lamp) takes its name from the British chemist Sir Humphry Davy (1778–1829). Davy invented the safety lamp for miners in 1816; its flame is enclosed in metal gauze to prevent the possible ignition of explosive gas. His other notable achievements included the isolation of the elements potassium, sodium, calcium and magnesium.

Davy Jones' locker

The bottom of the sea, thought of as the grave of those drowned or buried at sea, is known as Davy Jones' locker. Davy Jones is seen as a personification of the devil who rules over the evil spirits of the sea, and the expression has been part of sailor slang for over two hundred years; there are several different theories as to how it originated.

Some suggest that Jones is a corruption of the name of the biblical Jonah, thrown overboard from a ship and swallowed by a great fish. The name Davy is said to have been added by Welsh sailors, David being the patron saint of Wales.

Other sources say that Davy is an anglicisation of the West Indian word *duffy* or *duppy* meaning a malevolent ghost.

Still others hold that Davy Jones was originally the owner of a sixteenth-century London public house that was popular with sailors. The pub is said to have also served as a place for press-ganging unwary citizens into service: Davy Jones was thought to store more than just ale in the lockers at the back of the pub. The victims would be drugged and transferred to a ship, to awaken only when the ship had put to sea. Thus Davy Jones' locker came to be feared.

Debrett

Debrett – in full *Debrett's Peerage* – is the name of a directory of the British aristocracy. The listing bears the name of the London publisher who first issued it, John Debrett (*c.*1752–1822). The original compilation, published in 1802, was titled *A Peerage of England, Scotland, and Ireland*; it was followed six years later by *A Baronetage of England*.

decibel

The decibel is the unit that is used to compare two power levels, especially of the intensity of sound, on a logarithmic scale. The decibel is one-tenth of a bel, the latter being only rarely used. Both units are named after the Scottish-born American scientist Alexander Graham Bell (1847–1922).

Bell is famous for his invention of the telephone (1876); the first, historic, words that Bell spoke to his assistant Thomas Watson on the telephone were, 'Watson, come here, I want you.'

Delilah

A Delilah is a treacherous and seductive woman, especially a mistress or wife. The use of this name alludes to the story of the biblical character Delilah who was bribed by the Philistine rulers to discover the secret of Samson's great strength (Judges 16:4–22). Samson lied to her on three occasions, but when she continued to ask him, he grew so weary of her nagging that he told her the truth – that the source of his power lay in his long hair. Delilah then betrayed this secret to the Philistines, and while Samson slept upon her lap, his hair was shaved off, so depriving him of his strength.

See also **Samson**.

demijohn

A demijohn is a large narrow-necked bottle made of glass or stoneware. Usually having small handles at the neck, demijohns are often encased in wickerwork. The word demijohn probably derives from the French *dame-jeanne*, 'Lady Jane', from the resemblance between the shape of the large bulging bottle and that of a particular buxom French housewife or, more likely, with portly women in general.

Derby

The Derby is the name of the annual flat race for three-year-old horses run at Epsom Downs, Surrey. It is probably named after Edward Stanley, 12th Earl of Derby (1752–1834), who founded the horse-race in 1780. The American counterpart is the Kentucky Derby, founded in 1875.

Derby is also the American and Canadian word for a bowler hat (its first syllable being pronounced to rhyme with fur). It is said that some Americans, noticing the distinctive shape of the style of hat worn by English sportsmen, took some of the hats back to American manufacturers, asking them to copy the narrow-brimmed felt hats with a rounded crown that came to be sold as 'hats like the English wear at the Derby'.

derrick

The word derrick, now referring to a hoisting apparatus or crane, formerly described a gallows. The word derives from the seventeenth-century English hangman surnamed Derrick.

Derrick served under the command of Robert Devereux, 2nd Earl of Essex, in the sacking of Cadiz (1596), where he was charged with rape and found guilty. He was sentenced to death by hanging but was pardoned by Essex when he agreed to become executioner at Tyburn gallows, London, near what is now Marble Arch. A few years later, Essex was found guilty of treason after instigating a riot in London (1601) and was sentenced to death, and it fell to Derrick to execute him. On this occasion Derrick used an axe, requiring three attempts to cut off Essex's head. In all, Derrick is said to have carried out more than 3000 executions in his service as hangman, his name being applied to the gallows itself and then to the crane which the gallows resembled.

derringer

A derringer is a small, short-barrelled pistol of large calibre. It is named after its inventor, the American gunsmith Henry Deringer (1786–1868). Deringer's invention meant that he became one of America's largest manufacturers of arms. There were, however, many imitations of his gun, one of which was the European make of derringer – i.e. Deringer's name adapted with an additional 'r' to avoid patent laws – and it is the spelling derringer that has become generally accepted.

deutzia

Deutzia is the name of a genus of ornamental shrubs of the saxifrage family that bear white or pink bell-like flowers. It is named after the Dutch patron of botany Jean Deutz (*c.* 1743–*c.* 1784).

Dewar flask

A Dewar flask is the name given to a kind of vacuum flask used in scientific experiments to store a liquid or gas at a constant temperature. It is also known by the trademark Thermos flask or, non-technically, as a vacuum flask. A Dewar flask has two thin glass walls that are separated by a vacuum to reduce loss of heat by conduction. The inner surface is silvered to reduce loss of heat by radiation, and the vessel has a tight stopper to prevent evaporation.

The Dewar flask takes its name from the Scottish chemist and physicist Sir James Dewar (1842–1923) who invented this prototype of the modern vacuum flask in about 1872. Dewar is known for his research into gases – he was the first person to produce liquid hydrogen – and, with the British chemist Sir Frederick Augustus Abel (1827–1902), he invented the explosive cordite.

Dewey Decimal System

The book classification system known as the Dewey Decimal System is named after the American librarian Melvil Dewey (1851–1931). Dewey devised his book-classification system in 1876, while working as acting librarian at Amherst College, Massachusetts. In Dewey's system, books are classified according to their subject matter by a three-digit number showing the main class, followed by numbers after a decimal point, to show subdivisions. The Dewey system is widely used by libraries throughout the world, the classification being constantly revised.

Dickensian

The adjective Dickensian has a number of meanings: it suggests poverty, misery and the squalor of urban or industrial life in Victorian England; it suggests conviviality (an old-fashioned 'Dickensian' Christmas) and it means vividly caricatured, when used in connection with the figures he created. The word Dickensian comes of course from the name of the English novelist Charles (John Huffman) Dickens (1812–70). It was memories of his painful childhood – he himself had to go to work in a blacking warehouse at the age of twelve – that inspired a great deal of his writing. Some of the characters in his writings have also become eponymous, for example, **Scrooge** from *A Christmas Carol* and **gamp**, an umbrella, from Mrs Sarah Gamp in *Martin Chuzzlewit*.

It is a mistake, however, to consider that 'the dickens', in expressions such as 'what the dickens' and 'the dickens only knows' comes from the name of Charles Dickens. The dickens referred to here is a euphemism for the devil. In fact the expression was used centuries before Dickens;

Shakespeare used it in *The Merry Wives of Windsor* (Act 3, Scene 2): 'I cannot tell what the dickens his name is.'

diddle

The word diddle, meaning informally to cheat or swindle, comes from the name of the character Jeremy Diddler in the farce *Raising the Wind* (1803) by the Irish-born English dramatist James Kenney (1780–1849). Diddler, the chief character of the play, has the habit of constantly borrowing small sums of money that he never pays back. The play's success led to the quick acceptance of the verb diddle into the language.

diesel

A diesel engine is an internal-combustion engine in which fuel is ignited by highly compressed air. The word diesel comes from the name of the German mechanical engineer Rudolf Diesel (1858–1913), who invented the diesel engine in 1892. Diesel's design followed up earlier ideas of the French scientist Sadi Carnot (1796–1832). Diesel developed the engine at the Krupp factory in Essen; and he not only invented a new kind of engine, he also found the best kind of fuel, the relatively cheap semi-refined crude oil, to power the engine. Today the diesel engine is widely used in industry and road, rail and maritime transport.

Dionysian

Dionysus was the Greek god of wine, also of fruitfulness and vegetation; he is identified with the Roman god Bacchus. He was worshipped in five annual dramatic festivals (the Dionysia) by the people of Athens. Dionysian feastings were scenes of wild, orgiastic licentiousness and it is in allusion to such ecstatic frenzy that the words Dionysian (or Dionysiac) are sometimes used today.

Dioscorea

Dioscorea is the botanical name of the genus of plants in the yam family. This name was given by Linnaeus in honour of the Greek physician Dioscorides Pedanius (*c.*AD40–*c.*90). As a surgeon in the Roman army, Dioscorides travelled widely and he collected information about nearly six hundred plants and their medicinal properties which he recorded in *De materia medica* (*c.*AD77). He is commonly regarded as one of the founders of the science of botany.

Dives

Dives is the name given to the rich man in the story about the rich man and Lazarus told by Jesus (Luke 16: 19–31). In the story, Dives pays no attention to the plight of Lazarus, the beggar at his gate. After death Lazarus is carried to 'Abraham's bosom' and Dives to hell, but it is not possible for there to be any contact between them.

It is interesting to note that the rich man is not actually named in the English Bible text. It is in the Latin version of the New Testament that he is called *dives*, meaning 'rich', hence 'a rich man', and the word has come to be thought of as a proper noun.

The name of Dives has thus become proverbial for a very rich person, especially one who is unconcerned and hardened to others' needs.

Doberman pinscher

A Doberman pinscher is a breed of short-haired, medium-sized dog with a short tail. The name of the dog derives from the German Ludwig Dobermann (1834–94) and the German word *pinscher*, a breed of hunting dog. A tax collector as well as a dog breeder, Dobermann developed in the 1880s a particularly ferocious breed of dog to help him in his duties. Nowadays Dobermans are widely used as guard dogs.

dolomite

Dolomite is the name given to the mineral calcium magnesium carbonate, which has a hexagonal crystal structure and is used in the manufacture of cement and as a building stone. The term is also used to refer to a rock containing a high ratio of magnesium carbonate that is used as a building material. The word dolomite comes from the name of the French geologist Déodat de Dolomieu (1750–1801) who discovered the mineral.

doily

The word doily, for a small ornamental openwork mat made of paper, cloth, or plastic that is laid under dishes of food, comes from the name of a London draper. His name is variously spelt Doily, Doiley or Doyley – and he owned a London shop around the year 1700 in the Strand, where fabrics trimmed with embroidery or crochet work were sold. The decorative cloths were originally known as Doily napkins, then doilies.

Don Juan

A Don Juan is a man who tries to seduce many women, a man with an insatiable desire for women. The name is based on the legendary fourteenth-century Spanish aristocrat and womaniser, Don Juan Tenorio. According to the traditional Spanish story, Don Juan Tenorio of Seville kills the father of Doña, the young girl he is attempting to seduce. On visiting the tomb, Don Juan scornfully invites the statue to a feast; the statue accepts, seizes Don Juan and delivers him to hell.

Don Juan is the subject of numerous plays and operas: Molière's *Don Juan* (1665), Mozart's *Don Giovanni* (1787), Byron's *Don Juan* (1819–24) and Shaw's *Man and Superman* (1903).

Don Quixote see Quixotic

Doppler effect

The Doppler effect is the technical name for the change in the apparent frequency of the waves of sound, light, etc., when there is relative motion between the source and the observer. For instance, the sound of a low-flying aeroplane seems to drop in pitch as the plane passes the observer although it in fact remains constant.

The phenomenon is named after the Austrian physicist Christian Johann Doppler (1803–53), who first explained it in 1842. Doppler originally tried to apply his principle to explain the coloration of stars.

doubting Thomas

A doubting Thomas is someone who is sceptical, particularly someone who refuses to believe until he has seen proof of something or has been otherwise satisfied as to its truth. The expression alludes to one of Jesus's apostles, Thomas, who refused to believe in Christ's resurrection until he had seen and felt Christ's body for himself (John 20: 24–9).

Douglas fir

The Douglas fir is a very tall evergreen American tree that is grown both for ornament and for its high-quality timber. With needle-like leaves and large cylindrical hanging cones, the Douglas fir is named after the Scottish botanist David Douglas (1798–1834).

Sent to North America at the age of twenty three, Douglas crossed Canada on foot and travelled as far south as California. When he came across the tall trees (which are second in height only to the giant sequoias and redwoods) Douglas had to shoot some seeds down with a gun – and in the process was chased by American Indians. In all,

Douglas collected over two hundred plants and seeds that were unknown in Europe. He suffered an unusual death: he was gored by a wild bull while working in Hawaii.

Dow-Jones average

The Dow-Jones average (or index) is a daily index of the relative prices of shares on the New York Stock Exchange. Based on the prices of a representative number of shares, the index takes its name from two American financial statisticians, Charles Henry Dow (1851–1902) and Edward D. Jones (1856–1920). Dow and Jones founded Dow, Jones and Co. in 1882 to provide information to Wall Street finance houses. Since 1884 indexes of movements of selected stocks and shares have been calculated.

Downing Street

Downing Street is the name of the road in Westminster, London, that houses the official residences of the British prime minister (Number 10) and the chancellor of the exchequer (Number 11). The street is named after the English statesman Sir George Downing (1623–84). A nephew of a Massachusetts governor, Downing graduated from Harvard and returned to England where he served under both Cromwell and King Charles II. His warning to Charles II in 1657 that Cromwell wanted to capture him saved Charles's life. Downing was later given a grant of land in what is now Downing Street.

Down's syndrome

Down's syndrome is a congenital disease typically marked by mental retardation and the physical features of slanting eyes, a broad short skull and short fingers. Associated with the presence of one extra chromosome in each cell, the condition is named after the English physician John Langdon-Down (1828–96) who first adequately described it in 1866. The disease was formerly called mongolism because the characteristic facial appearance of the affected children was commonly thought to resemble that of the people of Mongolia.

draconian

Draconian means 'very harsh or severe' and is used to describe laws, measures or regulations. The word comes from Draco, the seventh-century-BC Athenian law-giver. In 621BC he drew up what was probably the first comprehensive code of laws in Athens; before that time the laws had been interpreted arbitrarily by members of the city's governing body.

Draco's code of laws was so severe – almost every named crime carried the death sentence – that draconian came to be used to describe laws of unreasonable cruelty. In 590BC the Athenian statesman Solon formulated a more lenient legal code.

Druse

The Druses (or Druzes) are members of a religious sect centred on the mountains of Syria and Lebanon. The name probably derives from the name of one of the sect's founders, Ismail al-Darazi, Ismail the tailor (*d.* 1019). The Druses' scriptures are based on the Bible, the Koran and Sufi writings. Druses believe in the deity of Al-Hakim, a caliph of Egypt.

dryasdust

A boring pedantic person is sometimes called a dryasdust. The name is that of the fictitious character the Reverend Dr Jonas Dryasdust, to whom the Scottish writer Sir Walter Scott (1771–1832) addressed the prefaces of some of his novels.

dunce

The word dunce, 'a person who is stupid or slow to learn', derives originally from the name of the Scottish theologian John Duns Scotus (*c.* 1265–1308). (The Duns in his name comes from his supposed birthplace near Roxburgh, Scotland.) A Franciscan, his teaching combined elements of Aristotle's and Augustine's doctrines, but he was opposed to the theology of St Thomas Aquinas, he being nicknamed 'the Subtle Doctor' and Aquinas 'the Angelic Doctor'. His teachings ('Scotism') were accepted by the Franciscans and were influential in the Middle Ages but were ridiculed in the sixteenth century by humanists and reformers who considered his followers (called Dunsmen or Dunses) reluctant to accept new theological ideas. The word dunce then came to refer to a person resistant to new ideas, hence to someone who is dull or stupid.

E

Eiffel Tower

The Eiffel Tower in Paris is named after its designer, the French engineer Alexandre Gustave Eiffel (1832–1923). Built for the Paris Universal Exposition of 1889, the 300-metre (984-foot) structure was the world's highest building until 1930, when it was displaced by the Chrysler Building in New York.

Eiffel also designed the interior structure of the Statue of Liberty, although the external structure was designed by the French architect Frédéric August Bartholdi (1834–1904).

einsteinium

Einsteinium is the name of a radioactive chemical element that is produced artificially; its atomic number is 99. The element, originally identified by the American physicist Albert Ghiorso and others in 1952 in fall-out from the first hydrogen bomb explosion, is named after the German-born American physicist Albert Einstein (1879–1955). Einstein is most famous for his formulation of the special theory of relativity (1905) and the general theory of relativity (1916) and was awarded the **Nobel prize** for physics in 1921.

Electra complex see Oedipus complex

Elgin Marbles

The Elgin Marbles is the name given to the collection of ancient Greek marble sculptures that between 1803 and 1812 were removed from the Parthenon in Athens by Thomas Bruce, the 7th Earl of Elgin (1766–1841). Elgin was British ambassador to Turkey at the time and he obtained them from the Turks who were then occupying Athens. Elgin sold the sculptures to the British government in 1816 for £35,500 and they are currently on display at the British Museum. Efforts are continuing on the part of the Greek government to have this part of their cultural heritage restored to them.

Elizabethan

The reign of Queen Elizabeth I (1533–1603; reigned 1558–1603) was marked by great achievements in literature, exploration and many other areas, for instance, by the life and work of poets such as Shakespeare and Spenser, the discoverers Raleigh and Drake and musicians such as William Byrd. It is this spirit of outstanding creativity and bold adventure that is evoked by use of the term Elizabethan. The adjective may also be applied to Queen Elizabeth II (born 1926), alluding to the possibility of a similarly great and imaginative age.

éminence grise

An *éminence grise* refers to someone who exercises power unofficially by influencing another person or group who appear to have authority. *Éminence grise* (French for 'grey eminence') was originally the nickname given to the French friar and diplomat Père Joseph (François le Clerc du Tremblay 1577–1638), private secretary and confidant to the French statesman Cardinal Richelieu. The nickname referred to the colour of Père Joseph's garments and also to the authority he wielded over the unsuspecting Richelieu.

epicure; Epicurean

A person who cultivates a discriminating taste in food or wine is known as an epicure. The word derives from the name of the Greek philosopher Epicurus (341–270BC). Epicurus taught that the highest good was pleasure, but because every joy entailed some pain, he taught his disciples (Epicureans) to exercise moderation in all things. Epicurus also taught that pleasure was gained not through sensual indulgence but by self-control and achieving tranquillity of mind. His teachings have been misunderstood at times, however, and some have seen them as defending the unashamed pursuit of bodily pleasure.

Erastianism

The theory that the state should have authority over the church in ecclesiastical matters is known as Erastianism. This term comes from the name of the Swiss theologian Thomas Erastus (1524–83), to whom such a theory was attributed. In fact, however, Erastus limited his argument only to 'the case of a state where but one religion is permitted'.

erotic

The word erotic, 'of or tending to arouse sexual desire', derives from Eros, the Greek god of love, and the Greek word *eros*, meaning love; (sexual) desire. The god Eros (Roman counterpart: Cupid) was the son of Aphrodite and was usually portrayed as a winged, blindfolded youth with a bow and arrows.

eschscholtzia

Eschscholtzia is the name of a genus of plants in the poppy family and is applied particularly to the California poppy (*Eschscholtzia californica*), grown for its yellow and orange flowers. The term Eschscholtzia honours the name of the Russian-born German naturalist Johann Friedrich von Eschscholtz (1793–1834), who accompanied the German navigator and explorer Otto von Kotzebue on his expeditions (1815–18, 1823).

Esperanto

Esperanto is the name of the artificial language invented by the Polish doctor and linguist Lazarus Ludwig Zamenhof (1859–1917) in 1887. The language takes its name from the pseudonym chosen by its inventor when he wrote his first book on the subject, *Linguo Internacia de la Doktoro Esperanto*. The word Esperanto itself comes from Latin *sperare* (to hope), thus his pseudonym means 'the hoping doctor'. The language's grammar is completely regular and each letter represents only one sound. It is the world's most successful artificial language.

Euclidean geometry

Euclidean geometry is a system of geometry based on the axioms of the third-century-BC Greek mathematician Euclid. These axioms are recorded in Euclid's books, *Stoicheia* (Elements), which remained the standard work on geometry for over 2000 years. It was not until the nineteenth century that the possibility of a non-Euclidean geometry was seriously contemplated.

Euclid defined a line as 'length without breath'; and he is also said to have warned King Ptolemy I that 'there is no royal road to geometry' when asked if there was a quicker and easier way to learn the subject. Besides referring to geometry, the adjective Euclidean is also sometimes used to mean clear and orderly in presentation and explanation.

euhemerism

Euhemerism is the theory that the gods described in mythology are in fact historical heroes who have come to be regarded as divine. The word euhemerism derives from the name of the fourth-century Sicilian Greek philosopher Euhemerus who advanced this theory in his philosophical romance *Sacred History*. Euhemerus asserted that he had come across an inscription that supported his theory on a gold pillar in a temple on an island in the Indian Ocean.

euphorbia

Euphorbia is the name of the genus of plants of the spurge family that have a milky sap and small flowers surrounded by conspicuous bracts. As well as being used for ornamentation, some of the species have been used medicinally. The description euphorbia derives ultimately from the name of the first-century-AD Greek physician Euphorbus. Euphorbus was physician to King Juba II of Mauritania, who is said to have named the plant after him.

euphuism

Euphuism – not to be confused with euphemism – is used to describe an artificial and highly ornate style of writing or speaking. Fashionable in the late sixteenth and early seventeenth centuries, euphuism derives from Euphues, a character in the prose romance in two parts *Euphues: The Anatomy of Wit* (1578) and *Euphues and his England* (1580) by the English writer John Lyly (*c.*1554–1606). *Euphues* is Greek for 'well endowed by nature' and Lyly's prose romance, marked by excessive use of antithesis, alliteration, historical or mythological allusion and other figures of speech, has given us the word euphuism to describe this elaborately embellished style.

Eustachian tube

The Eustachian tube is the name of the canal connecting the pharynx (throat) to the middle ear. Known also as the pharyngotympanic tube, it had already been discovered by the fifth-century-BC Greek physician Alcmaeon of Croton, but it was the Italian physician Bartolommeo Eustachio (*c.*1520–74) who first adequately described it. As well as undertaking anatomical research into the ear, Eustachio studied the heart, kidneys and nervous system.

Everest

The name of the world's highest mountain, Mount Everest, on the Nepal–Tibet border (8848 m; 29,028 ft), honours the surveyor-general of India, Sir George Everest (1790–1866). Everest was the first to undertake detailed mapping of the subcontinent, including the Himalayas.

Since 1920–1 expeditions to climb Mount Everest have been undertaken, the first successful one being the expedition led by Colonel John Hunt when the New Zealander Edmund Hillary and the Sherpa Tensing Norkay became the first to reach the summit on 29 May 1953.

In a derived application of the word, Everest is sometimes used to refer to the highest point of achievement.

everyman

Everyman is the name sometimes given to the typical or average person, 'the man in the street'. The description comes from the allegorical character Everyman in the sixteenth-century morality play of the same title. In the play, which is based on a slightly earlier Dutch counterpart *Ellckerlijc*, Everyman is summoned by Death, but he finds that none of his friends will go with him except Good Deeds. The lines of Knowledge in the play have become legendary:

> Everyman, I will go with thee and be thy guide,
> In thy most need to go by thy side.

F

Fabian

The adjective 'Fabian' is sometimes used to mean cautious in politics; avoiding direct confrontation. This sense derives from the policies of the Roman general Quintus Fabius Maximus (also known as Cunctator, the delayer; died 203BC). As a commander against Hannibal in the Second Punic War, Fabius continually harassed Hannibal's armies without ever risking a pitched battle. Fabius's cautious tactics contributed to Hannibal's eventual defeat.

The Fabian Society, an association of British socialists, took its name from Quintus Fabius Maximus. Founded in 1884 to establish democratic socialist principles gradually rather than by adopting revolutionary methods, its prominent personalities included George Bernard Shaw.

fagin

The name Fagin is sometimes used to describe an adult who teaches others, especially children, to steal goods, and also to describe a person who receives stolen goods. The allusions are to the fictional character Fagin, the head of a gang of thieves in the novel *Oliver Twist* (published 1837–8) by Charles Dickens.

Fahrenheit

Fahrenheit is the scale of temperatures in which 32° represents the freezing point of water and 212° the boiling point of water. It is named after its inventor, the German scientist Gabriel Daniel Fahrenheit (1686–1736), who set 0° as the lowest temperature he could scientifically derive, by mixing ice and common salt. The Fahrenheit scale is no longer in general use, having been replaced by the Celsius scale.

Fahrenheit was born in Danzig and lived most of his life in Holland and England. His father wanted him to be a merchant, but after a brief and unsuccessful attempt at this career, he turned to physics. Before he was twenty, Fahrenheit manufactured meteorological instruments. He initially used alcohol in his thermometers, but he soon substituted mercury, inventing the first mercury thermometer. He was elected to the Royal Society in 1724.

Falkland Islands

The British name of the Falkland Islands, the islands in the South Atlantic, commemorates Lucius Cary, 2nd Viscount Falkland (c. 1610–43), secretary of state (1642). The name Falklands was given by an English sailor, Captain John Strong, who in 1690 named the sound between the two main islands Falkland Sound.

The Argentine name for the islands, Islas Malvinas, does not come from Spanish, but French. Many of the sailors who went there in the early eighteenth century were from St Malo in Brittany, so the French called the islands Îles Malouines, which became the existing Argentine name in Spanish.

Fallopian tube

The Fallopian tubes are the two tubes that connect the uterus to the ovaries in female mammals. They are named after the Italian anatomist Gabriel Fallopius (1523–62) who first described them. A pupil of the Flemish anatomist Andreas Vesalius (1514–64), Fallopius was professor of anatomy at Pisa (1548–51), after which he taught at Padua University. He described features of the ear as well as the reproductive system in his *Observationes anatomicae* (1561).

Falstaffian

The adjective Falstaffian is sometimes used to describe someone who is plump, witty and self-indulgent. The word derives from the character Sir John Falstaff in Shakespeare's *Henry IV*, *Parts I* and *II* (1597 and 1598) and *The Merry Wives of Windsor* (1602).

farad; faraday; faradic; faradism

The English physicist and chemist Michael Faraday (1791–1867) was born into a poor London family and was apprenticed at an early age to a bookbinder. The books he came across having aroused his interest in science, he attended lectures at the Royal Institution and persuaded Sir Humphry Davy to engage him as his assistant (1813), eventually succeeding Davy as professor of chemistry there (1833). Faraday made many notable discoveries in different areas of the physical sciences, but it is particularly with electricity and electrochemistry that his name is perpetually linked. A farad is the basic metric unit of electrical capacitance; a faraday is a quantity of electricity used in electrolysis. He is known for his laws of electrolysis (1813–14) and his pioneering work on electromagnetic induction, hence the terms faradic and faradism.

Farmer Giles

Farmer Giles is sometimes used in a mildly humorous way as a generic name for a farmer. The name implies not only a rural simplicity but also a capacity for common sense. The name may be derived from Giles, the orphan farm labourer in the poem 'The Farmer's Boy' (1800) by Robert Bloomfield (1766–1823).

faro

Faro, a gambling game in which the players bet on the value of the cards the dealer will turn up, probably derives via French ultimately from Pharaoh, the title of ancient Egyptian rulers. It is possible that at one time in the history of the game a picture of one of the ruling pharaohs featured on the cards.

Fata Morgana

Fata Morgana is the name given to a mirage that traditionally is seen in the Straits of Messina from the Calabrian coast. In a derived sense, the term may be applied to any mirage or to a figment of the imagination. The name Fata Morgana (English, Morgan le Fay) comes from the Italian *fata*, 'fairy', and Morgana, who was the queen of Avalon, half-sister of King Arthur and evil sorceress of Arthurian legend. It was believed by the Norman settlers in England that she lived in Calabria, hence the application of the name to the apparition.

faun; fauna

A faun is a figure in Roman mythology that has the body of a human and the horns and legs of a goat. The word derives from Faunus, the Roman god of pastures and forests who was later identified with the Greek god Pan.

The name fauna, referring to animal life in general or that of a particular area or period (and often complementing **Flora**), was adopted by Linnaeus in 1746, Fauna being the sister of the god Faunus.

Faustian

Faust is the name of the semi-legendary medieval German scholar and magician who allegedly sold his soul to the Devil in exchange for knowledge and power. Stories of conjurors working with the Devil, linked with the historical figure of the wandering conjuror John Faust (*c.*1488–1540), have inspired many literary works including Marlowe's *Dr Faustus* (1604) and Goethe's *Faust* (1808, 1832). The adjective Faustian has thus come to describe different characteristics of Faust and Faustus, including the abandonment of spiritual values in order to gain material benefits, the relentless pursuit of knowledge and enjoyment, and spiritual disillusionment and dissatisfaction.

fermium

Fermium is an artificially produced radioactive element. Like **einsteinium**, it was first detected by the American physicist Albert Ghiorso in fall-out after the first hydrogen-bomb explosion (1952). It was named after the Italian-born American physicist Enrico Fermi (1901–54).

Fermi's early work in Italy was concerned with quantum statistics – the Fermi-Dirac statistics are named after himself and the British physicist Paul Adrien Maurice Dirac (1902–84). Fermi is best known for his work on nuclear physics: he was awarded the **Nobel prize** for physics in Stockholm in 1938. Owing to his antifascism and because his wife was Jewish, Fermi sailed directly from Stockholm with his family to the United States. In Chicago he led the group that produced the first controlled nuclear chain reaction (1942). As well as being known for a chemical element, Fermi's name is also honoured by the fermi (a former unit of length in nuclear physics), the so-called Fermi level, and fermion (an elementary particle).

Ferris wheel

A Ferris wheel is a large upright fairground wheel with seats that hang freely from its rim; the seats remain more or less horizontal as the power-driven wheel turns. It is named after the American engineer George Washington Gale Ferris (1859–96) and was introduced at the World's Columbian Exposition in Chicago (1893). The first Ferris wheel measured 250 feet (76 m) in diameter, and had thirty-six cars, each holding up to forty people. The 'big wheels' of today are more modest attractions, seating six to eight people in each car.

fiacre

A fiacre was a small, four-wheeled, horse-drawn carriage of the seventeenth and eighteenth centuries. The name of the cab derives from the townhouse where they were first hired out in 1648, the Hôtel de St Fiacre in Paris. Fiacre is the French version of the name of the Irish Prince Fiachrach (or Fiachra), who founded a monastery at Breuil, near Paris, in about 670.

Fibonacci sequence

The Fibonacci sequence is the name given to the sequence of numbers in which each number after the first two numbers is the sum of the previous two in the series. The sequence begins with the numbers (known as Fibonacci numbers) 0, 1, 1, 2, 3, 5, 8, 13, 21, 34. It is named after the Italian mathematician Leonardo Fibonacci (*c*.1170–*c*.1250), who is said to have invented it in 1225 in order to solve a puzzle about the breeding rate of rabbits. The sequence has been found to occur in nature, such as in the number of leaf buds on a plant stem and the number of spirals of seeds on the head of a sunflower.

Fibonacci is also credited with popularising the Arabic numerical notation in his *Book of the Abacus* (1202).

filbert

The filbert (*Corylus maxima*) is a tree that is closely related to the hazel. It is named after the Frankish abbot St Philibert (*d*.684), because his feast day (22 August) falls in the nutting season.

fink

The word fink is used chiefly in US and Canadian slang for a strikebreaker, informer or a contemptible or unpleasant person. There are a number of different theories as to the word's origin. One possible suggestion is that fink is an altered form of pink, which is short for Pinkerton, the name of the strikebreakers in the Homestead steel strike of 1892.

flora

The word flora refers to plant life in general or that of a particular area or period; it often complements **Fauna**. The term derives from Flora, the Roman goddess of flowers, youth and spring, whose name comes from the Latin *flos* (flower). The spring festival (Floralia) in her honour was established in 283BC and provided an excuse for wild, uninhibited conduct.

Florence Nightingale

The English nurse Florence Nightingale (1820–1910) is known for her work during the Crimean War. She led a party of nurses to work in the military hospital at Scutari (1854), where she sought to improve the living conditions of the patients, who dubbed her 'the Lady with the Lamp'. After the war, Florence Nightingale devoted herself to raising the status of the nursing profession. She was the first woman to receive the Order of Merit (1907). Her name is sometimes used when referring to a devoted and highly efficient nurse.

Fokker

The Fokker was the famous German fighter plane of the First World War, noted for its speed and climbing power. It is named after its designer and manufacturer the Dutch-born Anthony Herman Gerard Fokker (1890–1939). In 1912 Fokker set up an aircraft factory in Germany. He later became an American citizen.

forsythia

Forsythia is the name given to a genus of ornamental shrubs of the olive family that have bright yellow bell-shaped flowers which appear before the leaves in early spring. The name honours the British botanist William Forsyth (1737–1804). A Scottish gardener and horticulturist, Forsyth became superintendent of the Royal Gardens of St James's and Kensington. He may have personally brought the forsythia shrub from its native China and introduced it to Britain.

Fowler

'Fowler' is sometimes used to refer to the style manual *A Dictionary of Modern English Usage*, compiled by the British lexicographer Henry Watson Fowler (1858–1933).

Fowler began his career as a teacher at Sedburgh School, but after seventeen years resigned from the school, objecting to the compulsory preparation of boys for confirmation. He then sought to make a living as a writer. With his brother Frank George Fowler (1870–1918), he translated Lucian (1905) and wrote *The King's English* (1906) and *The Concise English Dictionary of Current English* (1911). By lying about his age, Fowler saw active service in the First World War, but was invalided out. After the war he wrote *A Dictionary of Modern English Usage* (1926), the book that was to make him 'a household word in all English-speaking countries' (Sir Ernest Gowers).

Fowler is today seen as a classic, prescriptive guide to usage; its success is generally considered to lie as much in its idiosyncratic style as in its detailed and discursive stylistic commentary.

Franciscan

Franciscans are members of the Order of Friars Minor founded by St Francis of Assisi in 1209. In its original form, the distinctive feature of this order was its insistence on complete poverty of individual friars and corporately of the whole order.

St Francis of Assisi (original name Giovanni di Bernardone; 1182–1226) was the son of a wealthy merchant, who renounced his worldly possessions in 1205, turning to a life of prayer. By 1209 he had gathered a band of disciples around him. He composed for himself and his associates a Primitive Rule – now lost, but it seems to have been composed mainly of passages from the Gospels. In 1212 he presented this rule to Pope Innocent III, who gave his approval to the new order. St Francis later travelled widely, retiring in 1220 from leadership of his order, and, according to tradition, receiving the stigmata of Christ in 1224. He is remembered for his deep humility and generosity, his simple faith and his love of God, his fellow-men and nature.

The Franciscan Order has known decline and division since St Francis' time, but has remained a missionary and charitable part of the church.

frangipane

Frangipane is a pastry filled with cream and almonds. The name (often spelt frangipani) is also applied to the shrub *Plumeria rubra* of the periwinkle family (red jasmine) and to a perfume prepared from this plant or resembling the odour of its flowers.

The origin of frangipane is uncertain. It seems that the word came via French from the sixteenth-century Italian nobleman, the Marquis Muzio Frangipani, who first invented a perfume for scenting gloves. It may well have been the marquis or a relative of his who originally prepared the pastry named in his honour.

Frankenstein

A 'Frankenstein's monster' is the product of an inventor that then destroys its creator. The expression comes originally from the name Baron Frankenstein in the novel *Frankenstein, or the Modern Prometheus* (1818) by the English novelist Mary Wollstonecraft Shelley (1797–1851). The novel describes how the hero, the philosopher Baron Frankenstein, creates an immense and repulsive monster out of inanimate matter; the monster gets out of control and eventually murders its creator. In contemporary usage, the name Frankenstein is often applied to the monster itself rather than its creator.

Fraunhofer lines

Joseph von Fraunhofer (1787–1826) was a German physicist and optician. In 1814 he observed numerous dark lines in the sun's spectrum, now known as the Fraunhofer lines. He also made significant improvements to the design of telescopes and other optical instruments.

Fraunhofer's success was due in part to a great misfortune. The son of a lens-maker, he was orphaned as a boy and apprenticed to an apothecary in Munich; but he was to be the only survivor when the dilapidated tenement in which he lived collapsed. Watching the rescue was the Elector of Bavaria, Charles Theodore, who was so moved by the boy's predicament that he bought him out of the apprenticeship, so enabling him to develop his knowledge and skills.

freesia

Freesia is the name of a genus of ornamental sweet-scented South African plants of the iris family, grown for their yellow, pink or white flowers. The plants are named after the German physician Friedrich Heinrich Theodor Freese (*d.* 1876).

Freudian slip

A Freudian slip is a slip of the tongue that is considered to reveal an unconscious thought of the speaker's mind. The expression is often used to describe a word that is uttered unintentionally but which is thought nearer to the truth than the word the speaker originally had in mind.

The expression 'Freudian slip' comes from the teachings of the Austrian psychiatrist Sigmund Freud (1856–1939), who pioneered psychoanalysis. Freud developed the method of free association – he encouraged his patients to pursue verbally a particular train of thought. His *Interpretation of Dreams* (1899) analysed dreams in terms of unconscious childhood experiences and desires. His insistence that mental disorders had sexual causes that originated in childhood led to his estrangement from many of his colleagues.

In basic psychoanalytic terms, a Freudian slip is seen as a momentary lapse in a person's defensive position; thoughts or feelings that have been repressed are then unintentionally expressed.

Friday

The name of the sixth day of the week comes from the Old English *Frigedaeg*, the day of the Norse goddess Frig (or Frigga), the wife of Woden and goddess of married love. In some legends she is identified with Freya, the Norse goddess of love and fertility and the counterpart of the Roman goddess Venus. It is said that as **Wednesday** and **Thursday** had been named after Frig's husband Woden and her son Thor, Friday was assigned to her in order to appease her.

A man Friday is a trustworthy, loyal male employed for general duties. The expression comes from the name of the native servant in the novel *Robinson Crusoe* (published 1719) by the English writer Daniel Defoe (c.1660–1731). The expression girl Friday is formed, on the analogy of man Friday, for female general assistant, particularly in an office.

fuchsia

Fuchsia is the name of a genus of ornamental shrubs and herbs native to Central and South America; they have showy drooping deep red, purple, pink or white flowers. The name honours the German botanist and physician Leonhard Fuchs (1501–66). Fuchs's book on medicinal plants, *De historia stirpium* (1503), was widely known at the time; he was professor of medicine at the University of Tübingen from 1535. The plant was named in honour of Fuchs in 1703 by the French monk and botanist Charles Plumier (1646–1704)

furphy

In informal, chiefly Australian, usage 'a furphy' is an unlikely or ridiculous rumour or story. The word probably derives from the name Furphy, a supplier of water and sanitation carts in Australia in the First World War. The name was printed on the water tanks and the latrine buckets used by the Australian troops; they therefore came to describe news of the war obtained at these centres of gossip as furphies. An alternative, less likely, theory suggests that the origin lies with the name of the Australian writer Joseph Furphy (1843–1913), who wrote stories under the pseudonym of Tom Collins.

G

gadolinite; gadolinium

The black or brown mineral known as gadolinite is a silicate of the metallic elements iron, beryllum and yttrium. It is named after the Finnish chemist Johann Gadolin (1760–1852), who discovered and analysed it at Stockholm in 1794.

The metallic element gadolinium, which occurs in gadolinite, is also named after Gadolin. The element was discovered by the Swiss chemist J. C. G. Marignac in 1880.

Galahad

In Arthurian legend, Sir Galahad is the most virtuous knight of the Round Table. He is the son of Lancelot and Elaine and is, in many romances, the only knight who succeeds in the quest for the Holy Grail. As one tradition has it, Galahad was added by Walter Map (c.1140-c.1209) to the Arthurian legends. The name of Galahad has come to stand for chivalrous male purity and nobility.

galenical

The ideas of the Greek physician Galen (AD129–199) dominated medicine for well over a thousand years after his death. He wrote numerous treatises on medical theory and practice; and although some of his views are now known to have been mistaken, his experiments and findings – for example that the spinal cord is important in muscle activity – proved significant in the study of medicine. His name is still remembered in the adjective galenical, for a medicine that is prepared from plant or animal tissue rather than being chemically synthesised.

gallium

The metallic element known as gallium was first identified in 1875 by the French chemist Paul Lecoq de Boisbaudran (d.1912). It is said that the name derives from the Latin translation (*gallus*) of the French *coq* (cock) in the name of its discoverer.

Gallup poll

A Gallup poll is a survey of the views of a representative sample of the population on a particular issue; it is used especially as a means of forecasting election results. The poll is named after the American statistician George Horace Gallup (1901–84), who originally devised the method for assessing public opinion in advertising. Following his successful prediction of the result of the 1936 American presidential election, his techniques have been widely used, and developed, by different organisations, not only to forecast voting patterns but also to provide the basis of many other statistical surveys.

galvanise; galvanometer

Galvanise means to cover iron or steel with a protective zinc coating and, in a derived sense, to stimulate into sudden action. The word comes from the name of the Italian physician Luigi Galvani (1737–98).

Galvani observed that the muscles of a frog twitched when they were touched by metal contacts. He thought this effect was caused by 'animal electricity', and it was his fellow-countryman Volta who later provided the correct explanation, that the current was produced by the contacts of the metals themselves. Nevertheless, Galvani undertook a great deal of research in the development of electricity, and his name is linked both with the verb galvanise and the noun galvanometer, an instrument used to measure small electric currents.

gamp

Gamp is sometimes used in informal British usage for a large umbrella, especially one that is loosely tied. The word comes from the name of the nurse Mrs Sarah Gamp in the novel *Martin Chuzzlewit* (1843–4) by Charles Dickens who is known for her large, untidily tied umbrella.

Garamond see Baskerville

gardenia

Gardenia is the name of a genus of ornamental tropical shrubs and trees cultivated for their large, fragrant, often white, flowers. The name does not come from the word garden, as might be thought, but from the Scottish-American botanist Alexander Garden (1730–91). Dr Garden was a physician who spent much of his life in Charleston, South Carolina. He not only practised medicine but devoted a great deal of his time to collecting specimens of different plants and animals. He is said to have discovered the conger eel and several snakes and herbs. He pursued a vigorous correspondence with Linnaeus and other European naturalists, even seeking to persuade Linnaeus to name a plant after him. Dr Garden's wishes were fulfilled: in 1760 Linnaeus named the genus in his honour.

gargantuan

The word gargantuan means 'enormous or colossal'; it derives from the name Gargantua, the gigantic king in the novel *Gargantua* (1534) by the French satirist François Rabelais (c. 1494–1553). Gargantua's appetite was so enormous that he once ate six pilgrims in a salad and it is to food and appetites that the adjective gargantuan is most often applied.

garibaldi

A garibaldi is a woman's loose, long-sleeved blouse or, alternatively, a kind of biscuit containing a layer of currants. The word derives from the name of the Italian patriot and soldier Giuseppe Garibaldi (1807–82). The blouse was so named because it resembled the red shirt worn by Garibaldi and his thousand Redshirt followers in the Risorgimento – the nineteenth-century Italian nationalist movement. Garibaldi led his thousand volunteers to conquer Sicily and Naples, so enabling South Italy to be reunited with the North (1860–1). It is said that the red shirts worn by Garibaldi and his men were presented to him by the government in Uruguay, while he was gathering troops there.

It is uncertain how the biscuit came to be named after him, although it may be that he was fond of such delicacies.

Gatling gun

A Gatling gun was an early type of machine-gun. Mounted on wheels, it had a revolving cluster of barrels, the gunner controlling its rate of fire by means of a hand crank. The gun is named after its inventor, the American Richard Jordan Gatling (1818–1903). Patented in 1862, the Gatling was used in the later stages of the American Civil War (1861–5); it was discarded before the beginning of the First World War.

The name survives in the word gat, slang for a revolver or pistol.

Gaullism; Gaullist

Gaullism refers to the French political movement devoted to supporting the principles and policies of General, later President, Charles (André Joseph Marie) de Gaulle (1890–1970). Promoted to general in the Second World War (1940), he became leader of the French forces organised in London and a symbol of French patriotism. After the war he was president of a provisional government (1945–6), and later, of the Fifth Republic (1958–69). As president of the Fifth Republic, de Gaulle emphasised the status of the presidency and the supremacy of national interest; his independent foreign policy was aimed at re-establishing France as a world power. Gaullist principles continue to be a dominant influence in contemporary French politics.

gauss

The gauss is the unit of magnetic flux density in the centimetre–gram–second system of measurement. The unit is named after the German mathematician Karl Friedrich Gauss (1777–1855). Gauss – who is regarded as one of the greatest mathematicians of all time – is known for significant mathematical work in the fields of probability theory and number theory; he also applied mathematics to electricity, magnetism and astronomy.

Gauss's name is also remembered in the word *degauss*, meaning 'to demagnetise'. During the Second World War, Germany developed a magnetic mine for use at sea, the mine being detonated by the magnetism of an approaching ship. Equipment was then designed to degauss the ship: to neutralise the magnetic field of the ship's hull.

Gay Lussac's Law see Charles's Law

Geiger counter

A Geiger counter is an electronic instrument that is used to measure the presence and intensity of radiation. The instrument is named after the German physicist Hans Geiger (1882–1945), who developed it with the help of the German scientist Walter M. Müller (b.1905). Research by Geiger and Müller built on investigations undertaken by the British physicist Ernest Rutherford (1871–1937). Geiger later became professor of physics at the Universities of Kiel (1925–29), and Tübingen (1929–36), and the Technische Hochschule, Berlin (from 1936).

gentian

Gentian is the name of a group of plants (genus: *Gentiana*) with showy, mainly blue, flowers; many alpine perennials are gentians. The name of the plant is said to derive from Gentius, the second-century-BC king of Illyria, an ancient region on the Adriatic. Gentius is believed to have discovered the medicinal properties of the plant now known as yellow gentian (*Gentiana lutea*).

Geordie; George

The word Geordie, for someone who comes from or lives on Tyneside, in north-east England, derives from the name George. This name is also used in the rather old-fashioned exclamation of surprise or disbelief, 'By George!' 'By George! you're right – how amazing!' – and in the language of air crews to refer to the automatic pilot in military and civil aircraft: 'Let George do it!' This latter comes from George, originally slang for an airman.

georgette

Georgette (or georgette crêpe) is a fine, thin, strong, silk crêpe used in clothing, especially for blouses and gowns. The fabric is named after the late-nineteenth-century Parisian dressmaker Madame Georgette de la Plante.

Georgia; Georgian

The American state of Georgia, on the south-east coast of the USA, is named after King George II (1683–1760). Founded in 1732, it was the last of the thirteen original states.

The Georgian style of architecture is that which was dominant in the reigns of the kings George I to George IV (1714–1830). The style is marked by well-proportioned gracefulness.

Georgian is also a term applied in a literary sense to the writers, especially poets, during the reign of King George V (1910–36).

Geronimo

'Geronimo', an exclamation of delight or surprise, was originally the cry of American airborne paratroopers as they jumped from their planes into battle. The name shouted is that of the American Apache Indian chief Geronimo (1829–1909), but there are different theories as to how the expression was adopted. One suggestion is that the cry was inspired by paratroopers in training seeing a film featuring the Apache Indian chief. Others suggest that Geronimo, being hotly pursued by the cavalry, shouted out his name as he plunged on horseback down an almost vertical cliff into a river below.

Geronimo, finally captured in 1886, became something of a celebrity when he visited the St Louis World's Fair and other expositions.

gerrymander

To gerrymander means to divide an area into new electoral districts in order to give one party an unfair advantage. It is also used in a derived sense to mean to manipulate to obtain an unfair advantage for oneself. The word comes from the name of the American politician Elbridge Gerry (1744–1814). While governor of Massachusetts (1810), Gerry sought to rearrange the electoral boundaries in favour of his own party in the forthcoming elections. It is said that one day the painter Gilbert Stuart came into the offices of the *Boston Sentinel* newspaper, and, seeing the newly redrawn district on a map, proceeded to draw a head, wings and claws round the district that was already in the shape of a salamander. 'That will do for a salamander,' declared the artist. 'A Gerrymander, you mean,' replied the editor, Benjamin Russell, and so the word was born. Gerry later went on to become vice-president of the USA (1813–14)

gib

A gib is a male cat, especially one that has been castrated. The word is probably originally a nickname for Gilbert. See also **Tom**.

Gideons

The Gideons are an interdenominational Christian group who have the aim of making the Bible freely available. Originally founded in Wisconsin, USA, in 1899, the organisation places Bibles in hotel rooms, hospital wards, etc. The name Gideon derives from the Old Testament judge noted for his leadership of a small army who triumphed over the Midianites (Judges 6–7).

gilbert

A gilbert is the unit of magnetomotive force in the centimetre–gram–second system of measurement. It is named after William Gilbert (1544–1603), English physicist and physician to Queen Elizabeth I. Gilbert is noted for his pioneering work on magnetism, especially his treatise *De Magnete* (1600), and he has come to be known as the father of electricity. Gilbert was responsible for introducing many new terms into the language, including electricity, electric force and magnetic pole.

Gilbertian

Gilbertian is used to refer to the satirical light humour of the English comic dramatist Sir William Schwenk Gilbert (1836–1911). Originally a barrister, in 1869 Gilbert met the composer Arthur Sullivan (1842–1900), for whom he wrote the librettos of fourteen operettas for D'Oyly Carte, including *Trial by Jury* (1873), *HMS Pinafore* (1878), *The Pirates of Penzance* (1879), *Iolanthe* (1882), *The Mikado* (1885),

Rudigore (1887), *The Yeoman of the Guard* (1888) and *The Gondoliers* (1889). Thus the adjective Gilbertian has come to mean 'fanciful, wittily humorous', in the style of these ever-popular Savoy Operas.

Gill see Baskerville

girl Friday see Friday

Gladstone bag

A Gladstone bag is an article of hand luggage: a bag that has flexible sides set on a rigid frame, it opens into two equal-sized compartments. The bag is named after the British statesman and prime minister William Ewart Gladstone, known as the Grand Old Man (1809–98), but he did not invent it. It seems that the article of hand luggage was named in Gladstone's honour because he undertook so much travelling in the course of his public career. The bag was designed for the purpose of being particularly convenient for travellers.

Goethian; goethite

The German Johann Wolfgang von Goethe (1749–1832) was not only a great poet and writer; he was also a scholar and scientist. His powerful writings, notably *Götz von Berlichingen*.(1773), *The Sorrows of Young Werther* (1774), *Iphigenie auf Tauris* (1787) and *Faust* (1808; 1832), have inspired the adjective Goethian, 'intellectual, yet kind and benevolent'.

His scientific work, for example *The Theory of Colours* (1810) and *Metamorphosis of Plants* (1817–24), led to a mineral being named after him: goethite, the yellow-brown mineral that is formed as a result of the oxidation and hydration of iron minerals.

golliwog

A golliwog is a soft children's doll, made of cloth, that has a black face and black hair that sticks our around its head. The word golliwog comes from the name, Golliwog, of an animated doll in children's books by the American writer Bertha Upton (*d.* 1912) and the American illustrator and portrait painter Florence Upton (*d.* 1922).

Gongorism

Gongorism is used to refer to an artificial literary style whose chief characteristics include elaborate constructions and obscure allusions and comparisons. It is named after the Spanish priest and lyric poet Luis de Góngora y Argote (1561–1627). Góngora's earlier works are not written in such a style, but his later works, including notably *Soledades* (1613), show many Gongoristic elements. The style resembles **Euphuism**.

Good Samaritan

A Good Samaritan is a kind person who selflessly helps people in distress. The allusion is to the biblical story told by Jesus (Luke 10:25–37); the Good Samaritan has come to stand for a helpful person who assists others, often to the point of inconvenience and without the slightest thought of personal gain.

By extension, the name Samaritans has been given to those who man the voluntary telephone service set up to help those in need. Established in Britain in 1953, the Samaritans provide a confidential and anonymous service to anyone in despair.

goodbye

Goodbye, the conventional expression said as two people part, was originally a contraction of the phrase 'God be with you.' The word good was substituted for the name God by analogy with the expressions good day and good night.

Gordian – cut the Gordian knot

The expression 'cut the Gordian knot' means to solve a complex problem by a single decisive, brilliant action. The phrase alludes to the story of Gordius, the peasant king of Phrygia in Asia Minor. Gordius dedicated his chariot to Jupiter, fastening the yoke to the beam of his chariot with such an intricate knot that no one could untie it. The legend developed that whoever could untie the knot would reign over the whole empire of Asia. When Alexander the Great passed through the town (333BC) he is said to have simply cut the knot with his sword and so claimed fulfilment of the legend in himself.

Gordon Bennett

The name Gordon Bennett is used as an exclamation to express great surprise: 'Gordon Bennett! It's Jack – how are you? It must be years since I've seen you!' The expression comes from the name Gordon Bennett (1841–1918), the proprietor of the *New York Herald*. He is famous for his sponsorship of balloon races at the beginning of the twentieth century. Like the slang expression 'gorblimey', Gordon (Bennett) was originally used as a euphemism to avoid using the name of God directly.

Gordon setter

The black and tan breed of dog known as the Gordon setter originated in Scotland. The breed was developed by the Scottish nobleman Alexander Gordon (1743–1827). Gordon was also a sportsman and a writer of folk ballads.

gorgon

A gorgon is sometimes used informally to refer to an ugly or repulsive woman. The word derives from the Gorgons of Greek mythology, the three winged females who had snakes for hair, claws and enormous teeth. Medusa was the only mortal of the three Gorgons: she was so hideous that anyone who looked at her was instantly turned into stone.

gossip

The Old English word from which gossip derives is *godsibb* which originally meant a godparent, from *God* plus *sibb* 'relation'. Gossips were the sponsors for children at baptism – Shakespeare in *Two Gentlemen of Verona* wrote: ' 'Tis not a maid, for she hath had gossips' (Act 3, Scene 1). Gradually the word came to be applied to familiar friends and acquaintances, and then to the contemporary sense of someone fond of idle talk. Interestingly, the Old English *sibb* is preserved in the modern word sibling, meaning a person's brother or sister.

Gothic

The word Gothic is used to describe a style of art or architecture used in Western Europe from the twelfth to the sixteenth centuries and imitated later in the so-called Gothic Revival of the eighteenth and nineteenth centuries. Features of Gothic architecture include the pointed arch, slender tall pillars and flying buttresses. The description 'Gothic' was originally used as a term of ridicule by Renaissance artists and architects: they considered the medieval style to be crude and barbarous, blaming the destruction of the superior classical art on the Goths. The Goths were a Germanic people who originated in Scandinavia and invaded many parts of the Roman Empire from the third to the fifth centuries AD. Although the Goths' artistic styles were certainly not 'Gothic', it is the name of this people that is remembered in the Gothic style of architecture.

Graafian follicle

A Graafian follicle is one of the small liquid-filled sacs in the ovary of a mammal that contains the developing egg. The name Graafian follicle honours their discoverer, the Dutch physician and anatomist Regnier de Graaf (1641–73).

gradgrind

A hard, utilitarian person who remorselessly pursues facts and statistics is sometimes known as a gradgrind. The word derives from Thomas Gradgrind, a character in the novel *Hard Times* (1854) by Charles Dickens. Gradgrind is a hardware merchant in Coketown, a drab northern industrial centre. Considering himself to be an 'eminently practical man', he suppresses the imaginative and spiritual aspects of the education of his children, Tom and Louisa.

graham flour

Graham flour is a Northern American term for wholemeal flour. The name derives from the American dietary reformer Sylvester Graham (1794–1851). Originally a Presbyterian minister, Graham advocated temperance and also campaigned widely for changes in Americans' diets, especially the use of unbolted wheat flour. His efforts were rewarded by the emergence in the 1830s of Graham food stores and Graham Societies. He is still remembered in America by graham crackers, graham bread and graham flour.

grangerise

The verb grangerise means to illustrate a book with pictures taken from other books or publications. The word comes from the name of the English writer and clergyman James Granger (1723–76), who in 1769 published a book entitled *Biographical History of England from Egbert the Great to the Revolution, Consisting of Characters Dispersed in Different Classes, and Adapted to a Methodical Catalogue of Engraved British Heads*. The book contained blank pages that were to be filled by cutting illustrations out of other books. A craze (Grangerism) developed, leading to the mutilation of many other valuable books.

Granny Smith

Granny Smith is the name of a variety of hard green apple that can be cooked or eaten raw. It is named after the Australian gardener Maria Ann Smith, known as Granny Smith (d. 1870). Granny Smith first grew the apple at Eastwood, Sydney in the 1860s.

Graves' disease

Graves' disease (exophthalmic goitre) is a disorder of the thyroid gland accompanied by protrusion of the eyeballs. It is named after the

Irish physician Robert James Graves (1796–1853) who first identified it in 1835.

Great Scott

The expression of great surprise, 'Great Scott!' probably alludes to General Winheld Scott (1786–1866). Scott was a hero of the Mexican War (1846–8) and candidate in the US presidential election in 1852. The exclamation may originally have been applied in praise of the hero's achievements.

greengage

The variety of greenish or greenish-yellow plums known as greengage comes from a combination of the word green and the name Gage. It was the English botanist Sir William Gage (1777–1864) who introduced the variety of plum to England from France about 1725.

Interestingly, the French word for a greengage is also eponymous. This variety of plum was brought in the early sixteenth century from Italy to France, where it was named *reine-claude* (Queen Claude) in honour of Queen Claudia, wife of King Francis I of France, the reigning monarch of the time.

Gregorian calendar

The old-style Julian calendar was the name given to the system introduced by Julius Caesar in 46BC in which three years, each of 365 days, were followed by a leap year of 366 days. The average length of the year was therefore 365¼ days. This was approximately eleven minutes longer than its actual length as derived from astronomical and seasonal data. In order to rectify this error Pope Gregory XIII introduced a new system in 1582 which became law in Britain and the colonies in 1752, and is now used throughout most of the world. To allow for the alteration to the new system, eleven days were omitted, 2 September in 1752 being followed by 14 September. Under the new-style Gregorian system, named in the Pope's honour, leap years are every year that is divisible by four and century years divisible by 400 (thus 2000, but not 1900).

Gregorian chant

The Gregorian chant is the official liturgical plainsong of the Roman Catholic Church. The term derives from the name of Pope Gregory I (c.AD540–604). It was under his papacy (590–604) that the whole subject of plainsong was reviewed, and the vocal, unaccompanied chant now known as the Gregorian chant was introduced.

Gresham's law

Sir Thomas Gresham (*c.*1519–79) was the English financier who founded the Royal Exchange (1568). He is perhaps better known for the so-called Gresham's law, attributed to him in the mid-nineteenth century. Gresham's law, usually formulated as 'Bad money drives out good money', means that if two different types of coin are in circulation, the less valuable will remain in circulation, while the more valuable will be hoarded and will eventually disappear from circulation.

Grimm's law

Grimm's law is a rule that describes the change of consonants in the Germanic and Indo-European languages. Named after its formulator, the German philologist Jakob Ludwig Karl Grimm (1785–1863), Grimm's law explains, for example, the change from Latin p-sounds to English f-sounds, as in the progression from Latin *piscis* to English fish.

Jakob Grimm is also known with his brother Wilhelm Karl (1786–1859) for their *Kinder und Hausmärchen*, a collection of German folk tales, published 1812–14, which came to be known in English as *Grimm's Fairy Tales*.

gringo

The derogatory term 'gringo', used by Latin Americans to refer to an English-speaking foreigner, probably comes from the Spanish *gringo* (gibberish) which is derived from *griego*, meaning 'Greek' or 'stranger'. (Compare the expression, 'It's all Greek to me,' meaning, 'It's all strange; I find it utterly incomprehensible.')

An alternative, more picturesque, suggestion is that the word gringo derives from the singing of the American soldiers in the Mexican War (1846–8). The soldiers are said to have sung the song 'Green grow the Lilacs' so much that the natives described the singers as green-grows or gringos.

grog

Grog is the term for diluted spirits, usually rum, as formerly given to sailors. The word comes from Old Grog, the nickname of the British admiral Sir Edward Vernon (1684–1757). Old Grog began the issue of diluted alcoholic spirits in 1740, in order to put an end to drunken brawling aboard his ship, and soon the sailors were calling the drink grog. The nickname Old Grog arose from the fact that in rough weather the admiral wore a cloak made of grogram – a coarse fabric, usually of wool and mohair or silk.

guillemot

A guillemot is a kind of narrow-billed sea-bird, an auk, that is found in coastal regions of the northern hemisphere. The name of the bird derives from the French Guillemot, an affectionate form of Guillaume, which is the French version of the English name William.

guillotine

The device for beheading people known as a guillotine consists of a heavy blade that slides down between two grooved upright posts. The name of the machine derives from the French physician Joseph Ignace Guillotin (1738–1814). Contrary to popular belief, Guillotin did not invent the device; it was designed as a development of similar instruments in use elsewhere in Europe by a colleague of Guillotin, Dr Antoine Louis (1723–92). Guillotin advocated the use of this machine on humanitarian grounds: it was a speedier and more efficient method than the former practice of putting common criminals to death by means of a clumsy sword. Guillotin therefore proposed to the French National Assembly that this device should be used as a means of capital punishment. The first person to be decapitated by the guillotine was a highwayman in April 1792.

gun

The word gun, first recorded in the fourteenth century, may come originally from the Old Norse female name Gunhildr, both elements of which mean 'war'. The list of weapons in the English Exchequer Accounts of 1330–1 records 'a large ballista [a catapult used to hurl stones] called Lady Gunhildr', a name derived from the Scandinavian Gunhildr. With the passage of time, the name became shortened to gunne and then to gun, the word's application also changing, on the invention of the cannon, from a weapon that threw missiles to one that discharged missiles by explosion.

Gunter's chain; gunter rig

A Gunter's chain is a measuring device 66 feet (20 m) long used, especially formerly, in surveying. The term derives from the name of the English mathematician and astronomer Edmund Gunter (1581–1626). Gunter's name is also honoured in the gunter rig, a kind of ship's rig with a sliding topmast, so called because it resembled a slide-rule invented by Gunter that was used in solving navigational problems.

guppy

A guppy is the name of a kind of freshwater fish that is popular in aquaria. The fish is named after the Trinidadian naturalist and clergyman Robert John Lechmere Guppy (1836–1916). Guppy sent specimens of the fish to the British Museum in 1868. The male guppy is brightly coloured – hence the alternative name rainbow fish; the female is a prolific breeder and produces live young, rather than eggs, every four weeks.

guy

The word guy referring in informal use to a man or fellow (or in recent American usage, in the plural, any group of people) comes from the first name of the English conspirator Guy Fawkes (1570–1606). Fawkes served as a mercenary in the Spanish army in the Netherlands and when he returned to England in 1604 became involved in the Gunpowder Plot. A convert to Roman Catholicism, Fawkes was outraged by the harshness of the anti-Catholic laws imposed by King James I. Together with a group of other Catholics, Fawkes plotted to blow up James I and Parliament on 5 November 1605. The conspirators were informed on and Fawkes was caught red-handed, with the gunpowder in a cellar of the Palace of Westminster. Guy Fawkes and six of the other conspirators were executed the following year. The anniversary of 5 November continues to be remembered in Britain, with firework displays and guys, stuffed effigies of Fawkes, being burnt on bonfires.

Gypsy

The wandering people known as Gypsies (or Gipsies) were thought at one time to have come from Egypt, and so were called Egyptians. In time, this came to be shortened to Gyptians, from which came the present word Gypsy. In fact, it seems that the people probably originally came from north-west India.

H

Hadrian's Wall

The fortified Roman wall across northern England known as Hadrian's Wall is named after the Emperor Hadrian (AD 76–138). The wall was built under Hadrian's orders about AD 122–130, in order, as Hadrian's biographer comments, 'to separate the Romans from the barbarians'. The wall extends 120 km (85 miles) from the Solway Firth in the west to the mouth of the River Tyne in the east. Substantial parts of Hadrian's Wall still stand and it is one of the largest Roman remains in the United Kingdom.

Hadrian (Latin name Publius Aelius Hadrianus) was the adopted son of Trajan. On his father's death in AD 117, Hadrian became emperor. From then onwards Hadrian travelled throughout the Roman Empire, consolidating the gains made by his predecessor, though some of Trajan's conquests, including Mesopotamia, had to be abandoned.

Halley's comet

The British astronomer Edmund Halley (1656–1742) was the first to realise that comets do not appear haphazardly but have orbital periods. Following his observations in 1682 of the comet that has been named after him, he correctly predicted it would reappear in 1758. Halley was a friend of Sir Isaac Newton and financed the publication of Newton's *Principia* (1686–7). Halley was appointed to the post of astronomer royal in 1720. The last appearance of Halley's comet was in 1985–6.

Hansard

Hansard is the official verbatim report of debates in the Houses of Parliament in the United Kingdom. The reports are so called after the name of the London printer Luke Hansard (1752–1828) who printed the *Journal of the House of Commons* from 1774 onwards. His eldest son, Thomas Curson Hansard (1776–1883), printed the first reports of parliamentary debates in 1803, and the Hansard family continued to print parliamentary reports up to the end of the nineteenth century. Now printed by HM Stationary Office, the official record of the debates is still known as *Hansard*.

hansom

The hansom cab, a light two-wheeled covered carriage, in which the driver sits high up at the back, is named after its designer, the English architect Joseph Aloysius Hansom (1803–82). Noted for his designs of public buildings and churches, Hansom designed the town hall of Birmingham in 1833. A year later he registered a 'Patent Safety Cab'. These hansom cabs – or hansoms – quickly became popular and were manufactured in various designs. Disraeli called them 'the gondolas of London'.

It seems that Hansom was not so skilled at handling financial arrangements as designing buildings and vehicles. He is said to have sold his patent rights for a mere £300, while the manufacturers of his designs made fat profits.

See also **brougham**.

Harlequin

The stock character of pantomime, Harlequin, has a shaved head, a mask over his face, and a diamond-patterned tight-fitting costume. The name may come from the Old French Hellequin, the name of a devil-horseman riding by night, which in turn may derive ultimately from Old English Herla Cynnig, King Herle, a legendary king who is identified with the god Odin (Woden).

The Harlequin has its origins in the Italian *commedia dell'arte*. In traditional English pantomime, Harlequin is the mute character who is the foppish lover of the beautiful Colombine. He is supposedly invisible to both the clown and pantaloon and rivals the clown in the affections of Columbine.

havelock

A havelock is the cloth cover for a soldier's cap with a long flap that extends down the back, designed to protect the wearer's head and neck from the heat of the sun. The word comes from the name of the English general Sir Henry Havelock (1795–1857).

Havelock served for over thirty-four years with the British army in India, taking only one period of home leave during that time. He is noted for his recapture of Kanpur (Cawnpore) and his holding of Lucknow until relieved by troops under Campbell (1857). It seems unlikely that Havelock actually invented the cloth cover named in his honour, a similar covering having been known for centuries before, but it was the havelock which he devised for his brigades that became known. Nowadays it may be seen in films depicting desert hostilities.

Heath Robinson

A Heath Robinson device or contraption is one that is absurdly complex in design. The description comes from the name of the English artist William Heath Robinson (1872–1944). Known for his drawings depicting ingenious devices used to perform trivial tasks, Robinson was also a serious artist whose illustrations accompanied poems in several books of verse. He also designed stage scenery.

Heaviside layer

The Heaviside layer is a former name for the E-layer of the earth's atmosphere – the charged level of the upper atmosphere that reflects medium-frequency radio waves. This layer is 90–150 km above the earth's surface. The Heaviside layer was so called because it was predicted and then discovered by the British physicist Oliver Heaviside (1850–1925).

The American electrical engineer Arthur Edwin Kennelly (1861–1939), working independently of Heaviside, made a similar prediction in 1902, the same year as Heaviside's prediction, and so the layer is also known as the Heaviside-Kennelly layer.

Heaviside is also noted for his development of the mathematical study of electric circuits and his work in vector analysis.

See also **Appleton layer**.

Heaviside lived the life of an eccentric hermit in Devon. Even after gaining public recognition for his scientific achievements, he was still so poor that at times he could not even afford to pay his gas bills.

hector

The word hector may be used as a noun to refer to a bully or as a verb to mean 'to bully or torment'. The word alludes to the Greek legendary character Hector, son of Priam and Hecuba, the Trojan hero of Homer's *Iliad* who was killed by Achilles.

Homer, and English literature up to the seventeenth century, depicted Hector as a gallant warrior. It seems that the derogatory meaning derives from a gang of disorderly youths in London at the end of the seventeenth century. This band of young men took the name Hectors, fancying themselves as models of bravery. In reality, however, their bullying, terrorising behaviour became infamous and the unfavourable meaning of the word hector became predominant.

henry

The henry is the derived metric unit of electric inductance; it is named after the American physicist Joseph Henry (1797–1878). Henry is famous for his contributions to electromagnetism, inventing the first electromagnetic motor; he discovered electromagnetic induction independently of the English scientist Michael Faraday.

The US Weather Bureau was established as a result of Henry's meteorological work while he was the first director of the Smithsonian Institute, Washington DC. He is considered the founder of weather forecasting from scientific data in the USA.

Hepplewhite

Hepplewhite is used to describe an eighteenth-century style of English furniture. The style is noted for its graceful, elegant curves, especially in chairs with straight tapering legs and oval or heart-shaped backs with openwork designs. The name of the style honours the English cabinet-maker George Hepplewhite (d.1786). Probably originally a Lancastrian, Hepplewhite worked from a shop at St Giles, Cripplegate, in London.

herculean

A herculean task is one that requires immense effort or strength. The word comes from Hercules (Greek, Heracles), the son of Zeus and Alcmena, and the greatest and strongest of the Greek demigods. While in the service of his rival Eurystheus, Hercules completed twelve supposedly impossible labours: he killed the Nemean lion and the Lernean water-snake Hydra; he captured the Arcadian stag and the Erymanthian boar; cleaned the Augean stables (see **Augean**); killed the ferocious Stymphalian birds; captured the white Cretan bull; caught the man-eating mares of Diomedes; stole the girdle of the Amazon Queen Hippolyte; captured the oxen of Geryon; took the golden apples of Hesperides; and finally brought the three-headed dog Cerberus (see **sop to Cerberus**) to its master, Hades. This last task was seen as representing victory over death itself.

hermaphrodite

A hermaphrodite is an animal or plant that has both female and male reproductive organs. The word comes from Hermaphroditos, the Greek mythical son of Hermes and Aphrodite, goddess of love. Hermaphroditos refused the love offered by the nymph Salmacis, in whose pool he was bathing. She embraced him, however, and prayed to the gods to make them indissolubly one. The gods answered her prayer and the body of both the nymph and Hermaphroditos grew together as one. From this story of the union of these two beings comes the word hermaphrodite.

hermetic

A hermetic seal is one that is airtight, the word hermetic deriving ultimately from the name Hermes Trismegistus ('Hermes, thrice-greatest'). This is the Greek name given to the Egyptian god of learning, Thoth, and also the name given after the third century AD to the author of certain writings on alchemy and mysticism. Hermes Trismegistus is traditionally believed to have invented a seal to keep containers airtight by using magical powers.

hertz

A hertz is the derived metric unit of frequency, equal to one cycle per second. (The term may be more familiar in the word kilohertz, meaning one thousand hertz or one thousand cycles per second.) The terms honour the German physicist Heinrich Rudolph Hertz (1857–94). Developing the work of the Scottish scientist James Clerk Maxwell, Hertz was the first person to detect radio waves (1888). The type of electromagnetic wave known as the herzian wave is also named after him.

Hilary term

The term that begins in January at Oxford University and certain other educational institutions is known as the Hilary term. The name is chosen because the feast day of St Hilary falls on 13 January. St Hilary of Poitiers (c.315–c.367) was converted to Christianity from Neoplatonism and became Bishop of Poitiers in about 353. The most highly regarded Latin theologian of his time, he was a leading critic of Arianism. His defence of orthodox beliefs led to his exile for four years. St Hilary's works include *De Trinitate* (a criticism of Arianism) and *De Synodis*.

Hindenburg line

The Hindenburg line was the German western line of fortifications in the First World War. It is named after the German general Paul von Beneckendorff und von Hindenburg (1847–1934). Recalled from re-tirement at the outbreak of the First World War, Hindenburg, together with Erich von Ludendorff (1865–1937), led Germany to a decisive victory over Russia at Tannenburg (August 1914). In 1915

Hindenburg and Ludendorff were given command of the western front. Together they directed the construction of the line of fortifications known as the Hindenburg line near the border between France and Belgium in 1916–17. It was breached by the Allies in 1918, by troops under the direction of Douglas Haig.

After Germany's defeat in 1918, Hindenburg again retired, but became president of the Weimar Republic in 1925. He was re-elected president in 1932, but with the growing prominence of Hitler was compelled to appoint Hitler as chancellor in January 1933.

Hippocratic oath

The Greek physician Hippocrates (c.460–c.377BC) is commonly regarded as the father of medicine. He has given his name to the Hippocratic oath traditionally taken by a doctor before commencing medical practice. The oath comprises a code of medical ethics probably followed by members of the school of Hippocrates.

Born on the island of Cos, Hippocrates was the most famous physician of the ancient world. Some of his writings still survive, including his *Aphorisms*, of which the most famous reads, in Chaucer's translation, 'The life so short, the craft so long to learn.'

Hitler

A person showing ruthless dictatorial characteristics may be described as a Hitler, with reference to the German dictator Adolf Hitler (1889–1945). Born in Austria, Hitler served in the First World War and became president of the National Socialist German Workers' (Nazi) Party in 1921. After an abortive coup (the Munich Putsch, 1923), Hitler spent several months in prison, during which time he wrote *Mein Kampf*, which expressed his political philosophy based on the innate superiority of the Aryan race and the inferiority of the Jews.

Hitler was appointed chancellor of Germany in 1933 and a year later assumed the title of Führer (leader). Germany became a totalitarian state, with Hitler establishing concentration camps to exterminate the Jews. The Second World War was precipitated by his invasion of Austria (1938), and Czechoslovakia and Poland (1939). He narrowly escaped assassination in 1944 and, in the face of an Allied victory in April 1945, committed suicide.

Ho Chi Minh City

Ho Chi Minh City (former name, Saigon) is a port in Vietnam, inland from the South China Sea. It is named after the Vietnamese statesman Ho Chi Minh (original name Nguyen That Thanh; 1890–69).

In 1941 Ho Chi Minh founded the Viet Minh, the Vietnamese organisation that fought against the Japanese and then the French in an attempt to create an independent Vietnamese republic. He was the first president of the Democratic Republic of Vietnam (1945–54) and of North Vietnam (1954–69). In 1959 he supported the Viet Cong guerrilla movement in the South, although he was not actively involved in the work of government. When Saigon yielded to the communists in 1975, it was renamed Ho Chi Minh City in his honour.

Hobson's choice

If you were in seventeenth-century England and wanted to hire a horse from Thomas Hobson of Cambridge, you would have had no choice at all over which horse you could take. The liveryman Thomas Hobson (1544–1631) is said not to have allowed his customers any right to pick one particular horse, insisting that they always choose the horse nearest the door. Hence the expression Hobson's choice, a situation in which there appear to be alternatives but, in fact, no real alternative is offered and there is only one thing you can do.

Hodgkin's disease

Hodgkin's disease (also known as lymphoma or lymphadenoma) is a cancerous disease marked by an enlargement of the lymph nodes, liver, etc. The disease is named after the English physician Thomas Hodgkin (1798–1866), who first described it in 1832. A physician at Guy's Hospital, London, Hodgkin was one of the most distinguished pathologists of his time.

Homer sometimes nods; Homeric

The expression 'Homer sometimes nods' means that even the wisest of people make mistakes. Homer is the presumed author of the great epic poems the *Iliad* and *Odyssey*, but little is in fact known about his life. He is believed to have lived in the eighth century BC and, according to legend, was blind.

The source of the expressions 'Homer sometimes nods' and 'even Homer nodded' are Horace: 'If Homer, usually good, nods for a moment, I think it shame' (*Ars Poetica*) and Byron (*Don Juan*):

> We learn from Horace, 'Homer sometimes sleeps';
> We feel without him, Wordsworth sometimes wakes.

The adjective Homeric is used to mean heroic, majestic or imposing.

hooker

Hooker is slang for a female prostitute. While it is possible that the word was popularised during the American Civil War – General Joseph Hooker, known as 'Fighting Joe' (1814–79), is said to have associated with prostitutes – earlier usages of the word have been recorded. For example, 1845, in N. E. Eliason *Tarheel Talk*: 'If he comes by way of Norfolk he will find any number of pretty Hookers in the Brick row not far from French's hotel.' (*Oxford English Dictionary*, Supplement)

hooligan

The origin of the word hooligan, meaning a rough lawless young person, seems to lie with the name Patrick Hooligan, an Irish criminal who was active in London in the 1890s. It is said that Pat Hooligan and his family – their real name may have been Houlihan – basing themselves at the Lamb and Flag, a public house in south London, attracted a gang of rowdy followers.

Hoover

Hoover is a trademark used to describe a type of vacuum cleaner. The name comes from the American William Henry Hoover (1849–1932). Hoover, however, did not invent this cleaner; he was a perceptive businessman who saw the possible sales of a new kind of cleaner that had been made by a J. Murray Spangler, a caretaker in an Ohio department store. Hoover persuaded Spangler to sell his rights to the invention and so, in 1908, it was the Hoover Suction Company that produced the first Hoover – selling for $70. Four years later vacuum cleaners made by Hoover were exported to Britain, where, in fact, the vacuum cleaner had been invented in 1901 by the Scotsman Hubert Cecil Booth (1871–1955). However, it is neither Booth's nor Spangler's name that is remembered today, Hoover now being used not only generically as a noun to refer to a vacuum cleaner but also as a verb to mean 'to clean with a vacuum cleaner'.

hotspur

The word hotspur, meaning a rash or fiery person, was originally applied to the English rebel Sir Henry Percy (1364–1403), known as Harry Hotspur. Together with his father, also Sir Henry Percy, 1st Earl of Northumberland, he led a revolt against King Henry IV, whom earlier he and his father had supported. Impetuous and headstrong – hence his nickname – he was killed at the Battle of Shrewsbury.

Shakespeare featured the rash, fearless character of Hotspur in *Richard II* and *Henry IV*.

Houdini – do a houdini

Someone who does a houdini succeeds in performing an astonishing act of escape or disappearance. The expression honours Harry Houdini, the stage name of the American magician and escapologist Ehrich Weiss (1874–1926). Of Hungarian–Jewish descent, Weiss assumed the name of Harry Houdini to echo the name of the great French magician Jean Eugene Robert Houdin (1805–71). Houdini became world famous for his ability to escape from handcuffs, straitjackets, locked chests, etc., even when under water.

Hoyle – according to Hoyle see Cocker

Huguenot

The Huguenots were Calvinist French Protestants, especially in the sixteenth and seventeenth centuries. The name of this religious movement comes from the Middle French dialect word *huguenot*, which is an alteration of the Swiss-German *eidgnoss*, 'confederate', influenced by the name of the Swiss political leader Besançon Hugues (*d.*1532). Hugues was a Protestant syndic and party leader in Geneva.

Huntingdon's chorea

Huntingdon's chorea is a rare hereditary disorder of the brain in which there is progressive involuntary spasmodic movement (chorea) and gradual mental deterioration. It is named after the American neurologist George S. Huntingdon (1851–1916) who described it.

husky

A husky – also called an Eskimo dog – is a breed of very strong sledge dog that has a double-layered coat. The word husky is probably an alteration and shortening of the Tinneh Indian – one of the Athapascan (American Indian) languages – *uskimi*, an Eskimo, or of *Esky*, English slang for Eskimo, or the English word *Eskimo*. The word Eskimo itself is of Algonquian origin, and is related to a Cree Indian word meaning 'eaters of raw flesh'. See also **Samoyed**.

hyacinth

The hyacinth, the fragrant plant of the lily family that bears clusters of typically blue, pink or white flowers takes its name from Hyacinthus, a youth in Greek mythology. Hyacinthus was so attractive that he was loved by both Apollo, god of the sun, and by Zephyrus, god of the west wind. Hyacinthus' preference for Apollo made Zephyrus intensely jealous, and while the three of them were playing games one day, Zephyrus hurled Apollo's quoit of iron at Hyacinthus, hitting him on the head and killing him. It is said that a flower grew from the blood of the wound, 'that sanguine flower inscribed with woe', as Milton describes it.

hygiene

The word hygiene, the science of maintaining good health, and the clean conditions that lead to good health, comes from Hygeia, the Greek goddess of health. Hygeia was worshipped with Aesculapius, the god of medicine, and is sometimes identified as his wife or daughter. Hygeia was typically depicted as feeding a serpent from a dish in her hand.

I

Iris

Iris is the name of a genus of plants that have sword-shaped leaves and large showy flowers made up of three upright petals and three drooping petals. The name of the plant comes from Iris, the Greek goddess of the rainbow, because of the flower's bright and varied colours. Messenger of Hera (the queen of the Olympian gods), Iris travelled along the colours of the rainbow to bring her messages to earth.

The name of iris is also used for the coloured part of the eye surrounding the pupil.

isabelline

The adjective isabelline, meaning greyish-yellow, comes from the name of the colour isabel or isabella. It is said that these words are derived from the colour of the underwear of Isabel Clara Eugenia, daughter of King Philip II of Spain, who in 1598 married Albert, Archduke of Austria. Tradition has it that at the siege of Ostend, she vowed not to change her underwear until the city was captured. The siege lasted for three years, so the colour of her under-garments must have been truly isabelline when the city was finally taken.

Other sources relate a similar story about Queen Isabella of Castile (1451–1504) and the siege of Granada.

Ishmael

An Ishmael is a social outcast. The expression comes from the Bible figure of Ishmael, the son of Abraham and Hagar, the Egyptian maidservant of Sarah. According to the biblical narrative (Genesis 16–25), when Sarah realised that she could not conceive children, she gave her maidservant to Abraham to conceive in her stead. When Hagar became pregnant, she began to despise her mistress who then drove her out of her home. An angel of Jehovah met Hagar and told her to return and submit to Sarah, also saying that her descendants through Ishmael would be innumerable. God assured Abraham that Ishmael would be the father of twelve rulers and ultimately of a great nation. When in due course Sarah bore a son, Isaac, by Abraham, she insisted that Ishmael and Hagar be expelled from the home. In the desert, the outcasts nearly perished for lack of water, but God provided them with a well to drink from. Ishmael grew up to become an archer and, Hagar having found him a wife, he did indeed become the father of twelve sons.

J

Jack

Jack is the commonest pet-form of the name John and is used in a large number of expressions, in many of which it stands simply for 'man', for example lumberjack and steeplejack, sometimes with derogatory connotations, as in cheapjack. It is also used to refer to a mechanical appliance used to lift a heavy weight such as a car, and as a verb to lift a car, etc., using such a device.

The generic use of the name Jack features in other expressions, including Jack Frost, a personification of frost, the surname Frost being chosen probably because it was well known; a jack in office, meaning a pretentious petty official; a jack in the box, the toy consisting of a small box out of which a figure springs when the lid is opened; Jack and Jack Tar referring to a sailor, tar probably being a shortening of tarpaulin; and the Union Jack, the national flag of the United Kingdom. 'I'm all right, Jack,' the slogan of the smug, complacent opportunist out to satisfy his or her own interest, was popularised by the film *I'm All Right, Jack* (1960). 'A Jack of all trades, and a master of none', refers to a person who can undertake various kinds of work, and is sometimes used to imply that the person has no great ability in any of the different trades. The informal expression 'every man Jack' is an idiom meaning every one of a large number of people, with no exceptions: 'He thinks that all politicians – every man Jack of them – are in it just for the power they have.' Finally, the phrase 'before you can say Jack Robinson' means very quickly – 'I'll be back before you can say Jack Robinson' – but it is not known who Jack Robinson actually was.

Jack Ketch

Jack Ketch was a seventeenth-century English public executioner who was notorious for his barbarism. He was appointed hangman in 1663 and was particularly infamous for his executions of Lord William Russell, a conspirator in the Rye House Plot against King Charles II (1683), and the Duke of Monmouth (1685).

Ketch was known for his bungling, cruel, work – he is said to have required several blows to sever Russell's head. The Duke of Monmouth's last words are reputed to have been, 'Do not hack me as you did my Lord Russell!' but it seems that he was slaughtered as ineptly if not even more clumsily than the earlier victim.

After his death in 1668, the name of Jack Ketch came into common use to refer to a public executioner, and it was later used for the hangman of the Punch and Judy puppet shows.

Jack Russell terrier

A Jack Russell terrier is a breed of dog with a stocky body, small drooping ears, short legs and a short white, black and tan coat. The breed of terrier is named after the English clergyman John (Jack) Russell (1795–1883) who developed the breed from the fox terrier. Russell was curate of Swimbridge, near Barnstaple, and was also master of the local foxhounds.

jackanapes

The word jackanapes is sometimes used to refer to an impudent or conceited person or a mischievous child. There are two theories of the origin of the word. Some suggest that it is an alteration of Jack Ape, a term of endearment for a pet monkey. Other sources suggest that it derives from Jack Napes, the nickname of William de la Pole, 1st Duke of Suffolk (1396–1450), whose symbol showed an ape with a ball and chain. In 1450 de la Pole was arrested and beheaded at sea, while being sent into exile for conspiring against King Henry VI. He was later nicknamed Jack Napes or Jackanapes.

Jacky Howe

The expression Jacky Howe is used in Australian English for a sleeveless shirt, as worn by sheep-shearers. It is named after John (Jacky) Howe (1855–1922). Howe was the world sheep-shearing champion for many years; in 1892 he shore 321 merinos in one day.

Jacobean

Jacobean refers to the styles of furniture and architecture current at the time of King James I of England, from the New Latin Jacobaeus for James. He was the first Stuart king of England and Ireland (1603–25) and, as King James VI, ruled Scotland (1567–1625). The Jacobean style of furniture is particularly noted for its use of dark brown carved oak. In architecture, the Jacobean style stands between the Elizabethan and the classical Palladian style of the English architect and designer Inigo Jones (1573–1652). It is marked by a combination of Renaissance forms such as ornamental gables, and the late Gothic preference for mullioned windows.

Jacobin

The Jacobins were an extremist group during the French Revolution. Founded in 1789, they were responsible, under the leadership of the French revolutionary Robespierre (1758–94), for the Reign of Terror, in which over a quarter of a million people were arrested, and nearly fifteen hundred guillotined. The name of the society comes from the group's original meeting place – a Dominican convent in Paris, near the church of St Jacques (St James). The word Jacobin has since passed into general use for a member of an extremist, radical or terrorist political group.

Jacobite

The Jacobites were followers of the Stuart King James II (New Latin, Jacobus) after his overthrow in 1688 (the Glorious Revolution), and of his descendants. The Jacobites made several attempts to enable the House of Stuart to regain the throne. Two Jacobite rebellions – in 1715, led by James Edward Stuart (James II's son, known as the Old Pretender) and in 1745, led by Charles Edward Stuart (the son of James Edward Stuart, known as the Young Pretender or romantically as Bonnie Prince Charlie) – were suppressed. At the Battle of Culloden (April 1746), Bonnie Prince Charlie was defeated by the Duke of Cumberland, so concluding the Jacobite rebellion.

Jacob's ladder

Jacob's ladder is the name given to two items – a ladder used on board ship and a plant. The Jacob's ladder that is used on board ship is made of rope or cable; it has wooden or metal rungs and is dropped over the side of a ship to allow people to ascend from or descend to small boats positioned alongside. The plant known as Jacob's ladder (*Polemonium caeruleum*) has blue or white flowers and a ladder-like arrangement of its light-green leaves.

The origin of the expression Jacob's ladder is to be found in the Bible (Genesis 28:12); it is the ladder, which rested on the earth and reached to heaven, that Jacob saw in a dream.

Jacquard loom

The Jacquard loom was a loom for weaving patterned fabrics. It is named after the French weaver and inventor Joseph Marie Jacquard (1752–1834), who completed its design in 1801. When first introduced in France, it was very unpopular, because it was so efficient that it made thousands of people redundant. Within eleven years of its introduction, however, over ten thousand Jacquard looms were in use in France. Napoleon bought the loom for the state, declaring it to be public property; he paid Jacquard a yearly pension of 3000 francs and also a small sum for each machine sold. The revolutionary loom was the first automatic machine that could weave patterns into fabrics. It was controlled by punched cards – a method that was later applied by the British mathematician Charles Babbage (1792–1871) in his development of the calculator and subsequently in the development of computers.

Jacquerie

Jacquerie is the name given to a peasants' revolt, particularly the revolt of the peasants of north-east France against the nobility in 1358. During the period of the Hundred Years' War between England and France, that rebellion had its roots in famine and plague and was quickly suppressed. The name Jacquerie derives from the contemptuous name given by the nobles to the typical French peasant Jacques Bonhomme, which, as Eric Partridge suggests, might be translated into English as 'goodman James' or 'simple, easy-going James'.

Jacuzzi

Jacuzzi is a trademark used to describe a system of underwater jets of water that massage the body. The name derives from its creator, the Italian-born Candido Jacuzzi (c.1903–86). Candido was born the youngest of seven brothers and six sisters. When the family emigrated to California early in the twentieth century, it seemed that they would prosper from aviation engineering. But in 1921, when the first Jacuzzi monoplane crashed on its first flight, the Jacuzzi boys were forbidden by their mother to develop these skills.

The brothers also worked in the field of fluid dynamics, patenting a jet pump, originally for use in ornamental gardens. When one of the children of the family was stricken by rheumatoid arthritis, they developed a pump that could be used to produce the therapeutic effects of swirling bubbly water in a home bath tub. In 1968, Roy Jacuzzi, a third-generation member of the Jacuzzi family, saw the commercial potential of the whirlpool bath: a pump was fixed to the bath's outer walls to force the water and air through four jets – and so the modern Jacuzzi came into being.

Jansenism

Jansenism was a Roman Catholic movement in the seventeenth and eighteenth centuries based on the teaching of the Dutch theologian Cornelius Otto Jansen (1585–1638). First director of the episcopal college in Louvain, and consecrated Bishop of Ypres (1636), Jansen is noted for his treatise *Augustinus* (1640), which he wrote after reading St Augustine's works many times. The teaching of Jansenism, as expressed in *Augustinus*, emphasised the more strictly predestinarian points of St Augustine's doctrines. The teaching brought the followers of Jansenism into conflict with the Jesuits and was condemned by Pope Innocent X as heretical (1653).

January

January, the first month of the year, comes from the name of the Roman god Janus. Janus was the god of doors, thresholds and bridges. He is usually portrayed as having two faces, one looking forwards and the other backwards. January is therefore seen as providing an opportunity for looking back to take stock and of gazing into the future to wonder what lies ahead. From the representation of Janus as having two faces also comes the expression Janus-faced, meaning two-faced or hypocritical.

The jay, the bird (*Carrulus glandarius*) of the crow family, probably derives its name ultimately from the Latin Gaius. It seems that this name may well have been used in a similar manner to Jack in English, namely as a familiar way of describing people generally.

JCB

A JCB is the trademark for a type of mechanical earth-mover. At the front of the vehicle is a hydraulically operated shovel and at the back, an excavator arm. The name of the earth-mover comes from the initials of its English manufacturer Joseph Cyril Bamford (*b.* 1916).

A skilled welder and fitter, Bamford built a farm trailer using materials surplus to war use in 1945. Various types of trailer were then constructed, and by the late 1940s and the early 1950s hydraulics were introduced in tipping trailers and loaders. The JCB company is currently headed by the eldest son of the original Bamford, Anthony P. Bamford.

Jehovah's Witness

A Jehovah's Witness is a member of a religious movement originally founded in 1872 by Charles Taze Russell (1852–1916). Members of the organisation aim to follow the literal sense of the Christian Bible, but they reject some basic tenets of established Christianity, especially the doctrine of the Trinity and the deity of Jesus Christ and the Holy Spirit. Jehovah's Witnesses are known for their zealous door-to-door personal evangelism.

Jehovah's Witnesses use the name Jehovah for God, applying the personal name of God, revealed to Moses on Mount Horeb (Exodus 3: 13–15). The word Jehovah (also Yahweh) comes from Hebrew *YHVH*. Because this name was regarded as too sacred to be pronounced, Jews from about 300BC onwards replaced the word by *Adonai* (Hebrew for 'Lord') when reading their Scriptures. The vowel sounds a, o, a, from *Adonai* were later inserted into the word YHVH, hence YaHoVaH and Jehovah.

Jekyll and Hyde

The phrase Jekyll and Hyde is used to describe a person who has two separate personalities, one good and the other evil. The expression derives from the name of the main character in the novel *The Strange Case of Dr Jekyll and Mr Hyde*, published 1886, by the Scottish writer Robert Louis Stevenson (1850–94).

In the story Doctor Jekyll discovers a drug that will change him into an evil dwarf, whom he calls Mr Hyde. At first, Doctor Jekyll is able to change from one personality to the other at will, but gradually the personality of Mr Hyde begins to predominate, and Hyde later commits murder. In the trial that follows the secret is made known and Hyde commits suicide. The expression is often used in front of a noun; for example, a Jekyll-and-Hyde personality.

jemmy

A jemmy (American English, jimmy) is a short steel crowbar, as used by burglars to force open doors and windows. The word comes from Jemmy, a nickname for James.

jennet

A jennet is the name given to a female donkey or ass or to a small Spanish riding horse. The word comes from the Catalan *ginet*, a horse used by the tribe of the Zenete, a Berber people famous for their horsemanship.

jenny

The word jenny – from the name Jenny, a nickname for Jane or Janet – has a number of different meanings including a female donkey, a wren, and the early type of spinning frame (spinning jenny).

jeremiad; jeremiah

A jeremiad is a lengthy lamentation or complaint. The word comes, via French, from the name Jeremiah, the Old Testament prophet. His book contains many prophecies of judgment, particularly against idolatry, immorality and false prophets, and he is sometimes known as the Prophet of Doom. Thus a Jeremiah has come to be used to refer to a pessimistic person who foresees a gloomy future or one who condemns the society he lives in.

jeroboam

A jeroboam is a very large wine bottle, one that holds the equivalent of four standard bottles. It seems that the expression was first humorously applied to such bottles in the nineteenth century, alluding to Jeroboam, the first king of the northern kingdom of Israel, whom the biblical text describes as 'a mighty man of valour' (I Kings 11:28) and who 'did sin, and who made Israel to sin' (I Kings 14: 16). The bottle is without doubt 'mighty' and the alcoholic drink contained in it could certainly lead to 'sin'.

Other Old Testament figures after whom bottles and large drinking vessels are named include: jorum, a large drinking bowl, from Joram, who brought to King David 'vessels of silver, and vessels of gold, and vessels of brass' (II Samuel 8:10); methuselah, a bottle holding eight times the standard amount from the patriarch Methuselah who lived to be 969 years old (Genesis 5:27); nebuchadnezzar, a very large bottle holding the equivalent of 20 standard bottles, after King Nebuchadnezzar of Babylon; and rehoboam, a wine bottle holding the equivalent of six standard bottles, from Rehoboam, a son of Solomon, last king of the united Israel and first king of Judah, and whose name means 'may the people expand'.

jerry-built

A building that is jerry-built is one that has been poorly built with cheap, low-quality materials. There are various theories of the origin of the expression. According to some sources jerry could refer to the tumbling walls of Jericho in the Bible (Joshua, chapter 6). An alternative theory states that jerry comes from the name of the prophet Jeremiah, who predicted decay and destruction. Still others suggest that jerry is a corruption of jury-mast, a makeshift wooden mast in use in English shipbuilding yards in the mid-nineteenth century.

jerry can

A jerry can is a narrow flat-sided container used for storing or carrying liquids, especially petrol. It has a capacity of about 25 litres (about 5 gallons). The expression comes from Jerry, the word for a German or German soldier. It was the Germans who designed this metal fuel container in the Second World War; and since its design was superior to the design of the can used by the Allied troops, it was copied, the new container being called a jerry can.

Jesuit

A Jesuit is a member of the Society of Jesus, a Roman Catholic religious order founded by St Ignatius Loyola in 1534. Its original aims were to defend Catholicism in the face of the Reformation and to undertake missionary work amongst the unbelieving world. The word Jesuit comes from Late Latin *Jesus* (Jesus Christ) and the suffix *-ita* meaning follower or supporter.

Because of a tendency of a few Jesuits, especially in the seventeenth century, to be concerned with politics, the word Jesuit and the adjective Jesuitical are sometimes used to refer to a person who is involved in subtle intrigue or cunning deception.

Jezebel

A Jezebel is a shameless, scheming or immoral woman. The word comes from the biblical figure of Jezebel, daughter of Ethbaal, king of Tyre and Sidon, who married Ahab, the king of Israel. Jezebel's notorious wickedness is described in I and II Kings. She worshipped the fertility god Baal and persuaded Ahab and his people to follow her religion. Under her orders, God's prophets were killed, and were replaced by the prophets of Baal. In answer to Elijah's prayer, God defeated Baal at Mount Carmel. Jezebel then resolved to kill Elijah, who was forced to go into hiding. After the incident over Naboth's vineyard, Elijah predicted Jezebel's violent end, and some time later she was thrown down from a high palace window.

jilt

If you jilt a lover, you end your relationship with that person, leaving and rejecting him or her in an unfeeling way and without previous warning. The earlier form of the word, *jillet*, indicated that it comes from the proper name Jill – a very common girl's name, used in the same way that Jack is used to refer to any boy or man.

jim crow

The phrase jim crow (or Jim Crow) was used in American English to refer to a Black person, and also to racial segregation imposed by Whites on Blacks. The phrase was very common in the 1880s and 1890s, but has been dated back to 1730, when Black people were first described as crows. In 1828 a White blackface minstrel Thomas D. Rice wrote the song 'Jim Crow', which was widely sung and danced in both Britain and the United States in the 1830s. Jim Crow was the Black person of the song-and-dance act. The song popularised the expression Jim Crow to mean a Black, a Jim Crow store being a shop with provisions that would be sold only to Blacks, and, later, Jim Crow laws being discriminatory laws against Black Americans.

Job – patience of Job; Job's comforter

The Old Testament character of Job was a man of upright character who lost his wealth, his ten children and his health. Satan brought these disasters on him with God's permission. The book of Job tells how Job kept his faith in God in the midst of all his afflictions. Thus, the patience of Job has become proverbial to stand for the enduring of difficulties, misfortunes or laborious tasks with supreme patience, courage and tolerance.

Job was visited by three friends who gave him the advice of popular opinion, emphasising particularly that his misfortunes were brought about by his own disobedience to God. From these friends, whom Job refers to as 'miserable comforters' (Job 16:2), comes the expression 'a Job's comforter', used to describe someone whose attempts to bring encouragement or sympathy have the opposite effects of discouragement and distress in reality.

jockey

The word for a jockey, a person who rides a horse, especially a professional rider in horse-races, comes from the name Jockey, originally the Scottish variant (Jock) of Jack. It seems that the name was chosen as a nickname for a young man who rode well. In the sixteenth century the word meant simply 'lad'.

Joe; Joe Bloggs; Joe Blow; Joe Public; Joe Soap

In British English, the name Joe Bloggs is used to refer to an average or typical man. Its American and Australian equivalent is Joe Blow. Joe Public is a member of the general public just as John Citizen is the ordinary person – as in *John Citizen and the Law* (published 1947) by the London lawyer Ronald Rubinstein (1896–1947). A Joe Soap is someone who is considered stupid or credulous and who can be imposed upon as a dupe or object of ridicule.

In American and Canadian English a Joe is a man or fellow ('a good Joe'); in American English a Joe or GI Joe is an American soldier, the equivalent of the British Tommy Atkins.

joey

The traditional name of a circus clown, Joey, comes from the famous English clown Joseph Grimaldi (1779–1837). He is said to have been only one year old when he made his début at the Drury Lane Theatre in London. He began as a dancer, and later became well known as a clown and pantomime artist. His memoirs (1838) were edited by Charles Dickens.

Joey, for a young kangaroo, is not a name, but comes from a native Australian language.

john; johnny

Particularly in American English, the word john is an informal term for a toilet. The first appearance of the word in print, according to William and Mary Morris (*Morris Dictionary of Word and Phrase Origins*) was in 1735, in an official rule of Harvard College. The word appeared in the full expression Cousin John: 'No Freshman shall go into the Fellows' Cousin John.'

A Dear John letter is an informal expression used to refer to a letter from a girl who wants to break off a love affair. The expression comes of course from the opening words of such a letter, but the original person named John has not been identified with a particular individual.

Johnny, the nickname for John, is used informally in British English to mean a man or fellow and also to refer to a condom. The word Johnny also occurs in some compounds, including johnnycake, an American cake or bread made with meal from maize (possibly originally journeycake or Shawneecake); Johnny-come-lately, a person who has recently joined a social or working group; and Johnny-jump-up, American for a violet or wild pansy.

Long johns are a pair of usually woollen underpants with long legs that extend to the ankles. The garment may be so called because a *long john* – originally a lanky man – looked particularly unusual wearing long johns.

John Barleycorn

John Barleycorn is a personification, usually in humorous usage, of alcoholic drink. The expression may have originated in the early seventeenth century, but it was popularised by the Scottish lyric poet Robert Burns (1759–96) in his narrative poem *Tam o'Shanter*:

> Inspiring bold John Barleycorn
> What dangers thou canst make us scorn!

John Bull

John Bull is a personification of the English nation or a typical Englishman. The expression was first used in the satirical pamphlet by the Scottish writer and physician John Arbuthnot (1667–1735), 'Law is a Bottomless Pit', published in 1712. The pamphlet was designed to ridicule the Duke of Marlborough and to express disgust at the continuing war against France.

In the pamphlet John Bull is an allegorical character representing England. He is straightforward, honest, independent, bold and quarrelsome. Other characters in the pamphlet are Humphrey Hocus (the Duke of Marlborough), Lewis Baboon (Louis XIV of France), Nicholas Frog (the Dutchman) and Lord Strutt (Philip of Spain). The pamphlet was originally one of a series and later the collection was reissued under the title *The History of John Bull*.

John Doe; Richard Roe

John Doe and Richard Roe are the names sometimes given to the two parties to legal proceedings. It seems unlikely that men by these names actually existed, the forenames being apparently chosen randomly because of their frequent occurrence. The surname Doe was probably chosen with reference to the gentle and pleasant character of a doe and Roe seems to have been chosen because it rhymes with Doe.

The names were used in legal documents since at least the fourteenth century – one source suggests that the names may even date back to Magna Carta (1215). Originally, prosecutors are said to have used these names when they could not find two genuine witnesses or when the true witnesses did not wish to disclose their real names. Later, the names came to be used instead of the real names of the parties to legal proceedings, John Doe usually being the plaintiff and Richard Roe the defendant.

John Dory

A John Dory is a golden yellow food fish, *Zeus faber*, with an oval compressed body, long spiny dorsal fins and a black spot on each side. The name John may have been chosen arbitrarily, and dory is probably simply derived from the Middle French *dorée*, 'gilded one'. An alternative theory suggests that the fish is named after a certain John Dory, an infamous privateer in the sixteenth century and the subject of a popular song, but this seems unlikely.

John Hancock; John Henry

The expressions John Hancock or John Henry are used particularly in American English to refer to a person's signature. John Hancock (1737–93) was the Boston merchant and revolutionary patriot who not only was the first to sign the American Declaration of Independence but also was the one who wrote his signature the most prominently and apparently the most aggressively, 'so big no Britisher would have to use his spectacles to read it'. Hancock later became president of the Continental Congress and governor of Massachusetts.

The alternative expression John Henry came originally from the cowboy slang of the American west.

johnny see John

Jolly Roger

The Jolly Roger is the traditional flag of pirates, consisting of a white skull and crossbones on a black background. It is said that the earliest flags of pirate ships were plain black cloth sheets, later some pirates adding the decoration of the white skull and crossbones. The expression 'Jolly Roger' seems to have come from thieves' slang, in which a Roger meant a beggar or rogue. In time the adjective jolly, meaning carefree, was added, so Jolly Roger came to stand for the flag of carefree rogues seeking booty.

The Blue Peter, a blue signal flag with a white square at the centre used to show that a vessel is ready to leave port, honours the name Peter. As Partridge comments, 'the choice of the name Peter was probably a matter of caprice'.

Jonah

A Jonah is a person who is believed to bring bad luck. The expression derives from the biblical Jonah, the Hebrew prophet who was held responsible for the storm that struck the ship he was travelling on

(Jonah 1: 4–7). Jonah was running away from God, disobeying his command to go to Nineveh to denounce its people.

Joneses – keeping up with the Joneses

The idiomatic expression 'keeping up with the Joneses' means trying to maintain the same living standards as one's richer neighbours. The expression derives from a comic strip by Arthur R. Momand with the title 'Keeping up with the Joneses' which began in the New York *Globe* in 1913 and was based on the experience of the author and his wife trying to maintain the same material standards as those living around them. Originally the author thought of calling the cartoon strip 'Keeping Up With the Smiths' but 'Keeping up with the Joneses' was eventually chosen 'as being more euphonious'.

jorum see jeroboam

joule

A joule is the metric unit of work or energy. The unit is named after the English physicist James Prescott Joule (1818–89). Born in Salford, Joule was a student of Dalton and performed experiments in the 1840s to determine the mechanical equivalent of heat. He is also known for his work on the heating effects of an electric current (Joule's law), his work on the effect on temperature that occurs when a gas expands under certain conditions (the Joule–Thomson effect or Joule–Kelvin effect), and his research that formed the basis of the theory of the conservation of energy.

Jove – by Jove; jovial

Jove was the Roman god Jupiter and the word is sometimes used in the exclamation 'by Jove' to express surprise or agreement, for example, 'By Jove, you're right!' Originally a euphemism for 'by God', the first recorded use of 'by Jove' is 1570.

Jovial, with its contemporary meaning of good-humoured, originally meant to have been born under the influence of the planet Jupiter, which astrologers considered to be the source of good humour.

Judas

A Judas is a traitor, a person who betrays a friend. The word comes from the name of Christ's betrayer, Judas Iscariot.

The name Judas occurs in a number of expressions that allude to betrayal or cunning. A Judas kiss is a show of affection that conceals treachery. A Judas slit is a peep-hole in a door through which guards can observe their prisoners. A Judas tree is an ornamental shrub or tree of the genus *Cercis*; its pinkish-purple flowers bloom before the leaves appear. The genus is so called because it is traditionally thought that Judas hanged himself on such a tree.

jug

A jug, a vessel for holding or pouring liquids, usually with a handle and a lip or spout, probably derives its name from a nickname of Joan. In informal usage, jug can also mean prison, as in 'ten years in jug'. This usage may well be influenced by Spanish *juzgado* meaning 'jailed'.

juggernaut

In contemporary English, a juggernaut is a large articulated lorry: 'Huge juggernauts roaring through country villages.' The original meaning of the word is an irresistible, overwhelming force or object: 'The inexorable juggernaut of government.' The word comes from Hinduism: Jagannath, Lord of the World, is one of the titles of the Hindu god Vishnu. At an annual festival, an idol of this god is carried in an enormous wheeled vehicle; devotees, it is said, formerly threw themselves under its wheels.

Julian calendar see Gregorian Calendar

July

The seventh month of the year is named after Julius Caesar.
    See also **August**.

jumbo

The adjective jumbo means enormous or very large, as for example in a jumbo packet of washing powder. Originally, Jumbo was the name of a very large, sixty-two-ton African elephant exhibited at London Zoo from 1865 to 1882.

    Despite an outcry, which included a personal protest from Queen Victoria, Jumbo was bought by the American showman P. T. Barnum in 1881. In the USA, Jumbo was exhibited in the Barnum and Bailey Greatest Show on Earth. Jumbo lived for three and a half years in America and during this time it is estimated that he carried a million children on his back. He died in 1885, when a railway train hit him while he was trying to rescue Tom Thumb, Barnum's smallest attraction.

    There are several different theories as to the origin of Jumbo's name. Some believe it comes from mumbo-jumbo, others that it is derived from the Swahili *jumbe*, meaning chief, while still others claim that its origin lies in *gullah jamba*, meaning elephant.

Whichever theory is correct, P. T. Barnum's showmanship resulted not only in the celebration of an outsize animal, but also in the introduction of a new word into the language, now seen also in the compound *jumbo* jet.

June; Junoesque

The name of the sixth month of the year may come from Junius, the name of the Roman family to which the murderers of Julius Caesar belonged. Other sources suggest that June derives from the name of the goddess of the moon, and women and marriage, Juno, whose festival fell in this month. She was both the wife and sister of Jupiter.

The adjective Junoesque derives from the name Juno and means beautiful in a stately or regal manner.

K

Kafkaesque

The adjective Kafkaesque is used to describe a nightmarish sense of unreality and helplessness in the face of an impersonal and sinister bureaucracy. The word derives from the name of the Czech-born Austrian novelist Franz Kafka (1883–1924). Virtually unknown as an author in his own lifetime, Kafka wanted his manuscripts to be destroyed at his death. However, his friend Max Brod undertook to publish his works posthumously. Among his best known writings are *Metamorphosis* (1912), *The Trial* (1925) and *The Castle* (1926).

kaiser see tsar

keeshond

The keeshond is a breed of small dog with a compact body, foxlike features and a shaggy grey coat. This breed is traditionally used by the Dutch as barge dogs. The word *keeshond* comes from the Dutch, probably from *Kees*, a nickname for Cornelius and *hond*, dog, but it is uncertain why the name Cornelius was chosen.

kelvin

The kelvin is the metric unit of thermodynamic temperature. The kelvin scale is a scale of temperature in which the hypothetically coldest temperature (absolute zero) is 0°K and the freezing-point of water is 273.16°K. It is named after the Scottish physicist William Thomson Kelvin, 1st Baron Kelvin (1824–1907), who was a professor at Glasgow University for fifty-three years.

As well as suggesting the temperature scale, Kelvin is noted for his work on electricity and the conservation of energy, his many inventions of instruments, including the modern compass, and his personal supervision of the laying of the first transatlantic cable in 1866.

King James Bible

The King James Bible is an alternative name for the Authorised

Version of the Bible, written under the patronage of King James I (1566–1625) and published in 1611.

At a conference at Hampton Court (1604) a suggestion was made by a Dr John Reynolds (1549-1607), a Puritan and president of Corpus Christi College, that a new translation of the Bible be undertaken. The proposal appealed to the king, who wanted a uniform translation written by scholars from Oxford and Cambridge Universities, to be considered by bishops and to be ratified by his authority. The translation was based on the earlier Bishops' Bible (1568), and other versions, especially the Geneva Bible (1560), and work by William Tyndale. The style and wording of the Authorised (King James) Version has had a unique influence on the English language, becoming the familiar version of the Bible for generations of English-speaking people. Many of its phrases have become part of the language, including 'an eye for an eye', 'a fly in the ointment', 'the powers that be' and 'the salt of the earth'.

knickerbockers

Knickerbockers are short, baggy breeches gathered in at the knee. The word comes from the name Dietrich Knickerbocker, the pseudonym under which the American author Washington Irving (1783–1859) wrote his *History of New York from the Beginning of the World to the End of the Dutch Dynasty*, published in 1809.

The name Knickerbocker came to stand for the typical, solid Dutch burgher, who was a descendant of the original Dutch settlers in New York. The word knickerbockers is said to have been used for the baggy breeches considered to have been the traditional dress of the Dutch settlers in America. This tradition arose from illustrations by the caricaturist George Cruikshank (1792–1878) in a British edition of Irving's book in the 1850s. Cruikshank portrayed the Dutch settlers as wearing baggy breeches and so the name knickerbockers came to be used.

See also **bloomers**.

Köchel number

A Köchel number is a serial number in a catalogue of the works of Mozart, for example Mozart's Clarinet Concerto in A major is K.622. Köchel numbers are named after the Austrian botanist and cataloguer Ludwig von Köchel (1800–77), whose catalogue of Mozart's works was first published in 1862. The letter K (or in German KV, for *Köchelverzeichnis*, 'Köchel index') followed by a number, shows the chronological order of Mozart's works.

L

Lady Bountiful

A Lady Bountiful is a woman who is noted for her generous bestowing of charity or favours in a condescending, patronising manner, as for example in: 'We don't need her coming round here to play Lady Bountiful; we can afford to buy our own food and clothes, thank you very much.' The expression comes from the character in the comedy *The Beaux' Stratagem* (1707) by the Irish dramatist George Farquhar (1678–1707). In the play, Lady Bountiful gives half her money to charity.

lambert

Born the son of an impoverished tailor, the German scientist Johann Heinrich Lambert (1728–77) is noted for his work in several disciplines, such as mathematics, physics, astronomy and philosophy. Lambert proved that pi was an irrational number; he derived the trigonometric hyperbolic functions; and he measured the amount of light emitted by stars and planets.

It is for his work in physics that Lambert is particularly honoured: the unit of illumination in the centimetre–gram–second system of measurement is named after him.

Larousse

The well-known French Larousse dictionaries are named after the French grammarian, lexicographer,and encyclopedist Pierre Athanase Larousse (1817–75). The son of a blacksmith, Larousse founded the reference-book publishing firm that bears his name in 1852. His most important work was the *Grand dictionnaire universal du XIXe siècle* (1866–76), issued originally in fortnightly parts and finally totalling fifteen volumes.

lawrencium

Lawrencium is a short-lived radioactive chemical element that is artificially produced from the element californium. It is named after the American physicist Ernest Orlando Lawrence (1901–58). As physics professor at the University of California (1930), Lawrence invented the cyclotron, a type of particle accelerator that produces high-energy particles, for which he was awarded the **Nobel prize** for physics in 1939.

lazaret; lazaretto

A lazaret or lazaretto is a hospital for people with contagious diseases, a building or ship used for quarantine, or a ship's storeroom. The terms derive from a combination of the words lazar and Nazaret. Lazar is an archaic word for a poor diseased person, especially a leper, and comes from Lazarus, the name of the beggar in Jesus's parable (Luke 16:20; see also **Dives**). Nazaret is short for Santa Maria di Nazaret, a church in Venice that maintained a hospital.

Leninism; Leningrad

The word Leninism is used to refer to the political, economic and social theories of communism propounded by the Russian statesman Vladimir Ilyich Lenin (1870–1924), whose original surname was Ulyanov. It was the close study of Marxism and the execution of his elder brother Aleksandr that set Lenin on his political career. In exile in Siberia for his revolutionary activities (1897–1900) he wrote his first book, and married a fellow Marxist, Nadezhda Krupskaya. He was one of the leaders of the unsuccessful revolution of 1905. After the Russian Revolution broke out in 1917, Lenin led the Bolsheviks in the overthrow of the provisional government. He made peace with Germany (1918) and fought off opposition in the civil war (1918–21). As head of state, he founded the Third International (1918) and instituted the New Economic Policy (1921) which allowed a small degree of free enterprise. After a series of strokes, he died in 1924. His embalmed body was put on display in a tomb in Red Square, Moscow.

The former capital of Russia known as St Petersburg (1703–1914) and Petrograd (1914–24) was renamed Leningrad after Lenin's death. It has recently reverted to the name St Petersburg.

See also **Marxism, Stalinism, Trotskyism.**

leotard

A leotard is a close-fitting, one-piece garment worn by acrobats, ballet dancers and others performing physical exercises. It is named after the French acrobat Jules Léotard (1842–70), who designed and introduced the original costume for the circus. Léotard was one of France's most famous acrobats, starring in circuses in Paris and London. He perfected the first aerial somersault and invented the flying trapeze; he inspired the popular song 'That Daring Young Man on the Flying Trapeze' (1860) by George Leybourne. At the age of twenty-eight he died of smallpox.

Levis

Levis is a trademark for a kind of jeans, from the name of Levi Strauss (1830–1902), a Bavarian immigrant to the USA and a San Francisco clothing merchant at the time of the Gold Rush. Strauss started to make durable jeans in the 1850s. He added rivets to the corners of the pockets in the mid-1870s, so that, it is said, the pockets would not tear when they were loaded with ore samples. As he became more well known, so these hard–wearing jeans came to be called Levis.

lewisite

The colourless, poisonous liquid known as lewisite causes blistering of the skin. It was developed (1917–18) by the American chemist Winford Lee Lewis (1878–1943), after whom it is named, as a gas to be used in chemical warfare.

life of Riley

A person who enjoys an easy, lazy and luxurious life may be said to be 'living the life of Riley'. There are a number of different theories as to the origin of this expression. Some sources state that the original Riley was the American poet James Whitcomb Riley (1849–1916), whose writings often concerned boys spending summer days in a carefree manner; others suggest that the phrase originates with the song 'The Best In the House is None Too Good for Reilly' by Lawlor and Blake; still others say that the original Riley was an O'Reilly of the song 'Are You the O'Reilly?' popularised by Pat Rooney in the 1880s: O'Reilly would one day strike it rich, and everyone would be prosperous.

Linnaean

Carolus Linnaeus (1707–78; original name Carl von Linné) was the Swedish botanist who established the system of naming living organisms. In his Linnaean system, all organisms have two names, the first identifies the genus to which the organism belongs, the second its species. For example. Linnaeus classified members of the human race as belonging to *Homo sapiens* ('wise man'), *Homo* being the genus, and *sapiens* the specific species.

The son of a Lutheran clergyman, Linnaeus had an early interest in nature – he was nicknamed 'the little botanist' at the age of eight. He became assistant professor of botany at Uppsala University, studied medicine in Holland, and later became professor of medicine and botany at Uppsala University in 1741.

Linnaeus's system is outlined in his books, especially *Systema naturae* (1735), *Genera plantarum* (1737) and *Species plantarum* (1753). His was the first significant attempt to bring all living things together in a systematic classification.

It is said that he believed he had been chosen by God to name and classify plants and animals. Not only did he indeed name more living organisms than any other person in history, but also his system of nomenclature formed the basis of modern classification.

lobelia

Lobelia is the name of a genus of flowers bearing showy lipped blue, red, yellow or white flowers. The genus is named after the Flemish botanist and physician Matthias de Lobel (1538–1616), who was physician to King James I.

loganberry

The loganberry, the large sweet purplish-red berry of the upright-growing raspberry plant (*Rubus loganobaccus*) takes its name from an American lawyer. It was judge James Harvey Logan (1841–1928) who developed the plant in his experimental orchard at his home in California in about 1881.

The boysenberry was developed in the 1920s or 1930s as a hybrid of the loganberry, blackberry and raspberry by Rudolph Boysen (died 1950), an American botanist and horticulturist.

long johns see john

Lonsdale belt

The belt awarded as a trophy to professional boxing champions is known as a Lonsdale belt. It is named after Hugh Cecil Lowther, 5th Earl of Lonsdale (1857–1944), who originated the awards. The Earl of Lonsdale was an all-round sportsman; he was president of the National Sporting Club. Not only was he a sparring partner to the heavyweight fighter John Lawrence Sullivan (1858–1918), he was also an expert huntsman, steeplechaser and yachtsman.

Lucullan

The Roman general Lucius Licinus Lucullus (*c.*110–57BC) was a Roman general and administrator. He waged war against Mithridates, gaining both riches and success. He retired to private life in Rome in about 66BC to enjoy a life of luxury; and his Lucullan (or Lucullian) feasts became proverbial for their lavishness.

Luddite

A Luddite is a person who is opposed to industrial innovation It is said that the name derives from a Ned Ludd, an eighteenth-century English labourer who in about 1779 destroyed labour-saving stocking frames at his workplace. The name Luddite was adopted by a group of workers between 1811 and 1816 who tried to destroy new mechanical textile appliances in the Midlands and the north of England. The workers saw the new machines as a threat to their livelihood. The movement was suppressed and some Luddites were hanged or transported. Distrust of innovation continues and the word Luddite is still used to refer to someone who opposes the latest technological changes.

lumber

The word lumber, old disused articles that are stored away, may come from Lombard, in the now obsolete sense of pawnbroker, after the Lombards, the merchants who came from Lombardy, a region in north Italy. A Germanic tribe known as the Longobardi or long-bearded (men) settled in that region about AD568.

It seems that the sense of disused articles may derive from the fact that the lumber (pawnshop) rooms were filled with evidence of unredeemed pledges – boxes, furniture and other miscellaneous articles.

The American English use of lumber to mean 'sawn timber' is also a development of this sense.

lush

Lush, slang for intoxicating liquor and also a drunken person, is said to have originally been a shortening of the name of an actors' drinking club in London, the City of Lushington. The club, founded in the mid-eighteenth century, met in the Harp Tavern in Great Russell Street until the 1890s. The name of the club may possibly have come from a chaplain, Dr Thomas Lushington (1590–1661), who was a drinking companion of Bishop Richard Corbet, although a number of alternative theories have been proposed, including the suggestion that the origin is *lush*, to eat and drink, in Shelta, the jargon of some Irish vagrants.

lynch

If an angry mob of people 'lynch' someone, they put that person to death without giving him or her a proper trial. The word comes from lynch law, the condemning and punishing of a person who has not been tried, but dictionary writers have long argued over which person with the name Lynch originated the expression. Most now agree, however, that it was probably William Lynch (1742–1820), an American who organised extra-legal trials in Virginia.

The evidence for this is an editorial on lynching by the American short-story writer Edgar Allen Poe (1809–49) in an issue of the *Southern Literary Messenger*, published in 1836. Poe wrote that the expression 'lynch law' originated in 1780 when Captain William Lynch led a group of his fellow citizens in Pennsylvania County, Virginia, to deal with a group of ruffians who were disturbing public order. Lynch had an agreement with his fellow vigilantes 'to inflict such corporeal punishment . . . as shall seem adequate to the crime committed or the damage sustained'. Thus lynch law came to refer to the administration of mob justice using non-legal means, and on occasions men were hanged for their alleged crimes.

The expressions lynch law and lynch also, no doubt, gained currency because of the practices of another person named Lynch, the planter and justice of the peace, Charles Lynch (1736–96), who took the law into his own hands and set up his own trials during the American War of Independence. However, there is no evidence that the administration of rough justice by this Lynch ever led to any hangings.

M

macabre

The adjective macabre, meaning 'grim or gruesome', is derived from the Old French *danse macabre*, 'dance of death', a medieval representation of a dance in which living people are taken, in order of their social standing, to their graves by a personification of death. The origin of the *danse macabre* may lie in a miracle play in which the martyrdom of the seven young Maccabee brothers under the Syrian (Seleucid) King Antiochus IV is depicted. This story is told in the Apochrypha in the second Book of the Maccabees, Chapter 7.

macadam

A macadamised road is one that has a surface made of macadam: compacted layers of small broken stones bound together with tar, asphalt, etc. The word macadam honours its inventor, the Scottish engineer John Loudon McAdam (1756–1836). It is said that as a small boy McAdam laid out model roads in his back garden – but it was years later, after spending some time on America, that he returned to Scotland, to discover that the roads in the estate that he had bought in Ayrshire were, like most roads, in a poor condition. McAdam set to work to improve the state of the roads, experimenting in Ayrshire and later in Falmouth. His efforts led to his appointment in 1815 to construct new roads around Bristol, and in 1827 he was made surveyor general of all British metropolitan roads.

Macadamising – covering the earth base with a layer of large, tightly packed, broken stones that were in turn covered by a layer of smaller stones – soon became the standard road-surfacing method. The trademark Tarmac is an abbreviation of Tarmacadam, a company formed in 1903 which perfected a technique of using tar and bitumen to bind together the stones in the surface.

McCarthyism

The name of the US Republican senator Joseph Raymond McCarthy (1909–57) is remembered for McCarthyism, a kind of political witchhunting in America in the early 1950s. In February 1950, McCarthy claimed he knew of over two hundred communists, or communist sympathisers, in the State Department. The investigations that followed marked a witchhunt that personally attacked individuals not only in politics but also in the television and film industries. McCarthy was, however, unable to prove his allegations. Eventually he was censured by the Senate in December 1954 and his witchhunt came to an end.

The term McCarthyism is still used, however, to refer to an obsessive opposition to individuals considered disloyal or who hold views considered to be subversive, especially when the charges against the individuals are not substantiated.

McCoy – the real McCoy

Someone or something that is described as the real McCoy (or the real Mackay) is certainly genuine; it is not an imitation or a fake. There are, however, many different theories as to the origin of the expression.

Some say it comes from Kid McCoy (professional name of the American Norman Selby, 1873–1940), welterweight boxing champion 1898–1900, who was said to have proved his identity by boxing with his doubters until they conceded he was 'the real McCoy'.

Others suggest a Chicago livestock trader Joseph McCoy (b. 1838) who changed the town of Abilene, Kansas, into a cow town in 1867 by taking cattle via the new railhead at Abilene to the cities of the north and east. It is said that he transported half a million cattle a year and he claimed that he was 'the real McCoy'.

Still further explanations of the origin of the expression include a chief of the Mackay clan; a Prohibition rum-runner named Bill McCoy; a character in an Irish ballad of the 1880s; the island of Macao (hence McCoy), where drug addicts are said to have demanded 'the real Macao' of the island's uncut heroin; and whisky dispatched from Glasgow to the United States by A. M. MacKay. This last explanation may well have increased the currency of the expression, since it seems that the phrases McCoy or the clear McCoy were originally (1908) used to refer to good whisky.

Mach number

A Mach number is a number that represents the ratio of the speed of a body to the speed of sound in the same medium. Thus Mach 1 corresponds to the speed of sound, a number less than 1 is subsonic, a number greater than 1 is supersonic, and a number greater than 5 is said to be hypersonic. The term 'Mach number' is named after the

Austrian physicist and philosopher Ernst Mach (1838–1916) for his research into airflow.

Mach was also known as a philosopher; he propounded the theory of sensationalism – that the only things that ultimately exist are sensations. This theory influenced the philosophical movement of logical positivism in the 1920s.

Machiavellian

The adjective Machiavellian has come to refer to cunning, double-dealing and opportunist methods and to describe a view that in politics the use of any means, however unscrupulous, can be justified in the pursuit of political ends. The term derives from the Italian political theorist Niccolò Machiavelli (1469–1527). Machiavelli served as a statesman and secretary to the Florentine Republic from 1498 to 1512. When the Medici family were restored to power, he was forced into exile, however. His most famous work was *Il Principe* (*The Prince*; published in 1532), in which he argued that all means are acceptable in the securing and maintenance of a stable state. It seems that his views have been unfairly exaggerated in the modern connotation of unprincipled trickery in the word Machiavellian.

mackintosh

A kind of raincoat made of rubberised cloth, a mackintosh (also mac or macintosh) is named after the Scottish chemist Charles Macintosh (1760–1843). It was, however, another Scotsman, James Syme (1799–1870), who first invented the process of making waterproof fabrics in 1823. A few months later, the fabric was patented by Macintosh, who went on to found a company in Glasgow, which produced the first mackintoshes in 1830. In Macintosh's process, a waterproof fabric was produced by sticking two layers of cloth together with rubber dissolved in naphtha. Nowadays, the word mackintosh is applied to any raincoat.

madeleine

A madeleine is a small, rich sponge cake that is baked in a mould. It is probably named after Madeleine Paulmier, the nineteenth-century French pastrycook who is said to have been the first to concoct this delicacy.

Mae West

A Mae West is an inflatable life jacket that was issued to airmen in the Second World War. When inflated, the life-jacket resembled a well-developed bust – hence the choice of the name of the American actress

Mae West (1892–1980), renowned for her full figure.

On learning that she was honoured in the name of the life jacket, she is said to have uttered, 'I've been in *Who's Who* and I know what's what, but it's the first time I ever made the dictionary.'

magdalen

The word magdalen (or magdalene) means a reformed prostitute or a house of refuge or of reform for prostitutes. It comes from the name Mary Magdalene, a woman rid by Jesus of evil spirits (Luke 8:2) and the first person to whom the risen Jesus appeared (John 20:1–18). Mary Magdalen is often also traditionally identified with the sinful woman of Luke 7:36–50, and considered to have been a reformed prostitute, though the biblical text does not justify such a conclusion.

Maginot line

The original Maginot line was a line of fortifications built by France to defend its north-east frontier with Germany from 1929 onwards, before the outbreak of the Second World War. The Maginot line is named after the French minister of war (1922–4, 1929–32) André Maginot (1877–1932). In the event, their blind confidence in the defences lulled the French into a false sense of security, and when in 1940 Germany invaded France, the Maginot line (which was not even continued to the coast) was easily by-passed by the flanking manoeuvres of the Germans through Belgium. Nowadays, a Maginot line is any defensive position in which blind confidence is placed.

magnolia

Magnolia is the name of a genus of evergreen or deciduous shrubs or trees with showy white, yellow, rose or purple flowers. The genus is named after the French botanist Pierre Magnol (1638–1715). Magnol, professor of botany at Montpellier University, is known for his systematic classification of plants.

malapropism

A malapropism is an instance of the unintentional confusion of words that produces a ridiculous effect. The word comes from the name of the character Mrs Malaprop in the play *The Rivals* (1775) by the Irish dramatist Richard Brinsley Sheridan (1751–1816). In the play, Mrs Malaprop – her name comes from the French *mal à propos*, meaning inappropriate – misapplies words on numerous occasions; for example, 'If I reprehend anything in this world, it is the use of my oracular tongue and a nice derangement of epitaphs!' (Act 3, Scene 3).

Other examples of malapropisms are 'under the affluence of alcohol' and 'teutonic ulcers'.

Malpighian

The name of the Italian physiologist Marcello Malpighi (1628–94) is relatively unknown, but he was a pioneer in the field of microscopic anatomy. In 1661 he identified the capillary system, confirming the theory of the English physician and anatomist William Harvey (1578–1657). Malpighi made several studies of organs of the body, and the Malpighian corpuscle, part of the kidney, and the Malpighian layer, a layer of skin, are named after him. Malpighi held professorships at Bologna, Pisa and Messina; he also served as private physician to Pope Innocent XII.

Malthusian

The adjective Malthusian refers to the population theories of the English economist Thomas Robert Malthus (1766–1834). In his *Essay on the Principle of Population*, which aroused great controversy throughout the world when it was published in 1798, Malthus argued that population increases at a faster rate than the means of subsistence. The inevitable result would be that the human race would remain near starvation unless the growth in population was checked by sexual restraint or by natural controls such as disease, famine or war.

man Friday see Friday

Manichaenism

Manichaenism is the religious movement named after its Persian founder, Mani (*c*.AD217–*c*.276). It combined elements from Buddhism, Zoroastrianism and Christianity. According to the teaching, the world and the human race are engaged in the struggle between good and evil (light and darkness, God and matter). By strict abstinence and prayer, Manichaeans believed that man could become aware of the light.

The religion spread throughout Asia and the Roman Empire and lasted until the thirteenth century. Mani, its founder, was martyred by the disciples of Zoroastrianism. St Augustine followed Manichaenism for a brief period before his conversion to Christianity.

mansard roof

A mansard roof has two slopes on both sides and ends, the lower slopes being almost vertical and the upper ones nearly horizontal. It is often used to provide a high ceiling to an attic. The roof is named after the

French classical architect François Mansart (1598–1666). Notable buildings that Mansart designed include the north wing of the Château de Blois (1635–8) and the Maisons Laffitte near Paris (1642). It is said that he was chosen to design the Louvre, but since he would not allow his design to be changed during the building, he was not appointed.

Maoism

The theory of Marxism–Leninism was developed in China by Mao Tse-tung (Chinese, Mao Zedong; 1893–1976). Born into a peasant family in Hunan province, Mao helped establish the Chinese Communist Party in 1921 and founded a Soviet republic in Jiangxi province in south-east China (1931)

He led the Long March, the flight of the Chinese communists from Jiangxi to north-west China (1934–6), and this established him as leader of the Communist Party. He joined forces with the Kuomintang (Nationalist Party) to bring about the defeat of Japan in the Sino-Japanese War (1937–45), but he then opposed and defeated the Kuomintang in the ensuing civil war.

In 1949, he founded the People's Republic of China and was chairman of the Communist Party from 1949 until his death. He instigated the economic Great Leap Forward (1958–60) and the Cultural Revolution (1966–9). Mao, one of the most significant revolutionary figures of the twentieth century, is remembered for, amongst other things, his emphasis on revolutionary guerrilla warfare of the peasant armies, his courageous political and social activities in transforming China, and his stress on moral exhortation and indoctrination, typified by the *Little Red Book* of his sayings.

See also **Marxism, Leninism.**

marcel

A marcel is a deep, soft, continuous wave made in the hair with a curling iron; to marcel the hair is to make such a wave in the hair. The word comes from the name of the French hairdresser Marcel Grateau (1852–1936). In 1875, Grateau devised the marcelling process; it is said that the hairstyle became so popular in France that Grateau amassed a great wealth, enabling him to retire before he was even thirty.

marigold

A marigold is one of several annual herbaceous plants grown for their yellow or orange flower heads. The word marigold comes from a combination of the name of the Virgin Mary, the mother of Jesus, and the word gold. The name marigold was probably first applied to the plant now known as a pot marigold (*Calendula officinalis*), once used for healing wounds and as a flavouring for soups and stews.

Mariotte's law see Boyle's law

Marshall Plan

The Marshall Plan (officially known as the European Recovery Programme) was the programme of US economic aid to Europe after the Second World War. The Marshall Plan is named after the US general and statesman George Catlett Marshall (1880–1959), who originally proposed it when he was secretary of state (1947–9). For this work, he was awarded the Nobel prize for peace in 1953. Earlier in his career, Marshall had been army chief of staff (1939–45) and was responsible for organising the expansion of American armed forces during the Second World War.

martin

A martin is a bird of the swallow family that has a square or slightly forked tail. Its name may come from the time of the birds' migration, reckoned to be about the time of Martinmas, 11 November, the festival of St Martin, the fourth-century Bishop of Tours.

martinet

A martinet is a strict disciplinarian. The word comes from the name of a French army officer during the reign of Louis XIV, Jean Martinet. Under Martinet's influence, the French army was transformed from an ill-disciplined body of men into an efficient military force by a rigorous system of drilling and training that even included punishing his soldiers with the cat-o'-nine tails. Thus Martinet's name became associated with harsh forms of discipline, and the term gradually entered non-military contexts.

Somewhat ironically, Martinet was 'accidentally' killed by his own forces. In the siege of Duisberg (1672), it is said that Martinet over-zealously entered the line of fire of his own rear ranks. But to those who had experienced the severity of Martinet's training methods, it seems quite possible that the event was not an accident.

Marxism

Marxism is the theory of socialism of the German political philosophers Karl Marx (1818–83) and Friedrich Engels (1820–95).

Born in Prussia, Marx was educated at the universities of Bonn and Berlin. He edited the radical Cologne newspaper, the *Rheinische*

Zeitung (1842–3), but after its suppression he left Germany. At first he stayed in Paris, where he met Engels; later in Brussels the *Communist Manifesto* (1848) was written. Marx settled in London in 1849, where he spent the rest of his life. He assumed leadership of the International Working Men's Association (the First International) in 1864. His theories of the class struggle and the economics of capitalism were developed in *Das Kapital* (first volume, 1867; the remaining two volumes published posthumously).

Marxism has come to stand for the theory that capitalism and the class struggle will give way to the dictatorship of the proletariat and then to the establishing of the classless society.

See also **Leninism, Stalinism, Trotskyism.**

masochism

The word masochism is used to describe the mental disorder that causes a person to derive pleasure (especially sexual) from the experience of self-inflicted pain, humiliation, etc. The word derives from the name of the Austrian novelist Leopold von Sacher-Masoch (1836–95), whose writings depicted this condition.

This form of obsession was reflected not only in the novels of Sacher-Masoch; it was also evident in his bizarre life – he was the self-appointed 'slave' of a number of mistresses and two wives in his lifetime. It was probably the German psychiatrist Richard von Krafft-Ebing (1840–1902) who coined the word masochism after studying Sacher-Masoch's works.

Mason–Dixon line

The Mason–Dixon line (originally Mason and Dixon's line) was the name given to the boundary between the states of Maryland and Pennsylvania, set in 1763–7. It is named after its English surveyors Charles Mason (*c.*1730–87) and Jeremiah Dixon. Before the American Civil War the line came to be regarded as the demarcation line between the North and South, the free states and the slave states.

maudlin

The word maudlin is sometimes used to refer to someone who is tearfully sentimental or foolishly drunk. The word comes originally from the name Mary Magdalene, traditionally portrayed in paintings as a weeping penitent. The biblical text relates that Mary weeps when she discovers the empty tomb after the resurrection of Jesus (John 20:1–18).

On the identity of Mary Magdalene, see **Magdalen.**

Mauser

Mauser is the trademark used to describe a type of pistol. The word comes from the name of the German firearms inventors Peter Paul von Mauser (1838–1914) and his older brother Wilhelm (1834–82). The Mauser rifle (or pistol) was used by the Germany army for many years from 1871; modified versions were used in World Wars I and II. The younger brother also invented the Mauser magazine rifle in 1897.

mausoleum

A mausoleum, a grand stately tomb, comes from the name of King Mausolus, ruler of Caria in ancient Greece. When he died in 353BC, his widow, Artemisia, built a huge magnificent tomb at Halicarnassus in his honour. The monument was probably a raised temple with decorative statues and a pyramid-like roof; it was considered one of the seven wonders of the ancient world. It is believed that the monument was destroyed by earthquake in the Middle Ages.

maverick

A person who is independent and who does not wish to conform or be identified with a group is sometimes called a maverick. The word comes from the name of the American pioneer Samuel Augustus Maverick (1803–70). Also known as a fighter for Texan independence and originally a lawyer, Maverick became a rancher when he gained a herd of cattle in settlement of a debt. He failed, however, to ensure that all his calves were branded, perhaps so that he could claim all unbranded calves as his own or so that neighbouring ranchers could put their own brands on them. In the course of time the word came to be used to refer not only to unbranded cattle but also to people who do not 'go with the herd', who do not give allegiance to a particular group, especially a political one.

Maxim gun

The Maxim gun is the name of the first fully automatic machine-gun – a water-cooled, single-barrelled weapon that used the recoil force of each shot to keep up the automatic firing. The machine-gun is named after the US-born British inventor Sir Hiram Stevens Maxim (1840-1916), who developed it in 1884.

Maxim originally served as chief engineer for America's first electric company, the United States Electric Lighting Company. He later applied his engineering skills to inventing his machine-gun, and also to other items such as a kind of mousetrap and a fire sprinkler.

maxwell

The maxwell is the unit of magnetic flux in the centimetre–gram–second system of measurement. The unit is named after the Scottish physicist James Clerk Maxwell (1831–79).

Maxwell wrote his first scientific paper at the age of fifteen; he later became professor of physics at the University of Aberdeen and then London. In 1871 he became the first professor of experimental physics at Cambridge. Maxwell made significant advances in physics, notably in his unifying of electricity, magnetism and light into one set of equations (Maxwell's equations, published 1873 in his *Treatise on Electricity and Magnetism*), which form the basis of electrodynamics. Maxwell also made important contributions to the kinetic theory of gases and to the understanding of colour vision.

March

The name of the third month of the year comes from the name of the Roman god Mars, the god of war. Before the time of Julius Caesar, the Roman year began in March. This month was considered the beginning of not only a new year but also a new season of waging war; so the month was committed to Mars and named in his honour.

May

The fifth month of the year takes its name from the Roman goddess Maia, the goddess of spring and fertility, and daughter of Faunus and wife of Vulcan.

The Old English name for the month is said to have been of a more practical nature: Thrimilce, because in the longer days of spring, the cows could be milked three times between sunrise and sunset.

Medes – laws of the Medes and Persians

The laws of the Medes and Persians are unchangeable laws that are to be strictly followed: 'She need not be so inflexible – after all, it's not a law of the Medes and Persians that lunch has to be eaten at 1 o'clock every day.' The expression comes from the Bible (Daniel 6:8): 'Now, O King, establish the decree, and sign the writing, that it be not changed, according to the law of the Medes and Persians, which altereth not.'

The Medes were inhabitants of Media, north-east of Mesopotamia, between the Black Sea and the Caspian Sea. In 550BC the Persian King Cyrus the Great defeated his overlord and father-in-law Astyages to gain control of the Median empire. Many Medes were then granted high positions in the Persian court and the Medes' customs and laws were amalgamated with those of the Persians – hence the expression the laws of the Medes and the Persians.

medusa

A medusa is the name given to a type of jellyfish and also to the free-swimming form in the life-cycle of a coelenterate animal. The word comes from the name Medusa, one of the Greek mythological **Gorgons**. When the goddess Athena was incensed by Medusa's giving her favours to Poseidon, she changed Medusa's locks into serpents and made her face so hideous that everyone who looked at her was turned to stone. The name of the jellyfish comes from the resemblance of its tentacles to the serpent-like curls of the Gorgon.

Melba toast; peach melba

Melba toast (thinly sliced toasted bread) and peach melba (a dessert of peaches, ice-cream and raspberry sauce) owe their origin to the stage name of the Australian operatic soprano singer Dame Nellie Melba (1838–1914)

Born as Helen Porter Mitchell, and later adopting the name Melba (from Melbourne, near which she was born), the singer made her début in *Rigoletto* (Brussels, 1887) and went on to star in London, Paris and New York. It is said that Melba toast originated at the Savoy Hotel in London when Dame Nellie Melba ordered toast and was served with several pieces that were unusually thin and crisp and almost burnt; such toast was then named after her. Peach melba is said to have been originally made by the French chef Auguste Escoffier (1846–1935) in her honour.

mendelevium

The artificially produced radioactive metallic chemical element known as mendelevium is named in honour of the Russian chemist Dmitri Ivanovich Mendeleyev (1834–1907). Mendeleyev was professor of organic chemistry at St Petersburg (1866–90). After listening to a lecture on the subject of atomic weights by the Italian chemist Stanislao Cannizzaro (1826–1910), Mendeleyev became interested in a classification of the elements and in 1869 he devised the first version of the periodic table of the chemical elements.

Mendel's laws

Mendel's laws are the basic principles of heredity proposed by the Austrian botanist Gregor Johann Mendel (1822–84). Mendel was originally a monk; however, because of his earlier scientific training and interest in botany he began to experiment with the hybrid breeding of pea plants in the monastery garden at Brno, Moravia. His conclusions were formulated in two principles – Mendel's laws – in 1865, but remained unrecognised until 1900, when they were rediscovered by Hugo de Vries and others. Mendel is now recognised as the founder of the science of genetics.

mentor

Mentor, the word for a wise and trusted adviser, comes from the name of Mentor, Odysseus's loyal friend who was also tutor to his son, the young Telemachus, in Homer's *Odyssey*. Mentor's identity is assumed by Athene, the goddess of wisdom; she accompanies Telemachus in his search for his father. The currency of the word in English is probably due to the prominence of the character in *Les Aventures de Télémaque* (1699) by the French theologian and writer François de Salignac de la Mothe Fénelon (1651–1715).

Mephistopheles; Mephistophelean

A person may be described as a Mephistopheles or as being Mephistophelean if he or she is diabolical or evil in a sinister, persuasive manner. The term comes from the Mephistopheles of German legend – the contemptuous, merciless, tempting evil spirit to whom Faust sold his soul. The origin of the word Mephistopheles itself is uncertain; it is said to have been used by magicians and alchemists in spells. The earliest form of the word is Mephostophiles (*Faustbuch*, 1587), possibly meaning 'not loving the light'.

Mercator projection

Mercator (or Mercator's) projection is the form of map projection in which lines of latitude and longitude are straight lines that intersect at right angles and all lines of latitude are the same length as the equator. The projection is used for navigation charts but it has the disadvantage of distorting outlines and exaggerating sizes at increasing distances from the equator.

This form of map projection is named after the Flemish geographer Gerardus Mercator (original name Gerhard Kremer; 1512–94) who devised it in 1568. Originally working in Louvain, Mercator had to flee to Protestant Germany in 1552 to escape charges of heresy.

See also **Atlas**.

mesmerise

If you are mesmerised by something you are extremely fascinated, spellbound or even hypnotised by it. The word comes from the name of the Austrian physician and hypnotist Franz Anton Mesmer (1734–1815), who induced a hypnotic state in his patients. Born in Austria, Mesmer studied and later practised medicine in Vienna. He considered his medical success was due to his method (so-called 'animal magnetism') of stroking his patients with magnets.

In spite of the support of those he had treated, Mesmer was compelled by the Austrian authorities to leave Vienna, so he moved to Paris in 1778. Here, his healing technique became very fashionable. Wearing purple robes, he would wave his magic wand, and seek to treat individuals in a gathered group.

In 1784 Louis XVI appointed a scientific commission to investigate the practices; they concluded that Mesmer was a charlatan and an imposter. This led him to flee from Paris and he spent the rest of his life in obscurity in Switzerland. Mesmer believed that his success was due to the supernatural; today we would acknowledge that it was due to his hypnotic powers.

Messerschmitt

The Messerschmitt planes (particularly the Me-109 and the first mass-produced jet-fighter, the Me-262) of the Second World War are named after the German aircraft designer Willy Messerschmitt (1898–1978). Messerschmitt built his first aeroplane at the age of eighteen and owned his own factory by the time he was twenty-five. In 1927 he was appointed chief designer at the Bayerische Flugzeugwerke; in 1937 he received the Lilienthal prize for research into aviation.

Methuselah – as old as Methuselah

The expression 'as old as Methuselah', meaning very old, refers to the age of the Old Testament patriarch. According to Genesis, chapter 5, Methuselah was the son of Enoch and grandfather of Noah and lived to be 969 years old.

See also Jeroboam.

Micawber

Someone who is described as a Micawber or as being Micawberish is a person who does not make provision for the future, optimistically trusting that 'something is bound to turn up'. The name comes from the character Wilkins Micawber in the novel *David Copperfield* (published

1849–50) by Charles Dickens. By the end of the story, Micawber, relieved of his debts and having emigrated to Australia, appears as a highly regarded colonial magistrate.

Michaelmas

Michaelmas is the feast of St Michael the Archangel, 29 September, and is one of the four quarter days when certain business payments become due. The autumnal celebration of St Michael is recalled in the naming of the Michaelmas daisy, an autumn-blooming aster, and Michaelmas term, another name for the autumn term at some universities.

See also **Hilary**.

mickey – take the mickey out of ; Mickey Finn

If you take the mickey out of someone, you make fun of him or her. The origin of the word is not known, but it could derive from the derogatory use of the name Mick (from Michael) to refer to an Irishman, Michael being a common Irish first name.

A Mickey Finn is slang for an alcoholic drink containing a drug to render someone unconscious. The expression is said to derive from a Chicago saloon-keeper at the end of the nineteenth century called Mickey Finn. He would add a knock-out drug to the drinks of his unsuspecting victims, and would rob them once they had passed out. It is possible that the original Mickey Finn was a laxative for horses.

Mickey Mouse

Something may be described as being Mickey Mouse if it is trivial or trite. The expression derives from the name of the simple-minded cartoon character Mickey Mouse created by the American film producer and animator Walt Disney (1901–66).

Disney first drew Mickey Mouse in 1928; it seems that the character was based on his former pet mouse, Mortimer. Mickey Mouse made his début in the first animated sound cartoon *Steamboat Willie* (November 1928), in which Disney used his own voice for Mickey's high-pitched speech. The mouse became an instant success, and by 1931 Mickey Mouse clubs had a million members throughout the USA.

Midas – the Midas touch

Someone who has the Midas touch makes an easy financial success of all his or her business undertakings. The expression comes from King Midas of Phrygia in Greek legend. In gratitude to King Midas for his hospitality towards the satyr Silenus, the god Dionysus promised to fulfil any wish King Midas might make. The king told Dionysus that he wanted everything he touched to be turned to gold. Dionysus granted this – but on discovering that even his food and drink turned to gold, Midas asked that the gift be taken away. Dionysus then ordered King Midas to bathe in the River Pactolus and he was washed clean of his power.

mint

The word for the place where money is coined, a mint, comes from the Latin word for money, *moneta*. The Romans coined their money in the temple of the Roman goddess Juno, who was known by the title Moneta, 'the admonisher'; so it was that the mint and its product came to be known by this name.

mithridatism

The word mithridatism is used to refer to an immunity to poison that is acquired by a gradual drinking of increasing doses. The expression comes from the name of the king of Pontus, Mithridates VI, called the Great (*c.*132–63BC), who allegedly produced this condition in himself.

King Mithridates engaged the Romans in many significant battles, but was eventually defeated by Pompey in 66BC. During his whole lifetime he is said to have guarded himself from being poisoned by gradually drinking increasing amounts of poison, so rendering himself more and more immune to its effect. On his defeat by Pompey he decided to commit suicide only to discover that he had mithridatised himself too successfully. He was completely immune to poison and so ordered a mercenary to kill him with his sword.

Möbius strip

A Möbius strip is a one-sided continuous surface that is made by twisting a strip of paper through 180° and joining the ends. It is named after the German mathematician August Ferdinand Möbius (1780–1868), who discovered it. The Möbius strip is significant because its unexpected properties are of interest in topology: if it is cut lengthways, it remains in one piece.

mogul

A Mogul was a member of the Muslim dynasty of rulers in India in the sixteenth to eighteenth centuries, and (with a small 'm') is an important or very rich person: for instance, a film mogul. The founder of the dynasty was the Emperor Barbur (1483–1530). Both usages of the word have their origin in Persian *Mughul*, which in turn comes from

Mongolian *Mongol*. The figurative sense probably comes from the Great Moguls, the first six rulers of the dynasty.

Mohammed – if the mountain will not come to Mohammed, Mohammed must go to the mountain

The idiomatic expression 'if the mountain will not come to Mohammed, Mohammed must go to the mountain' means that if a person or set of circumstances will not change or be adapted to suit one's own wishes, then one must oneself change or adapt to suit them. The expression derives from the life of Mohammed, the prophet and founder of Islam (*c.*AD 570–632). It is said that when he brought his message of Islam to the Arabs, they demanded a miracle to prove his claims. Mohammed then ordered Mount Safa to come towards him. When it failed to do so, he explained that God had been merciful: if the mountain had moved, it would have fallen on them and destroyed them. Mohammed then proposed that instead he would go to the mountain, and give thanks to God for his mercy.

molly

The molly is a brightly coloured tropical fish that belongs to the genus *Mollienesia*, and is valued as an aquarium fish. The molly takes its name from the French statesman Comte Nicolas-François Mollien (1758–1850). Mollien served as financial adviser to Napoleon, although it seems his advice was often rejected. It is not clear why the fish is named after this French statesman; he was not even a collector of tropical fish.

Molotov cocktail

The Soviet statesman Vyacheslav Mikhailovich Molotov (original surname Scriabin; 1890–1986) played a substantial role in the growth of the Soviet Union as a superpower. After the Bolshevik Revolution of October 1917, Molotov held a series of posts in the ranks of the Party, becoming (1921) a secretary to the Central Committee; in 1922 he was instrumental in promoting Stalin to general secretary. He was prime minister (1930–41) and foreign minister (1939–49; 1953–6). He negotiated the Soviet–German non-aggression treaty (1939), and after the Germans invaded the Soviet Union he negotiated alliances with the Allies. He was also a prominent figure in the Cold War between the USA and the Soviet Union after the Second World War. Disagreements with Khrushchev led, however, to his dismissal from office in 1956 and in 1962 his expulsion from the Communist Party, although he was readmitted to the party in 1984.

The crude petrol bomb known as the Molotov cocktail is named after the Russian statesman. It consists of a bottle filled with a flammable liquid, such as petrol, and stoppered with a saturated rag; the rag is ignited as the bottle is thrown. It seems that the device may have been used as early as 1934 but the term Molotov cocktail was not applied to the device until 1940, when the Finns used them against the tanks of the invading Russians.

Monroe doctrine

The US president James Monroe (1785–1831) is remembered for his proclamation to Congress on 2 December 1823 that has come to be known as the Monroe doctrine. In this statement he warned the European nations against trying to interfere in or influence the affairs of the Americas; in return the USA would not intervene in Europe. The Monroe doctrine, largely the work of secretary of state John Quincy Adams, became a fundamental principle in the foreign policy of the USA.

Earlier, Monroe had fought and been wounded in the American Revolution; he had also served as minister to France (1794–6) and Britain (1803–7). His two terms in office (1817–25) as president are known as the 'era of good feelings'; during this time Florida was acquired and five states were added to the Union.

Monrovia, the capital and main port of the African country of Liberia, is also named in honour of Monroe. The country was founded during Monroe's presidency, in 1822, as a settlement for freed American slaves.

Montbretia

A montbretia is a plant of the *Iris* family that bears showy orange or yellow flowers. The plant is named after the French botanist A. F. E. Coquebert de Montbret (1780–1801).

Montessori method

The Italian physicist and educator Maria Montessori (1870–1952) is remembered for the development of an educational method that is named after her. In this method the creative potential of young children is developed; they are provided with different sensory materials in a prepared environment, and they progress at their own rate through free but guided play.

Born into a noble family, Montessori studied medicine at the University of Rome and became the first woman in Italy to receive a degree in medicine (1896). She then began to work with retarded children, later opening a school for children of normal intelligence in a slum area of Rome (1907). The success of her methods led to the founding of other schools in Europe and Asia. With some refinements, Montessori's ideas have had an important influence on the modern education of children.

Moog synthesiser

Moog is the trademark for a type of synthesiser. Robert Arthur Moog (b.1934) is an American physicist, engineer and electrician who designed the synthesiser that bears his name. Working with the composer H. A. Deutsch, Moog developed his device that could electronically reproduce the sounds of conventional musical instruments and also produce a variety of artificial tones. The Moog synthesiser was patented in 1965.

Moonie

Moonie is the name given to a member of the Unification Church founded by the Korean industrialist Sun Myung Moon (original name Yong Myung Moon; b.1920).

The religious group was established in 1954; its members believe that the 'Reverend' Moon has been given the responsibility, begun by Adam and Jesus, to unite the human race into a perfect family. The movement is also known for its indoctrination of potential recruits and its methods of fund raising.

Mormon

A Mormon is a member of the Church of Jesus Christ of Latter-Day Saints, founded in 1830 by Joseph Smith (1805–44) in New York state. Smith claimed that led by visions he had, in 1927, discovered some gold plates which contained the *Book of Mormon*. This sacred book is named after its compiler, and, according to Mormon belief, was buried in the fifth century AD.

Smith published the book in 1830; Mormons see it as one of a series of scriptures that supplement the Bible. Following Smith's murder in Illinois, the movement was led by Brigham Young (1801–77), and their headquarters were established at Salt Lake City, Utah, in 1847. The Mormons' practice of polygamy brought them into conflict with the Federal authorities until 1890 when it was disallowed.

morphine

Morphine (or morphia) is an addictive narcotic drug used medicinally to alleviate pain and to induce sleep. The word is derived from the name Morpheus, the god of dreams in Greek mythology. He was the son of Somnus, the god of sleep.

Morris chair

The Morris chair, an armchair that has an adjustable back and large loose cushions, is named after its designer, the English poet, artist and socialist writer William Morris (1834–96). Morris founded a firm of designers and decorators in 1861 and he designed furniture, wallpaper and stained glass of a style different from that of the contemporary Victorian era. The work of William Morris and his Pre-Raphaelite associates led to the development of the Arts and Crafts movement in England.

Morris is also noted for his development of the private press, with his founding of the Kelmscott Press (1890) for his poetry and prose writings, and for his establishing of the Socialist League in England.

morris dance

A morris dance is a traditional English dance performed in the open air by costumed men – morris men – wearing bells and often carrying sticks. The name morris dance is thought to have originally been Moorish dance; it is said that the dances derived from the ancient dances of the Moors and were introduced from Spain into England about 1350. The dances often illustrate a legend or portray an activity.

Morrison shelter see Anderson shelter

Morse code

Morse code is a telegraphic system of signalling in which letters and numbers are represented by dots and dashes. The code is named after its inventor, the American artist and inventor Samuel Finley Breese Morse (1791–1872).

Morse was originally an artist: he exhibited paintings at the Royal Academy in London and enjoyed a good reputation as a portrait painter. He founded and became the first president of the National Academy of Design in New York in 1826, and then was appointed professor of painting and sculpture at New York University.

Morse's interests gradually turned to electric telegraphy. His work was only very slowly recognised, but following financial backing from Congress, the first line, between Washington and Baltimore, was built (1843–4). The words 'What hath God wrought?' constituted the first communication in Morse code sent on 24 May 1844. Following a series of legal battles, Morse patented his system in 1854, and the Morse code is still in use today.

mosaic

A mosaic is a decorative design or picture that is made by inlaying different coloured pieces of material, especially glass or stone. The word mosaic comes via French and Italian from the Medieval Latin *mosaicus*, which in turn is derived from Greek *Mousa*, a Muse. In Greek mythology, the Muses were nine sister goddesses who were patrons of the arts and sciences. The English words museum and music also derive from the same Greek word for a Muse.

Moses basket

A portable shallow wickerwork cradle for a baby is sometimes known as a Moses basket. This expression alludes to the papyrus cradle in which the infant Moses was hidden among the reeds by the River Nile (Exodus 2:3).

Mother Carey's chickens

Mother Carey's chickens are storm petrels – small sea-birds with dark plumage and paler underparts. It is not known who the original Mother Carey was; it is possible that the expression is a corruption of the Latin *Mater Cara* (Beloved Mother), a name for the Virgin Mary, considered to be the protector of sailors. An alternative suggestion is that the expression is an alteration of a nautical Spanish or Italian name.

Mother Goose

A Mother Goose rhyme is a nursery rhyme. The name derives from the title of the collection of fairytales by the French writer Charles Perrault (1628–1703), *Contes de ma Mère L'Oye*, published in 1697, and translated into English as *Tales of Mother Goose* (1729)

Mrs Grundy

A Mrs Grundy is a narrow-minded person noted for prudish conventionality in personal behaviour. The name comes from a character in the play *Speed the Plough* (1798) by the English dramatist Thomas Morton (*c.*1764–1838). From the name Mrs Grundy the word grundyism is derived, referring to a disapproving or censorious, prudish attitude.

Mrs Mop

Mrs Mop is an informal expression for a lady who cleans a house or office. The name, often used in a facetious or derogatory way, derives from the character (Mrs Mopp) in the BBC radio programme ITMA broadcast during the years of the Second World War. Mrs Mopp was a

Cockney charlady who first featured in the radio show on 10 October 1940. Her original question was, 'Can I do for you now, sir?' This was later shortened, by omitting the 'for', to the expression that has become a familiar catch-phrase, 'Can I do you now, sir?'

muggins

The word muggins is sometimes used in informal English to refer to someone when he or she has been foolish. Often the person referred to is oneself: 'I'm sorry but muggins here has forgotten to bring the tickets!' The expression probably derives from the surname Muggins, and is influenced by mug, in the sense of a fool or someone who can be deceived easily, and juggins, an old-fashioned informal word for a simple person.

Murphy's Law

'If anything can go wrong, it will' – this is the pithy wisdom of Murphy's (or Sod's) Law. Other humorous rules of thumb that go under the name of Murphy's Law include: 'Nothing is as easy as it looks,' and, 'Everything takes longer than you think it will.' It is not certain who the original Murphy was; quotations of the 'law' in print date back to the 1950s.

museum; music see mosaic

myrmidon

Myrmidons are loyal followers, especially those who carry out orders without questioning. The word derives from the Myrmidons, the people of Greek legend from Thessaly. It is said that Zeus made the Myrmidons from a race of ants (Greek *murmex*, an ant). They were well known for their loyal devotion to Achilles in the Trojan War.

N

namby-pamby

Someone or something that is described as namby-pamby is thought of as being very sentimental in an insipid manner. The word was originally a nickname for the English poet Ambrose Philips (1674–1749). His verses about children (such as 'Dimply damsel, sweetly smiling' and 'Timely blossom, infant fair, Fondling of a happy pair') were mocked by writers such as Pope and Carey for their weak sentimentality. It was Henry Carey (c.1687–1743) who is credited with the coining of the word namby-pamby: amby comes from the poet's first name and the alliterative p from his surname.

nancy

The use of the word nancy for an effeminate boy or man or a homosexual dates back to the early twentieth century. The word comes from the girl's name Nancy, originally a diminutive of the name Ann, derived from a Hebrew word meaning grace. A nanny goat, a female goat, comes from Nancy. A billy goat, a male goat, takes the name Billy, a nickname for William.

nap; napoleon; Napoleonic

Nap is a card game that is similar to whist in which the number of tricks that a player expects to win is declared. The longer version of the name of the card game is napoleon, which reveals the word's origin: the French Emperor Napoleon Bonaparte (1769–1821). It is, however, uncertain why the game is named after him.

The adjective Napoleonic is sometimes used with allusion to the Emperor's masterly tactics or the vastness of his ambitions.

Napierian

The mathematical functions known as logarithms, used in calculations of multiplication and division, were invented by the Scottish mathematician John Napier (1550–1647). He published his table of logarithms in 1614; these came to be known as Napierian or natural logarithms. A modified version of these mathematical functions (common logarithms) came into use later.

Napier also devised a simple calculating machine that consisted of a series of graduated rods known as Napier's bones.

narcissism

Extreme interest in or love for oneself is known as narcissism. This word comes from Narcissus, the beautiful young man in Greek mythology who, after spurning all offers of love, including that of the nymph Echo, was punished by falling in love with his own reflection in the waters of a fountain, thinking that it was a nymph. His attempts to approach the beautiful object were to no avail, however. He was driven to despair and pined away, finally being transformed into the flower that bears his name.

nebuchadnezzar see jeroboam

negus

A negus is a drink of wine (usually port or sherry), hot water, lemon juice, sugar and nutmeg. It is named after the English soldier and politician in the reign of Queen Anne, Colonel Francis Negus (*d.*1732), who is reputed to have invented it.

The Dictionary of National Biography records that on a certain occasion, Negus averted a fracas between Whigs and Tories 'by recommending the dilution of the wine with hot water and sugar. Attention was diverted from the point of issue to a discussion of the merits of wine and water, which ended in the compound being nicknamed "Negus".'

nemesis

Nemesis means vengeance or something that is thought to be or to bring retribution. The word derives from Nemesis, the Greek mythological goddess of retribution. Nemesis personified the gods' resentment at, and just punishment of, human arrogance, pride and insolence. According to the early Greek poet Hesiod, Nemesis was a child of Night.

nestor

A nestor is a wise old man or a sage. Nestor was the king of Pylos in Greek legend. The *Iliad* describes him as being the oldest – he was about seventy – and most experienced of the Greek commanders in the Trojan War, who advised moderation to the quarrelling Greek leaders.

He was well known for his wise advice and the narration of his deeds in earlier days, in spite of his wordiness.

newton

Newton, the metric unit of force, comes from the name of the British physicist and mathematician Sir Isaac Newton (1642–1727), one of the world's greatest scientists. Newton is particularly noted for his law of gravitation – said, as is well known, to have been inspired by the falling of an apple on his head – his laws of motion and his studies of calculus and the theory of light.

Newton was also a member of parliament (1689–90), and master of the mint from 1699 to 1727, during which time he undertook a reform of the coinage. From 1703 he was president of the Royal Society and he was knighted in 1705. His last words are said to have been: 'I don't know what I may seem to the world. But as to myself I seem to have been only like a boy playing on the seashore and diverting myself in now and then finding a smoother pebble or prettier shell than ordinary, whilst the great ocean of truth lay all undiscovered before me.'

nicotine

Nicotine, the chemical compound found in tobacco, comes from the name of the French diplomat Jean Nicot (1530–1600). Nicot was ambassador in Lisbon at the time that Portuguese explorers were bringing back seeds of tobacco from the newly discovered continent of America. In 1560, Nicot was given a plant from Florida, which he grew, sending tobacco seeds to the French nobility. When Nicot returned to France in 1561, he took a cargo load of tobacco with him. The powder quickly became so well known that the tobacco plant itself was named after Nicot: *Herba nicotiana*. It was in the early years of the nineteenth century that the liquid nicotine was isolated and named in Nicot's honour.

Nimrod

The name Nimrod is sometimes used to describe a great, skilful hunter. Use of this word derives from the biblical Nimrod, the son of Cush, a warrior or hero of Babylon. Genesis 10:9 describes him as 'a mighty hunter before the Lord'.

Nimrod is credited with the founding of the cities of Ninevah and Calah (modern Nimrud) in Assyria.

Nissen hut

A Nissen hut is a prefabricated military shelter that has a semicircular arched roof of corrugated iron sheeting and a cement floor. The hut was named after its inventor, the British mining engineer Lieutenant Colonel Peter Norman Nissen (1871–1930) and was used in both World Wars.

The American equivalent is the Quonset hut, given its trademark name after Quonset Point, Rhode Island, where the huts were first made.

Nobel prize; nobelium

The Swedish chemist, manufacturer and philanthropist Alfred Bernhard Nobel (1833–96) is noted for his invention of dynamite (1866). A pacifist, Nobel believed that his explosives would be the foundation of a country's defence system and, acting as a deterrent towards belligerent countries, would bring about peace.

Nobel amassed a great fortune from the manufacture and sale of explosives and also from his exploitation of oil interests. His great wealth went towards the funding of the Nobel prizes – prizes awarded annually for outstanding contributions to the service of humanity in the fields of physics, chemistry, medicine, literature and peace. The first of these annual awards was given in 1901; in 1969 a prize for economics was added.

The artificially produced element nobelium, discovered in 1957, is also named after Nobel.

nosey parker

A nosey (or nosy) parker is someone who pries very inquisitively into other people's affairs. It is said that the origin of the expression lies in the way of life of the Anglican churchman Matthew Parker (1504–75)

Having moderate Protestant views, Parker was forced to flee to Germany during the reign of Queen Mary. Later, he was appointed Archbishop of Canterbury (1559–75) and participated in the issue of the Thirty-nine Articles. He also directed the compilation of a new version of the Bible, the Bishops' Bible (published 1568), essentially a revision of the Great Bible.

Various sources point to different aspects of Parker's life in attributing the origin of the expression nosey parker to him; some note his over-long nose while others describe his intense curiosity about other people's affairs.

O

obsidian

Obsidian is a dark, glassy, volcanic rock that is formed by the fast cooling of molten lava. It has sharp edges and was originally used for weapons. The word obsidian is said to have come from a wrong manuscript reading of Latin *obsianus lapis*, stone of obsius, a 'd' being incorrectly inserted in the spelling. According to Pliny the Elder in his *Natural History*, Obsius was the first person to discover the rock, in Ethiopia.

Ockham's razor

The philosophical principle known as Ockham's (or Occam's) razor is usually formulated as, 'Entities are not to be multiplied unnecessarily.' This means that an explanation should contain the simplest elements that are necessary, with as little reference as possible to unknown or assumed matters. This statement is attributed to the English philosopher and Franciscan William of Ockham (*c.*1285–1349), but these actual words have not been found in his writings.

Ockham was a pupil of Duns Scotus (see **dunce**), but later became his rival. He is known for his nominalist views, holding that general (or universal) terms have no real existence that is independent from the individual things denoted by the terms. The expression Ockham's Razor is therefore to be seen as an attack on the proposed existence of universals by the realists.

odyssey

An odyssey is a long quest or wandering that is full of adventures. The word comes from the *Odyssey*, the ancient Greek epic poem by Homer that describes the many adventures of the Greek king and hero Odysseus (Latin name, Ulysses) on his journey home from the Trojan War.

Oedipus complex

An Oedipus complex is the unconscious sexual attraction of a child (especially a boy) to the parent of the opposite sex, while having jealous, aggressive feelings towards the parent of the same sex.

The expression derives from Oedipus, the character in Greek mythology, who is the son of Laius and Jocasta, the king and queen of Thebes. When an oracle informed Laius that he was to perish at the hands of his son, he ordered his son to be destroyed, but Oedipus was rescued by a shepherd. Later, unaware of the identity of his parents, Oedipus killed his father, subsequently marrying his mother and having four children by her.

The expression is most commonly used to refer to the attraction of a male child to his mother. In cases when a female child is attracted to her father and shows hostility to her mother, the term Electra complex is more commonly used. In Greek mythology, Electra was the daughter of Agamemnon and Clytemnestra. She persuaded her brother Orestes to avenge their father's murder by killing her mother Clytemnestra and her lover, Aegisthus.

oersted

The oersted is the unit of magnetic field strength in the centimetre–gram–second system of measurement. The unit honours the Danish physicist Hans Christian Oersted (1777–1851) who was a professor at Copenhagen University. Oersted discovered the magnetic effect of an electric current in 1819, thus founding the science of electromagnetism.

ohm

The ohm, the metric unit of electrical resistance, is named after the German physicist Georg Simon Ohm (1787–1854). In 1827 he discovered that the electric current that passes through a conductor is directly proportional to the potential difference between its ends; this formulation became known as Ohm's law.

After gaining a doctorate in physics, Ohm prepared to teach but failed to find sufficient financial support. It is said that following the publication of his first book – which included discussion of what is now known as Ohm's law – he sent copies to several of the ruling European monarchs. It was the king of Prussia who decided to give him financial backing. In 1841 he was awarded the Copley Medal of the British Royal Society, and at the International Electrical Congress of 1893 it was decided to honour Ohm by naming the unit of electrical resistance after him. See also **Siemens**.

old Adam see Adam's apple

Old Bill

Old Bill, the slang expression for a policeman or the police, probably comes from the name of a character in cartoons current at the time of the First World War. In the cartoons by the Indian-born British cartoonist and author Charles Bruce Bairnsfather (1888–1959), Old Bill was the name of a grousing old soldier with a large moustache. One particular cartoon depicts two British infantrymen Bert and Bill with water up to their knees in a shellhole. To Bert's complaint about the inconvenience of their situation, Old Bill answers, 'If you know of a better 'ole, go to it.' During the Second World War, Bairnsfather became an official war cartoonist.

Old Nick

There are several different theories of the origin of the expression Old Nick, the informal or jocular name for the devil. Some suggest that Nick, being the nickname for Nicholas, derives from the name of St Nicholas, the fourth-century bishop of Asia Minor. The patron saint of Russia, sailors and children, he is said to have brought gifts of gold to three poor girls for their dowries. Those who support this view however fail to show the link between the good-natured saint and the 'prince of evil'.

Others propose that Nick refers to the Florentine statesman and philosopher Niccolò Machiavelli (1469–1527). His supposed political unscrupulousness is said to have been the origin of the satanic reference to Old Nick. Still others point to non-eponymous sources, such as a shortening of the German *nickel*, meaning goblin.

onanism

Onanism is used to refer to two sexual practices: coitus interruptus and masturbation. The word derives from the biblical character Onan who 'spilled his seed on the ground' (Genesis 38:9), though it seems that the biblical passage describes coitus interruptus rather than masturbation. When Onan's elder brother, Er, died, Judah commanded Onan to take his brother's wife, Tamar, under the custom of levirate law which said that if a married man died without a child, his brother was expected to take his wife. Onan, however, was not willing to follow this practice and did not fully consummate the union.

Orangeman

An Orangeman is a member of a society (the Orange Order) originally established in Ireland in 1795 to uphold the Protestant religion and defend the British monarch. The word Orangeman derives from the Protestant King William III of England (1650–1702), known as William of Orange. At the Battle of the Boyne, north of Dublin (July 1690), William defeated the Roman Catholic King James II. On 12 July, Protestants in Northern Ireland still celebrate the anniversary of this battle.

orrery

An orrery is a device that shows the relative positions and movements of planets, stars and other heavenly bodies round the sun. The first orrery was invented by the mathematician George Graham (1673–1751) in about the year 1700. Graham sent the device to an instrument maker, John Rowley, who built a copy of such an apparatus, presenting it to his patron, Charles Boyle, the 4th Earl of Orrery (1676–1731), and naming the device in his honour.

Orwellian

The adjective Orwellian is used to describe aspects of life that are thought to be typical of the writings of the English novelist George Orwell (real name, Eric Arthur Blair; 1903–50). The adjective is most commonly used with reference to the nightmarish way of life that is experienced in a totalitarian state – for example, 'an Orwellian vision of total uniformity' – particularly as described in Orwell's novel *Nineteen Eighty-Four* (published 1949), in which life is controlled by the ever-present Big Brother, the head of the Party.

Oscar

An Oscar is one of several gold statuettes awarded annually by the Academy of Motion Picture Arts and Sciences in the USA for outstanding achievements in the cinema.

The idea for the presentation of trophies came in 1927; the first were awarded in 1929; but they were not called Oscars until 1931, when, so the story goes, the Academy's librarian, Margaret Herrick, is alleged to have remarked that the statuettes reminded her of her Uncle Oscar. It is said that a newspaper reporter happened to be listening and he passed on the news to his readers that 'Employees of the Academy have affectionately dubbed their famous statuette "Oscar".' It seems that Herrick's uncle was Oscar Pierce, a wheat and fruit grower formerly of Texas, who later lived in California.

Otto engine

The German engineer Nikolaus August Otto (1832–91) devised in 1876 the four-stroke petrol engine, the Otto engine, which represented the first practical internal-combustion engine. In Otto's engine, with the induction, compression, power and exhaust strokes, gas was used as a fuel. Subsequently, oil was used and the Otto engine became the source of power for motor cars. A variation of the Otto engine is the Diesel engine.

ottoman

An ottoman, a heavily padded box used as a seat and usually without a back, originated in Turkey. The word ottoman comes from the French *ottomane*, which in turn comes via Arabic from the Turkish *Othman*. This was originally the name of the Turkish sultan Osman I (1259–1326) who founded the Ottoman Empire, which ruled in Europe, Asia and Africa from the fourteenth to the twentieth centuries.

out-herod Herod

The expression 'to out-herod Herod' means to exceed someone in a particular quality, especially wickedness or cruelty. The Herod referred to is Herod the Great (c.73–4BC), the ruler of Judaea who had all the baby boys of Bethlehem killed (Matthew 2:16). The source of the expression itself is *Hamlet* (Act 3, Scene 2): 'I would have such a fellow whipped for o'erdoing Termagant: it out-herods Herod: pray you, avoid it.'

P

paean; peony

Nowadays, a paean is a piece of music or writing or a film that expresses praise, triumph, joy, etc. Originally, a paean was a hymn to Apollo, the god of healing and physician of the gods in Greek mythology. Apollo bore the title Paion. Songs or hymns were sung to Apollo to ask or give thanks for his healing favours. From this developed the modern sense of the word.

The herb or shrub-known as peony, grown for its large, showy pink, red or white flowers, also comes from Paion: the plants were once widely used in medicine.

Palladian

The Palladian style of architecture is characterised by symmetry and free-standing classical columns in façades. The style is named after the Italian architect Andrea Palladio (1508–80), who based his work on the architecture and principles of the first-century Roman architect Vitruvius. Originally a stonemason, Palladio began his successful career as an architect by embarking on the remodelling of the basilica in his home town of Vicenza in 1549. He designed many villas, palaces and churches, especially in the vicinity of Vicenza and in Venice. His treatise *Four Books on Architecture* (1570) helped spread his ideas. It was the English architect Inigo Jones (1573–1652) who introduced Palladianism into England.

palladium

A palladium, something that gives protection, was originally the wooden statue of the Greek goddess Pallas Athene that was kept in the citadel of Troy. It was believed that the statue had been sent from heaven by Zeus and that the safety of the city of Troy depended on its protection. The word palladium later came to refer to anything, such as the constitution or the freedom of the press or religion, on which the safety of a country might be thought to depend.

pamphlet

The word for a pamphlet, an unbound printed publication with a paper cover, comes originally from a twelfth-century love poem, 'Pamphilus seu De Amore' (Pamphilus or On Love), Pamphilus being a masculine proper name. This short Latin love poem evidently became so popular that it came to be known simply as Pamphilet, later pamflet, and eventually pamphlet. The sense of a brief treatise on a matter of current interest was added in the sixteenth century.

pander

If you pander to someone's wishes, you do everything that he or she wants. This verb sense comes from the rarer noun form of the word, meaning a go-between in love affairs, a procurer and someone who exploits evil desires. The noun sense derives from the character Pandarus, who takes a role devised by the Italian Giovanni Boccaccio in his poem *Filostrato*, and who features in a number of romances, particularly Chaucer's *Troilus and Criseyde* and Shakespeare's *Troilus and Cressida*. Pandarus is the intermediary between the two lovers, procuring Cressida for Troilus.

The Pandarus of Greek legend is a Trojan archer who shot the Greek commander Menelaus with an arrow and was killed by Diomedes in the battle that followed.

Pandora's box

A Pandora's box is a source of great troubles; if it is opened, then difficulties that were previously unknown or under control are unleashed. The expression derives from the story in Greek mythology of Pandora, the first woman. Pandora ('all gifts') was given a box into which all the powers that would eventually bring about the downfall of mankind had been put; the box was to be given to the man that Pandora married. There are several different conclusions to the story. According to one version, her husband Epimetheus opened the box against her advice, to release all the misfortunes that have beset the human race. Another version has Pandora herself opening the box out of curiosity and letting out all the ills that afflict mankind, leaving only hope inside.

panic

Panic, the state of sudden overwhelming terror or fright, derives ultimately from Pan, the name of the Greek god of woods, shepherds and flocks. He is usually depicted as having a human body and the ears, horns and legs of a goat. Pan was, it seems, known for the mischievous trick he would play of suddenly springing out from the undergrowth to inspire panic in those walking by. The god was also considered the source of the weird noises that could be heard in the forests at night, filling lost wanderers with panic.

pantaloon; pants

The fourth-century Venetian physician and saint San Pantaleone is remembered for a number of words that do not seem compatible with the saint's mild personality. There was the stock character in the Italian *commedia dell'arte*, the lecherous old man known as pantaloon, who wore spectacles, slippers and tight breeches. In time, 'pantaloons' came to describe trousers; later the word was shortened to 'pants', meaning in American English, trousers, and in British English, underpants.

Pap test (or smear)

A Pap test is an examination for the early detection of cancer in which cells in a smear of bodily secretions, especially from the uterus or vagina, are examined. The test takes its name from the Greek-born American anatomist George Nicholas Papanicolaou (1883–1962), who devised it.

Pareto principle

Sometimes referred to as the 80:20 rule, the Pareto principle (or law) is seen, for example, in company sales: 80 per cent of the sales may come from 20 per cent of the customers. The expression derives from the name of the Italian economist and sociologist Vilfredo Frederico Pareto (1848–1923).

Pareto worked as director of Italian railways and superintendent of mines before being appointed professor of economics in 1892. His studies led him to analyse consumer demand and to formulate a law of the distribution of income within a society.

Pareto's law has since come to be formulated as the 80:20 rule and to apply to spheres outside economics and business; for example, one could speak of taking 80 per cent of the time to teach 20 per cent of the students.

Parkinson's disease

Parkinson's disease is a disease that is marked by a tremor of the limbs, weakness of the muscles and a peculiar gait. Also known as *paralysis agitans*, the disease is named after the British physician, James Parkinson (1755–1824), who first described it in 1817.

Parkinson's law

The observation in office organisation known as Parkinson's law states that: 'Work expands so as to fill the time available for its completion.' This was first formulated in the 1950s by the English historian and author Cyril Northcote Parkinson (*b.*1909). In Parkinson's Law (published 1957), Parkinson also noted that: 'Subordinates multiply at a fixed rate regardless of the amount of work produced,' and that according to the law of triviality: 'The time spent on any item on the agenda will be in inverse proportion to the sum involved.'

Pascal

The French mathematician and philosopher Blaise Pascal (1623–62) had an early interest in mathematics that led to his formulation of what has become known as Pascal's triangle, used in probability theory. He later made discoveries in fluid mechanics and also invented a hydraulic press and a calculating machine. Coming under Jansenist influence, he entered the convent at Port Royal in 1655. His most well-known writings are *Lettres provinciales* (1656–7), a defence of Jansenism, and *Pensées sur la religion* (1670), fragments of a defence of Christianity. Pascal is also remembered by having the pascal, the metric unit of pressure, and Pascal, the high-level computer programming language, named in his honour.

pasteurise

When milk or another drink or a food is pasteurised, bacteria in it are destroyed by a special heating process. The word pasteurise derives from the name of the French chemist and bacteriologist Louis Pasteur (1822–95).

The son of a tanner, Pasteur studied chemistry, but was graded as only a mediocre student. He became a teacher and lecturer, and in 1854 was appointed dean of the faculty of science at Lille University. Pasteur first developed the process now known as pasteurisation on wine and beer. He found that certain micro-organisms caused wine to ferment very quickly and that the fermentation could be prevented if the wine was subjected to heat and then cooled rapidly.

Pasteur also devised methods of immunisation (pasteurism or Pasteur treatment) against anthrax and rabies.

Paul Jones

The dance known as the Paul Jones, in which couples change their partners, is probably named after the American naval commander John

Paul Jones (original name John Paul; 1747–92).

Born in Scotland, Jones went to America where he was commissioned into the American navy and was involved in several naval exploits against the British in the American War of Independence. In 1779, commanding the ship the *Bon Homme Richard*, Jones defeated the British frigate *Serapis* in a long battle. Refusing to surrender, even though his ship was on the verge of sinking, Jones is said to have uttered to the British captain Richard Pearson, 'I have not yet begun to fight.'

After the War of Independence, Jones served in the navies of Russia and France. The dance was probably named after Paul Jones in honour of his exploits.

Paul Pry

A Paul Pry, someone who is inquisitive and interfering, comes from the character of that name in the farce *Paul Pry* (published 1825) by the English dramatist John Poole (*c.*1786–1872). Brewer describes the figure Paul Pry as 'an idle, meddlesome fellow, who has no occupation of his own, and is always interfering with other folk's business.' He constantly enters with the apology, 'I hope I don't intrude.'

pavlova

The Russian ballerina Anna Pavlova (1885–1931) is remembered for her popularising of ballet throughout the world. At the age of twenty-one she was the prima ballerina at the Russian Imperial Ballet and later she joined Diaghilev's Ballet Russe for a short time. From 1914, Pavlova began to tour throughout the world with her own company, and she is particularly remembered for her roles in *Giselle* and *The Dying Swan*. To celebrate her ballet performances in Australia and New Zealand, chefs in these countries popularised pavlova – a meringue cake topped with cream and fruit.

Pavlovian

The Russian physiologist Ivan Petrovich Pavlov (1849–1936) is remembered for his studies of digestion and conditioned reflexes. In his experiments with dogs Pavlov showed that a reflex response could be evoked by a stimulus that was different from the one that usually produced it. He found that dogs produced saliva in response to the sight of food accompanied by a bell. Eventually they would learn to associate the bell with the appearance of food and would produce saliva in response to hearing the bell alone. The adjective Pavlovian has therefore come to refer to something that is predictable or is evoked automatically as a response to a stimulus (a Pavlovian reaction).

Pavlov later applied his theories to cover other aspects of human and animal behaviour, such as learning. Although he persistently criticised the communist regime, the authorities continued to fund his work, and his studies have influenced the behaviourist school of psychology.

peach melba see melba toast

pecksniffian

The character Seth Pecksniff in the novel *Martin Chuzzlewit* by Charles Dickens (published 1843–4) has given his name to the adjective pecksniffian. In the story, Pecksniff is a smooth-talking hypocritical figure who gives an appearance of kindness and benevolence but is in reality mean, selfish and treacherous.

peeping Tom

A peeping Tom, a voyeur or a man who takes pleasure in secretly looking at women undressing, derives from the name of a legendary English tailor. The traditional story relates how Leofric, the eleventh-century Lord of Coventry, imposed crippling taxes on his people. Leofric's wife, Lady Godiva, pleaded with him to ease the tax burden on the citizens. Eventually he said he would on condition that Lady Godiva rode naked through the streets. Lady Godiva agreed and, having asked the citizens to keep the shutters on their windows closed, she rode naked through the streets on a white horse. Everyone respected her request except for the tailor, Tom, who peeped – only to be struck blind for his brazenness.

Pennsylvania

Pennsylvania, the state in the north-eastern USA, is named not, as is sometimes believed, after William Penn, founder of the original colony, but after his father Sir William Penn (1621–70), an admiral in the British navy. It seems that the younger William Penn asked King Charles II for an area of land in America in settlement of a debt owed by the king to Penn's father. The land was to become a colony for Protestant Quakers who were being persecuted. Penn suggested the name Sylvania and the king, in honour of Penn's father, added Penn to it. The younger Penn tried to get the name changed but to no avail.

peony see paean

Père David's deer see buddleia

Pestalozzi

The emphasis of the Swiss educationalist Johann Heinrich Pestalozzi (1746–1827) on observation in learning has had a profound influence on primary education. Born in Zurich into a wealthy family, Pestalozzi studied the writings of Rousseau and later attempted to establish schools for poor children. In spite of the apparent failure of the schools, his writings, including his book *Wie Gertrud ihre Kinder lehrt* (1801), have affected later educational developments. Pestalozzi International Children's Villages have also been established, for example in Sedlescombe, East Sussex.

Peter Pan

A Peter Pan is a man who never seems to grow up or who is unwilling to give up boyish or immature ways. The name is taken from the character in the play *Peter Pan, or The Boy Who Would Not Grow Up* by the Scottish dramatist and novelist Sir James Matthew Barrie (1860–1937). The play, an immediate success when first performed at the Duke of York's Theatre in London, was developed from fantasy stories Barrie had created for the young sons of friends. Barrie became famous because of his writings, especially *Peter Pan*, and was made a baronet (1913) and awarded the Order of Merit (1922) and several honorary degrees. From 1930 he was chancellor of Edinburgh University.

See also **Wendy house.**

Peter principle

'In a hierarchy, every employee tends to rise to the level of his incompetence.' This humorous semi-scientific statement is known as the Peter principle, after the Canadian educator Dr Laurence J. Peter (*b.*1919) who with Raymond Hull (*b.*1919) wrote the book *The Peter Principle – Why Things Always Go Wrong*, published in 1969.

Peter's pence

Peter's pence was originally an annual tax of one penny formerly levied on all English householders for the maintenance of the Pope. Dating from the ninth century, it was abolished by King Henry VIII in 1534; it is now a voluntary contribution made by Roman Catholics to the Pope. The phrase derives from the tradition that the apostle Peter was the first Pope.

petersham

Petersham, a tough, corded ribbon used, for example, in belts and hatbands takes its name from the English army officer Charles Stanhope, Viscount Petersham, 4th Earl of Harrington (1780–1851).

Viscount Petersham, it seems, was something of a dandy; he designed and popularised a kind of overcoat made of a heavy woollen cloth. The coat cloth and then the ribbon came to be known by his name. It is also said that he invented an original mixture of snuff.

Petrarchan sonnet

The Petrarchan sonnet, also called the Italian sonnet, originated in thirteenth-century Italy and was associated with the Italian poet Petrarch (Italian name, Francesco Petrarca; 1304–74). The fourteen-line poem is divided into two parts: the first eight lines rhyme abbaabba and the remaining six lines rhyme cdecde.

Born the son of a notary in Florence, Petrarch spent most of his life in Provence. He travelled throughout Europe and is particularly noted for *Canzoniere*, a series of love poems addressed to Laura, and also his humanist and spiritual writings. In 1341 he was crowned poet laureate in Rome.

See also **Shakespearean**.

philippic

Philippic, meaning bitter and biting denunciation, derives from the name of the speeches in defence of Athenian liberty by the Athenian orator and statesman *Demosthenes* (384–322BC) against King Philip II of Macedon (382–336BC). In the three orations, known as the *Philippics* ('speeches relating to Philip'; 351, 344, 341BC), Demosthenes attacked Philip's ambitions to make Athens part of his kingdom, and attempted to arouse the citizens against their cruel ruler. Philip, however, defeated Athens at the Battle of Chaeronea in 338, thus ending the self-government of the Greek city states and making his conquests of Greece complete. Philip was, however, assassinated two years later.

Later, Cicero's eloquent speeches against Mark Antony were referred to as philippics, and now philippic refers to passionate speech against anyone.

Pickwickian

The adjective Pickwickian is used in allusion to the character Mr Pickwick in the novel *Pickwick Papers* by Charles Dickens (first published 1836–7). In particular, Pickwickian is used to mean kind and generous in a simple manner and, also, to describe a word or expression that is not used in its ordinary or literal sense, from the scene in the opening chapter in which Mr Pickwick and Mr Blotton appear to insult each other, whereas in reality they respected each other greatly.

pinchbeck

Pinchbeck, was originally an alloy of copper and zinc – five parts copper and one part zinc – used to imitate gold in cheap jewellery. The word derives from the name of the English watchmaker Christopher Pinchbeck (*c.*1670–1732). Pinchbeck used the alloy in the manufacture of watches and jewellery. Later, the word came to be used for anything counterfeit or shoddy, probably partly because the 'pinch' in the name has associations with cheapness.

Plantin see Baskerville

platonic

A platonic relationship is a close relationship between a man and a woman that does not involve sex. Such platonic love – spiritual or intellectual in contrast to physical – was first described by the Greek philosopher Plato (*c.*427–347BC), in his *Symposium*, originally with reference to the pure love of Socrates towards young men.

Born into a wealthy Athenian family, Plato was known as a poet and athlete before becoming a follower of Socrates. Following Socrates' death, Plato travelled widely before returning to Athens to found his Academy in about 385BC, teaching philosophy, mathematics and government. Many of his writings survive, in which ethical and philosophical matters are discussed.

Plimsoll line; plimsoll

The Plimsoll line is a set of markings on the side of a ship that show the various levels that the ship may safely be loaded to. The pattern of lines is named in honour of the English leader of shipping reform Samuel Plimsoll (1824–98).

Originally the manager of a brewery, then a coal dealer, Plimsoll was elected MP for Derby in 1868. He called the overloaded ships of his day coffin-ships and determined to make maritime transport safer. His book *Our Seamen* was published in 1872 and, following his insistent efforts, a bill providing for rigorous inspection of ships became law in 1876. The Plimsoll line was adopted in that same year to mark the limit to which a ship may be loaded.

Plimsoll is also honoured in the light rubber-soled canvas shoe that bears his name, since the top edge of the rubber was thought to resemble a Plimsoll line.

poinsettia

The traditional Christmas evergreen plant known as a poinsettia takes its name from the American diplomat Noel Roberts Poinsett (1779–1851). Born in Charleston, South Carolina, Poinsett was educated in Europe. He left his medical and legal studies, however, preferring to travel. During the course of his wanderings he is said to have met several political leaders including Napoleon, Metternich and the Tsar of Russia. When Poinsett returned to the United States, he was sent by President Madison to be consul to South America, where, however, he supported the Chilean revolutionaries.

Following several years' service as a congressman, he was appointed as American minister to Mexico (1825). He is said to have sent back to the United States specimens of the fiery plant now named after him, although it seems that it had already been introduced into the country. Because Poinsett was a well-known public figure at that time, the plant was named in his honour.

Poinsett later became secretary of war in the cabinet of Van Buren and a Unionist leader in the Civil War.

Pollyanna

A person who is constantly optimistic is sometimes described as a Pollyanna. The name was originally that of the heroine in the novel *Pollyanna* (published in 1913) by the American writer Eleanor Porter (1868–1920).

Pollyanna is an eleven-year-old orphan who is sent to her very strait-laced Aunt Polly – who only takes her in as it is her duty. When she was younger, to cope with the very poor life they lived as a missionary family, her father taught Pollyanna the 'glad game' – always to look for something to be glad about in whatever unhappy circumstances one finds oneself. The result is that she is always a happy, smiling child.

Pollyanna passes on the 'glad game' to every needy person she meets in the village of Beldingsville with some quite startling results. A Pollyanna is therefore someone who can find something good in even the blackest circumstances.

pompadour

The word pompadour was used originally for a woman's hairstyle that was fashionable in the early eighteenth century, in which the hair was raised back, usually over a pad, into loose rolls round the face. A similar later style, in which the hair is combed straight up from the forehead, came to be worn by men and women. The name of the hairstyle derives from the Marquise de Pompadour, the title of Jeanne Antoinette Poisson (1721–64), mistress of Louis XV of France. From 1745 until her death, Mme de Pompadour exerted great influence on political matters. She was to a great extent responsible for the French defeats in the Seven Years' War (1756–63). Mme de Pompadour also served as patron to scholars such as Voltaire and Diderot.

The French court was renowned for its wasteful extravagance at that time, and after being reproved for such excesses, Mme de Pompadour is said to have replied with the now famous words, '*Après nous le déluge*' – literally, 'After us the flood.'

praline

A praline, a confection of nuts – usually almonds – and sugar, is named after César de Choiseul, Count Plessis-Praslin (1598–1675). Count Plessis-Praslin was a French field marshal, and it seems that it was his chef who first concocted the confection. Later, the count served as minister of state under Louis XIV. Originally known as a praslin, in time its spelling became praline.

Pre-Raphaelite

A Pre-Raphaelite is the term used for a member of a particular artistic group known as the Pre-Raphaelite Brotherhood (PRB), a group of artists, including Dante Gabriel Rossetti, John Everett Millais, and William Holman Hunt, founded in 1848. This group aimed to emulate the earlier Italian schools, in reaction to the contemporary taste for the Italian painter Raphael (original name Raffaello Santi; 1483–1520). The Pre-Raphaelite Brotherhood sought to oppose what they saw as the superficial conventionalism of much painting at that time by returning to a faithfulness to nature. Their works depict moral or religious scenes, and are marked by fine detail and vivid colours.

Prince Albert

A Prince Albert is a man's long double-breasted frock coat. It is named after Prince Albert Edward, later King Edward VII of England (1841–1910). He is said to have worn the formal coat at afternoon social functions and so established it as a fashionable garment.

Procrustean

Procrustes was a robber in Greek mythology who forced his victims to lie on a bed. If they were too long, he would lop off their limbs; if they were too short, he would stretch their bodies to the necessary length until they fitted the bed. The word *prokroustes* literally means 'the stretcher', and the adjective Procrustean has come to describe something designed to enforce or produce conformity to a particular teaching by violent or arbitrary methods. Similarly, a Procrustean bed (or a bed of Procrustes) has come to refer to a predetermined system or standard to which a person or thing is forced to conform exactly.

Promethean

The adjective Promethean is used to describe something that is exceptionally creative or original. The word derives from Prometheus, a demigod in Greek mythology who is known for his bold, skilful acts: he made mankind out of clay, stole fire from Olympus and gave it to man and taught man many arts and sciences. Zeus punished him by chaining him to a rock in the Caucasus mountains where during the day an eagle fed on his liver only for it to grow again each night. Eventually Prometheus was freed from this torture by Hercules.

protean

Proteus was the sea-god of Greek mythology who tended the flocks of Poseidon. He was noted for his ability to take on different shapes at will. The adjective protean, deriving from his name, has therefore come to mean 'variable or diverse' or 'capable of assuming different shapes, sizes, or roles', as in a protean personality.

Pulitzer prize

The Pulitzer prizes are prizes awarded annually for outstanding achievements in journalism, literature and music. The awards take their name from the Hungarian born US newspaper publisher Joseph Pulitzer (1847–1911). Persuaded to emigrate in 1864, Pulitzer served for a year in the Union army before settling in St Louis, where he set up the *Post-Dispatch* newspaper in 1878. He later moved to New York where he founded the *World* (1883). The prizes were established by Pulitzer's will, in which he provided a fund to Columbia University for the setting up and endowment of a school of journalism. The prizes have been awarded since 1917; since 1943 a prize for musical composition has also been presented.

Pullman

A Pullman, the luxurious railway passenger coach, is named after the American inventor George Mortimer Pullman (1831–97). Originally a cabinet-maker, Pullman began improving railway coach accommodation in the 1850s and, with his colleague Ben Field, built the first sleeping car, the *Pioneer*, in 1864. This cost $20,000 and had chandeliers, walnut woodwork, painted ceilings, a heavy-pile carpet and folding upper berths for the sleeping accommodation.

It was the assassination of President Lincoln in 1865 that brought the *Pioneer* and Pullman – to fame. Every area brought out its finest railway transport and so the *Pioneer* was brought into service to form part of the presidential funeral train. Bridges were raised and platforms narrowed to accommodate the *Pioneer*; it proved so popular that other railway companies wanted similar carriages. Pullman then formed a company, the Pullman Palace Car Company, to manufacture sleeping and dining cars, the profits from which made him a multi-millionaire.

Next, Pullman had a model town built in Chicago, but he was discredited when the courts found that the rents he was charging were much higher than those for the houses in the surrounding area.

Towards the end of his life Pullman suffered a further blow – the railway workers' strike and riots of 1893–4 in which at least twelve people died. His name is, however, still remembered for the special trains that provide comfortable and luxurious accommodation.

Pyrrhic victory; Cadmean victory

A Pyrrhic victory is a victory won at such a great cost that it amounts to no victory at all. It is named after Pyrrhus, king of Epirus (312–272BC), who won several victories against Rome, particularly that of Asculum (279BC) in which he lost very many of his men. After this battle he is said to have uttered, 'One more such victory and we are undone!'

A Pyrrhic victory is also sometimes known as a Cadmean victory. In Greek mythology Prince Cadmus killed a dragon and planted its teeth, from which a race of armed warriors sprang up. Cadmus set the warriors fighting by throwing a stone among them, and only five escaped death. A Cadmean victory thus refers to a victory that is secured at an almost ruinous cost, the allusion being to the victory of the five survivors in the conflict with the multitude of other warriors.

It is interesting to note that this story also gave rise to the expression sow the dragon's teeth. One can take a course of action that is intended to be peaceful, such as disposing of the dragon's teeth by burying them, but in reality the course of action leads to dissension or warfare.

Pythagoras's theorem

Pythagoras's theorem states that in a right-angled triangle the square on the hypotenuse is equal to the sum of the squares on the other two sides. The theory is named after the sixth-century-BC Greek philosopher and mathematician Pythagoras, whose work had a significant effect on the development of mathematics, music and astronomy. It seems, however, that the ancient Egyptian surveyors, and also the Babylonians at least a hundred years before Pythagoras, were already familiar with such triangles, but it was Pythagoras or one of his followers who developed the actual theorem that has been named after him.

python

The large non-venomous snake that winds itself around its prey and then crushes it by constriction is known as a python. The word derives from the name of the monstrous serpent Python of Greek mythology. This dragon arose from the mud after the flood that Deucalion survived and guarded Delphi. It was after killing Python that Apollo set up his oracle at Delphi.

quassia

Quassia is used to refer to the genus of tropical trees and shrubs that have a bitter bark and wood, and also the bitter drug obtained from this bark and wood. The drug was formerly used as a tonic and vermifuge and is now used as an insecticide. The name *quassia* honours an eighteenth-century Surinam negro slave, Graman Quassi, who in about 1730 discovered the medicinal value of the tree.

Queen Anne is dead; Queen Anne

'Queen Anne is dead' is a saying used as a reply to mean, 'Your news is stale; everyone knows this.' Born in 1665, Queen Anne was queen of England and Scotland (known as Great Britain from 1707) and Ireland (1702–14). The last of the Stuart monarchs, she died in 1714; her death led to the coming of the Hanoverians. The expression 'Queen Anne is dead' is first recorded in a ballad of 1722, eight years after her death. Obviously everyone knew of the monarch's passing; to tell stale news needed to be met with such a slighting rejoinder.

Queen Anne is the term used to describe a style of furniture popular in the eighteenth century, marked by plain curves, walnut veneer and cabriole-legged chairs, and also a style of early-eighteenth-century architecture marked by plain red brickwork in a restrained classical form.

Queensberry rules

The Queensberry rules, representing the basis of modern boxing, were written under the sponsorship of John Sholto Douglas, the 8th Marquess of Queensberry (1844–1900), and were published in 1867. The Queensberry rules established the use of padded gloves – up to that time fighting had been with bare fists – rounds of three minutes and limitations on the kinds of blows permitted.

The expression 'Queensberry rules' in also sometimes used to stand for fair play or proper behaviour in sport in general – or elsewhere.

quisling

A quisling is a traitor who collaborates with an invading enemy. The word derives from Vidkun Abraham Quisling (1887–1945), the Norwegian politician who collaborated with the Germans in the Second World War.

Having served as a military attaché in Russia and France, Major Quisling worked for the League of Nations, entering politics as a zealous anti-communist in 1929. A defence minister in the Norwegian government (1931–3), Quisling resigned to form his right-wing National Unity party in 1933, which met with little success, however.

When Hitler invaded Norway in April 1940, Quisling became 'puppet' prime minister, and later minister president. Under his rule, a thousand Jews were sent to concentration camps. He lived in a reinforced forty-six-room villa on an island near Oslo; he was so paranoid that all the food he ate had to be previously sampled by others.

When the Germans surrendered in Norway on 15 May 1945, Quisling was arrested. He was found guilty of war crimes and was shot by a firing squad on 24 October 1945.

Quixotic; Don Quixote

Someone who is carried away by the impractical pursuit of romantic ideals and who has extravagant notions of chivalry is sometimes referred to as quixotic. The word comes from the name of Don Quixote, hero of the novel *Don Quixote de la Mancha* (published in two parts 1605, 1615) by the Spanish novelist Miguel de Cervantes Saavedra (1547–1616). The novel tells how Don Quixote, infatuated with stories of chivalry, feels himself called to roam the world in pursuit of noble adventures.

The expression 'tilt at windmills', to attack an imaginary enemy in the belief that it is real, comes from part 1, chapter 8, of the romance. Don Quixote travels through the countryside attacking windmills, in the belief that they are giants.

Quonset hut see Nissen hut

R

Rabelaisian

Rabelaisian is sometimes used to describe coarse humour or, less commonly, fantastic extravagance or sharp satire. These features are considered characteristics of the works of the French writer François Rabelais (1483–1553).

A Franciscan and then a Benedictine monk, Rabelais left the monastery to become a physician. Renowned for his fine scholarship and satirical wit, he wrote many works, of which the most famous are *Pantagruel* (1532) and *Gargantua* (1534) – the source of the word **gargantuan**.

Rachmanism

The unscrupulous exploitation of tenants by a landlord known as Rachmanism takes its name from Peter (Perec) Rachman (1920–62), a Polish-born British landlord, who indulged in such a practice.

Under the 1957 Rent Act, rents in Britain were kept at an artificially low level compared with the market value of property as long as the property remained in the hands of the tenant. This led to unscrupulous practices by some landlords who harassed tenants in order to evict them. The property could then be sold or relet at an exorbitantly high rent.

Rachman was one such landlord who bought cheaply rented houses in London in the early 1960s and used blackmail, intimidation and physical violence to evict the tenants. He then let the properties out at very high rates to prostitutes, etc., or sold them to businesses, making a great profit.

Rafflesia

The genus of parasitic Asian herbs known as *Raifflesia* is named after the British colonial administrator Sir Thomas Stamford Raffles (1781–1826) who discovered it. After a renowned administrative career in Penang and Java, Raffles acquired Singapore for the East India Company in 1819. The famous Raffles Hotel in Singapore is named after him.

The species *Rafflesia arnoldi* has the largest bloom in the world, measuring up to three feet in diameter and weighing up to 15 pounds. This mottled orange-brown and white flower – also known as stinking-corpse lily – grows on the roots of vines in south-east Asia. Only the bloom of the plant can be seen above the ground. Its growing fungus below the ground smells of rotting meat and attracts carrion flies that act as pollinators.

raglan

A raglan, a loose-fitting coat that has sleeves (raglan sleeves) that extend to the collar without shoulder seams, is named after the British field marshal Fitzroy James Henry Somerset, 1st Baron Raglan (1788-1855). Raglan served in the Napoleonic Wars, and when he was wounded at the Battle of Waterloo and had his arm amputated, he is alleged to have said, 'I say, bring back my arm – the ring my wife gave me is on the finger!'

Raglan later became secretary to the Duke of Wellington (then commander-in-chief of the British forces) and field marshal. Despite his success at the Battle of Inkerman in the Crimean War, his tactics at the Battle of Balaclava were heavily criticised. It was during the Crimean War that Raglan became known for wearing his raglan overcoat.

See also **cardigan**.

raise Cain; the mark of Cain; the curse of Cain

The expression 'to raise Cain' – to behave in a wild, noisy manner; to cause a loud disturbance; to protest angrily – derives from the biblical Cain, the eldest son of Adam and Eve, the brother of Abel and the first murderer in the Bible (Genesis 4:3–12). It seems that in earlier times, Cain was a euphemism for the devil, religious people preferring 'raise Cain' to 'raise the devil'.

Two expressions derive from the judgment of God on Cain after he killed Abel. The 'curse of Cain', the fate of someone who is forced to lead a fugitive life, wandering restlessly from place to place, derives from the punishment mentioned in Genesis 4: 11-12: 'And now art thou cursed from the earth . . . a fugitive and a vagabond shalt thou be in the earth.' The 'mark of Cain' is a stain of a crime on one's reputation, with reference to the protective mark God gave him to prevent him from being killed himself, mentioned in Genesis 4:15: 'And the Lord set a mark upon Cain, lest any finding him should kill him.'

Rastafarian

Haile Selassie (1892–1975) became Emperor of Ethiopia in 1930. His title Ras Tafari (*Ras* meaning 'Lord' and *Tafari*, a family name) was adopted by Black West Indians, who venerated Haile Selassie as God, and wanted deliverance for the Black race and the founding of a homeland in Ethiopia. Rastafarian beliefs were developed by the Jamaican founder of the Back to Africa Movement, Marcus Garvey (1887–1940).

Haile Selassie lived in exile in England from 1936 to 1941 during the Italian occupation of Ethiopia. He was finally deposed in a military rising in 1974.

Réaumur scale

The Réaumur scale is a scale of temperature in which the freezing-point of water is 0° and the boiling-point of water 80°. It is named after the French scientist, Réne Antoine Ferchault de Réaumur (1683–1757) who devised it. A naturalist as well as a physicist, Réaumur studied the chemical processes of animal digestion and also developed a method of tinning iron that was used in French industry.

rehoboam see jeroboam

Reuters

Baron Paul Julius von Reuter (original name Israel Beer Josaphat; 1816–99) founded the first news agency. Born in Germany, Reuter began a continental pigeon post in 1850 to fly stock-market prices between Brussels and Aachen to complete the final part in the growing European telegraph system. In 1851 Reuter moved to London, taking advantage of the opening of the Dover–Calais submarine cable to send stock prices between Paris and London. He then extended his coverage to include general news items to many European newspapers. In 1865 Reuters Telegraph Company was registered; it became a private company, Reuters Ltd, in 1916 and in 1984 it became a public company, Reuters Holdings plc.

rhesus monkey; Rh factor

A rhesus monkey, *Macaca mulatta*, is a south Asian monkey that is widely used in medical research. It seems that the description rhesus was chosen arbitrarily in honour of Rhesus, king of Thrace, in Greek mythology. The Greek hero Odysseus and King Diomedes killed Rhesus and twelve of his men, carrying off his splendid horses, because an oracle had said that if Rhesus's horses had tasted Trojan pasture and drunk of the River Scamander, Troy would not fall.

The Rh (or rhesus) factor in blood is called after the rhesus monkeys in which it was first discovered. The Rh factor is a blood protein that is present in the red cells of most people, those who do have it being classified as Rh-positive and those who do not Rh-negative. It can cause strong reactions in the blood during pregnancy or blood transfusions.

Richard Roe see John Doe

Richter scale

The Richter scale, a scale for expressing the magnitude of earthquakes, is named after the American seismologist Charles Richter (1900–85). Richter devised the scale in 1935 in association with the German Beno Gutenberg (1889–1960), thus it is sometimes called the Gutenberg–Richter scale. The logarithmic scale ranges from 0 to 10; a value of 2 can just be sensed as a tremor, while earthquakes that measure values greater than 6 cause damage to buildings. The strongest earthquake so far recorded measured 8.6 on the Richter scale.

Rip van Winkle

Someone who has outdated views and is completely out of touch with contemporary ideas is sometimes referred to as a Rip van Winkle. The description comes from the character in the story *Rip Van Winkle* (published in 1819) by the American author Washington Irving (1783–1859). In the story, Rip van Winkle falls asleep for twenty years and wakes to find his home in ruins and the world utterly different.

Washington Irving used to write using the pseudonym Knickerbocker: see knickerbockers.

ritzy

The adjective ritzy is used in informal English to mean smart, especially in a showy manner. This usage derives from Ritz hotels, a chain of luxury hotels established by the Swiss hotelier César Ritz (1850–1918).

The original Ritz hotels in Paris (founded 1898) and London (1906) were known for their elegance and luxury. The 1920s saw the growth of 'Plazas and Astorias and Ritzes all over the hinterland' (H. L. Mencken), and also the development of the word ritzy in association with ostentatious smartness. The word ritz also featured in the song by Irving Berlin 'Putting on the Ritz', sung by Fred Astaire.

robin

The British robin, the songbird related to the thrush that has an orange-red breast and brown back, was originally called a robin redbreast. It seems that the name Robin, nickname for Robert, was chosen arbitrarily to stand for this bird. The name is now used for a number of different species of red-breasted birds in different countries.

Roland – a Roland for an Oliver

Roland and Oliver were two of the legendary twelve peers or paladins who attended Charlemagne, king of the Franks (c. AD 742–814). Roland, Charlemagne's nephew, once fought Oliver in a duel that lasted several days. The knights were so evenly matched, each man answering the other's blows in kind, that the duel was declared a draw and the two knights became ardent friends. The expression 'a Roland for an Oliver' thus came to mean an effective retaliation or tit for tat.

Both knights were slain at Roncesvalles in north-east Spain in 778. The early-twelfth-century French epic poem *Chanson de Roland* describes the heroic stand of the knights at this battle.

Rolls-Royce

Rolls-Royce, the trademark for a type of luxurious car of outstanding quality, is also applied to something that is considered to be the foremost of its kind. The car is named after its designers, Charles Stewart Rolls (1877–1910) and Sir Frederick Henry Royce (1836–1933).

Royce originally established an engineering business in Manchester in 1884, where he manufactured electric dynamos and cranes. In 1904 he began to build cars and so impressed Rolls that they formed a partnership, the Rolls-Royce Company, in 1906. Royce was the engineer, while Rolls promoted the cars.

The partnership ended abruptly when Rolls was killed in a flying accident in 1910. Royce was forced, because of poor health, to move to the South of France, where he designed some of their most famous cars and also the aero-engine that was developed into the Merlin engine that was used in Spitfires in the Second World War.

Romeo

A romantic lover is sometimes known as a Romeo, after the hero in Shakespeare's tragedy *Romeo and Juliet*. The two most important families of Verona, the Montagues and the Capulets, were great rivals; Romeo, son of Lord Montague, fell in love with Capulet's daughter,

Juliet. Shakespeare based his play on Arthur Brooke's poem *The Tragicall Historye of Romeus and Juliet* (1562).

röntgen

A röntgen (roentgen), the former unit of dose of ionising radiation, is named after the German physicist Wilhelm Konrad Röntgen (1845–1923). Röntgen was awarded the first Nobel prize for physics in 1901 for the outstanding achievement of the discovery of X-rays (formerly known as roentgen rays). While professor of physics at Würzburg University, Bavaria, Röntgen accidentally discovered the mysterious rays when he was undertaking research into the luminescence of cathode rays in 1895. Because the phenomenon of X-rays was unknown to him, he borrowed the symbol X from algebra to describe them. The discovery that X-rays pass through matter was quickly appreciated by the medical world and they soon became used in medical diagnosis.

Rorschach test

The Rorschach test is a psychological test in which the interpretation by a subject of a series of inkblots reveals aspects of the subject's personality. The test is named after the Swiss psychiatrist Hermann Rorschach (1884–1922), who devised it in 1921.

Roscius; Roscian

Quintus Roscius Gallus (*c.*126–62BC), was a famous Roman actor. A friend of Cicero, he became regarded as the most distinguished Roman comic actor. The name Roscius is thus sometimes applied to an outstanding actor; and a Roscian performance is one that displays great theatrical mastery.

Rubik's cube

Rubik's cube is a puzzle consisting of a cube, each face of which is divided into nine small coloured squares that can rotate around a central square. The aim of the puzzle is to rotate the squares on the cube so that the whole of each face shows one colour only. The total number of positions that can be reached on the Rubik's cube is 43,252,003,274,489,856,000.

Rubik's cube is named after its inventor, the Hungarian designer, sculptor and architect Ernö Rubik (*b.*1944). Originally intended to help Rubik's students understand three-dimensional design, it first became generally known to mathematicians at a Mathematical Congress at Helsinki in 1978. In the following few years it quickly became a craze throughout the world.

Rudbeckia

The *Rudbeckia* genus of flowers has showy flowers with yellow rays and dark-brown to black conical centres. Also called cone-flowers, several of the plants of the genus, particularly *Rudbeckia hirta*, are known as black-eyed Susan.

The name *Rudbeckia* derives from the Swedish botanist Olof Rudbeck (1630–1702) and his son, also Olof Rudbeck (1660–1740). Olof Rudbeck senior was noted for his discovery of the lymphatic system, and also his book *Atlantica* in which he argued that Sweden had been the site of Plato's Atlantis.

rutherford

The rutherford, a unit of radioactivity, honours the British physicist Ernest Rutherford, 1st Baron Rutherford (1871–1937).

Born in New Zealand, Rutherford was educated at Christchurch and later Cambridge. He is known for his pioneering research into the nature of radioactivity – initially in Montreal, then in Manchester and Cambridge, where he was director of the Cavendish Laboratory. Most well known for his discovery of the atomic nucleus in 1911, he was awarded the **Nobel prize** for chemistry in 1908, the Order of Merit in 1925 and made a baron in 1931.

S

Sabin vaccine; Salk vaccine

The American microbiologist Jonas Edward Salk (b.1914) developed the first successful vaccine against polio, which came to be named after him and was used initially in 1954. The Salk vaccine was widely used but by the 1960s it was replaced by the Sabin vaccine, which provided greater immunity from polio and for a longer period. The Sabin vaccine is named after the Polish-born American microbiologist Albert Bruce Sabin (b.1906), who developed it in 1955. Sabin vaccine is administered orally.

sadism

Sadism – the pleasure derived from inflicting pain on others – is named after the French soldier and writer Count Donatien Alphonse François de Sade, known as Marquis de Sade (1740–1814). De Sade's writings depict sexual perversion. His most famous writings, including *Les 120 Journées de Sodome* (1785) and *Justine* (1791), were composed during the 1780s and 1790s while he spent many years imprisoned for sexual offences. The final years of de Sade's life were spent in a mental asylum in Charenton.

St Anthony fire

St Anthony's fire is the name of a disease causing inflammation or gangrene. Known technically as ergotism or erysipelas, the disease was named after St Anthony in the sixteenth century because it was believed that praying to him led to healing.

St Anthony of Egypt (c.AD251–356) was known as a hermit and also as the founder of Christian monasticism. At the age of about eighteen, he gave up all his possessions and some years later withdrew to the desert, there to be tempted by demons disguised as wild animals. He emerged in about AD305 to organise his followers into a monastic community.

St Bernard dog

The Italian churchman St Bernard of Menthon (923–1008) founded hospices on two alpine passes, which came to be named after him, the Great St Bernard Pass between Italy and Switzerland and the Little St Bernard Pass between Italy and France. The monks of the hospice at the Great St Bernard Pass used to keep a breed of large working dog that was trained to track down travellers lost in blizzards and the breed came to be named after the founder of the hospice.

The breed is the heaviest breed of domestic dog in the world, the heaviest recorded example weighing 22 stone 2 pounds (140.6 kg).

St Elmo's fire

The expression St Elmo's fire refers to the luminous discharge sometimes seen in stormy weather at points that project into the atmosphere, such as a church spire or the mast of a ship. Known technically as corposant, the luminous appearance derives from small electrical discharges.

St Elmo's fire is probably so called because it was associated with St Elmo, an Italian alteration of the name St Erasmus (*d.*303BC), the Italian bishop and patron saint of Mediterranean sailors. According to one legend, in reward for being saved from drowning by a sailor, Erasmus is said to have promised that a light would be displayed to indicate an impending storm.

St Leger

The St Leger horse-race is a flat race for three-year-old colts run annually in September on the Town Moor, Doncaster, South Yorkshire. Founded in 1776, it is named after a leading local sportsman of that time, Lieutenant General St Leger of Park Hill, Doncaster.

St Luke's summer; St Martin's summer

St Luke's summer and St Martin's summer both refer to periods of exceptionally warm weather in the autumn. The summery weather is associated with the saints because of the dates of their feast-days, St Luke's Day being 18 October and St Martin's Day 11 November.

St Luke, traditionally regarded as the author of the third Gospel and also the Acts of the Apostles, was the Gentile doctor who accompanied Paul on his missionary journeys. St Martin (*c.*315–397) was Bishop of Tours. Born into a non-believing family, it is said that he became a Christian after dividing his cloak into two to give half to a beggar.

St Vitus' dance

St Vitus' dance is the non-technical name for chorea, the disease of the central nervous system marked by involuntary jerky movements. The disease is named after St Vitus, a child who was martyred with his nurse and tutor during the persecution of Christians by the Roman Emperor Diocletian in about 303. The description of the disease as St Vitus' dance arose in the seventeenth century, when sufferers prayed to St Vitus for healing, dancing around a statue of him.

Salk vaccine see Sabin vaccine

Sally Lunn

A Sally Lunn, a slightly sweetened tea-cake, is said to have been named after a late-eighteenth-century English baker. It seems that Sally Lunn used to advertise her wares by shouting out her name in the city of Bath. A resourceful local baker named Dalmer developed mass production of the buns and also wrote a song to express their delights; so their fame spread.

salmonella; salmonellosis

Salmonella is the name of the rod-shaped bacteria that cause diseases, including food poisoning (salmonellosis), in humans. The genus of bacteria has nothing to do with the fish but is named after the American veterinary surgeon Daniel Elmer Salmon (1850–1914), who first identified it. Many cases of salmonellosis are thought to have been caused by inadequate thawing of frozen poultry before cooking.

Sam Browne belt

A Sam Browne belt is the military officer's leather belt supported by a light strap that passes over the right shoulder and designed originally as a belt for supporting a sword or pistol. The belt is named after the British army officer Sir Samuel J. Browne (1824–1901) who designed it.

Born in India, Browne had a distinguished military career. His decisive role in the Indian Mutiny (1857–9) earned him the Victoria Cross and in 1888 he was promoted to general.

A version of the belt is worn by cyclists, etc., to increase their visibility.

samarskite

Samarskite, the velvet-black mineral discovered in Russia in 1857, is named after a Russian mine official Colonel M. von Samarski. When, in 1879, the French chemist Lecoq de Boisbaudrian discovered a new lanthanide element spectroscopically, he named the element samarium after samarskite, since it contained this mineral. Thus a little-known mine official is remembered by having a chemical element named in his honour.

Samoyed

Samoyeds are a breed of working dogs, strongly built with husky-like features and a dense white or cream coat. The dogs take their name from the Samoyed people, a group of Siberian people who live in the coastal regions of north central USSR. See also **husky**.

Samson

A man of great strength is sometimes known as a Samson, with reference to the biblical judge of Israel. Samson's outstanding feats of strength included the tearing of a lion apart with his bare hands, catching three hundred foxes and then tying them tail to tail in pairs, and striking down a thousand men with the jawbone of a donkey.

When the treacherous **Delilah** eventually discovered that the secret of his strength lay in his hair, she had it all shaved off so that his strength left him and the Philistines seized him, gouging out his eyes. However, as his hair grew back his strength returned and Samson's final act was to take revenge on the Philistines at the temple of Dagon. Calling upon God, he braced himself against the two central pillars that supported the temple, in which about three thousand people had assembled to bait him. Pushing with all his strength, he brought down the whole edifice, killing himself but at the moment of his death killing more Philistines than during his life.

sandwich

Sandwich is one of the most famous eponyms in the English language. The name of the snack consisting of two slices of buttered bread with a filling between them derives from the English diplomat John Montagu, 4th Earl of Sandwich (1718–92).

The earl was addicted to gambling, some of his gambling sessions lasting as long as two days non-stop. He was so compulsive a gambler that, rather than leave the gaming table to take food and so interrupt the game, he would order his valet to bring him food. Invariably, he would be brought slices of cold beef between two slices of bread. Within a few years the snack became generally known as a sandwich, although it had of course been eaten before this time.

The Earl of Sandwich was also notorious for his part in the

prosecution of his former friend John Wilkes, and the inadequacy of the English navy during the American War of Independence is attributed to the corruption that was rife while he was first lord of the Admiralty.

Sanforized

Sanforized is the trademark used for the process of pre-shrinking a fabric before it is made into articles, such as clothes. In the process, the fibres are compressed mechanically. The word derives from the name Sanford Lockwood Cluett (1874–1968), the American director of engineering and research of a firm of shirt and collar manufacturers, Cluett, Peabody and Co., of Troy, New York.

Saturday

Saturday, the seventh day of the week, derives its name from the Roman god of agriculture Saturn. The Old English name *Sæternes dæg* was a translation of the Latin *Saturni dies*, day of Saturn.

saxophone

The saxophone, the keyed woodwind instrument with a brass body and a single-reed mouthpiece, is named after its inventor, the Belgian musical-instrument maker Adolphe Sax (1814–94). It seems that it was while working in the musical-instrument workshop of his father Charles Joseph Sax (1791–1865) in the early 1840s that Adolphe invented several instruments, the most famous of which was to become known as the saxophone.

The instrument was first shown to the public in 1844, and enjoyed a great deal of success. Composers such as Berlioz and Bizet wrote music for the instrument and today the sax is most commonly used for jazz and dance music.

Scrooge

A miserly person is sometimes called a Scrooge, after the character Ebenezer Scrooge in the story *A Christmas Carol* (published in 1843) by Charles Dickens. On Christmas Eve Scrooge is visited by the ghost of his former business partner Marley. He sees visions of the past, present and future, including one depicting his own death unless he quickly changes his ways, which he then proceeds to do.

Scylla – between Scylla and Charybdis

The expression 'between Scylla and Charybdis' is used to refer to a situation in which one is faced with two equally dangerous alternatives: avoiding one danger immediately exposes one to the other. The

expression originally referred to the narrow sea passage, the Straits of
Messina, between Italy and Sicily. In Greek mythology, the female sea
monster Scylla was believed to live there in a cave off the Italian coast.
On the Sicilian side lived Charybdis, the monster in the whirlpool.
Thus, sailors who tried to avoid one danger were exposed to the other.

sequoia

The most massive tree in the world, the Giant Sequoia, is named after
the American Indian Sequoya (c.1770–1843). The name Sequoia,
referring in fact to either of two giant Californian coniferous trees, the
big tree (Giant Sequoia) or the redwood, was chosen by the Hungarian
botanist Stephen Ladislaus Endlicher in 1847.

Sequoya – who believed himself to be the son of a white trader and so
adopted the name George Guess – was sure that the power of the white
man lay in his possession of a written language. He therefore set about
writing down his own language. Over a period of twelve years, Sequoya
established a writing system of eighty-six characters that represented all
the sounds in the Cherokee language. Thousands of Cherokees quickly
mastered the writing system and soon a weekly Cherokee newspaper
was published and a constitution written in the Cherokee language.

Shakespearean

The adjective Shakespearean (or Shakespearian) is used in reference to
William Shakespeare (1564–1616) or his writings, particularly when
considered to show great vision and power. The name of the famous
English dramatist and poet is also remembered in the Shakespearean
sonnet, a fourteen-line poem in the form abab cdcd efef gg. Also
known as the English sonnet, it is a variant of the **Petrarchan sonnet**.

Shavian

The adjective Shavian describes the life, works or ideas of the Irish
dramatist and socialist George Bernard Shaw (1856–1950). GBS, as he
was known, disliked the adjective Shawian, so coined Shavius as the
Latin form of Shaw, then derived the adjective Shavian from it. Shavian
wit is sometimes used to describe the particular style of humour of
Shaw's plays.

Sheraton

The English furniture-maker Thomas Sheraton (1751–1806) is remembered for a style of furniture named in his honour. The style is
known for its elegance, straight lines and inlaid decoration.

Sheraton is particularly famous for his writings, especially *The*

Cabinet-Maker and Upholsterer's Drawing Book (published in four volumes, 1791–4) and *The Cabinet Dictionary* (1802). He taught drawing, but there is no record that he ever owned a workshop where he undertook furniture design.

shrapnel

The explosive device known as a shrapnel shell, the projectile that contains bullets or fragments of metal and a charge that is exploded before impact, takes its name from the English artillery officer Henry Shrapnel (1761–1842) who invented it.

Shrapnel spent many years developing this deadly weapon, which was originally known as the spherical-case shot; it was eventually adopted in about 1803. It was first used in action against the Dutch in Surinam (Dutch Guiana) and was important in the defeat of Napoleon at Waterloo in 1815.

Shrapnel gained promotion for his efforts – he was finally a general – but he received scant financial reward for all his work.

shyster

A shyster is a person who is unscrupulous in the pursuit of his or her profession; the word is used chiefly in American English to describe a lawyer or a politician. The word possibly derives from the name Scheuster, a mid-nineteenth-century lawyer who on several occasions was admonished in a New York court for pettifoggery. Other authorities suggest the ultimate origin as the German *Scheisse* meaning excrement.

Shylock

A pitiless and extortionate moneylender is sometimes referred to as a Shylock. The name was originally that of the ruthless usurer in Shakespeare's *Merchant of Venice*. The expression 'have [get, etc.] one's pound of flesh' also derives from the play. Shylock agreed to lend the merchant Antonio money against the security of a pound of Antonio's flesh, but as the debt could not be repaid when due, Shylock demanded his pound of flesh.

sideburns

Sideburns are the strips of hair that grow down the sides of a man's face reaching from the hairline to below the ears. The word comes from Ambrose Everett Burnside (1824–81).

After a short time as a tailor's apprentice and a brief period of military service, Burnside set up in business to manufacture a breech-loading rifle that he had invented. The business failed, however.

Later, he became a general, fighting for the Union in the American Civil War, and was renowned for the defeats under his command at Fredericksburg (1862) and Petersburg (1864). Despite these failures, Burnside remained popular and was elected governor of Rhode Island (1866–9) and a US senator from 1875.

The general is notably remembered for his shaving habits: he sported so-called burnsides, full side whiskers joining the moustache. With the passage of time, the side whiskers became shorter and the two parts of the word mysteriously changed places to give sideburns.

siemens

Siemens, the metric unit of electrical conductance, is named after the German electrical engineer Ernst Werner von Siemens (1816–92). A pioneer in telegraphy, Siemens is known for his work in laying a government telegraph line from Berlin to Frankfurt. With his three brothers, Friedrich Siemens (1826–1904), Sir William Siemens (Karl Wilhelm Siemens; 1828–83) – who invented the open-hearth process of making steel – and Karl Siemens (1829–1906) he created the immense Siemens industrial empire.

It is curious that the siemens unit was formerly known as a mho – a word formed by reversing the letters of another eponymous word, ohm.

silhouette

A silhouette, the outline of a dark shape set on a light background, takes its name from the French politician Étienne de Silhouette (1709–67), but the precise reason for this is uncertain.

As controller of finances (1759), Silhouette had to restore the French economy after the Seven Years' War. He therefore instituted a series of stringent tax revisions, which made him unpopular. His measures were seen as niggardly and the phrase *à la silhouette* meaning 'on the cheap' became current. The sense of parsimony was then applied to the partial shadow portraits that were fashionable at that time.

Other sources suggest that the brevity of Silhouette's period of office as controller-general – he was forced to resign after only nine months – is the origin of the incompleteness of the portraits.

Still others claim that Silhouette's hobby was in fact making such outlines and he is said to have displayed many examples of this art form in his château.

silly-billy

The term silly-billy is sometimes used in informal English – particularly by or to children – to describe someone who is foolish or silly. The expression, deriving from Billy, the nickname for William, may well have first been applied to King William IV of England, formerly Duke of Clarence (1765–1837). He was known as silly billy, from, it seems, his carefree attitude towards his royal responsibilities. The nickname was also given to the nobleman William Frederick, Duke of Gloucester (1776–1834).

simony

Simony, the practice of buying or selling of church or spiritual benefits or offices, derives from Simon Magus, a first-century-AD sorcerer. After becoming a Christian, Simon tried to buy the gift of spiritual power from the Apostles, but was strongly rebuked by Peter (Acts 8:9–24).

slave

The word slave came via Old French from the Medieval Latin *Sclavus*, meaning quite simply, 'a Slav'. In the Middle Ages a large number of Slavonic people in central Europe were conquered and held in bondage, so the name *Sclavus* gained the additional sense of 'slave'.

smart alec

A smart alec (or aleck) is a conceited know-all: 'I don't want any smart alec coming in here to tell me how to run my business, thank you very much.'

The expression can be traced back to about the 1860–5, but it is not recorded who the first smart Alec was; he seems to have been intelligent enough to conceal all evidence as to his identity. An expression with the same meaning is 'clever Dick'.

smithsonite; Smithsonian Institution

Smithsonite, the whitish mineral that is an important ore of zinc, takes its name from the English chemist James Smithson (original name James Lewes Macie; 1765–1829).

Smithson left a bequest that an institution named after him should be set up in Washington DC, 'for the increase and diffusion of knowledge among men'. The American Congress spent many years discussing whether to accept the bequest and finally agreed to do so. The Smithsonian Institution was founded in 1846, and today conducts scientific research and maintains several art galleries and museums.

Socratic method; Socratic irony

The Greek philosopher Socrates (c.470–399BC) wrote no philosophical works himself, his beliefs only being known through the works of his pupils, Plato and Xenophon. His supposed method of reasoning (Socratic method) involved questions and answers designed to evoke truths that he considered every rational person knew, even if only implicitly.

The expression Socratic irony derives from his pretended ignorance in arguments, so leading the person answering his questions to be easily defeated by his skilful interrogation.

In 399BC Socrates was condemned to death by the Athenian government for impiety and corruption of youth. He was forced to commit suicide by drinking hemlock.

Sod's law see Murphy's law

Solomon – the wisdom of Solomon; Solomon's seal

Solomon, the tenth-century-BC king of Israel and son of David and Bathsheba, was noted for his great wisdom and wealth. His wisdom has become proverbial, being evoked in expressions such as 'need the wisdom of Solomon' and 'as wise as Solomon', and was demonstrated when two women came to him each claiming that a particular baby was her own. Solomon's suggestion that the baby be divided in two revealed the true mother: the one who would rather hand the baby over to her rival than see the baby killed (I Kings 3: 16–28).

Solomon's seal is the name given to any of the genus *Polygonatum* of the lily family that have greenish-white flowers, long smooth leaves, and a fleshy white underground stem. The underground stem is marked with prominent leaf scars, which are said to resemble seals – hence the name. Solomon's seal is also the name of a mystic symbol, the Star of David, that is traditionally associated with Solomon.

sop to Cerberus

In Greek mythology, Cerberus was the three-headed dog that guarded the entrance to Hades. Cerberus allowed the dead to enter; some were greeted in a friendly manner, others were met with ferocious snarls. Friends used to put a cake in the hands of those who died, for them to give to Cerberus in order to secure safe passage. So it is that figuratively 'a sop to Cerberus' is a bribe or gift given to appease a potential source of trouble or danger.

sophist; sophistry; sophism

The sophists were ancient Greek itinerant teachers of the fifth and fourth centuries BC who taught various subjects, particularly public speaking and philosophy. Although their name comes from a Greek word meaning wise man or expert, because of the methods of some of the teachers, the word sophist came to stand for someone who used unscrupulously clever arguments in persuasion. Thus our modern word sophistry means deceptively subtle reasoning and sophism is an instance of this.

soubise

Soubise, a white or brown sauce containing a purée of onions, takes its name from the French nobleman Charles de Rohan, Prince de Soubise (1715–87). It seems that the sauce was probably named in the prince's honour by his chef Marin. The Prince de Soubise was a renowned military leader and general and became marshal of France in 1758 through the influence of Madame de Pompadour.

sousaphone

A sousaphone, the large tuba that encircles the player with a forward-facing bell, is named after its inventor, the American bandmaster and composer John Philip Sousa (1854–1932).

Known as 'the march king', Sousa was appointed leader of the US Marine Corps band in 1880, and twelve years later formed his own Sousa Band, which toured the world, gaining him great fame. Sousa composed over a hundred popular marches, including 'The Stars and Stripes Forever', 'The Washington Post' and 'Liberty Bell'.

spaniel

Spaniel, the name of any of several breeds of smallish short-legged dog that have long drooping ears, comes ultimately from the Old French word *espaigneul* or *espaignol*, meaning 'Spanish'. The dog is thought to have originally come from Spain.

Spartacist

In 73BC a Thracian gladiator named Spartacus successfully led a slave revolt against Rome. Two years later he and his followers were defeated by the Roman politician Marcus Licinius Crassus.

During the First World War the German socialists Karl Liebknecht and Rosa Luxemburg formed a radical socialist group known as the Spartacus League (which developed into the German Communist

Party), Karl Liebknecht adopting the name Spartacus. Members of the group were called Spartacists. Both leaders were murdered following the unsuccessful communist revolt of 1919.

spencer

A spencer – a short, waist-length, close-fitting jacket, which was fashionable in the late eighteenth and early nineteenth centuries – takes its name from the English politician George John Spencer, 2nd Earl of Spencer (1758–1834). According to one account, the earl won a bet that he could set a new fashion simply by appearing in the streets wearing a new kind of garment.

While lord of the admiralty under the prime ministership of William Pitt the Younger, Earl Spencer chose Nelson to command the Fleet in the Mediterranean – which led to the British victory in the Battle of the Nile (August 1798).

Spenserian stanza; Spenserian sonnet

The English poet Edmund Spenser (c.1552–99) is noted for his moral allegory *The Faerie Queen* (1590; 1596). It consists of nine-line stanzas that have come to be known as Spenserian stanzas: eight lines in iambic pentameter followed by an iambic line of six feet, rhyming ababbcbcc. Spenser also developed a form of sonnet with the rhyming scheme abab bcbc cdcd ee, which came to be known as the Spenserian sonnet.

spinet

The spinet, a type of small harpsichord with one manual, may take its name from the sixteenth-century Italian musical instrument maker Giovanni Spinetti. It is said that Spinetti invented this instrument at the beginning of the sixteenth century. Alternatively, the word spinet may possibly derive from Italian *spina*, a thorn, with reference to the thorn-like quills used in plucking the strings of the instrument.

Spode

The British potter Josiah Spode (1754–1827) was famous for a type of porcelain that came to bear his name.

His father, also Josiah Spode (1733–97), had started his own works at Stoke-on-Trent in 1770. The son succeeded his father in 1797, developing porcelain (1800), by introducing bones into the paste as well as feldspar, and stone china tableware in about 1805.

spoonerism

The Reverend William Archibald Spooner (1844–1930) was, it seems, renowned for slips of the tongue in which the initial sounds of words were accidentally transposed, often with a comical effect. Some examples of such 'spoonerisms', as they came to be called, attributed to the clergyman include: a half-warmed fish instead of a half-formed wish; kinkering congs instead of conquering kings; a well-boiled icicle instead of a well-oiled bicycle; reference to God as a shoving leopard instead of a loving shepherd; and to Queen Victoria as our queer old dean instead of our dear old queen.

Stakhanovite

A Stakhanovite is an industrial worker in the USSR who is offered special incentives for producing an output that is greater than the norm. The word Stakhanovite, a member of the movement known as Stakhanovism, derives from the Russian coal-miner Alexei Grigorievich Stakhanov (1906–77). In 1935 Stakhanov reorganised his coal-mining team, so greatly increasing the production.

Stalinism

Stalinism describes the form of communism developed by the Soviet leader Joseph Stalin (original name Josef Vissarionovich Dzhugashvili; 1879–1953). A variant of Marxism–Leninism, Stalinism is marked by a policy of establishing socialism in one country, strict bureaucracy, extensive use of terror, and devotion to Russian nationalism.

Succeeding Lenin as head of the Communist Party, Stalin (his name means 'steel') created a totalitarian state in the USSR. He introduced rapid collectivisation of industry and agriculture. Notorious for his ruthless dictatorship, Stalin crushed all opposition, particularly in the purges of the 1930s. By the outbreak of the Second World War Stalin was in complete control of the country. By the time of his death the Soviet Union had been transformed into a world power.

After his death, Khrushchev denounced Stalin and a process of de-Stalinisation followed. Stalin's body was transferred from Lenin's mausoleum and the names of all places honouring him were changed.

See also **Leninism, Marxism, Trotskyism**.

Star of David see Solomon

Sten gun

The Sten gun, the light 9-millimetre sub-machine-gun used in the Second World War, was named using the initials of the surnames of its inventors: Major R. V. Shepherd, a twentieth-century English army officer, and H. J. Turpin, a civil servant, plus the 'en' of England (or Enfield, London).

stentorian

If someone speaks in stentorian tones, he or she is speaking extremely loudly. The adjective derives from the name of Stentor, the herald in Greek mythology who, according to Homer's *Iliad*, had a voice as loud as the voices of fifty men. Stentor died when he lost a shouting contest with Hermes, herald of the gods.

stetson

The stetson, the wide-brimmed, high-crowned, felt hat, was named after the American hat-maker John Bauerson Stetson (1830–1906) who designed it.

When Stetson travelled in the western USA at the time of the Civil War, it occurred to him that hats suitable for the needs of the cowboys were not being manufactured. When he returned to Philadelphia in 1865, therefore, he started to mass-produce a wide-brimmed hat that became popular with cowboys and was known as a stetson or a John B.

stoic

If someone behaves in a stoic or stoical way, then he or she endures hardship or pain without letting their feelings show. The word derives from the Stoics, a school of ancient Greek philosophers taught by Zeno of Citium. Amongst the teachings of Stoicism were the suppression of emotion and the belief that wisdom lay in mastery of oneself.

The school was known as the Stoic school, since it met at the Painted Portico (in Greek, *Stoa Poikile*) in Athens.

stonewall

If you stonewall, then you act in an obstructive or defensive manner. The expression gained currency as a result of the nickname of the US Confederate general in the American Civil War, Thomas Jonathan Jackson, known as Stonewall Jackson (1824–63). In the first Battle of Bull Run (1861), he and his forces were described as 'standing like a stone wall' against the Federal troops.

From Jackson's name derives 'stonewalling', the act of obstructing something with stubborn resistance. The word is found particularly in cricket, to describe cautious defensive batting, and also in discussion, where a speaker talks for a long time expressly to stop other people from voicing their opinion.

Swedenborgian

The Swedish scientist and theologian Emanuel Swedenborg (original surname Svedberg; 1668–1772) is known for his system of teachings showing the importance of the spiritual structure of the universe.

Originally a mining engineer and mineralogist, Swedenborg became more spiritually orientated in about 1743, claiming to have mystical visions. His works include *Arcana Coelestia* (1756) and *Divine Love and Wisdom* (1763). The religious group known as the New Jerusalem Church, also known as the New Church or Swedenborgians, was established after his death in 1787.

sweet Fanny Adams

Sweet Fanny Adams now means 'nothing at all': 'What's been happening while I've been away?' – 'Sweet Fanny Adams.' It is sometimes shortened to sweet f.a.

The expression comes originally from the name of a girl who was murdered in Alton, Hampshire in 1812. Her body was found in the River Wey, cut into pieces.

Fanny's name became popularised by sailors talking about a distasteful meal of tinned mutton – it is said that a sailor found a button in a tin of mutton and with gruesome humour called the tin's contents Fanny Adams. From this slang usage, the meaning of the word developed to refer to something of little value and then the current meaning.

Swiftian

Swiftian is sometimes used to mean satirical in a keen and bitter way: 'The appointment of a mathematician to lead the enquiry into the teaching of English language shows an undeniable Swiftian logic.' The adjective clearly derives from the name of the Anglo-Irish clergyman, poet and satirist Jonathan Swift (1667–1745), whose numerous writings included *A Tale of a Tub* (1704), a satire 'on corruptions in religion and learning', and the famous *Gulliver's Travels* (1726), a satire on the human condition, particularly the politics of that period.

sword of Damocles

In classical legend, the courtier Damocles declared enviously that the tyrant of Syracuse, Dionysius the Elder (405–367BC), was the happiest of men. Flattered by this remark but wanting to teach Damocles a lesson, Dionysius invited Damocles to a banquet, where he could see the ruler's happiness. Damocles accepted the invitation, and sat down to a sumptuous feast, but above him was a sword, suspended by a single hair. Damocles was so troubled that he could not enjoy the banquet.

The moral was that fears and threats of danger constantly prevent those that have power from fully enjoying that power. The expression 'sword of Damocles' has thus come to refer to impending disaster.

syphilis

The venereal disease syphilis derives from the name of a character in a poem published in 1530 with the title *Syphilis sive Morbus Gallicus* (Syphilis or the French Disease) by the Italian physician and poet Girolamo Fracastro (1483–1553).

In the poem, Syphilis, the hero of the book and a shepherd, angers the sun god to such an extent that he is struck down by this disease. Fracastro probably coined the name Syphilis from the Greek *suphilos*, 'lover of pigs' or 'swineherd'.

T

tam o' shanter

Tam o' shanter, the brimless cap of Scottish origin that usually has a pom-pom on the top, is named after the hero of the poem *Tam o' Shanter* (published 1791), by the Scottish poet Robert Burns (1759–96). Often shortened to tam or tammy, it is possibly the only item of male headgear that takes its name from a poem.

Tammany Hall

Tammany Hall is the headquarters of the Tammany Society, the central organisation of the Democratic Party in New York City. Originally founded in 1789, it was notorious for its political corruption in the nineteenth and early twentieth centuries.

The society is named after Tammanend (also known as Tammenund or Tammany), a Delaware Indian chief, who, it seems, may have negotiated with William Penn over the transfer of land that eventually became **Pennsylvania**.

tantalise

Tantalise, to tease someone by offering something desirable to view and then withholding it, derives from Greek mythology. Tantalus, the mythical king of Phrygia, was punished for offences against the gods. In Hades he was condemned to stand in water that receded whenever he tried to drink it and under branches of fruit that moved away whenever he tried to grasp them.

Tarmac see **macadam**

tartar

A person who is thought to be very formidable, fearsome or exacting is sometimes known as a tartar. The world tartar comes from the Tatars, a Mongoloid people who conquered Asia and eastern Europe to establish an immense and mighty empire from the thirteenth to the sixteenth centuries.

It seems that the change from Tatar to Tartar came about in the Middle Ages under the influence of the spelling of *tartarus*, Latin for 'hell', since their deeds were so savage that it seemed as if they had come from hell.

Tasmania

Tasmania, the island in the south Pacific, south of mainland Australia, is named after the Dutch navigator Abel Janszoon Tasman (1603-59). Appointed by the Dutch colonial administrator Anthony van Dieman (1593–1645), Tasman explored the south Pacific Ocean for trading purposes (1642–4). Tasman sighted the island that is now named in his honour, originally calling it Van Dieman's Land after his patron. The island was known as this until 1856, when its name was changed to Tasmania.

tawdry

The queen of Northumbria, St Audrey (Ethelrida; *d.*679), was patron saint of Ely. In olden times a fair was held annually on 17 October in her honour. The fair was noted for its good-quality jewellery and fine silk scarves, which in time came to be known as St Audrey's laces. Later, however, the fine scarves were replaced by cheap, gaudy imitations and so the word tawdry developed, a shortening and alteration of (Sain)t Audrey('s laces), a term that is now applied to anything that is cheap and showy.

Some versions of the story add that St Audrey died of a tumour in her throat, which she considered a punishment for wearing showy jewel necklaces as a child.

teddy bear

The teddy bear, the soft stuffed toy bear, takes its name from the US president Theodore Roosevelt (1858–1919), who was nicknamed Teddy. Well known as a hunter of bears, it is said that on one occasion Roosevelt spared the life of a brown bear cub while on a hunting expedition. The story was later depicted in a cartoon in the *Washington Post* by the cartoonist Clifford K. Berryman, and stuffed toy bears became known as teddy bears.

The president's association with teddies remained. He presented several bears to the Bronx Zoo, and when, in 1911, he received an honorary degree at Cambridge University, a large teddy bear was lowered from the ceiling on to his head while he stood on the platform.

Teddy boy

Teddy boys, young men in the Britain of the 1950s, wore tightly fitting trousers and long jackets reminiscent of fashions during the reign of King Edward VII (1841–1910; reign 1901–10), Teddy being the nickname for Edward.

Associated with early rock-and-roll music, the Teddy boys were known for their unruly or violent behaviour. Young men who nowadays wear clothes in this style are also sometimes known as Teddy boys, and the association with bad or rebellious behaviour remains.

tesla

Tesla, the metric unit of magnetic flux density, is named after the Croatian-born American electrician and inventor Nikola Tesla (1857–1943). Tesla is known for his work on the distribution of alternating electrical current and many inventions including a transformer, a dynamo and a generator.

Thatcherism

Thatcherism is the term used to describe the policies of the Conservative government of the UK under the prime ministership of Margaret Thatcher, from 1979–90.

Born in Grantham in 1925, Margaret Hilda Thatcher studied chemistry at Oxford University. After studying and practising law, she was elected MP for Finchley in 1959. She served as secretary of state for education and science (1970–74) and became leader of the Conservative Party in 1975 and prime minister in 1979.

As prime minister, she led a firm government that adopted a monetarist economic policy, seeking generally to reduce public expenditure, and policies of privatising nationalised services and industries.

Thespian

The late-sixth-century-BC Greek poet Thespis is traditionally thought to have been the founder of Greek tragic drama. Up to that time performances had been given only by a chorus; he is said to have introduced an actor who represented a historical or legendary figure. Thespis is also said to have toured the country with his plays. From his name comes thespian, used as a word for an actor, and as an adjective to refer to drama.

Thursday

The name of the fifth day of the week comes from the Old English *Thursdaeg*, the day of Thor, the Norse god of thunder. Thor is said to have made thunder with a chariot that was pulled by he-goats across the sky. Armed with a massive hammer, he was considered the strongest and bravest of the Norse gods.

titan; titanic

The Titans were twelve primeval gigantic gods and goddesses in Greek mythology, the children of Uranus (sky or heaven) and Gaea (earth). There were six Titans (Oceanus, Coeus, Crius, Hyperion, Japetus and Cronus) and six Titanesses (Thea, Rhea, Themis, Mnemosyne, Phoebe and Tethys).

The Greeks believed that the Titans once ruled over the earth in a golden age. The youngest of the twelve, Cronus, became their leader when he overthrew his father Uranus. Later, Cronus was himself overthrown by his son, Zeus.

The noun titan and the adjective titanic have come to describe a person or thing that is extremely large or strong. The *Titanic* was, of course, the luxury passenger ship that struck an iceberg near Newfoundland on its maiden voyage on the night of 14–15 April 1912, with the loss of 1513 lives.

titchy

Someone or something that is described as titchy is very small. The word derives from Little Tich, the stage name of the English actor Harry Relph (1867–1928). The word Tich may derive from the Tichborne case, a legal case of the 1870s, in which a certain podgy Arthur Orton was found to have impersonated a Roger Charles Tichborne (1829–54), the heir to a vast fortune, who was presumed lost at sea. Eventually Orton was discredited and imprisoned (1874–84)

Titian

The adjective Titian is sometimes used to describe bright golden-auburn hair. The word derives from the Italian painter Titian (original name Tiziano Vecellio; c.1487–1576). A renowned artist of the Venetian school, Titian is noted for his mythological and religious works, frescoes and portraits. In many of his works, Titian depicted a model with hair of a reddish-brown hue that came to be named after him.

tom; Tom, Dick or Harry; Tom Thumb

The male of various animals, especially the cat, is known as a tom, a shortened form and nickname of Thomas. The name Tom also occurs in such words as tomboy and tomfoolery.

The expression Tom, Dick or Harry refers to different kinds of ordinary people, often unsuitable or unqualified: 'We won't allow any Tom, Dick or Harry to come and set up a stall in the market.'

A Tom Thumb, a person of restricted growth, derives from the tiny hero of nursery tales. General Tom Thumb was the stage name of the American person of restricted growth, Charles Sherwood Stratton (1838–83), who was exhibited by P. T. Barnum in his circuses. He was 3ft 4in (102 cm) tall.

Tom Collins

A Tom Collins – the tall iced drink consisting of gin, lime (or lemon) juice, sugar and soda water – is said to have been named after a bartender, but his exact identity is unclear. A possible candidate is the nineteenth-century bartender at Limmer's public house in London.

tommy; Tommy Atkins; Tommy gun

Tommy, a representative British soldier, especially a private, is the shortened form of the name Thomas Atkins. Use of the name Thomas Atkins dates back to the early nineteenth century: it first appeared on sample army enlistment forms in 1815.

The name of the lightweight sub-machine-gun known as a Tommy gun comes from a different source. It was invented by the American army general John Taliaferro Thompson, hence Tommy (1860–1940), the American navy commander John N. Blish and others towards the end of the First World War. First manufactured in 1921, the Tommy gun was popularised by the Chicago gangsters of the Prohibition era (1920–33).

tontine

Tontine, a financial scheme that provides life annuities to a group of subscribers, is named after the Italian banker Lorenzo Tonti (1635–90), who devised the scheme and introduced it to France in 1653. Under the scheme, a number of people subscribe to the tontine. When one of the subscribers dies, his share is divided among the remaining members, until the last surviving member takes the whole income. The scheme was used by governments to raise money, particularly in the seventeenth and eighteenth centuries.

Tony

Tony, the medallion awarded annually for 'distinguished achievement' in the American theatre, is named after the American actress Antoinette Perry (1888–1946), known familiarly as Tony. Making her début in 1905, Perry became a successful actress and producer and was appointed to the chair of the American Theatre Council.

tradescantia

The genus of flowering plants known as *Tradescantia*, which has striped leaves and is usually grown as house plants, includes the popular varieties known as wandering Jew and spiderwort. The genus is named after the English traveller and gardener John Tradescant (*c.*1570–1638), who was gardener to Charles I. John Tradescant travelled widely with his son, also John Tradescant (1608–62), and introduced into Britain many vegetables, fruits, trees and flowers, including figs, runner beans, oranges, lupins and the lilac. He established his own nursery in Lambeth in London.

trilby

Trilby, the soft felt hat with an indented crown, derives from the dramatised version of *Trilby*, the novel (published in 1894) by the English artist and writer George du Maurier (1834–96). In the original stage version of the novel (1895), the heroine, Trilby O'Ferrall, wore such a hat.

Trotskyism

Trotskyism is the theory of communism propounded by Russian revolutionary Leon Trotsky (original name Lev Davidovich Bronstein; 1879–1940). Trotsky called for permanent worldwide revolution, in contrast to Stalin's insistence on the establishing of socialism in one country in isolation.

A leader with Lenin of the October Revolution (1917), Trotsky was commissar of foreign affairs and war (1917–24) and built up the Red Army. On Lenin's death, he was ousted by Stalin, and was expelled from the Communist Party in 1927. Banished from the Soviet Union, he eventually settled in Mexico, where he was assassinated, probably by Soviet agents.

See also **Leninism, Marxism, Stalinism**.

tsar

Tsar (or czar), used as a title of the rulers of Russia from 1547 to 1917 or to describe someone who exercises authority, derives ultimately from the Latin use of the name Caesar to mean emperor.

The title kaiser, adopted by the emperor of the Holy Roman Empire and also the emperors of Germany and Austria, similarly derives from Caesar.

Opinions are divided, however, as to which Roman statesman is the source of this usage. Some propose (Gaius) Julius Caesar (100–44BC); others, more plausibly, suggest his adopted son, Augustus, known as Gaius Julius Caesar Octavianus (63BC–AD14), the first to be proclaimed Emperor of Rome (see also **August**).

trudgen

The trudgen (or trudgen stroke) is a type of swimming stroke that uses a double overarm action and a scissors kick. It is named after the English swimmer John Arthur Trudgen (1860–1940), who introduced it in 1893.

Tuesday

The name of the third day of the week comes from the Old English *Tiwesdaeg*, the day of Tiw (or Tyr), the Anglo-Saxon god of war and the sky. Latin writers, beginning with Tacitus, identified Tiw with Mars, the Roman god of war – hence the Latin name for Tuesday, *dies Martis*, day of Mars.

Tweedledum and Tweedledee

Tweedledum and Tweedledee – two individuals or groups that can scarcely be distinguished – was a description first applied to the musicians George Frederick Handel (1685–1759) and Giovanni Bononcini (1670–1747), when a rivalry arose between them. The probable first occurrence is in an epigram by John Byrom (1692–1763),

> Some say compared to Bononcini
> That mynheer Handel's but a ninny;
> Others aver that he to Handel
> Is scarcely fit to hold a candle.
> Strange that such high dispute should be
> 'Twixt Tweedledum and Tweedledee.

The names were popularised by the fat twin characters in *Through the Looking Glass* (published in 1872) by the English writer Lewis Carroll (1832–98).

U

Uncle Sam

Uncle Sam is a personification of the United States of America, its people, government or national spirit. The expression is probably a humorous expansion of the letters US (abbreviation of United States) stamped on the side of containers of military provisions. It is also noted that in 1812 a meat-packer named Samuel Wilson (1766–1854) at Troy, New York, was jocularly called Uncle Sam by his employees, in reference to the US stamped on the cases.

The expression Uncle Sam spread quickly during the War of 1812, to oppose John Bull, the symbol of the British Army. It was nearly sixty years later, however, that the first picture of Uncle Sam as he is recognised today appeared in *Harper's Weekly*. Uncle Sam was depicted as clothed in top hat and striped suit and enjoying his victory over John Bull.

Uncle Tom

Uncle Tom is a derogatory term for a Black person who wants to co-operate with and win the favour of Whites. The name was originally that of the Black slave in the abolitionist novel *Uncle Tom's Cabin* (published in 1852) by the American author Harriet Beecher Stowe (1811–96). The novel aroused strong anti-slavery feelings; and Abraham Lincoln is alleged to have said that the novel helped to start the Civil War.

V

valentine

A valentine – a card sent anonymously to one's sweetheart on 14 February – derives from either of two third-century-AD Christian martyrs. One St Valentine was a Roman priest who was martyred for assisting persecuted believers. He is said to have been martyred on the Flaminian Way, the road from Rome to Ariminum (Rimini) in about 270. The other St Valentine was a bishop of Terni, martyred in Rome at about the same time.

The connection between the feast of St Valentine (14 February) and courtship is not associated with either saint, however. The traditions linked with St Valentine go back to the Roman feast of Lupercalia (15 February) and the popular belief that 14 February is the date that birds select their mates.

Van Allen belts

The Van Allen belts, two regions of electrically charged particles surrounding the earth in the outer atmosphere, are named after the American physicist James Alfred Van Allen (*b.*1914). It was during the International Geophysical Year of 1958 that, as the Carver Professor of Physics at Iowa University, Van Allen inferred the existence of two belts of radiation. By examining the readings recorded by the Explorer satellites, he explained the existence of two belts of radiation, one at 1000–5000 km (620–3100 miles) and the other at 15,000–25,000 km (9300–15,500 miles) above the equator.

vandal

Someone who deliberately destroys or damages property is known as a vandal. The word derives from the Vandals, the Germanic people who moved southwards from Scandinavia in the first four centuries AD, overrunning Gaul, Spain and North Africa in the fifth century and sacking Rome in 455. The devastation that they caused was so severe that their name has ever since stood for those who bring about wanton destruction.

vandyke beard; vandyke brown; vandyke collar

The Flemish painter Sir Anthony Van Dyck (or Vandyke; 1599–1641) was court painter to King Charles I. His portraits are noted for their depiction of subjects wearing a trim pointed beard (vandyke beard) and a wide collar with deeply indented points forming a border (vandyke collar). Vandyke brown is the dark brown colour that the artist liked to use.

Born one of twelve children to a rich silk merchant, Van Dyck was by the age of nineteen an assistant to Rubens. In 1620 he first came to England and worked for King James I. After travels round Europe, he returned to England in 1632 to be court painter to Charles I (1632–41), who conferred on him a knighthood.

venereal; Venus

The word venereal is most often used in the expression venereal disease, a disease spread by sexual intercourse, for example gonorrhoea or syphilis. The word venereal derives from Latin *venus* meaning sexual love, from Venus, the Italian goddess. Originally the goddess of gardens and fertility, Venus became identified with the Greek Aphrodite as goddess of love: see also **aphrodisiac**.

Venus occurs in many compounds, particularly in the names of flowers and plants, such as Venus's flytrap (*Dionaea muscipula*), and even the small creature Venus's flower basket, a deep-sea sponge, genus *Euplectella*.

Venn diagram

A diagram in which circles and other shapes are drawn to overlap at certain points to represent mathematical and logical relationships is known as a Venn diagram. The name honours the English mathematician and logician John Venn (1834–1923), who devised the system.

Venus see venereal

vernier; vernier rocket

A vernier is a small additional scale that is attached to a measuring instrument to allow measurements to be taken that are finer than those on the main scale. The scale is named after the French mathematician Pierre Vernier (1580–1637), who described it in a treatise that he wrote in 1631. The scale was in fact a development of the *nonius*, invented by, and named after, the Portuguese mathematician Pedro Nuñez (1492–1577).

A vernier rocket (or vernier engine) is an alternative term for a rocket thruster, the small engine or gas nozzle that makes fine adjustments to the speed, altitude or direction of a space vehicle or missile.

Very light; Very pistol

The Very light is a coloured or white flare used as a signal. It is fired from a special pistol, a Very pistol. The light and pistol are named after the American naval officer Edward W. Very (1847–1910), who invented them in 1877.

vesta; vestal

The kind of short match known as a vesta is named after the Roman goddess Vesta. Vesta was the goddess of the hearth, who was venerated by every Roman household. The Vestal virgins were the virgin priestesses who kept the sacred fire at the altar in the Temple of Vesta constantly aflame.

Victorian

The adjective Victorian is sometimes used to refer to the moral standards or behaviour popularly associated with the reign of Queen Victoria (1819–1901; reign, 1837–1901). Some examples of the use of the word are: 'She rebelled against her strait-laced Victorian upbringing'; 'traditional Victorian values'; 'the solid Victorian virtues of self-help and hard work'. The qualities regarded as typically Victorian are thus seen to emphasise 'good' morals, often to the point of prudery, and strict discipline. The divergence between moral standards and practices during Queen Victoria's reign is reflected in the word's further associations of narrow-mindedness and hypocrisy.

Queen Victoria instituted the Victoria Cross (VC) in 1856, the highest military decoration capable of being awarded to members of the armed forces of Britain and the Commonwealth for bravery in battle. The queen also gave her name to numerous places, including the Victoria Falls, Victoria state and Lake Victoria.

Queen Victoria is further honoured in the word victoria itself which is used variously to refer to a light, four-wheeled carriage with a folding hood, a kind of water-lily and a large sweet variety of plum (victoria plum).

volcano; vulcanise

A volcano, an opening in the earth's crust out of which molten matter issues in an eruption, derives from Vulcan the Roman god of fire and metalworking. As Ernest Weekley comments, 'There was . . . for the ancient world, only one volcano . . . Etna . . . in the bowels of which Vulcan and the Cyclopes forged the thunderbolts of Jupiter' (*Words and Names*).

To vulcanise – to treat natural rubber chemically, in order to increase its elasticity, hardness, etc. – also derives from the god Vulcan.

volt

Volt, the metric unit of (electric) potential, is named after the Italian physicist Count Alessandro Volta (1745–1827). Volta is particularly noted for his invention (1800) of what was the first real battery (the voltaic cell or pile), and the electrophorus (1775) a device that accumulates electric charge. Widely praised for his experiments, he received numerous awards and medals from many countries; Napoleon conferred a countship on him in 1801.

vulcanise see volcano

W

Wagnerian

The adjective Wagnerian, used to mean grandiose or intense in a dramatic manner, derives from the music of the German composer Wilhelm Richard Wagner (1813–83). Particularly noted for his origination of the music drama, Wagner's operatic cycle *Der Ring des Nibelungen* was first produced in 1876.

Walter Mitty

The expression Walter Mitty is used to refer to an ordinary person who indulges in extravagant day-dreaming and fantasies in an attempt to escape from reality. The description derives from the hero of the short story *The Secret Life of Walter Mitty* by the American humorist and cartoonist James Grover Thurber (1894–1961).

Wankel engine

The Wankel engine, a type of internal-combustion engine that has a triangular-shaped rotating piston with slightly curved convex sides, is named after its inventor, the German engineer, Felix Wankel (*b.*1902).

Wankel gained his engineering skills in private study and through correspondence courses. His interest in a rotary engine dates back to 1924 and he developed the engine before and during the Second World War. Cars powered by the Wankel engine were produced by the early 1960s but the engine's inherent design problems have never been fully overcome.

Washington

The name of the American statesman and first president of the United States, George Washington (1732–99; president 1789–97), is the most frequently used place name in the USA. The capital of the USA, Washington state, Lake Washington, Mount Washington . . . all honour him. In Britain, Washington (new town) in Tyne and Wear was the home of George Washington's forebears before they moved to Sulgrave, Northamptonshire.

Born into a rich Virginian family, Washington was a surveyor before serving in the French Indian War (1754–63). He became a strong opponent of British government policy in the Continental Congresses and when the American War of Independence broke out, he was appointed commander-in-chief of the American forces. Having gained the final victory over Cornwallis at Yorktown in 1781, Washington became president of the Constitutional Convention in 1787.

The popular story that the young George Washington virtuously admitted to his father that he had felled the cherry tree is probably an invention. He is alleged to have said, 'Father, I cannot tell a lie. I did it.' The story seems to have originated in the biography of Washington by the American clergyman Mason Locke Weems, first published in the fifth edition of the book (1806).

Wassermann test

The Wassermann test (or reaction), a test for detecting syphilis, is named after the German bacteriologist August von Wassermann (1866–1925), who invented it. An assistant to Robert Koch at his Institute for Infectious Diseases in Berlin, Wassermann late became director of the department of experimental therapy and serum research. In 1906, he developed a test for syphilis, which, using the 'complement-fixation' technique, indicates the presence or absence in the blood of a specific antibody. Wassermann is also noted for his development of a diagnostic test for tuberculosis.

Watt

Watt, the metric unit of power, is named after the Scottish engineer and inventor James Watt (1736–1819). Watt is particularly famous for his development of the steam engine.

Born at Greenock, Scotland, Watt worked at Glasgow University. While repairing a model of the Newcomen steam engine (1765), Watt realised that it would be more efficient if it were fitted with a separate condenser. Thus Watt's steam engine, developed in 1769, soon replaced the Newcomen model. From 1774–5 he worked in partnership with the businessman and engineer Matthew Boulton (1728–1809) to manufacture steam engines.

Watt's other inventions included a centrifugal governor and manuscript copying machine. The term horsepower was coined by him and Boulton.

Watteau back; Watteau hat

A Watteau back (or dress) has broad back pleats that fall from the neckline to the hem without a girdle. A Watteau hat is one that has a shallow crown and a wide brim that is turned up at the back to hold decorative flowers. Both features are named after the French painter Antoine Watteau (1684–1721), in imitation of characteristics of his art.

Originally training as a painter of scenery for the theatre, Watteau later had the opportunity of studying Rubens' work, which proved to be highly influential in the development of his style. He became famous in England and France for his scenes of gallantry (*fêtes galantes*).

Wedgwood

Wedgwood is a trademark used to describe a kind of ceramic ware made originally by the English potter Josiah Wedgwood (1730–95). Wedgwood pottery is known for its classical ornamentation in white relief particularly on a blue (Wedgwood blue) background.

Born at Burslem, Staffordshire, Wedgwood was handicapped as a child when his right leg had to be amputated, but he nevertheless experimented with clays and firing and worked in the family's small pottery shop. He eventually founded a firm in Staffordshire which produced a wide range of ceramic ware that was to become famous throughout the world. He collaborated with the sculptor John Flaxman (1755–1826) and built a factory (and a village for his workers) at Etruria in Staffordshire.

Wednesday

The fourth day of the week comes from the Old English *Wodnesdaeg*, Woden's day. Known also as Odin, Woden was the god of wisdom, culture and war. He was also the god of the heroes who died in battle and were brought to Valhalla by his personal attendants, the Valkyries. His yearning for wisdom was so great that he surrendered his right eye so that he could drink from Mimir's fountain of knowledge.

wellington boot

The wellington boot was originally a leather boot which covered the front of the knee and was cut away at the back. Nowadays the wellington is a waterproof rubber boot, without fastenings, that reaches to the knee. The boot is, of course, named after the British soldier and statesman Arthur Wellesley, 1st Duke of Wellington (known as the Iron Duke; 1769–1852). Wellington is known for his victory against the French in the Peninsular War (1814) and, with Blücher, for the final defeat of Napoleon at Waterloo (1815). He served as prime minister (1828–30) but his opposition to parliamentary reform led to his resignation. He was commander-in-chief of the British army (1827–8; 1842–52).

Apart from the boots named in his honour – he is said to have worn the boots during his military and political careers – the capital of New Zealand is named after the Duke, as is the wellingtonia, the giant Californian coniferous tree, known also as the 'big tree'.

Wendy house

A Wendy house is a small model house that children can play in. It is named after the house built for Wendy, the girl in the play *Peter Pan, or The Boy Who Would Not Grow Up* by the Scottish dramatist and novelist Sir James Matthew Barrie (1860–1937).

See also **Peter Pan**.

Wesleyan

John Wesley (1703–91) was the English preacher who founded Methodism, the word being used to describe his followers, especially in the branch of Methodism known as Wesleyan Methodism.

Born the fifteenth son of a rector in Epworth (now Humberside), John was ordained in 1735. After a conversion experience in 1738, he determined to devote the rest of his life to evangelistic work. From 1742 he travelled throughout Britain, and is said to have preached over 40,000 sermons and travelled 250,000 miles before he died.

His brother Charles (1707–88) is known for his composition of several thousand hymns, including 'Jesus, lover of my soul'; 'Love divine, all loves excelling'; and 'And can it be that I should gain'.

Wightman Cup

The Wightman Cup, the annual tennis competition between British and US women's teams, is named after the donor of the trophy, Hazel Hotchkiss Wightman (1886–1974). A very successful tennis player herself (she was American national singles champion 1901–11) Wightman bought the silver cup in about 1920, when preliminary efforts were underway to stage a competition similar to the Davis Cup. These plans proved fruitless but in 1923 a competition was arranged between British and US women's teams, which has been played every year since.

See also **Davis Cup**.

will-o'-the-wisp

The expression will-o'-the-wisp is used to describe a light that some-times appears over marshy ground at night. Known also by a variety of other terms – friar's lantern, jack-o'-lantern and *ignis fatuus* – the light is believed to be caused by the spontaneous combustion of gases formed by organic decomposing matter. Figuratively, the expression will-o'-the-wisp is used to refer to an elusive person or someone who cannot be depended on. The original seventeenth-century expression was 'Will with the wisp', Will – the short form for William – being chosen as alliterative with wisp – a twist of hay, etc., burning as a bright light.

Winchester rifle

Winchester rifle is the trademark of a type of repeating rifle with a tubular magazine below the barrel. The name derives from its American manufacturer Oliver Fisher Winchester (1810–80). The Winchester was first made in 1866, at his factory in New Haven, Connecticut. The Winchester became well known as a cowboy rifle in the Wild West period of American history.

Winchester's original line of business was the manufacture of men's shirts; his special competence lay in the adaptation of the inventions of others. In fact, the Winchester rifle was a development of the Henry rifle, a repeating rifle invented by Benjamin Tyler Henry (1821–98).

wisteria

Wistaria, the genus of twining climbing plants with purple flowers in hanging clusters, are named after the American anatomist Caspar Wistar (1761–1818).

The son of a well-known glass-maker, Wistar was a Philadelphian Quaker who was professor of anatomy at the University of Pennsylvania. He wrote America's first textbook on anatomy. It was, it seems, an error by Thomas Nuttal, the curator of the botanical garden in Harvard in 1818, that resulted in the misspelling of Wistar's surname in the designating of the plant as wisteria.

Xanthippe

Socrates' wife, Xanthippe, was notorious for being bad-tempered and nagging; so an ill-tempered or irritable woman or wife is sometimes referred to in the same way. Shakespeare refers to her in *The Taming of the Shrew* (Act 1, Scene 2) –

> Be she as foul as was Florentius' love,
> As old as Sibyl, and as curst and shrewd
> As Socrates' Xanthippe, or a worse,
> She moves me not.

Xanthippe's nagging is discussed in different ways by various authors. Some see it as the cause of Socrates' delight in outdoor discussions, while others argue that Socrates was such an unconventional husband that living with him must have taken up all his wife's patience.

Y

Yale lock

Yale, the trademark for a type of cylinder lock, is named after the American locksmith Linus Yale (1821–68) who invented it. Yale invented numerous other kinds of locks in the 1840s–1860s, but it is for the lock which has a revolving barrel that he is particularly remembered. Yale set up a company, the Yale Lock Manufacturing Company, to produce locks at Stamford, Connecticut in 1868.

Yankee

Yankee – someone from the USA in British English in a derogatory sense, and someone from the northern USA (particularly New England) in American English – probably comes from a Dutch name. Yankee may well originally have been Jan Kass, a derogatory nickname for a Hollander, meaning 'John Cheese'.

After the Dutch settled in New York, they applied the term to the neighbouring English settlers in north Connecticut. By the time of the American War of Independence, the term was used by the British to describe any colonist. (The song 'Yankee Doodle' originally mocked the poorly clad colonial forces, but the colonial troops changed the song's lyrics and used it as a marching song.)

In the American Civil War, the South used Yankee as a derisive term for a Union soldier, and by the outbreak of the First World War, all American soldiers were known as Yankees (or Yanks) by the rest of the world. From that time on, Yankee and Yank have been used to describe an American.

yarborough

A yarborough is a hand in bridge or whist in which none of the cards is higher than nine. The word comes from Charles Anderson Worsley, 2nd Earl of Yarborough (d. 1897). An enthusiastic card-game player, Lord Yarborough is said to have betted 1000 to 1 against the dealing of such a hand. In fact, the true mathematical odds have been calculated as 1827 to 1 against.

Z

zany

Something that is comical, especially in a fantastic or absurd way, may be described as zany. The word comes from Italian *zanni*, originally a traditional masked clown in the Italian *commedia dell'arte*. The buffoon was known as Zanni – an alteration of the name Giovanni (John), one of the traditional names for a clown. Zanni's role was to mimic the clown's tricks and generally to play the fool.

Zeppelin

A Zeppelin is an airship, and in particular a large rigid cylindrical airship built in Germany in the early twentieth century. It takes its name from the German general and aeronautical pioneer Count Ferdinand von Zeppelin (1838–1917). Zeppelin served in the American Civil War and the Franco-Prussian War. On retiring from the army in 1891, he developed his earlier interest in airships and by 1900 had built the first rigid airship. Between 1910 and 1914 Zeppelins were widely used in Germany to carry passengers. During the First World War, the Germans used these airships to bomb Britain, the first raid being over Great Yarmouth in 1915. From that time onwards, the story of airships was generally one of disaster – notably the British R101 disaster (1930) and the German Hindenburg (1937) – but in more recent times, airships are again being used, using non-flammable gas.

zinnia

Zinnia, the genus of annual or perennial plants native to tropical America of the family Compositae, is named after the German botanist and anatomist Johann Gottfried Zinn (1727–59). A professor of medicine, Zinn published in 1753 what is reported to have been the first book to describe the anatomy of the eye.

Zoroastrianism

The pre-Islamic Persian religion of Zoroastrianism was founded in the sixth century BC by the prophet Zoroaster (in Avestan, Zarathustra).

Zoroaster (c.660–583BC) received at the age of about thirty a vision of Ahura Mazda who inspired him to teach a new religion proclaiming that he was the god of light.

Zoroastrianism recognises two principles, good and evil, which are personified by Ahura Mazda (god of light, wisdom) and Ahriman (or Angra Mainyu; prince of darkness; the destroyer). Life is considered as a struggle between these two spirits, which will be won by the eventual triumph of good over evil.

The scriptures of Zoroastrianism are the Avesta. Written in Old Iranian, its five books contain prayers, hymns and songs (Gathas), and teaching on ritual, worship and law. Zoroastrianism survives in India amongst the Parsees and in Iran.

Zwinglian

Zwinglian is used to describe the teachings of the Swiss theologian Ulrich Zwingli (1484–1531), especially his understanding of the holy communion. In contrast to Luther, Zwingli had a purely symbolic interpretation of the eucharist.

Ordained as priest in 1506, Zwingli became a preacher in Zurich in 1519, strongly criticising Roman Catholic teachings. His New Testament lectures marked the beginning of the Swiss Reformation. His conflict with Luther was seen at the Colloquy of Marburg (1529), which failed to bring about a union between the two men and a united Protestantism became impossible. The Reformation divided Switzerland and in the civil war that followed, Zwingli, serving as a chaplain, was killed.